D1538696

CLIMBING JACOB'S LADDER

CLIMBING JACOB'S LADDER

The Arrival of Negroes in Southern Politics

PAT WATTERS

REESE CLEGHORN

HARCOURT, BRACE & WORLD, INC.
NEW YORK

Copyright © 1967 by Southern Regional Council, Inc.
All rights reserved. No part of this publication may be reproduced
or transmitted in any form or by any means, electronic or mechanical,
including photocopy, recording, or any information storage and
retrieval system, without permission in writing from the publisher.
First edition
Library of Congress Catalog Card Number: 67-20324
Printed in the United States of America

*To all those who have given of themselves in the voter
effort's struggle to achieve democracy in the South, among them
the thirteen known killed from 1962 to 1967:*

MEDGAR W. EVERS

CLIFTON WALKER

MICHAEL H. SCHWERNER

JAMES E. CHANEY

ANDREW GOODMAN

LEWIS ALLEN

JIMMIE LEE JACKSON

JAMES REEB

VIOLA GREGG LIUZZO

SAMUEL YOUNGE, JR.

JONATHAN M. DANIELS

FREDDIE LEE THOMAS

VERNON DAHMER

CONTENTS

FOREWORD

FOREWORD

The title Pat Watters and Reese Cleghorn have given their book might remind one of some sentences of Harold Isaac's:

If an artist were to try to catch a picture of Negro Americans caught at this moment [1963] as on a wide mural, he would put at the forward end the young men and women, mostly students at Negro colleges in the South, who began writing their own climactic chapter to this history only in 1960 when they launched the sit-in movement. . . . Just behind, pushing these young people ahead, he would paint in the plain men and women of Montgomery, Alabama, who walked to and from work for a year in 1955–56 . . . [Next] would come the young adults who have led the way into the white universities of the South. Here too would come the children who have been walking the gantlet into their desegregated classes, and their parents, led by the little-sung plaintiffs in the court cases . . . and the NAACP lawyers and their supporting organizers and workers . . . After them would come the new young ministers in the old Negro churches, a whole new species come to replace those who in a past time could only preach endurance. All together they still make a painfully thin vanguard of people who are where they are because a still smaller but still more

persistent band of predecessors fought to open the roads they have traveled
—all of them carrying a tremendous weight of commitment, not only pushing against a great and resistant society in front of them but also pulling
a great and sluggish mass behind them. These are the people who believe
that there is a self-respecting status for them to win in the American society and that they are at last winning it. Because they believe this is so,
the young Negro novelist Julian Mayfield, who does not believe it, has
called these Negroes in sad and bitter words, "the last defenders of the
American dream." *

I think it is important to see that during the 1960's there was a
deep tension within the Negro community, as well as tension between
Negroes and whites, between South and non-South, between civil
rights forces and conservatives everywhere. I am not referring to rivalries among the civil rights organizations (because until early 1966 all
of those were allied on fundamental goals), but to the cleavage between those who "believe that there is a self-respecting status for
them to win in the American society" and those who denied that
proposition.

It is also important to see that after every victory of the civil rights
movement the number and strength of the deniers has increased, so
that after six years (1960–65) of one decisive victory after another, bitterness had widely replaced anger, rejection had succeeded hope. This
has certainly not become as yet the prevailing mood, but we are misled if we overlook its spread and intensity. For every victory has demonstrated to Negroes how deeply and firmly imbedded in our social
system are the causes of their disadvantage, and many have grown
weary of victories, purchased by turmoil and yielding too little to re-
quite all that went into their gaining.

One of the achievements of the book Watters and Cleghorn have
written is the illumination they give to this development. They show
us something else as well, and that is data—not card-punched social
science data but data just the same—on the alliance formed during
the early 1960's between the civil rights movement and the general
radicalism of American youth. White youth came into the movement
in the early 1960's. They came to do the work and the will of the
Negro organizations. They came also as the most active expression of
liberal white concern. Increasingly, they gave their work and their serv-

* *The New World of Negro Americans* (New York: John Day Co., 1963),
pp. 330–331.

ice to the more militant of the Negro organizations and leaders. After the Selma march and as the Vietnam war picked up, they typically turned their attention away from single-minded concern with the civil rights movement and toward a general revaluation of American society. The old alliance between radical youth and the civil rights militants still holds, but now it is the civil rights militants, surfeited with the frustrations of victory, who join the radical youth. From this alliance is likely coming the shape of American liberalism in the last third of the century. There is good probability that most of the felt economic and social ills of today's disadvantaged are already in the process of being cured by secular progress. The even more probable fact is, however, that just as the radicalism of the 1930's forged the stock of ideas and attitudes that have become by now American orthodoxy, so that itself is now being undone by new dissent fashioned in the idealism of the civil rights movement and the revulsion over Vietnam.

But the subject of this book is those who believed in and worked for the American dream within the existing order. The civil rights movement was basically—as are most liberal strivings—a conservative effort, peopled by those who believed that American institutions and processes could be made to work. This book is about them, though it is full of a questioning of that premise, a questioning that always permeated the movement. Perhaps it is, in truth, a book about "the last defenders of the American dream."

Some would say—with much reason—that the civil rights movement came to its end between the summer of 1965 and the spring of 1966. More would agree that that did happen and at that time than would, by any means, agree on the cause. It does not seem to me intellectual cowardice to look not for a cause, or even a set of one-directional causes, but to look instead for a variety of suddenly congregating influences which combined to weaken the movement from within while reducing the nation's tolerance of and interest in it and its mission.

In rough chronological order there was first the passage in July of the Voting Rights Act of 1965 which, following on the Civil Rights Act of 1964, represented the fulfillment of the prime articulated demands (*not* the goals) of the movement, and also transferred initiative for further advance against the classical problems of voter, educational, employment, and service discrimination from the movement itself to the federal government. Moreover, by summer 1965, the federal antipoverty program was beginning to unfold and to be felt. Many from the leadership cadre of the movement lessened their concentration on grand goals and threw themselves into struggle over the nature and control of local community action programs. Something else entered here too: jobs. The anti-poverty program of the 1960's has not been a mass producer of jobs, but it has bred a sizable lot of positions for administrators, organizers, and research and information people. For the first time, there was patronage available and seeking for precisely the kinds of persons who had staffed the civil rights organizations.

On the heels of the Voting Rights Act came Watts. The riot there —and the others that sprang up elsewhere—did undoubtedly shatter the nerve and increase the resistance of many whites. Some liberals were scared off. But the movement of 1960–65 had overcome other serious crises of popular confidence; riots in Northern cities had been also bad in 1964; and for as long as one can remember the culpable inadequacy of "liberals" has been a favorite conversation piece of the movement. A greater harm of Watts was that the civil rights leadership was unprepared for it and stayed confused by it. The civil rights laws had transferred much of the responsibility for further tangible progress to the White House; now in their blurred response to Watts, the movement's leadership forfeited large portions of the tremendous moral leadership it then had. It could not either accept or effectively repudiate "Burn, baby, burn," and could never find a way to escape that either/or. And so the civil rights movement lapsed from its magnificent expressiveness into loud unintelligibility.

The White House Conferences in November 1965 and May 1966 seem, in retrospect, not only failures but disasters, because they forced people who desperately and above all, at that period, needed a private time to find new thoughts, to nag at each other in a lurid spotlight, and to drag down a lovely, cleanly phrased movement into a whirlpool of sullen meaningless talk, from which rescue has hardly yet begun. This was the backdrop of the fatuous "black power" controversy. In all our history, no Americans ever acted with more dignity and —yes—style than those who led the way from Selma to Montgomery. Less than a year later, that movement which they had led and for which they had spoken was shattered, and large elements of it were driving pell-mell toward a new era, an era of the chant rather than the song, of the incantation rather than the thought, of the buffoon instead of the hero, and of an explicit rejection of the movement's holy things —love, integration, and respect for the person.

I have said that we should look for a climate, a context, within which the civil rights revolution found its unquiet and unfulfilled end, not look for a cause. Yet I am not sure that the movement could not have withstood all else had it not been for the hectic increase during this same period of the Vietnam war. No wistful or demagogic—as the case might be—contentions that we could as a nation pay the costs of both a large-scale war in a distant land and a systematic drive against discrimination and poverty could conceal the truth that we would not do it; nor would there be any relevance to self-serving claims that we *would* have, had only others not acted badly and unwisely. It seems clear now that when the President's celebrated "peace offensive" collapsed in the early weeks of 1966, the civil rights movement was impliedly dissolved, its revolution effectively terminated. The churning moral and political dilemmas of that war chewed up its clear-sightedness and relentless advance.

The point of all this is to contend that Watters and Cleghorn here write history—not, let it be noted, anything that can call itself contemporary history, because the events they chronicle and portray took place in a past era, even though so close at hand. They write, principally, about a time before the legislative victory of 1965, but also before Watts, demagoguery, and the full horror of Vietnam. They write about the final days of an era, not the first days of a new one.

The book is, primarily, about the voter registration campaign of 1962–64, and is, therefore, involved, as was that campaign, in two historical contexts—that of the South and that of the civil rights movement. If one writes a history of the recent South he will try to tell how it spawned and was changed by the civil rights movement. If one writes a history of the civil rights movement he will try to tell how it found itself in the South. But if one writes of a single interlocking problem (just as if, say, he chose to write about the making of the atomic bomb and not about, primarily, either World War II or modern physics), he will have to find his way and show the reader his way through both contexts; in this case, through the civil rights movement *and* the South, and Watters and Cleghorn do this superbly.

If we try to make clear what we mean when we speak of the "civil rights movement," I think we must say that it was defined by Southern problems and given character by the qualities of Negro Southerners. The movement did, of course, spread beyond the South, but always the cohesion was the South. The Northerners who came down to aid the Southern cause did not in the first years disturb the Southerness of its intellectual and spiritual thrust; indeed, part of the style of those workers from the North was a heartfelt wish to act and think as did their Negro hosts. The movement spoke and thought in an idiom that was about one half Biblical, and about one fourth each copy-book Americanism and social science—though the latter hardly got beyond the ritualistic and yet somehow sincerely felt incorporation of abstractions such as "the power structure" and "alienation." In time, the younger movement people popularized also existentialist themes, and then, as the movement began to breed cults and dark corners, some of them smothered it all in Dylanesque mockery.

But until then, the civil rights movement had been a very bright flame in American history, warming the hopes of a nation. The movement was never, however, illusionary. Watters and Cleghorn give heavy emphasis to the student wing of the movement, especially the Student Nonviolent Coordinating Committee. They are right to have done so because, though others may have registered far more voters or done or achieved other objective things, here within its student wing the movement distilled its essential character. SNCC did not by any means embrace all of the youth, and wherever students were, there was the same compound of idealism and hard thought, of fierceness and compassion, and, perhaps above all, of ingrained suspicion of broad programs and concern for individual cases. At the great Washington march of August 28, 1963, John Lewis, an Alabama farm boy who had become chairman of SNCC, spoke alongside the other leaders to the assembled throng and to the vast television audience. His prepared remarks had been read in advance by some of his colleagues and had upset their plans for the tone of the day; so they had pressed Lewis strongly to soften his speech, and he finally, with compassion and courtesy for them, complied. Here are some of the blunt, demanding, non-praising, old-SNCC style statements from his original manuscript.

We march today for jobs and freedom, but we have nothing to be proud of.—

In good conscience, we cannot support, wholeheartedly, the administration's civil rights bill, for it is too little, and too late. There's not one thing in the bill that will protect our people from police brutality.

The voting section of this bill will not help thousands of black citizens who want to vote. It will not help the citizens of Mississippi, of Alabama, and Georgia, who are qualified to vote, but lack a sixth grade education.

"One man, one vote," is the African cry. It is ours, too. . . . What is there in this bill to insure the equality of a maid who earns $5 a week in the home of a family whose income is $100,000 a year?

We are now involved in a serious revolution. This nation is still a place of cheap political leaders who build their careers on immoral compromises and ally themselves with open forms of political, economic, and social exploitation. . . . The party of Kennedy is also the party of Eastland. The party of Javits is also the party of Goldwater. Where is *our* party?

The revolution is at hand, and we must free ourselves of the chains of political and economic slavery. . . . We cannot depend on any political party, for both the Democrats and the Republicans have betrayed the basic principles of the Declaration of Independence.
We all recognize the fact that if any radical social, political, and economic changes are to take place in our society, the people, the masses, must bring them about. In the struggle we must seek more than mere civil rights; we must work for the community of love, peace, and true brotherhood. Our minds, souls, and hearts cannot rest until freedom and justice exist for *all the people.*
. . . Listen, Mr. Kennedy. Listen, Mr. Congressman, listen fellow citizens, the black masses are on the march for jobs and freedom . . .

We won't stop now. All of the forces of Eastland, Barnett, Wallace, and Thurmond won't stop this revolution. The time will come when we will not confine our marching to Washington. We will march through the South, through the heart of Dixie, the way Sherman did. We shall pursue our own "scorched earth" policy and burn Jim Crow to the ground—nonviolently. We shall fragment the South into a thousand pieces and put them back together in the image of democracy. We will make the action of the past few months look pretty. And I say to you, WAKE UP AMERICA!!!

Climbing Jacob's Ladder explicates this Lewisan idealism-plus-hardness as it brightened and set to moving numberless persons of the South. I have quoted at some length, because the statement seems to me to recall clearly and well the tone and point of view of the civil rights movement at its peak, and that is to say, at the time chronicled by this book. Here was how the anger and the hope both were felt, even in days *before* the Birmingham bombing, the assassination of a believed-in President, the squalid brutality of St. Augustine, the Mississippi Summer of 1964, and all that happened in Selma and its aftermath.

The voter registration campaign was not the whole of the civil rights movement, but it expressed it all. The movement we knew is over but it had an intrinsic worth, independent of how it may have changed its future or shaped our present. But though the movement never did "fragment the South" and put it "back together in the image of democracy," it did make of the South and the nation a greatly different land. In the doing of that, the voter registration campaign had the biggest part.

The civil rights movement, as we knew it in the early sixties, is ended. The grand assemblage held together by a determination to erase the Southern blight is no more. Whether it can reassemble for other crusades is a question for the future. To say that the civil rights movement is over is not to say, however, that the Second Reconstruction of the South is ended. On that, I am more the optimist than is C. Vann Woodward in his celebrated article, "What Happened to the Civil Rights Movement?" (*Harper's Magazine,* January 1967). I believe that at the worst the evidence is still coming in, and that such evidence as we now have shows that, despite everything epitomized by the Wallaces of Alabama, the South is now and will continue to be a different and better place. What made the crucial difference, what made it possible to cross the border into a social order where a just multiracial society is now a true possibility was the civil rights movement. That that movement is now in disarray does not change the fact that it was a magnificent success.

The Southern Regional Council's role was central in the 1962–64 (and subsequent) voter registration campaigns, and this book is based in large part on its files. This is not, however, a usual program report. The Southern Regional Council has always seen itself as part of its environment, and this is, fittingly, primarily a report of those events within which the program took place. Watters and Cleghorn have written, I believe, a basic book for the understanding of recent Southern life and politics.

LESLIE W. DUNBAR

March 1967

CLIMBING JACOB'S LADDER

Little bands sang and prayed their way to the courage they needed to register to vote, to assert that they were men, and that they would overcome. Usually they did it in churches. In a tiny town of Terrell County, Georgia, a painting of Jesus hung over the pulpit of the little wooden building called the Mount Olive Baptist Church. On another wall hung a calendar with President Kennedy's picture and, small around him, pictures of all the other American presidents.

Car doors slammed outside on a hot July night in 1962 as the Reverend Charles Sherrod, young, thin-faced, led the people who had braved the night to talk about voting in a county where even talk about it was dangerous: "Yea, though I walk through the valley of the shadow of death, I will fear no evil. . . ." He stopped. "If they come in," he said, "I'm going to read this over again."

Fifteen white men, four of them local law-enforcement officers, came through the door and stood in a grim-faced row. "If God be for us," Sherrod intoned in prayer as they stood there, "who will be against us? Into Thy hand we commend our minds and souls and our lives every day. . . ." In the back, the sheriff of Terrell County, seventy-one years old, rough-looking, closed his eyes and bowed his head. The Negroes began to sing. Voices that were weak at first gained strength as they moved up the scale with the old, familiar words:

> We are climbing
> Jacob's Ladder
>
> . . .
>
> Every round goes
> higher, higher
>
> . . .
>
> We are climbing
> Jacob's Ladder
>
> . . .

Sherrod spoke again, softly, almost singing the words. "All we want our white brothers to understand is that Thou who made us, made us all." Another voice spoke: "Everybody is welcome. This is a voter registration meeting. . . ."

Now the old sheriff of Terrell County came to the front of the Mount Olive Church. He explained how happy Negroes were in Terrell. "We want our colored people to live like they've been living," he said. "There was never any trouble before all this started." As he spoke, the whites moved through the church, confronting little groups of Negroes. Finally, the whites left. The Negroes began to sing the strains of another old Baptist hymn, one with some new words and some old, the rising anthem now of the whole movement: "We shall overcome . . . We shall overcome . . . Oh, ohhh, deep . . . in my heart . . . I do be-lieve . . . we shall overcome . . . some day. . . ." The intruders were in their cars now, leaving, as the Negroes inside the church gathered their courage to go out into the night. "We are not afraid," they sang, loudly.

A few nights later, three small Negro churches in Terrell County, one of them the Mount Olive Baptist, with Jesus and the American presidents on its walls, were burned to the ground.

1)
New Life for Old Truths

They spoke mainly not to the state but to society, and what they said was not new. The words and the thoughts had been there all along, deeply imbedded in the canons of liberal democracy. Long before the great American civil rights struggle, in the dawn of mass democracy in England, John Stuart Mill had known and spoken these values and urgencies. The masses must share in power, he said, but more. He was concerned not so much with politics and power as with the fiber of society itself, and the character of men. "The worth of the state," he wrote in concluding *On Liberty*, "in the long run, is the worth of the individuals composing it; and a state which postpones the interest of their mental expansion and elevation to a little more of administrative skill . . . ; a state which dwarfs its men . . . will find that with small men no great thing can be accomplished; and that the perfection of machinery to which it has sacrificed everything will in the end avail it nothing. . . ." To Mill, the deepening of democracy by broadening the electorate would prove desirable even if it did not produce more proficient government. He saw the extension of political freedom as valuable chiefly because it helped bring a fullness and a strength to the

moral character of men. Political rearrangement, accommodating institutions to the citizenry, was simply not his first concern. His words
whisper to us now, for he wrote much in the vein of those who spoke
for the unfolding civil rights movement in America in the late 1950's
and in the first half of the 1960's. As others were concerned with the
political oppression of masses by the state, he was concerned with the
expansion of individuals; he dreaded the potential oppression of individuals by the mass, by society itself. There could be no liberal government, he knew, without a liberal society, not simply tolerating but valu-
ing differences, open always to new ideas, genuinely pledged to the
fullest development of each man.

Mill believed that those of his day who were voting for the first time
—for the first time participating in democracy's rational ways—might
develop thereby a more "intrinsically humane, civilized kind of character." Perhaps they did: we stand on the other side in time and know
better the ills of men on our side. Or perhaps Mill placed too much
emphasis upon the exalting influence that might spring from the
momentary act of participation itself, at the ballot box. Even so, his
interest was in the direction of what the student wing of the civil rights
struggle in this country in the early 1960's called "people development."
This was something beyond shaping institutions to people; it had to do
with what *kind* of people.

In Mill's democratic theory, politics and the qualities of men became
entwined as never before. People must participate not simply because
the participation itself was good for them—the alerting to issues that
affected their lives, the decision-making, the invigorating entry into the
rapids that flow into society's mainstream. The more important participation was to be not just at the moment when the ballot was cast but
in all the moments that led to that moment. Mill spoke about this in
nineteenth-century language. He talked about "character," and although we did not hear that word, with its connotations of formal
moral code, from the student activists of the early 1960's, they were in
fact and in their way concerned with the same thing. Mill was a
theoretician; but those who dealt in his currency in the cotton fields, the
sharecropper shanties, and the rutted roads of the back sides of a thousand Southern towns—these were not theoreticians but activists. As it
all unfolded, we saw an experiment in the actualities of Mill's theory.
The experiment was small and ephemeral, but it was compelling because of its roots, its certainty and its ambitions. It came first from the

youth movement fresh upon the scene, seemingly unfettered by the past. The spirit spread. This was seeding in a seedtime.

Charles Sherrod, a young Negro minister who went to the angriest part of Georgia's Black Belt to combat white supremacy, wrote a memorandum in 1962 that noted the church burnings, jailings, physical attacks, and economic reprisals in southwest Georgia during voter registration efforts. "We feel that we are engaged in a psychological battle for the minds of the enslaved," he said. "Our criterion for success is not how many people we register, but how many people we can get to begin initiating decisions solely on the basis of their personal opinion." [1] The refrain is constant in reports from the small, hounded band, mainly students, that burrowed into the structure of the Black Belt in the early 1960's. "The people who make up the Greenville Student Movement, for the most part, are those we recruited off the block, in the pool halls, and out of the cafés and juke joints . . . ," Charles Cobb of the Student Nonviolent Coordinating Committee reported in 1963 from Mississippi. "They have toned themselves down considerably over the past couple of months . . . One day, some day, they'll have to make a choice between us and the Block. But they work, every day, the dull drudgery of canvassing in hot streets, as long as we work, they work." That choice between "the Block" and "the movement" was then already a bigger part of the civil rights struggle than most people understood, and the choice was to become more and more imperative as the movement drew on. This choice raised by the movement was to end, ironically, as a divide taking people both ways; some in the movement were to be seduced, ultimately, by the violence and self-destructive irrationalism of "the Block."

As headlines played upon the frontal assaults on white supremacy's barricades, another structure, built around the Negro's acceptance of his inferiority and his hopelessness, was being undermined. This was what often was called "people development." Elizabeth Wyckoff, a white academician who served the movement in southwest Georgia, wrote in the winter of 1962: "On the strictly pragmatic level it is true that a greatly enlarged Negro electorate is the key to the solution of these problems which bedevil the South. But no urban Northerner like myself can be under the illusion that unhampered Negro suffrage brings the day of Freedom. It is a prerequisite, and no more. . . . To move from the pragmatic level, many of the Negroes with whom we have been in touch in southwest Georgia have moved into freedom of the mind, and it is now theirs for life, even if they should never succeed in their efforts to persuade a semi-literate, hostile registrar to put their names on a roll which gives them the option of voting for the less unpleasant of two repulsive candidates."

Wherever Negroes have "moved into freedom of the mind," they have gone one better than the ballot box in realizing the dream of that thunderous old spiritual of human release: "Free at last! Free at last! Thank God a'mighty we'll be free at last!" This was the best part of the struggle. The fact that so much of this opening of minds came through the reach for the ballot lent that struggle a higher purpose than it has ever had with any other group of left-out Americans.

One had only to hear in the mass meetings of the Negro movement in the South the expression of the fundamentals of American democracy, the loving reiteration of the words ("All men *are* created equal . . . AMEN . . . and *do* have inalienable rights . . . YES YES"), to understand how new life was breathed into old truths, and how the truths became alive in the people, giving them a strength and courage. This had happened before, one knew; these stirrings had formed a huge part of the modern history of the West, and the more recent history of the emerging nations. But in the American South, with all the symbolic meaning for the nation, it had a special poignancy, a special beauty. This time, one felt, such great release, such hope will not be disappointed.

Negroes propelled *themselves* into the mainstream of American politics (if not into the mainstream of American society). The Negro ballot, more than any other single power, moved the nation to resume the task of implementing its own century-old constitutional amendments. It had not been easy. Long before Martin Luther King, there had been a Frederick Douglass, and one reason he could not succeed was the absence of a political lever to pull. In fact, one leader after Douglass who could pull levers, Booker T. Washington, had even publicly renounced interest in the political lever; he accepted the reality that politics again had become white folks' business. William E. B. Du Bois could strongly protest that renunciation of politics, but to little effect. There were no votes. There was no political leverage. The history of the advance of the Negro cause since the Civil War has followed closely behind the history of Negro voting. It would be a gross misreading to isolate the vote as the only strong force of change; but it was the most powerful.

Before the Civil War, although there were a few Negro office-holders outside the South, Negro votes were not important anywhere. The war gave Negroes political influence and might, and their sudden emergence was accompanied for a while by the political demise of the traditional white South. Radical Republican dominance in Washington was made possible by that demise, a result never even approximated again to this day. Between 1875 and 1890, however, the traditional white South reclaimed, through massive violence, fraud, legal gymnastics, and economic coercion, the power that had been torn from it under military rule and unprecedented federal edicts. For half a century Negroes were removed as a political force, not just in the South, but nationally. The old South again dropped anchor in the Potomac, an unmoving Merrimac around which nothing vital to its interests might easily pass. It had votes, in the Capitol, in the electoral college, at the Democratic convention, and in those places, in the face of federal weakness, it stayed hard; this was not the power to rule, but the power to stop rulers.

Congressional Reconstruction by 1867 and 1868 had enfranchised more than 703,000 Negroes at a time when the total white registration was some 627,000 in the reconstructed states. This seemed likely to assure a radical Republican posterity. (The New South was to be not only Republican, but Radical.) The resurgence of the traditional South by the end of the century killed such prospects; Negro political power was dead.

The death of the Negro vote created a strange void. In it, the personal attitudes of presidents, more than their assessments of votes, largely determined federal policy on civil rights. The Negroes' rights, which had been involved with a savage war that tore the nation apart, now became part of the trivia of American politics. The Republicans, in the aftermath of the Radical Republicanism of Thaddeus Stevens and Charles Sumner, offered little more than did the secessionist-tinged Democrats. The latter were so feared that the election in 1884 of Grover Cleveland, the first Democratic president since the Civil War, moved a number of Negroes to flee the South, fearing that Cleveland would unleash the Southern white-supremacy Democrats even more than had his Republican predecessors since 1877. But Cleveland proved to be no enemy. His personal attitude in racial matters was one of fairness and equanimity, so that some white Southerners were outraged to find Negroes among those invited to White House functions. Even that arch-Republican Frederick Douglass had kind words for the President. Yet Cleveland's way was hardly that of the next Democrat in the White House, Woodrow Wilson, who permitted the Washington bureaucracy to be resegregated, even though he had received a sizable lot of such Negro votes as there were. Negro political strength was simply so insignificant that it was ignored.

The point at which it was revived may be argued, but certainly the election of 1928 spoke the prologue. For as long as the white South was solid, Negro votes mattered little. Negroes could even, sometimes, and in some places, be allowed to vote freely in federal elections, since their states were going Democratic anyway. But in 1928, with the Catholic, "wet," urban, and almost-immigrant Al Smith running as a Democrat against the Protestant, "dry," Western, and nativist Herbert Hoover as a Republican, the white Democratic South suddenly was divided. The results were in doubt in all but three or four states. Negroes found their votes courted by regular Democrats, regular Republicans, and even Democrats for Hoover.[2] Though their impact upon the election was slight, they had become a force. The prospect had arisen that they could be a balance of power if the white Solid South broke up. The meaning was simply that at last their votes could possibly matter, and so at last they truly had votes.

The 1928 prologue was followed by the party-switching of Negroes in 1932 and 1936, leading toward their emergence in 1944 as a decisive force in a presidential election. It was in this period that Negro votes and public policy at the presidential level became, in significant degree, cause and effect. The personal predilections of presidents became less important than the usual force of politics. And so was born the national political power that made Washington, rather than state capitols, city halls, and courthouses, the focal point of Negro protest; and made the presidency—whether filled by Democrat or Republican—especially responsive to the interests and demands of Negroes. Except for this political realignment, this detachment of the presidency from the Southern orbit of power, the nation might have been so paralyzed politically that Negro Americans' "revolution of rising expectations" could well have outpaced political response, and sour, deep-running chaos could have become pervasive and predominant.

In 1928 Mr. Hoover had received probably 80 per cent of the Negro vote, simply because he was a Republican. But what he saw in the returns was something quite different: he had carried five Southern states. And so was born again the old Republican hunger for a place in the South. This time, it was unlike the hunger of Thaddeus Stevens and his friends, whose vision was of a Radical South, led by Negro votes. Now Hoover—as Dwight Eisenhower was to do in the fifties and Richard Nixon in 1960—saw a Republican South led by conservative white voters. (In 1964, Barry Goldwater was to see even beyond this—to a whole nation so led; and the Republican Party, which Frederick Douglass had called "the ship; all else is the sea," was to learn again how treacherous to it was the Southern sea.) Hoover disowned the discredited, Negro-led Republican patronage organizations in Southern states, but in most cases he merely substituted lily-white patronage structures more interested in post office appointments from Republican administrations in Washington than in building a true mass party in the South. This adventure was a short-run failure that became a long-run disaster for the party. Mr. Hoover's general insensitivity about racial matters and lack of interest in them provoked an exodus of Negroes from his party. The Depression, a calamity for low-income Negro masses, was another mighty factor. In 1932, the party failed to carry any Southern states, and at the same time it lost half the Negro votes nationally. In 1936, Franklin D. Roosevelt made Democrats of a large majority of Negroes. Four years later, the Democratic platform mentioned Negroes for the first time, promising to uphold due process and equal protection of the laws. By this time it was clear that Negro votes were not of merely peripheral interest, but nationally were potentially more important to the Democrats than was the white South.

An analysis of the 1944 election results shows why.[3] It is always questionable to say that, in a close election, one group of voters or another made the difference, since a shift of others also would have changed the outcome. It is nevertheless of primary importance to say that if in 1944 Mr. Roosevelt had received no larger proportion of Negro votes than had his Democratic predecessors, Thomas E. Dewey would have been president. A reversal of Negro votes would have switched these states and their 68 electoral votes to Governor Dewey: New York, New Jersey, Michigan, Illinois, Pennsylvania, Maryland, and Missouri. Negro votes also helped President Roosevelt substantially in a number of other states. This kind of analysis is not mere electoral gamesmanship. It is the real stuff of political strategy, and frequently the basis of public policy.

What Negroes gained from Roosevelt was not immediate, massive desegregation but programs that benefited a broad spectrum of Americans: low-rent housing, far-reaching farm programs, and training under new agencies such as the Civilian Conservation Corps and the National Youth Administration. Most important, a liberal Supreme Court came into being. Before Roosevelt's death, it had outlawed the white primary, clearly the most important step since Reconstruction toward restoration of Negro political liberty in the South. In a series of other decisions during Roosevelt's years, it set the judiciary irrevocably on a collision course with segregation as a public institution.

The massive emigration of Negroes to Northern cities had made the difference in the value of Negro votes. Big cities are mostly in big states. The electoral system, under which all of New York's bloc of 47 votes went to the ticket that carried only a feather's weight plurality, multiplied the balance-of-power potential of Negro votes in a way that never could have been possible under a simple popular-vote method of electing a president. In 1900, less than 10 per cent of the nation's almost nine million Negroes were outside the former slave states. Philadelphia, with 62,000 of these, had more than any other Northern city. New York had 60,700; Detroit, 4,100. By 1944, New York had 458,444; Philadelphia, 250,880; Detroit, 149,119; and Chicago, 277,731.[4] The votes of Negroes outside the South were potentially decisive in sixteen states with 278 electoral votes; the old Confederate states all told commanded only 127. Not only was this true, but most of the white South seemed safely in the Democratic camp, barring extraordinary events, and so it thereby lost political leverage. Negro votes had gained importance in Congress, as well as in the White House: they had become potentially decisive in at least 75 congressional districts outside the South.[5]

This was the situation in 1944. The prologue of 1928 had been followed by the shifts of population and votes in the 1930's and early 1940's, and the great turning point of power was reached as World War II was coming to a close. There had not yet been a revolution in deep-running results, but there had been a revolution in the power to obtain results. For before, the Negro had had none; now he not only had a little, but he was clearly going to have more. He was obtaining a handhold, at last, on the political lever. In 1948, he pulled it for Harry S. Truman. Again, a reversal of Negro votes would have elected Dewey.[6]

This accumulating political power nurtured, if it did not create, the civil rights movement. The bus integration sought by the Montgomery bus boycott of 1955 was eventually won through a federal court order. Following the student sit-ins of 1960, federal courts ultimately gave protection to those arrested. When the Freedom Riders moved through the South in 1961, they forced the Interstate Commerce Commission to enforce its ban against segregated interstate travel facilities. These formative actions, which gave character and direction to the movement, were sustained by a federal judiciary and executive branch that were becoming allied to the Negro cause.

Political power, more than any other single kind of influence, had assured this. More specifically, it had been Negro political power. That is not to say that votes in Chicago desegregated the Montgomery buses or the bus terminals where Freedom Riders were beaten. But had there not been a large Negro vote in Northern cities, the traditional South's ability to block the federal reach might have stayed the ICC. And it seems certain that without that vote, the nation's political coloration would have been different and the Supreme Court would not have been moving so steadily in the direction reflected by the Montgomery ruling and many others.

Could even a concentration of Negroes in politically important places have brought all this about? Not alone; these voters could not have prevailed over a far greater majority if that majority had said no. What these voters were able to do was to play upon the nation's prior promise, most of which had existed for almost two hundred years. They were not trying to force upon the country a new set of ideals, founded in new formulations of theory. In the loose way in which those things are done in politics, which deals not in specifics of theory but in specifics of power, they were demanding that "equal protection" be made to mean equal protection and that "inalienable rights" be treated as inalienable rights, and that a part of the citizenry be let in. They were joined by many others who earnestly desired the same end. But nothing really happened before Negroes got votes.

In examining the Negro vote in the South and its political impact, we begin, then, with the death of the Negro vote in the South a long time ago and its birth as a power in the North within the past three decades. We begin also with recognition that the vote can make a difference. This is not to be assumed without empirical evidence; a large part of the world rejects the assumption. In the Marxist view, popular voting in a capitalist state is of little or no consequence, because the real power lies elsewhere. (Karl Marx called it "an old, democratic litany.") In our own country, implicit in some of the power-structure studies of recent years has been the assumption that votes merely ratify decisions made by an elite whose powers are beyond votes. Certainly the endemic conspiracy syndromes of our time, of the right, left, and center, rest firmly upon the proposition that some "they" and not we decide.

Return, then, to John Stuart Mill and his concern, shared by the civil rights movement of the mid-twentieth century, that there be not merely the freedom to vote but full political participation. It was reasonable, once, for civil rights leaders to look principally to Washington for relief. Bound powerless, Negroes had no other recourse. They could not untie themselves. But once government has discharged its obligation truly to clear the way to the ballot box, full participation of Negroes will depend mainly upon factors that remain uncertain in 1967: the strength, versatility, and pragmatic sophistication of Negro political leadership and community organization. That strength requires a conviction on the part of most Negroes that votes *do* matter; but even creating that conviction is primarily a job for those who represent Negroes. The entire country has a stake in their success. One effective political leader in a Watts ghetto of Los Angeles or a Hough section of Cleveland may be worth more, in directing pressures toward orderly solutions, than a host of federal officials, delegations from city hall, and workers from human relations councils. That is what politicians are for. It is altogether possible that even a corrupt ward boss may bring to such a community more cohesion, more self-respect, than a pile of federal anti-poverty money. What is needed most by Negro communities throughout the country, and needed badly by the country as a whole, is Negro political leaders free and able to lead. In early 1967, no one knew whether they would appear in time. They could not be taken for granted. Little optimism could be derived from knowledge of the structures of Negro communities, which were as ramshackle as shanties on concrete blocks, from Los Angeles to the most rural Southern counties.

Optimism, however, could be felt in seeing the unsuspected strengths that had come, like flowers growing in rusty cans on the front porch of a Negro slum shanty, out of the Negro communities over the South during the rights movement's earlier arousal of masses. Aside from Dr. Martin Luther King, Jr., and a very few others, the new leaders' names did not become widely known. They were a collection of preachers, student activists from the crippled but struggling Negro colleges of the South, old-time business and political leaders able to make the quantum leap forward with the activists, and younger leaders attuned to the spirit and drive of the movement. They called every turn during the period of the South's greatest turning; white Southern leadership, whether by forfeit or by honest adjustment or by violent reaction of the George Wallace kind, was only responding to Negro initiatives. Negroes were setting the pace and shaping the future direction of the South. There is no exact parallel in American history for what they did, coming out of inauspicious backgrounds with unexpected qualities their miracles to perform.

The word miracle is used purposefully. Because the best-known leaders were religious, because so much of the metaphor and physical setting of the Southern movement was religious, and because of the dimly perceived spiritual depth of the movement, there was, all along, a tendency to look upon what was accomplished as truly a latter-day miracle. The Lord's will being worked by His agents was the feeling of it, the poetic sense of it breaking upon the consciousness of the nation and the world. Here was a mighty force in a nation that had only begun to emerge from wallowing in McCarthy's good-guy, bad-guy political simplicities, and from being pampered by the blank, moralistic reassurances of the Eisenhower years. This was a force which—perhaps out of the same wistfulness that had motivated these other phenomena—was able still to rejoice that His will would be done, as it was in days of old.

But a great deal of hard work and careful planning, shrewd psychological insight and knowledge, and an instinct for leadership that sometimes seemed genius-touched went into the working of the miracles. The small traditionally pro-Negro minority in the white South played, at best, a supporting role. White moderates and liberals, when they did understand and support fully the direct-action movement, knew also that history, in this endeavor, had left them standing to the side. They supported what they saw; they even, a few of them, with symbolic importance, joined the lines of pickets and marchers. But they knew, the Negroes knew, and the world knew that this was a Negro show. It was in a Negro idiom and style, the largest part of which rose out of the little churches, the religious feeling of the Southern Negro heart. And it was this that added the essential final ingredient to enable the movement to work its miracles, with bodies offered in a context of genuine sacrifice and courage.

Not all Negro Southerners were involved, not the majority even in the communities where the calls for bodies and braveness were made. But there were enough. Even after years of it, when many victories already had been won, civil rights workers found their way into Black Belt communities which the movement had not touched, and found in the churches, at the mass meetings, this same simple and yet ultimately complex religious readiness to believe, and to act on belief. Strangers still come away from such places awed and, sometimes, ennobled.

This was the culture and this the leadership that both made a revolution and made it non-violently. No one need believe that this same culture can spawn a great political leadership—except that no one might have believed it could have done what it did earlier, either.

What will be the effects of extended Negro political influence on the nation as a whole? Many Negroes outside the South have been pulling the levers of voting machines for a long time with notable effects. But even their votes have been less than full votes. Blessed by chance with a mechanical advantage in the electoral college system, they still were not whole politically because of the deprival of Negro voting in the South. Politics is alliances, and any group deprived of its lawful allies is dismembered politically. So, even by 1967, nowhere in America had a Negro voter yet really had full political equality. But this was changing, and the change was not simply an addition of Negro political power to existing Negro political power. The whole was likely to be much greater than the sum of the former parts. And through the whole, it seemed probable, there would be an infusion into the national public life of qualities genuinely new to it.

"I can see a new day," a young Negro Mississippian wrote from a rural registration post in 1962. "The gossip for the women has become politics." Robert Moses, the young Negro intellectual who started the grass-roots student movement in Mississippi, wrote from Greenwood to Chicago friends, as he distributed food after county officials had cut off federal food-surplus distribution: "When a thousand people stand in line for a few cans of food, then it is possible to tell a thousand people they are poor, that they are trapped in poverty, that they *must* move if they are to escape. . . ." No one can doubt the difference in thrust and tone which such people will bring to public life in Mississippi, or, for that matter, in Chicago.

Will they move? Right beside them are historical examples of others who did. It was most notably the poorer people of the white South who rose from somnolence, under the flagellations of demagogues, to give their most ardent personal devotion to the Theodore Bilbos, "Cotton Ed" Smiths, and Gene Talmadges. All that was required for many of them, in their frustrations, was a pledge like James K. Vardaman's to "put the bottom rung on top." There will be some black Bilbos and Vardamans. But no hard look at the population of the South or at the motivating forces in Negro communities would suggest they will predominate or attain such exalted states of power as have their white predecessors.

Mere allusion to these white predecessors is sobering, however, for it reminds us of the abject failure of Southern politics. The magnitude of it is seen in the simple listing of the wants that depleted generation after generation of Southerners of both races. Beginning with the basic necessities—food, shelter, and clothing—and continuing through to the necessities for adequate life in modern industrial society, education, health services, job opportunity, income, research, the eleven states of the old Confederacy are consistently at or near the bottom of the ranking of the states. Not all of this, of course, is the fault of political leadership. But the continuing failure to face the facts of these rankings (almost as true in the 1960's as when W. J. Cash wrote *The Mind of the South* in the 1930's) and to attack the causes intelligently is the fault and failure of Southern leadership, past and present.

The subject of mass political failure is worth examining here because it is a specter hanging over Negroes' coming immersion in politics. Theodore Bilbo, James K. Vardaman, Cole Blease, "Cotton Ed" Smith, "Tom-Tom" Heflin, "Pitchfork Ben" Tillman, Eugene Talmadge, John Rankin, the Orval Faubus of 1957 and a few years thereafter, the Herman Talmadge of the 1940's and 1950's, James F. Byrnes, Marvin Griffin, John Patterson, Ross Barnett, George Wallace—all deserve special recognition for the peculiar fact that not only did they fail to give constructive leadership at the state level to a troubled people, but they lent their full weight to making democratic solutions almost impossible without a dangerous wrenching of the federal system itself and of the whole concept of the Constitution's supremacy. Not all Southern politicians have positively rejected open options. These did. Each had the option in his time to refrain from enlarging the crisis to the extent that he did. In each case another man might have moderated the difficulties in ways these did not. So while they cannot be charged with full responsibility for the tempers they played upon, they can be charged with responsibility for firing those tempers rather than moderating them. Their failure in public duty as politicians was complete.

There were and are other types, of course; the Southern politician is not pure-bred. Senator Richard B. Russell of Georgia may well and fairly represent the best and the worst of all of those of prior years. As the "leader of the South" in Washington, he accepted the role of being chief defender of the Southern veto and of white supremacy, though he did not use the blunt language of more vulgar representatives of the cause. He had the option of contributing to solutions rather than to the problem, and he rejected it; never did he in retreat work, even quietly, toward positive solutions at home. With a violence of thought and language that often is overlooked, he contributed to the South's stresses. Senator Russell has been a tragic figure. As an effective young governor, an early New Dealer, and a Senate power of presidential pretensions, he won the admiration of many throughout the country. He presented an aspect of steadfast character, and of admirable personal disdain for much of what is unworthy of U.S. senators but not uncommon among them. Yet as much as anyone over a span of two decades, Senator Russell led the South back to Gettysburg.

The sad truth about Senator Russell seems to be that he was a believer, a true believer, in the racist rigmarole he preached in legalistic cant through the years. In the mid-sixties, after the death of Senator Harry F. Byrd of Virginia and the defection of others, Senator Russell seemed perhaps destined to be a lone giant survivor of what was once a whole tribe of intellectual, political, philosophical, and religious apologists and advocates of Southern racism. Perhaps, in fact, he was the last of that long line of lone, forlorn survivors the South has given every generation of America, true sons of the romantic, anti-rational streak that went awry in the South, gallantly ready for self-ruination—not, as might have been done in all honor, against the name of those things in the North which opposed the human spirit and the best nature of the South, but in the name of the South's least worthy traits. There is a grandeur in self-destructive romanticism wandered out of the bounds of the merely mistaken into the irrational, but it is a kind of sad grandeur that must be measured against all the needless suffering that it brings upon blameless human beings.

We need to note at least the chance that the new Negro political leadership, emerging from the same South that made a venerable and loved fetish of political failure, could prove to be so shackled by this part of romanticism and mysticism that it, too, fails as a political class. (Is there a kinship between the extraordinarily personal clan loyalty and anti-institutional paranoia that came from the inherited tribalism of beleaguered Scotch-Irish, and that which came from beleaguered men taken from the rain forests of Africa?) White Southerners as politicians were partly crippled by the uncontrolled excesses of the public dialogue which they helped create. A failure of Negro leaders as politicians could come from the same cause. How much Negro political leaders will be buffeted by excesses in the public exchange is not yet known. But severe strain in Negro communities and the continuing resistance of many white persons suggest substantial temptations to excess for Negro politicians. They, like their white counterparts, will have to be appraised according to whether they enlarge solutions or enlarge the problem.

Politics will probably be more "liberal" in label with more Negroes voting. Will it be more liberal in fact? Will it reflect more the qualities of a liberal society such as Mill envisioned, wherein public opinion is genuinely tolerant and the extent of conformity and enforced agreement is limited, and wherein the unconventional is respected and divergence is not suppressed even by overwhelming majorities? Will there be a liberal society behind a liberal government, or will there be even a genuinely liberal government?

From Hattiesburg, Mississippi, a young voter registration worker wrote in the fall of 1963 about a Negro man who had come to his office and blurted out his thoughts. "The basic thing we need is freedom of speech," the man said, speaking rapidly, as if in desperation. He thus underscored the urgency of what most take for granted but what is often repressed everywhere by forces too subtle to describe. The registration worker, Carl Arnold, added his thoughts about the conversation with this disturbed and disturbing visitor: "He is simply an intelligent man who, because of the type of society in which he lives, has been caused such mental and psychological damage that it may not be repaired in a lifetime. I'm working on voter registration but I felt that I must tell of this man. Voter registration is only two words describing the immediate goals we aim for. We must dig deeper; we have to dig deeper into the individual. We can canvass, make speeches, point paper, and use a number of physical techniques, but we must go further. . . ."

The man who is free to register, as this man eventually was, and yet knows he is not truly free to speak may be a rare man in our society, not because he is not free to speak but because he knows he is not. Someone may tell him why that is, what hidden barriers now are built within him because of his race or because he is a twentieth-century American. But neither that knowledge nor the vote will deliver freedom to him. Only another society that he may or may not help build can do that, and it only can deliver that partial freedom that is freedom to quest. Whether he and millions like him will help to build it or prevent it, at a time when we are all increasingly at bay against the mass, the impersonal, and the unconscious arrogance of self-conscious institutions, is a question of such import that it ensnares us all.

Nowhere, at any time in the history of the nation, has political activity been so intimately involved with questions of personal values and personal freeness as in the voter registration movement in the South in the 1960's. The mere mechanics of successful voter registration did not require this. Hundreds of successful registration drives have been conducted without it, and were again in many places in the sixties. Much of the explanation lies in the resistance met by the movement when it sought the vote. One has to read the earnest, elaborate battle plans of the activists going into a new part of the hard-core resistance areas for voter registration work—a feel in them of guerrilla warfare, anticipating non-cooperative voting officials, hoodlumism, police inter-ference—to understand the dynamics of it.

They made a movement out of a registration campaign, a movement hardened and unified by trouble, deeply personal in its internal life as in its outward extension. Will the work of this period, already fading from easy view, be blown away, like another past now gone with the wind? If the answer depends upon the constancy of activist missionaries in the South over a span of decades, then the wind will surely prevail. The hard core of so-called professional workers in the civil rights movement has been a wisp, always wind-blown, never more than a thin mist on an old and durable meadow, subject to sudden gusts that sweep it away in moments. It never, in truth, has touched many places for very long. Across all the South, it has been a substantial, continuing presence in only a few cities and counties. Once it is granted credit for forcing extra-ordinary national change by local confrontations, we must wonder whether it is lastingly important. Will it change, or has it changed, more than structure and procedures? Has it helped to shift more than conven-tional power conventionally used?

Once again we come to the unique quality of this part of the revolution of the 1960's: the intimacy of political movement and personal expansion. "I can't see working to get large numbers of individual people registered and ignoring basic changes in the spirit of individual people and the community," a young Negro Northerner wrote from Albany, Georgia, in 1962. And Elizabeth Wyckoff wrote from the same Student Nonviolent Coordinating Committee (SNCC) voter project, which had been toiling in southwest Georgia counties that at least equaled Mississippi in repression and constant violence: "A returning visitor to the Lee [County] meetings is especially struck by the increased sureness of the principal figures of the Lee County Movement. They were always impressive personalities whose bearing and eloquence of expression matched the quality of their heroism, but now they are developed and experienced leaders. Lee County is the most remarkable example I have seen of the catalytic action that SNCC's presence can have in starting a community toward using its own undeveloped potential."

If these were only isolated sentiments of a handful of idealists in contemporary America, they might be taken as moving expressions of concern but not as evidence of a formative force. But they are not isolated. While these people may be untypical, those who speak such words are one blood with many others who have been drawn along by the existential forces of the 1960's. It is not sufficient simply to count the votes of Negroes. Negroes usually have had important effects upon the country more because of what was done to them and about them than because of what they have done. As passive agents on the scene a century ago, they gave rise to rigidities that precipitated a civil war. As passive agents on the scene in the South, they have been so central that on them has been shaped a whole culture that is unique in the nation. They have now become active agents, and it is difficult for a Robert Penn Warren to speak for Negroes when a James Baldwin can do it; or for a white liberal politician to speak for them when a Negro politician can; or for white votes to speak for them when Negro votes can. Still, through their mere presence, they will continue to be moulders of the destiny of the country because of what that presence causes others to do.

The white South always had a Negro, and so it had to deal with him. Politically, as in many other ways, it dealt with him by locking him up. With the out-migration of the twentieth century and the intrusion of the Negro as an active agent in national politics, the nation now has a

Negro. It cannot deal with him politically, socially, and economically by locking him up. It could not rid itself of him even if it were desperate enough to try to do that. The white South's public character and private soul were altered by the attempt to keep him locked up.

The nation, which now has a Negro, will likely look at itself in a different way. Some of its greatest pretensions are already extraordinarily self-conscious if not eroded and abandoned. It has become more aware, largely as a result of the Negro movement, of the implications of poverty, national and international. It has sensed a more intimate, personal meaning in the litanies of national patriotism and idealism. And it has, perhaps most importantly of all, seen demonstrated the surprising strength in the human potential that can confront, control, and change what had come to seem unchangeable, uncontrollable problems of modern existence. "We shall overcome" has become imbedded in its unconscious.

Around the mere presence of the Negro, William Faulkner dealt with the old, universal moral themes of life; that, too, was no accidental choice, for in the South which he wrote about it is impossible to ponder these matters without pondering the Negro. Now as the white South begins to ponder him more honestly, with more freedom than it has known before, the nation is constrained to ponder him, too, and to deal with his presence. So it is not simply by a numerical count of ballots that the country will be greatly influenced. It is because of something the Negro American has in large part produced: America's confrontation of itself. This suggests a creative circumspection that has to do with the fiber and the spirit of individuals, white and Negro. Largely because of Negro votes in the cities, the country comes to this new encounter free of the political paralysis of the past. It moves on, to new freedom or new paralysis. This is a hopeful moment in its history, and an awesome one. In the South of the 1960's, where this meshing of politics and personal expansion is seeding in a seedtime, we may glimpse at least the questions of the future.

NOTES

1. Quoted from a report to the Voter Education Project of the Southern Regional Council in Atlanta. Quotations from voter registration workers cited here are from the reports in the project's files unless otherwise attributed.

2. For further discussion of some of these political courtships, see Paul Lewinson,

Race, Class, and Party (New York: Grosset and Dunlap, Universal Library Edition, 1965; originally published 1932), p. 158. Lewinson comments at some length on the significance of the 1928 campaign in breaking the Solid South.

3. Reliable estimates of Negro voting in national elections in the 1930's have depended in large part upon information gathered by the National Association for the Advancement of Colored People (NAACP). In particular, for analysis of the 1944 election we are indebted to Henry Lee Moon of that organization, whose *Balance of Power* (Garden City, New York: Doubleday and Company, Inc., 1948) contains a valuable commentary on Negro voting and the consequences in the years of the New Deal.

4. *The Negro Handbook*, 1946–47.

5. Moon, p. 9.

6. Moon, p. 10.

2)
The Death of
Black Belt Power

The white South has not yet lost its yardman. Nor has it seen, as Senator Theodore G. Bilbo of Mississippi feared, the end of segregation "spoil a good field hand and make an insolent cook." But if it has not spoiled its field hand nor lost its yardman, it has lost its nigger. He is departing. James Baldwin may say he never existed—only men existed, and the white man invented the nigger, and this fact tells more about the white man than it tells about Negroes. But the white South at least thought it had a nigger. Many of its politicians helped it think so.

"No one is ever going to out-nigger me again," an animated little man in shirtsleeves said in 1958. He had just been defeated in a race for governor. His opponent, with no more evidence than has ever been required for such allegations, had successfully stamped him as "weak on segregation" and won the votes. The little man was George Wallace, and he was what passed, in 1958, for a Southern "moderate." Four years later he let no one "out-nigger" him. He became governor of Alabama, and shortly the nation's foremost representative of racism in politics.[1]

In the mid-1960's, many Southern politicians were changing their songs, as George Wallace had done in another way just a few years earlier. More politicians had begun to ask Negroes for their votes, appoint Negroes to public offices, and spend time solicitously looking after the particular needs of Negro constituents. More importantly, the entire framework within which a Southern politician must live and perform, from the time he explores tentatively to find whether he should run until the time he takes a stand on some issue as an office-holder, had been re-made.

A strange nexus of power, the Black Belt,[2] arching through parts of Southern states from Virginia to eastern Texas, had extended its hold in remarkable fashion over the larger remaining area of the South. Since these states themselves often had extended their power in remarkable fashion over the nation and the democratic institutions, the power of the Black Belt was heavy in Washington. But the framework has changed. The entire South and the nation have changed as a result. It had been the Black Belt that gave the older South political cohesion. Outside the Belt, in the "hill country" and the coast of Mississippi, the Tennessee Valley section, the mountains of Georgia, the Piedmont of South Carolina, and so on, another South yielded to the Black Belt on a matter which seemed more important to whites of the Belt than to anyone else: the matter of controlling the Negro. To the Black Belt's cries for help in throwing off the Negro voting majorities of Reconstruction, the "white counties" often responded, though sometimes they extracted their own political payoffs. Sometimes, too, they unsuccessfully fought the Belt on such matters as state literacy tests and disfranchisement itself. And sometimes they lost all the way around: when Alabama's Black Belt whites brought about the disfranchisement of Negroes in 1901–2, they successfully contended that their areas thus were losing votes and statewide influence and in return they should be given more legislative representation than their population merited. The Black Belt won on both sides of that "compromise" with the white counties.

In 1938 Senator Walter F. George of Georgia ran successfully in spite of an effort by President Roosevelt to defeat him by endorsing a challenger in the Democratic primary. Senator George told Georgia voters what the issue really was. It was, of course, the Negro. The liberals were trying to pass a bill in Congress which, he said, threatened the South. It would make lynching a federal offense. If this bill passed, more would come. It would be a forerunner of an iniquitous civil liberties law that would vitally affect the vote of every Southern (white) man and woman.

Appropriately, Georgia's oldest daily newspaper, the Augusta *Chronicle*, best explained the import of threat to which Senator George had referred:

The Senator did not say so in plain words, but what he meant, we are quite certain, was that the next step after the passage of the anti-lynching bill would be the enactment of some kind of measure to kill the Democratic white primary in the South. What Senator George meant was that if the Communist Party . . . and Walter White, head of the National Association for the Advancement of Colored People, are successful in "purging" the Democratic Party of a few stalwart Southern Democratic congressmen, that it will only be another step to destroy the Democratic white primary in Georgia and other Southern states. That, fellow Georgians, is no fable; it is a fact. Only through the tenacity of a small group of Southern Democrats was the vicious, vote-getting, anti-lynching bill defeated at the last session of Congress.[3]

This hortatory emission is no modern parody of the way it was. It was typical of the main flow of Southern politics in 1938, and for a good many years after that. A law to establish the right to vote was a communist plot that threatened the South. A law even against lynching was a plot that threatened the South. And the South was always saved by "a few stalwart Southern Democratic congressmen." In personal terms, what it meant was the debilitation of Southern politicians and their ruination as potential leaders in the face of a monstrous problem.

The Negro, who has not requested or enjoyed the ride, is being removed from the backs of Southern politicians. Since 1960, rising Negro political power has undulated through the South with more effect than in any other period of this century. In 1930, the number of Negro Southerners who voted was, except in a few communities, insignificant. One authority wrote at that time that it could not be demonstrated that this registration had increased at all during the previous thirty years,[4] since the period of massive disfranchisement.

Approximately 688,000 Negroes registered to vote in the eleven states of the South between April 1962, and November 1, 1964, under the Voter Education Project of the Southern Regional Council.[5] This was the largest and first notable increase in Southern Negro voter registration since the first wave of heavy registration that followed the Supreme

Court's outlawing the white primary in 1944.[6] In the years following that important collapse of what had become the South's most formidable legal fortress against Negro voting, registration of Negroes increased from 250,000 (the 1940 total) to 1,008,614 in 1952. This was from something like 5 per cent of the total Negro voting-age population to 20 per cent. But from 1952 to 1962, the rate of increase diminished considerably. In that decade, the increase was slightly less than half a million voters, bringing the total to 1,476,200. Thus, from 1962 to 1964, Negro registration increased more (688,000) than it had in all the ten years preceding (467,586), and by half as much as in all the 22 years preceding (1,226,200).

In the tragic clamor to resist the Supreme Court school decision, with the Citizens Councils launched on their brief but deadly career (they lasted only a decade; white-collar klansmanship seemed about done in by 1964), the South suddenly regressed to a phase of concerted, deliberate oppression of its Negro population. In the thirties and forties, despite ominous stirrings, the order of things between the races had seemed to most of the white South satisfactorily and permanently settled, foot on neck. With the Depression and later war, and with the postwar coming of the industrial revolution and urbanization to the South, the mind of the Southern white was distracted from its obsession with Negroes. Oppression had been casual. It had come to be, like church-going in the Bible Belt, more habitual than meaningful. When the 1954 school decision brought race back to the center of Southern existence and put oppression of Negroes back on an organized, well-schemed basis, it was natural that Negro voting—fear and hatred of which had been the inspiration for the whole post-Reconstruction rigmarole of segregation and caste ritual—would suffer badly.

A study turned up 530 cases of violence, reprisal, and intimidation between 1955 and 1958 in the aftermath of the school decision.[7] This report did not, of course, reflect *all* the violence, reprisal, and intimidation, for much of this activity never was noted beyond its immediate vicinity, where its message was clear to all. "The threats and illegal activities aimed at individual Negroes and whites who questioned the South's tradition of segregation undoubtedly deterred other Negroes from asserting their rights, including the right to vote," wrote Margaret Price. She added an observation that remains true: "An instance of racial violence in the South is rarely an isolated event—it serves as a reminder to Negroes that what has happened can happen again." [8]

There was also economic coercion, intimidation, and reprisal against Negro registration and voting. And beyond physical and economic harm, barriers were built into the administrative procedures of registration and voting. Qualification tests were the device relied upon most heavily after the white primary was outlawed. They could be difficult enough to prevent most Negroes from registering. They would have prevented most whites from registering, too, except that whites, including illiterates, usually were allowed to pass. Where Negroes came along extraordinary enough to pass, they could be eliminated by technical errors either on their test forms or on the registration application. Voting lists were sometimes purged to cut off Negroes who had managed to register in other years; this activity reached a peak in Louisiana, with the Citizens Councils in the forefront.[9] There also were "slowdowns" by registrars, including infrequent opening of their offices, and sometimes outright refusal to process a Negro's application.

It was no wonder, then, that in the eight states where the Southern Regional Council was able to obtain reliable figures, there was a 45,845 decrease in Negro registration from 1956 to 1958: among the missing states in the figures, moreover, were Mississippi and Alabama.[10] The same methods of physical and economic intimidation and administrative blocks were still being used during the Voter Education Project of 1962 to 1964. Indeed, one of the most significant results of that drive was to force federal legislation to eliminate these obstacles and open the registration process fully to Negroes.

After the passage of the Voting Rights Act of 1965, registration increased even more rapidly in states where recalcitrance had been greatest. In Mississippi, where registration had been estimated at 22,000 as the voting bill was nearing passage, it reached 150,000 within four months after the act took effect. Imperfect though it was and even though it was initially evaded in part, the new law did break the worst kind of resistance. Most state registrars who had been using discriminatory practices were forced to stop. The law also voided literacy tests in the states that had practiced discrimination. The message of the law was clear: no effort at evasion, none of the old sleight-of-hand at many registrars' offices, could prevent most Negroes from voting.

This was the end of an era in which the white South, to keep white supremacy, had forced itself for a century into legalistic contortions and the desperate building of backfires that had burned off much of the best in the region. Negroes had voted heavily between 1865 and 1876, but by

1910 every Southern state had systematically disfranchised them. Fraud and intimidation had been the chief means in the earlier stages,[11] but legalistic devices eventually became more important: the grandfather clause (permitting the descendants of all pre-1867 voters to vote without property or literacy qualifications), the poll tax, and literacy tests, all administered with proper care for race. But as these began to fall in the courts, the most effective single tool became the all-white state Democratic Party and the "white primary," in which Negroes were prevented from voting by party regulation rather than by statutory law.[12]

For four decades, Southern politicians reminded their constituents that only through the Democratic Party—"our Democratic white primary" was the phrase—could white supremacy be preserved, and that nothing worse could befall the white people of the South than a two-party competition in which Negro votes might matter. When the U.S. Supreme Court at last struck the blow, so long feared, that killed the white primary, the South went through a convulsion similar to, though not nearly as severe as, the one that began when the court outlawed school segregation ten years later. In 1944, the court in *Smith* v. *Alwright* ruled against the white primary in Texas, and in other decisions that soon followed it struck down white primaries in other states. The Deep South states then moved, as if by habit, to evade the court's decisions. The optimism of those who had seen the white-primary decisions as the final, fatal blow against Southern white supremacy soon faded.

There has been no one point at which Negro votes freed Southern politicians from being made or broken by racism. But there were times before the 1960's when this, at last, seemed possible in certain places. The example of Georgia is an adequate illustration. Georgia did not adapt its practices to the Supreme Court's white-primary ruling immediately after the decision was handed down in 1944; but neither did it rush to erect new legislative defenses. When in 1946 the federal courts applied the earlier ruling specifically to the white primary in Georgia, the state government did not seek long delay by evasive acts. So Negro registration began.

Registration drives were organized; response was widespread and spontaneous. By the end of 1946, Georgia had about 125,000 Negro voters, 18.8 per cent of the adult Negro population. This was numerically by far the largest Negro registration in the South. As a percentage of Negro adults it was second only to the 25.8 per cent in Tennessee, a state where racist tempers were not as strong and in which only seven counties had a population more than one-third Negro. Mississippi, by contrast with Georgia, had 5,000 Negro voters, 0.9 per cent of the Negro adults; Alabama, 6,000, 1.2 per cent; Louisiana, 10,000, 2.6 per cent; and Virginia, 48,000, 13.2 per cent.[13]

Georgia's sudden change was attributable largely to a combination of moderate forces led by Governor Ellis Arnall, a shrewd young lawyer who had defeated Eugene Talmadge in 1942. While neighboring states were trying to turn the clock back, Arnall was accepting Negro voters as allies. That year he supported a young industrialist, James V. Carmichael, to succeed him, and in the subsequent campaign between Carmichael and Eugene Talmadge, Negroes voted overwhelmingly for Carmichael. Their votes gave him, in fact, a popular majority. He thus would have been the first governor in the Deep South in this century elected because of Negro support. By the normal rules related to the seizure of political advantage, it may be supposed that a climate for continuing increase in Negro political strength would have followed under his administration. But he was not the winner. Talmadge won the election because he had the majority of "county unit" votes under Georgia's county-unit system of elections, which was biased heavily in favor of rural counties.[14] Although Talmadge died before taking office, his forces rallied successfully and in 1948 his son, Herman, was elected governor. The progress of Negroes toward further political participation was virtually halted in Georgia; the state took a strongly segregationist tack; Negroes' votes were not sought by candidates for statewide office, and so Negro voting influence on the state level was small.

These circumstances are worth noting now as an example of how close one Deep South state seemed to come even in the mid-1940's to a political reorientation that might have given Negroes their place in the democracy. We cannot know how history might have turned if Georgia had continued in that direction and if Negroes had begun to make a difference in state elections. Under those circumstances, Georgia might not have been fitted into the Southern defiance of the 1950's. And, of course, if the same turn had come in other states on the simple matter of Negro voting, a whole era of Southern and American history might have been different. Georgia missed the turn because the arithmetic was not right. If somehow 40 or 45 per cent of the age-eligible Negroes had been registered in 1946 rather than 18.5, these percentage points alone might have made a difference ever since.

The lesson to be drawn from this is that up to a point, in a racist climate at least, even a substantial Negro registration can be neutralized and negated. In Georgia, the Talmadge faction was able to whip up enough racist temper and resentment of Negro votes to negate them and the largely urban and mountain-county white votes that had been allied with them. The 125,000 registered Negro voters thus became, subsequently, only potentially important. In fact, for the next decade, the impact of Negro voting was perhaps negative, because the Talmadge forces had used fear of it to greatly strengthen anti-Negro sentiment, and this in turn had fortified a teetering Talmadge camp. By the mid-1960's, however, many Southern politicians believed a turning point had been reached at which Negro votes mattered more than anti-Negro votes. In Georgia, by 1966, the 125,000 Negro registration had risen to 272,000. Although a rise in racist sentiment was evidenced in that year's governor's election, it seemed likely that the arithmetic was becoming "right" for the interests of Negro voters.

Negro votes now were worth more, too, because Black Belt white votes were worth less. The whites of the Black Belt always had profited politically from Negroes' presence. Although Negroes did not count as votes there, they counted as population, and thus the Black Belt had many more congressional districts, judicial districts, legislative districts, and officeholders than its white population alone would have warranted. The end of slavery actually had helped to give Black Belt whites more power, since a slave had been counted as three-fifths of a person in determining congressional representation. So Negroes bestowed political benefits upon the areas that were their worst enemies. Those places also generally benefited from all the ills of malapportionment. Most Black Belt counties have been among the parts of the rural South which have steadily lost population in this century, but which usually have not accordingly lost political representation. When the federal courts finally broke that grip with the reapportionment decisions beginning in 1962, each Georgia House of Representatives member from Fulton County (Atlanta) represented more than 150,000 people; a House member from rural Echols County represented fewer than 2,000. The formula for representation had been established in 1917, when the state's political temper was very much that of its Black Belt counties. Such malapportionment was common around the country. What made it especially hurtful in the Deep South was that the principal beneficiaries of this political hammerlock were areas where whites were most determined to keep Negroes politically suppressed, to keep Negro labor cheap, and to give Negroes as little in educational and other government services as possible.

It probably was not an accident but a logical and symbolic outcome that the most "liberal" of Alabama's modern governors, Jim Folsom, was from a northern county with only 1 per cent Negro population and the most histrionically racist among its modern governors, George Wallace, was from a Black Belt county with 52 per cent Negro population. By the same token, however, a future governor from Wallace's Barbour County is likely to be more "liberal" on racial matters than a future governor from Folsom's Cullman County. Probably no one would be running seriously for governor from Barbour County if he were not entrenched at home, in his home area, and a new, heavy Negro registration in Barbour and nearby counties by 1966 made it seem unlikely that a future base for statewide office could be attained in that area without at least some Negro support.

What are the prospects for Negro control of Southern political divisions by majority voting? Sometimes they are vastly exaggerated. In no Southern state are Negroes a majority. In the 1960 census, they came closest in Mississippi, which was 42.3 per cent Negro; but Mississippi's voting-age Negro population that year was only 36.1 per cent. (This kind of discrepancy is common in the South because of its export of Negro young adults to the rest of the country.) Only in Mississippi, in fact, did Negroes constitute as much as a third of the voting-age population. (See APPENDIX II.) The next highest percentages were in South Carolina, 29.3 per cent, and Louisiana, 28.5 per cent. As long as racial identification remains a primary consideration, then, the eventual prospects of Negroes' electing governors, senators, and others chosen on a statewide basis depended upon more than numbers. As for congressmen: In late 1966, no congressional district among 106 in the South had a Negro voting-age majority, on the basis of the 1960 census, and none had a Negro registration majority. The districts with the highest percentages of voting-age Negroes were Mississippi's First, 44.3 per cent; Mississippi's Third, 39.6 per cent; South Carolina's Sixth, 39.2 per cent; South Carolina's First, 38.0 per cent; Georgia's Second, 36.4 per cent; and Mississippi's Second, 35.9 per cent. Negroes were a voting-age majority in 85 of the 1,139 counties (including Virginia's 32 independent cities) in the 11 Southern states: 21 of Mississippi's 82; 19 of Georgia's 159; 10 of Alabama's 67; 9 of South Carolina's 46; 7 of Virginia's 130 (counties and independent cities); 5 of North Carolina's 100; 5 of

Louisiana's 64; 5 of Arkansas's 75; 2 of Tennessee's 95; 2 of Florida's 67; and none of Texas' 254.

All of this suggests that the impact of Negro majorities and the election of Negro candidates by these majorities alone is not likely to be the overriding fact about Southern local and state government, or Southern congressional representation. The migration of Negroes out of the South, which began during World War I and resumed heavily during World War II, totaling 1.5 million Negroes during the decade from 1940 to 1950 and another 1.5 million between 1950 and 1960, has seen to that. The exodus has continued since 1960, according to Census Bureau and Labor Department studies. This was increasingly attributable to the mechanization of Southern plantations, a fact behind heavy migration also from farms to Southern cities during the same period.

Negro voting influence across racial lines, in predominantly white electorates, is another matter. In no less than half of all Southern congressional districts, Negroes are at least one-fifth of the people. In eight states and in most sizable Southern cities they are more than a fifth. Politicians ordinarily do not long ignore 20 per cent of their constituencies, if there is any cohesion at all in that segment, and the more cohesion the less ignoring.[15] About matters that affect them because of their race, great cohesion is possible among Negro voters. On other matters, less cohesion is possible. The more Negroes in large numbers improve their economic status, as an example, the more they will be subject to the usual differences of viewpoint that prevail in an economically diverse white society.

A cohesive vote can change political arithmetic dramatically. In 1965, before Negro registration had neared its potential, one prospective Alabama political candidate had calculated that with full Negro support and without even any further registration, he might win a majority in a statewide race the next year with only 38 per cent of the white votes. When a politician knows he can afford to lose 62 per cent of the old electorate, a figure which usually has been regarded as a landslide, all his bearings are suddenly shifted. In New Orleans, two young and moderate politicians were saying separately at approximately the same time that in the future they could win with 40 per cent of the city's whites. What lends significance to these particular calculations is that in 1966 this arithmetic was at the forefront of politicians' minds over the region. Such calculations not only may determine victors on election day but also the field that is running.

Slim majorities and pluralities are the rule rather than the exception in our political system because of its tendency toward the center, and because of the large number of voters who shift sides from one election to the next. Thus a small weight may tilt the whole structure, as did the white people of the Black Belt of the South in the past.

The tilting of Southern politicians as Negro votes increased and the 1950's white massive resistance died has occurred, in some cases, with a sudden sense of urgency. The balloting of congressmen on the Voting Rights Act itself tells much of the story. Seven Southern congressmen switched their votes from "no" to "yes" on the voting bill between the time it passed the House on July 9, 1965, and the time it returned to the floor from a conference committee and was approved on August 3. Altogether, 31 of the 106 congressmen from 11 Southern states voted for the bill on final passage. The Southern "yes" votes were distributed this way: 7 of Tennessee's 9 congressmen; 11 of Texas' 23; 7 of Florida's 12; 2 of Georgia's 10; 2 of Louisiana's 7 (with one vacancy); 1 of Virginia's 10; and 1 of Arkansas's 4. There were no "yes" votes from Mississippi, Alabama, South Carolina, or North Carolina.

The distribution of the "yes" votes is an almost precise reflection of the areas (such as Florida and Tennessee) where racist sentiments have been less important than in the traditional Deep South, and of areas where Negro voting has weakened the impact of racist sentiments (as in the two Georgia congressional districts dominated by Atlanta). These are the areas which might have been expected to break first from the old Southern solidarity in opposing civil rights measures in Congress. But the extent of the break was especially noteworthy: almost one-third of the congressmen from the old Confederate states voted for the bill. Only one year earlier, Representative Charles L. Weltner of Georgia, alone among congressmen from the Deep South tier and accompanied by few colleagues from other Southern states, had voted for the 1964 Civil Rights Act.[16]

Throughout the South similar shifts were occurring. Governor Orval Faubus of Arkansas, who had precipitated the first of the great federal-state collisions when he blocked the court-ordered desegregation of a Little Rock high school in 1957, intently began in 1965 to make peace with Negro voters. In November he announced the employment of more Negroes for state jobs and disclosed plans for the appointment, for the first time, of Negroes to state boards and commissions.

In Tennessee, as Negro registration rose rapidly at that same time, Governor Frank Clement was making plans to run again for the U.S.

Senate. Governor Clement's political career had risen and fallen with
Negro votes. He won the Democratic nomination for governor in 1962
with a margin supplied by Negro voters. He lost a 1964 Senate race to
Ross Bass, who had just voted for the Civil Rights Act and whose
margin of victory was more than accounted for by his overwhelming
Negro support. Senator Bass, who had been filling the remainder of the
late Senator Estes Kefauver's term, was up for re-election in 1966 and
Governor Clement obviously was working to prevent a repetition of the
Negro voting of 1964. Before 1965 had ended, he had appointed a
Negro criminal court judge in Memphis, added Negroes to the all-white
state highway patrol, and given two Negroes personnel department
assignments to find qualified Negroes for state jobs. Governor Clement's
appeals to Negroes in Memphis, especially the appointment of the
Negro judge there, paid off well in the Tennessee Democratic primary
in 1966. When the governor challenged Bass, Negro support in most of
the state went overwhelmingly for the senator. But in Memphis,
Clement broke the pattern. The number of Negro votes he won there
exceeded the margin of his statewide primary victory over Senator Bass.
In the subsequent general election, however, Howard Baker, a moderate
Republican, defeated Clement, winning most of the Negro votes. Even
if Clement had received a heavy Negro vote against Baker, he would not
have won. But except in that race, invariably Clement's political success
in the 1960's had been determined by Negro votes.

In Louisiana, Governor John McKeithen was facing perhaps the most
arduous task of any Southern politician: the necessity of completely
reversing himself within a two-year period. Governor McKeithen had
been elected in 1964 as the more uncompromising segregationist in a
runoff and apparently had won because of that position. Then, within
two months after the Voting Rights Act went into effect, 40,000 Negroes registered in Louisiana. By November the state's Negro registration was 210,000, and rising. Governor McKeithen's timing in the face
of all this was adroit. He wanted the legislature to pass an amendment
allowing him to succeed himself. Amendments usually are not approved
by the legislature until the year when they will be voted upon by the
people. But the governor pushed the amendment through the legislature a year early, winning the required two-thirds majorities, and then
he went busily about winning Negro support. He had used his legislative
strength when it was at a peak, before he had offended the segregationists. Now he needed to find votes elsewhere, popular votes for the

succession amendment. He named an official state bi-racial commission and startled some of its Negro members by saying he would do whatever it recommended.[17] His public tone by this time was distinctly one of moderation and compromise. Negro leaders soon were speaking favorably of Governor McKeithen, and many whites were impressed that he had "kept peaceful relations." His succession amendment was approved overwhelmingly.

In Georgia, while these events were transpiring in Tennessee and Louisiana, one particular little vignette was revealing. Governor Carl Sanders, under color of racial moderation, had defeated segregationist former Governor Marvin Griffin in 1962. Yet he was saying afterward, when pressed, that he was simply a segregationist by preference who believed in abiding by the law. By 1965, word came to Governor Sanders that Senator Herman Talmadge had accepted an invitation to speak to the Hungry Club, a luncheon group of influential Atlanta Negroes. No state-level politician had addressed the club before, and perhaps there was something to be gained from being first. Governor Sanders' Negro allies, hearing of the Talmadge plan, swiftly arranged for a special meeting so that the governor might be there first. Of such was the new jockeying for the support of Negro voters. Senator Talmadge, who once had truculently remarked that he would not reply to something said by Representative Adam Clayton Powell because he did not debate with Negro congressmen, was interviewed close to the time of the Hungry Club affair. He said he would not object if President Johnson proposed the appointment of a qualified Negro lawyer as a federal judge in Georgia.[18]

The last of the old South's powerful instruments of bargaining, the "solid South" phenomenon, was shattered in 1964. Some of it had gone when the Democratic Party under Roosevelt abandoned the requirement that its presidential nominees obtain approval of two-thirds of the convention delegates. More had gone as the Republican Party made inroads in some states, taking away the wholeness of the solid South. But until 1964, there still was a South around which a presidential candidate and a major party could build a strategy. Senator Barry Goldwater's "Southern strategy," rooted in the idea that a candidate starting with all the South could win without the states where Negro votes and liberal programs counted heavily, was not new. It was the Democratic tactic of old, which granted the white South its required concessions in order to start with that base, the "solid South." The 1964 results showed, however, that although a national party in future years may have a "Southern strategy," it cannot be successful even in the South if it is based on the old *quid pro quo* of leaving the white South alone to handle its own affairs in its own way. It cannot, simply because with the coming of Negro votes there is no longer any "solid South" on racial matters.

There was no "solid South" in 1964. President Lyndon B. Johnson carried more of the South than did Mr. Goldwater. Negro Southerners gave Mr. Johnson more than 1,400,000 of his 16,000,000 popular vote majority nationwide. Mr. Goldwater did not carry the Southern states that had been going Republican in national elections; he carried only some of the states that usually had not. These are pieces of the story. But the special meaning of the 1964 election for the South lay in this fact: in every Southern state where more than 45 per cent of the adult Negroes were registered to vote, Johnson won. Negro votes prevented Goldwater from carrying Arkansas, Florida, Tennessee, Virginia, and probably North Carolina. If Goldwater had carried these five states, along with South Carolina, Georgia, Alabama, Mississippi, and Louisiana, a "solid South" would have remained and possibly a "Southern strategy" would have survived. (The Negro vote also elected two Democratic senators and was decisive in sending at least half a dozen Democratic representatives to Washington.) The outcome without Negro votes would have encouraged the Goldwater wing of the Republican Party and strengthened the old South's forces in Washington. The old South's stalwart Democrats could have said the party must pay more attention to its Southern conservatives and less attention to the interests of Negroes.

Negro votes destroyed the last of the solid South in 1964, just as they had gradually destroyed the Southern veto in Washington during the previous two decades. For the nation, the meanings of the election were manifold, but in the South there was one overriding truth for the region's future. The South of the Black Belt was gone, and not only Negro Southerners but another South that had been present all along had overcome. No presidential candidate or major national party or political interest in Congress could speak easily again of "the South" when what it meant was "part of the white South." This is a change which profoundly affects the political life of the whole nation.

NOTES

1. Governor Wallace continued to carry racism's banner in the Alabama guberna-torial election of 1966 and indicated plans to run for president in 1968, as an entry in Democratic presidential primaries or as a third-party candidate. His forces failed in an effort to change the state constitution so that he might succeed himself as governor. In 1966, his wife, Lurleen, entered the governor's race as his stand-in. Wallace made it clear he would function as governor in all but the technical sense if she were elected. She won in the Democratic primary without a runoff and over-whelmingly defeated a Republican, James Martin, in the general election.

2. Definitions of the Black Belt vary. The name is derived from the fertile black soil, much of it "bottom land" but much of it, also, the clay-rich soil of the uplands. Because of its fertility and the ease with which it could be cultivated in great tracts, it had the heaviest concentration of slaves and it became the area where the plantation social and economic system, as well as plantation values, were strongest. Today a demographic map showing racial distribution may be considered a suggestive, though imperfect, delineation of the Black Belt. (Some counties with heavy Negro popula-tions were not part of Black Belt as defined by soil.) In a general way, then, the Belt may be said to begin in coastal Virginia and extend in a corridor through coastal North Carolina, along the coast and further inland in South Carolina, broadly across the mid-sections of Georgia and Alabama, and across the mid-section of Mississippi but broadening to take in the Mississippi "Delta," and into smaller regions of Louisiana and Arkansas, with pockets in Tennessee and Texas. (In Mississippi, the Delta is the deep triangle of land stretching north from Vicksburg between the Missis-sippi and Yazoo rivers, and should not be confused with the Mississippi River delta at the mouth of the Mississippi, in Louisiana.)

3. The Augusta *Chronicle*, August 27, 1938.

4. Lewinson, p. 198.

5. Unless otherwise noted, registration statistics are based on estimates of the Voter Education Project of the Southern Regional Council. These are, wherever possible, drawn from official figures. Where such are not available, newspaper clippings, in-formed sources, and other informal methods are used. These estimates have, over the years, proved the most complete, most accurate available. They are often used by the federal government.

6. It is interesting to note that after the white primary ruling the pattern of eva-sion, trickery, and disobedience of law, later summed up in the term "massive resis-tance" and so corrosive of civic morality in the South, was not the spontaneous reac-tion of all the South; it was, however, the reaction in most of the Deep South. See V. O. Key, Jr., *Southern Politics in State and Nation* (New York: Alfred A. Knopf, 1949), pp. 625–643.

7. Cited in "The Negro and the Ballot" by Margaret Price (Atlanta: The Southern Regional Council, August 1959), p. 15.

8. Price, p. 15.

9. An earlier pamphlet, "The Negro Voter in the South" by Margaret Price (At-lanta: Southern Regional Council, September 1957), tells of a scrutiny of white regis-tration cards made by the Colfax *Chronicle*, of Colfax, Louisiana, after a thorough purge of Negro registration by the local White Citizens Council: "The *Chronicle* checked the first 100 white registrations in one ward and found only one card which

would meet the standards set by the WCC for Negroes. Four, including the superintendent of schools, figured their ages incorrectly. In a further check, the *Chronicle* discovered that not a single member of a Citizens Council committee had filled in correctly all the blanks. Needless to say, only the Negroes were challenged." (p. 15)

10. Price, "The Negro and the Ballot," pp. 8–9. Both the Price pamphlets indicate that resistance to registration was general over the South, but much stronger in the Black Belt areas than otherwise, as would be expected. The best general receptivity in the aftermath of the school decision for registration seems to have been in Texas, Tennessee, and North Carolina.

11. A Mississippi judge, J. B. Chrisman, was quoted by the Jackson *Clarion-Ledger* on September 11, 1890, as declaring: "Sir, it is no secret that there has not been a full vote and a fair count in Mississippi since 1875—that we have been preserving the ascendancy of the white people by revolutionary methods. In plain words, we have been stuffing ballot boxes, committing perjury, and here and there in the state carrying the elections by fraud and violence until the whole machinery for elections was about to rot down." In 1890, Mississippi whites shifted from such methods as these to the legalistic methods that were to prevail for more than half a century. A constitutional convention adopted the poll tax and other devices, including a literacy test with interpretation of the Constitution as an alternative. The interpretation provision was designed to allow registrars to enroll white illiterates while turning away Negroes. In 1867, almost 70 per cent of Mississippi's Negro adults were registered. By 1892, under the new laws, less than 6 per cent were.

12. Nothing is ever simple in the South. In South Carolina, as late as the 1930's, a few Negroes were still voting in the Democratic white primary. They were called "Hampton Negroes," and they were allowed to vote because in 1876 they had voted for Wade Hampton and had been Democrats ever since; they thus were preferable to other Negroes, who might be assumed to be Republican. Here and there in various other Southern Democratic primaries, trickles of Negroes were allowed to vote for one reason or another.

13. Key, p. 523.

14. Under the county-unit system, which fell before the Supreme Court ruling in *Wesberry v. Sanders* in 1962, each county's vote for governor, senator, and a number of other statehouse officeholders in the Democratic primary was determined by its representation in the Georgia House of Representatives. Each county had two votes for each House member; and every county had at least one House member. The result was that each of the eight largest counties had three House members and six unit votes; the next 30 counties in population each had two House members and four unit votes; and the remaining 121 counties each had one House member and two unit votes. Thus three small counties had as large a vote in a governor's race as Fulton County, which includes Atlanta. In an unsuccessful effort to save the unit system, shortly before the *Wesberry v. Sanders* decision, this formula was revised to give the larger counties greater, though still disproportionately small, numbers of unit votes.

15. Even a few Negro votes in the Black Belt have been important on rare occasion. In Terrell County, Georgia, one of the most difficult of all Southern counties for voter registration workers and the site of the first federal prosecution under the voting provisions of the 1957 Civil Rights Act, a school superintendent opposed by Negroes lost by 200 votes in 1964. Some 238 Negroes were registered at the time.

16. Congressman Weltner, who had been identified with the moderate reform element as a young lawyer in Atlanta, was elected in 1962 with the aid of Negro votes. When the Civil Rights Bill was before the House on February 10, 1964, he voted

against it. A week later, the Supreme Court ordered congressional redistricting in Georgia. The state legislature already had begun the task, and on March 10 the new district plan was signed into law. It divided Mr. Weltner's Fifth District. The percentage of Negroes rose from 26.5 in the old Fifth to 33.3 in the new Fifth. In July, when the House was called upon to vote again on the Civil Rights Bill following Senate amendments, Mr. Weltner voted for it. Despite a substantial "white backlash" for a weak opponent in the Democratic primary of 1964, the congressman was nominated again. He then defeated a Republican opponent by a margin substantially less than his Negro vote. In the Fifth District, Negro votes had made the difference in a congressional race as early as 1946. In 1964, they made the difference not only in Mr. Weltner's race but also in the other Atlanta-area district. There another moderate reformer, James Mackay, won with Negro help. Weltner and Mackay were the two Georgia congressmen who voted the next year for the Voting Rights Act. In 1966, after winning renomination in the Democratic primary, Representative Weltner withdrew. He said he could not support the man who had been nominated by the Democrats for governor, Lester Maddox, an ultra-segregationist.

17. The day on which Governor McKeithen made this pronouncement was assuredly a significant date in Louisiana history. Within hours after the governor spoke to the new bi-racial Commission on Human Rights, Duties and Responsibilities on September 1, 1965, the mayor of New Orleans, Victor Schiro, also was breaking new ground. Running for re-election, he assembled thirty-five leading Negro citizens at the Seafarers' Hall in New Orleans for drinks and food. At this closed session, the first of its kind ever held by a New Orleans mayor, Schiro was pressed to make a number of specific pledges for Negro support. He asserted that the segregationist label applied to him in his last race was wrong and not of his making. He promised to open City Hall completely for Negro employment, to hire at least ten more Negro policemen if qualified prospects were presented, and to name a Negro to the next opening on the city's housing board. When pressed to do so, he promised to name at least two Negro assistant attorneys. Even as he declared he would not bargain about such matters, he gave the Negro leadership a more complete set of promises than it had ever had before. New Orleans at that time was probably the most segregated big city in the Deep South. But at the time the mayor and the governor were speaking, lines of Negroes, three and four hundred strong, were moving all day every day through a marble-lined first-floor corridor at the New Orleans City Hall, to the registrar's office. On one day an elected judge who saw future allies there called the people heading the Negro registration drive to warn them that the line was growing short.

18. Senator Talmadge's remarks were made in an interview with Charles Pou, political editor of the Atlanta *Journal*, published December 17, 1965.

3)

The Movement and
the Vote

During the 1950's, candidates accused one another of "wooing the Negro vote" and "catering to the NAACP," with the result that the Negro vote, where large enough to be once bargained for, came to be spurned, a liability because of the larger number of white votes it would alienate. Evocation of the dread initials of the National Association for the Advancement of Colored People was indeed an effective epithet in the political lexicon of those days. When the mind of the white South is finally successfully analyzed, one part of the case history may dwell on the extreme fear of Negro organizations and, as a part of phobia, the continuing refusal to learn about and understand them. To most white Southerners, the Negro organizations all looked alike.

A delight of the segregationist political stump-speaking folklore was to confuse initials, deadpan, "the N-A-C-C-P, or whatever they call it," and more fanciful variations, N double-P AC, NCPPA, and so forth, as though not to get the letters straight was somehow to dismember the organization.[1] More, however, than sympathetic magic was relied upon. Alabama outlawed the NAACP outright by court injunction; the state of Georgia embroiled it in litigation over tax exemption; the Virginia legislature passed six bills likened to the Alien and Sedition Acts to curb it; Texas obtained an injunction against its continued operation; and the South Carolina legislature barred its members from employment by school districts and state, county, and municipal governments.[2] This was a part of repression that followed the 1954 Supreme Court school decision, and as a result the NAACP suffered in most Southern states. Membership dropped heavily. The membership card became a secret badge of honor and good faith, and local NAACP officers in little towns, never heard from between one year and the next, continued resolutely (and covertly) to send in annual lists and membership fees from a faithful few.

Who can say what the repression of the NAACP contributed to the summoning forth of direct action? And direct action—essentially the controlled resort to the streets—not only created eminence for the then newly formed SCLC (Southern Christian Leadership Conference) and Northern-based CORE (Congress of Racial Equality), but also gave birth to SNCC (Student Nonviolent Coordinating Committee). All three organizations approach more closely the darkest dreads (who said that fears are only wishes disguised?) of the white Southern mind than did the NAACP in the mid-1950's.[3] All four organizations were an abstraction, sometimes quite thin, of the underlying will of the Negro people of the South. At its most basic, this was a will that citizenship no longer be denied them, as in the suppression of the NAACP, or in seating restrictions on the buses.

The word "revolution" is too easily flung about and mostly misused about the Negro movement in the South, which was restorative, not innovative. In its effect on *time*, however, this was a truly revolutionary movement. It began spontaneously out of just grievances and dissatisfaction, as revolutions will. But it was not against the government; it was against the amount of time it was taking to accomplish what the nation had, since before World War II, seemed to be promising Negroes. *Now* was the key word in the slogan "Freedom Now."

The normal process by which Negro Southerners might have acted to speed up their government was blocked; politics was denied most of them. Direct action—the non-violent demonstrations and techniques, the sit-ins, freedom rides, boycotts, marches—was, in effect, substituted. At first, the demonstrations were aimed at indignities imposed by businesses with which the Negroes traded—buses, ten-cent stores. Here Negroes did have a lever. Perhaps, too, even if only unconsciously, they were aware that business is at least as powerful as government in the ordering of society. And soon the demonstrations were aimed at whole towns and cities to force political action. Later, when Negroes through the Voting Rights Act had something nearer normal participation in politics, they tended to turn to the vote and not demonstrations as their natural lever of power. By the same token, when politics seemed to have proven unresponsive to the needs of the Northern ghettoes, the riots—a more spontaneous, more desperate, a less ingenious and leaderless protest—broke out. And there was no guarantee this might not be the next step in the South. None of this is to say that Negroes planned it that way; it is simply to suggest that the substitution of direct action for the vote was the effect of what they did, and that thereby direct action was entered, with the strike, the recall and the referendum, into the repertoire of extreme remedy in the American political process. Gunnar Myrdal had said that a major failing of white Southern liberals was their thralldom to the notion that "the Southern public must not be enraged into resistance" on racial matters. Direct action met fully his prescription of what these liberals had to learn—that "political actions, which for the moment amount to little more than mere demonstrations and which may actually cause a reaction in the individual case, in the long view may have been tremendously important as powerful stimuli to progressive thinking." [4]

Direct action was the great leap; with the coming of the sit-ins came a new birth of freedom, literally, to the South. Not merely Negroes of all classes and situations, but whites stifled and hopeless in the staleness of democracy denied, however many there might have been, were freed. Never again after the 1960 sit-ins was a large portion of the South's white liberals or moderates or Negroes to be completely trapped in that most real fear of enraging the beast of racist violence lurking in all the picturesque farm lands, lethargic cities, and pleasant little towns, threatening to howl through every warm, mystical night. How had the sit-in students, these agents of freedom to their elders, become so free? Too much from outside the minds of these nameless young heroes has already been written, but this guess is hazarded: Little Rock had occurred, and Clinton—fearful confrontations of the Southern beast in some of his less awesome lairs. He had snarled; he had reared; his attendants had egged him on; his mate had screamed fishwife curses, and he had belched his smoke and flame of night-time bombs, much of this at children. But the children had survived. The South had not devoured itself. It took the army; it took marshals; it took foot-dragging local police work and the manipulations of suddenly awakened business elements, but the beast was out in public, beaten and shown in all his ugly, bombastic backwardness and stupidity. In Montgomery, Alabama, with a bus boycott, he had similarly been backed away, and out in Oklahoma, in 1958 and 1959, he had been demoralized—by NAACP sit-ins.[5] Never again would he completely cower the people. He could still evoke fear, and inflict defeat. But he could no longer paralyze action over the whole South as he did when everyone conspired to keep him hidden.

In the coming years, the rest of the nation was to make fuller acquaintance with the South's beast, often with the opposite of the Southern overestimation of him. Too often representatives of the national government appeared, as at the University of Mississippi, to be engaging the beast with the expectation that he would react like a rational animal. On the other hand, one sensed lurking in the ambiguities of the early days of enforcement of new civil rights laws by the Johnson administration, in the bending over backwards to follow the mandates for encouraging voluntary compliance, some of that old fear of stirring the Southern racist beast. It is interesting to note that the Southern liberalism represented in the administration, including its topmost figure, largely came out of the pre-sit-in South, having been mostly in Washington during the years of the South's thunderclap reorientations by the movement. Perhaps this was a basic reason the federal government's deference to the beast resembled the traditional response of the moderate white South.

The Voter Education Project

The sweep of the movement was in epochs of compacted time, each year like an historical age, each with its own distinct character, achievements, and tone. After the year dominated by the sit-ins came the year of the freedom rides. These succeeded in forcing the federal government to enforce ICC and Supreme Court rulings against segregation of buses and terminals in interstate travel.

A change of tone rode in on the freedom rides. Gone to a large degree were the impeccable manners and dress of the sit-in students. Here come upon the South was the menace of the unshaven, the invasion of the unkempt, shortcomings seized upon through the rest of the history of the movement by Southern moralists who were less vocal about assault and murder of demonstrators, even those without beards. The Freedom Riders included the first large infusion of young Northerners, whites among them, into the Southern movement. What had been a largely spontaneous uprising by young Negro Southerners became a national movement. The influence of the Freedom Riders was to be important from then on, particularly in the youthful wing. Many of them, once released from Mississippi's Parchman state penitentiary and other places of incarceration, stayed on, as had some sit-inners before them, in the ranks of the "professional" freedom fighters, mainly as workers for SNCC and CORE.

If there had been hope in the heart of the white South that the sit-ins were the whole drama of direct action, and not merely the opening engagement of a revolution (and there was such hope), the freedom rides dispelled it. If the mannerly students, carrying their textbooks to jail with them, drew stern and self-righteous imprecations for daring to provoke racist violence, the bearded, "outside agitator" Freedom Riders sent segregationists of all degrees, including many editorialists who should have known better, into fits and frenzies. Where would it all end?

But others less culpable were pondering closely related questions, including the South's white liberals and its older body of Negro leadership, and including the attorney general of the United States, Robert F. Kennedy, who had called unsuccessfully for a cooling-off period during the freedom rides.[6] Here is how a Southern Regional Council pamphlet described the situation that confronted the movement after the freedom rides:

The titanic energies enlisted by the sit-ins and the freedom rides—where were they to go? To some, it seemed that they could best go into making the South the kind of place which could and would solve its own problems, i.e., a huge effort to get the full measure of Negro Southerners registered to vote, thus establishing for the first time the possibility of true representative government in the South. During the late spring and the summer of 1961, it was hardly a secret that the Department of Justice was among those quietly, but strongly, urging this emphasis.[7]

Out of such suggestions, after a year of planning, developed the Voter Education Project of the Southern Regional Council. Beginning in

March of 1962 and ending in the fall of 1964, it financed voter registration campaigns across the South, in the cities, small towns, and rural farmlands. A main purpose of VEP was research to determine the causes and remedies of the abnormally low voter registration in the South. But the method of research was the very direct one of encouraging persons not registered to attempt to register. Whites were not excluded from the VEP aim, but the main emphasis was on Negro registration, and organized drives to increase it. These were conducted by the civil rights organizations, NAACP, SCLC, SNCC, and CORE, with some participation by the National Urban League, and, very importantly, by local Negro organizations, acting on their own.

Thus the change in what was thought possible—in two years. In 1959, voter registration campaigns seemed risky and mostly futile. In 1962, such a project as the VEP seemed not only plausible and sure of reasonable success, but a relatively tame, mild direction for the civil rights movement to take.

Awareness of the tameness was high within the movement, particularly the youthful wing. Voter registration, after all, had been part of the old, discredited gradualist approach. A debate of considerable import ensued, creating two distinct factions within SNCC. Among these young people who had done on their own what a century of adult good intentions could not do, there was suspicion of this largely adult-inspired suggestion; a large element in SNCC felt that this was a white middle-class trick to get the movement out of direct action. The organization's main thrust until then had been from outside normal processes, to force them to change. With its belief in equality, it had also professed a similar allegiance to democracy, but this latter allegiance was tempered by considerable distrust and wariness of government and politics. Without clear analysis or explanation (that would come later), many SNCC chieftains vaguely but deeply felt the question that Marx in his day and "power structure" theorists of our day have raised about the relevancy of the vote.

An airing of views between SNCC and VEP staff workers was described in a VEP field report. One who was there finally said that although differences in ultimate goals might exist, there was no disagreement about voter registration as the means, so why not work together on it? Means or end, the franchise became a goal toward which SNCC NAACP, CORE, and SCLC could coordinate, if not join, efforts in the first VEP from spring 1962 to fall 1964, and again in a second VEP started in early 1966. (In the latter, all four organizations requested grants, but SNCC's in the first year were not approved.)

The Voter Education Project is interesting in several respects. First, it grew out of the discussions initiated by administration leaders in the wake of the freedom rides. These leaders participated in nearly all of the processes of decision-making up to March 1962. They were remembered to have promised that the Department of Justice would diligently support and protect registration workers, a promise—if it was one—which was not later fulfilled.

Second, VEP was to be as American as apple pie—for not only would the problems and the people be inescapably American, but nowhere else would old capitalist fortunes, now preserved in foundation trusts, be asked to finance such a venture.

Third, VEP was to be subsequently denied in some measure by nearly all who heralded and formed it. The foundations never put in as much money as was intimated would be forthcoming. The federal government never gave the support it had pledged. The civil rights groups soon abandoned even half-hearted attempts at joint registration programs, and the work became (for the most part) a series of separated programs, coordinated only by being kept—by the VEP staff—out of each other's way.

Despite these facts, VEP did telescope into two and a half years a Negro registration increase which could not otherwise have been predicted in less than ten years. It moved Negro registration off dead center, where it had been for most of the previous decade, and reestablished momentum. This it did in advance of an effective federal voting law.

The importance of VEP extended far beyond its being simply a sizable program temporarily engaging Negro organizations. It was, very significantly, the first extended program attempting to tie together all of the five major civil rights organizations. Subtly, as well as overtly and obviously, this fact had a mighty impact on the movement. VEP also led to the discovery, identification, and development of a broadened Negro community leadership throughout the South. It thus inevitably affected for many years to come the whole structure of Negro leadership in the region. (In South Carolina, as only one example, it led to the first statewide Negro organization of substance for political purpose.) VEP was not just a program to be delegated to committees of Negro organizations here and there; it frequently was a program that created not only the committee but the organization and, in fact, a whole series of leadership relationships that would affect many other phases of the lives of Negro communities, and thus white communities, in the South.

For this achievement, much of the credit is due to the qualities of the man chosen as director. By the nature of things, a man in charge of the allocation of several hundred thousands of dollars to the dollar-hungry Negro civil rights organizations and local civic and voter registration groups was to be a powerful man. He was also to be a sorely beset one, for the competition among Negro organizations of any kind is a phenomenon that impresses the most casual observer. He also had to be a man in whom all, tough-minded and hard-driving directors and workers of the civil rights organizations, and over-burdened, often-threatened local leaders alike, had confidence. And he had to be possessed of broad and minute knowledge of the Negro South, its over-all psychology and its state-by-state, town-by-town variations, and, most important of all, a knowledge of who in what place could be relied on, and what in which place was a feasible possibility. The name of Wiley A. Branton, a thirty-eight-year-old attorney from Pine Bluff, Arkansas, member of a leading family in the Negro community there, and the counsel for the youngsters who desegregated schools in Little Rock, was submitted to the leaders of the five civil rights organizations. He was approved.

A mark of the kind of problems he had to face and of a courage of special sorts he showed is illustrated in two of his actions during the course of the project—the cutting off of funds to SCLC for about a nine-month period until that organization could get its program soundly organized and its record-keeping and reports on voter activity in shape; and the decision in early 1964 to invest no more money in then futile efforts to register Negroes in Mississippi. The latter decision affected the NAACP, SCLC, SNCC, and CORE under the umbrella-group called COFO (Council of Federated Organizations), but most particularly it affected SNCC because almost half of SNCC's voter efforts had been in Mississippi. Mr. Branton, at the end of the first VEP, emerged from the job with his prestige in the movement intact. He later joined the federal government in Washington. His successor, Vernon Jordan, a thirty-one-year-old Negro attorney from Atlanta, was proving himself similarly in the second VEP.

The funds contributed to VEP were tax exempt. The registration drive was non-partisan; endorsement from the national committees of both parties was obtained at the outset. Until the emergence of lily-white Republicanism in the Goldwater campaign of 1964, both parties on a national scale had chances of gain from an increase to normal proportions of the number of Negro voters.

The two-and-a-half-year voter registration campaign eventually cost $870,371. Most of the funds were provided by the Taconic Foundation, the Field Foundation, and the Edgar Stern Family Fund. Their contributions, respectively, were $339,000; $225,000; and $219,000. Small amounts were contributed by a number of individuals and organizations, including churches, labor unions, and the National Association of Intergroup Relations Officers (NAIRO), the latter for an internship program in voter registration work.

Registration drives were not a new thing on the Southern scene. They had been going on, intermittently, since the outlawing of the white primary in 1944. Local Negro political organizations had sprung up over the South in the wake of that decision, and much of their exertion was simply to get Negroes registered. The NAACP, shortly after passage of the 1957 Civil Rights Act, conducted a campaign in four hundred cities and counties. Its goal was 3,000,000 registered Negroes by 1960, a goal not reached even by 1966. Dr. King's SCLC was organized in 1957 as a "crusade for citizenship" with an announced aim of aiding and encouraging Negro registration and of reporting facts of resistance to constituted authorities.

Not all of the Negro registration increase recorded between 1962 and 1964 can be attributed to VEP drives, but a majority can, as well as the prevention of thousands of other voters from being disqualified. Perhaps the VEP requirement of reporting induced some better organization. Whether this was so, it can be here appropriately noted that VEP required the many projects connected with it to file frequent and regular reports (which are, in fact, the fundament of much of this book). In all the annals of formal fact-gathering, particularly in the age of computers, there probably has never been a research project like this one, or such "data" for study as came constantly in. From some (to whom the authors of this report will be forever grateful) came hard data, figures, dates, calls made, money spent. From others—deeply involved in the emotional mood and clamor of mass meetings, or in the visitations on front porches of city slum shacks where workers patiently went over and over the vagaries of local tricks to prevent voting, or over and over the democratic imperatives for overcoming custom and fear to go down and "reddish," [8] or other visitations in the cotton fields of plantations where both teacher and pupil kept a wary eye out for the truck of the owner —came a flow of narrative reports of remarkable substance. They were not exactly material for computer programming,[9] but the stuff of which the movement was made, and they reached into levels of understanding seldom encountered about the South.

A most important research finding of the project was its demonstration, day by day for two and a half years, of the need for federal legislation if Negro enfranchisement were ever to be fully achieved for the present generations in the South. For there was rarely success, no Negro registration to amount to anything in any place where whites seriously resisted it. Neither legal cases of the federal government nor the dedicated work of the registration drives could prevail against the resistance until the 1965 Voting Rights Law was passed. Even then, the resistance could be at least partially effective.

Registration and Direct Action

For the most part, the voter registration phases of the movement's history has been an untold story. "I feel," wrote Charles Sherrod of SNCC, after more than a year's experience as director of registration activities in the hard-core resistance area of southwest Georgia, "that we who are writing some type of history with our feet are really losing the point with our hands and minds. We have not interpreted with depth. In fact, we have done little or no interpretation of what we are about." He was trying. Every project and every phase of the movement had its style. The style of southwest Georgia SNCC was insouciant, almost gay, in itself and in its description of others, and merciless in careful introspection of selves. Veteran newsmen were later to say that they never before or later heard singing quite like that in the Albany mass meetings. The authors of this book, who have had the great privilege of reading through the reports that came from all over the South, remember those that came from southwest Georgia for the special sense they conveyed of setting off on a journey that would be hard, but could become only glorious and good.

Certainly the nation was little aware of the quiet, day-by-day, grueling work that went on alongside the headline-making demonstrations and crises of direct action. Only when voter registration erupted into or coincided with such disgrace and hyperbole as Selma and the March to Montgomery in March 1965, did voter registration as an issue impress itself on the American consciousness. Voter registration efforts had set the stage often for direct-action campaigns, as in Albany and Greenwood, Mississippi. Usually, when this happened, one of the civil rights organizations was involved, but in Savannah in 1963 a strictly local voter registration drive flashed into fierce demonstrations.

A good number of the VEP reports told of communities that, aroused to the spirit of the movement by voter registration and to strong frustration over obstacles to registration, moved over to direct action and then back to voter registration. A CORE report from a Louisiana parish in January 1964 is typical:

Their [Negro leaders'] comments at the meeting indicate that they are moving beyond purely a "VEP outlook," and are beginning to see the necessity of using direct non-violent tactics against the registrar and the white power structure.

The young, particularly, would grow impatient with the drudgery of voter work and the frustrations of resistance, and push for direct action. On the other hand, many registration drives followed massive campaigns of direct action, capitalizing on the solidarity and awareness created by them. It became an axiom that not much voter registration could be expected during a direct-action campaign, although it would be urged at mass meetings and the like. But once the fever pitch of direct action ended, voter campaigns immediately afterward were notably successful. There were strictly observed restrictions against using VEP money for direct action, but from 1962 onward, voter registration and direct action were counterpoint phases of the civil rights drive. Their paths intertwined and occasionally merged into one, but their methods and impact were, in some important ways, different.

Negroes who were involved directly in direct action experienced something not quite like anything that we know normally in American life and history, something of mysticism and exaltation, and thus perhaps something more akin to early Christianity than to Western democracy. Part of this was the finding of a belief and courage at mass meetings that, individually, they might not have been able to muster. It is not likely that those who participated in such moments will lose in a lifetime what they found. Whites like the police who struggled with marchers and the jailers who confined them, whether they would ever admit it, were touched by the experience too, not unlike, it seems fair to say, the Roman persecutors of the early Christians; and there are some few tales of white toughs who encountered the spirit of non-violent love and resistance and came away changed.

But in both instances, Negroes and whites directly touched by direct action were relatively few, a small proportion of the South's population. It is important to know that, despite the way it seemed in television and other journalistic coverage, the South during the movement years was not a society consumed in jerky sequences of violent encounter, interspersed occasionally with the whining drawls of pained-faced white politicians in the throes of self-righteous indignation, spittle-spewing defiance, or doublethink lying. The truth is that the South in its time of greatest political and social upheaval and change has been, on the easy-going surface, pretty much as it had always been, and except for regional variations still notable, pretty much like the rest of the nation.

The nationally spotlighted, grim, and desperate struggle that took place in Albany, Georgia, during 1961 and 1962 never involved any more than a few thousand Negroes—in a population of 26,000 Negroes—who sang, with a sweetness never to be forgotten, their way to the courage to march, and a considerably smaller number of town police, who pitted against the marchers and a handful of white troublemakers alike the techniques and terrors of the police state.

In that pleasant-faced small city of broad streets and flat landscape, at the height of one of the most severe crises of that campaign, a white civic club met routinely not a block away from the turmoil of the day's demonstration and arrests. Members went through its ritual and buffoonery and solemn prayer and pledge to the flag and speechmaking with never, even in the slow-murmuring table talk, an acknowledgment of what was happening in and to their town, or a hint of awareness of the irony of the presentation of "citizenship awards" to two fine white high-schoolers while a block away their black counterparts, expressing their own citizenship, were being put into buses to be hauled to convict camps in feared and brutal rural counties nearby.

A Negro high-school band in gold-embroidered uniforms thumped and trumpeted through a regular practice session, with limber-legged majorettes strutting before it, not a block away from where another kind of march was forming in the small Shiloh Baptist Church. There the mass meetings kept up their exhortations all day, their singing forth of the movement's credo in all the forms of folklore and the preacher's poetry. ("Nobody can enjoin God. The City of Albany was not meant only for white folks. Albany does not belong to the Democratic Party of the state of Georgia. Albany does not belong to the Republicans. Albany does not belong to Governor Vandiver. Albany does not belong to the white people of the state of Georgia. All-benny . . . belongs to God. The earth is the *Lord's*. And the fullness thereof. This is God's Albany, and God tells us that out of one blood he created all the nations of the earth to dwell on the face of the earth. . . .") The faithful listened and prepared themselves—one a crippled old lady on crutches, bent and dwarfed, in the lead—to march into the white section of town, facing the fear bred into them with all the force of lifetime conditioning, to put themselves in the power of the dreaded police and go to jail.

But these were the few. The many Negroes went about their lives aware of what was happening but not intimately a part of it, old ladies sitting on their porches, rocking, inscrutable, and men at their jobs saying, "Yassuh, sho' is a nice day." Across town, on a broad street in a comfortable, tree-softened neighborhood, a sweet-faced white grandmother—whose life by nearly all the standards by which our civilization judges people had been good and useful and fulfilled—said, "Ah, we don't let it bother us. We just don't pay any attention. I don't know anybody who's even ridden over there to see. We're all too busy with Christmas."

Unlike direct action, the voter registration effort did reach directly more than a comparative few of the South's Negro population. There are no complete statistics on exactly how many, but judging from the reports on the number of them who were actually registered, and from the reports on the number who tried and were turned down, and from the indications of the number who just couldn't be compelled to try, it would not be too far off to guess that a majority of the unregistered had at least been confronted with registration's challenge.

Even in areas where there was no evidence of overt opposition, this was a challenge—as in direct action—to take on courage, to overcome the fears of a lifetime. Often the fears were founded on very real threats of severe harm, physical and economic. But the registration challenge came in a far more difficult context than that of the mass meetings. It came to the individual alone and unsupported. It was a challenge to many other things, indeed, all that goes into the way a human being adjusts to his environment. "When you ask a man to join you," mused a registration worker in southwest Georgia, "you are asking for a confession that his life up until now has been lived upside down."

The grandeur of the voter registration effort becomes apparent in the lonesome effort of will involved in the registration of thousands of Negro Southerners, and the unsuccessful efforts—some individuals trying again and again, ten, fifteen, twenty times—of thousands of others. It must be regarded also as requiring an act of faith in the efficacy of self-government. Mrs. Mattie Pilcher, a mother of five, was asked during one of the more dangerous periods for registering in Mississippi why she attempted to register. She answered: "I think it's important to vote because that will give us all our equal rights and equal payments when we work. And then my children would have better schools. Then I feel like a job would be more of a job for colored people; I mean there would be more jobs altogether for the colored people if we vote."

Voter registration involved closer touch than direct action with the lives of the people with whom the movement worked. It went to the homes; not a small amount of its energy was diverted by the small, personal problems that loom so large in such homes. Field reports were rife with long descriptions of these problems, case studies in illness unattended, in the various ways powerless, already poor people are swindled of what little money or land they might accumulate, in the simple inability of some families to secure the basics of food, clothing, warmth, shelter. A theme of quiet pathos running through some of the Mississippi reports was the suspicion that Robert Moses, the SNCC leader there, occasionally allowed VEP funds to be used to feed hungry families cut off from jobs because of attempts to register to vote. Who was to arraign him if such misappropriation occurred?

The voter effort thus dealt intimately with poverty, coming probably as close as any organized effort could to the details of the life of the rural poor in the South. The South's poverty is not a pretty reality, rural or urban. It bears tragic testimony to the evil men do through the almost abstract actions involved in the ordering of their societies, the running of their governments, the non-malevolent seeking after their everyday interests, all unaware of the results in human suffering and the crushing of dignity and potential which are the meaning of life.

"I will close this report with one observation about the poverty of Terrell County," Miss Prathia Hall of Philadelphia, Pennsylvania, wrote in February 1963 from southwest Georgia. "When I compare it with the slums of the cities, it seems that here, even the poverty is primitive.

The big city slums are complicated, mechanized, industrial ugliness, woven in an intricate pattern which has threads around many men. But here the shacks are low and makeshift—not the leftover houses of the wealthy or middle class but the shabby heirlooms which were built shabbily and have been passed on from slave to slave, from generation to generation. The shacks are low, the food simple, the work back-breaking, the poverty degrading. When you look up at the beautiful pure sky above, your glance has to come a long way down to see the unadulterated ugliness of the system on the ground."

Prologue for Radicalism

This close contact with the poverty of the South, an unplanned by-product of the voter effort but probably its most important, was a large contributing factor to the radicalism that grew up in the youth wing of the movement. Also contributing to the growth of radicalism was dis-illusioning experience with the federal government. The bitterness that developed against the federal role in the movement's rapid advances is often cited as ironic, since so much was accomplished by and through the federal government. The irony becomes easier to understand, how-ever, when it is remembered that the drive of the movement was for sudden, sweeping change through legislation, while the action of the government had to be confined—until such legislation was won—to slower administrative and judicial approaches under existing law. But still there was the fact that the federal government did not do all that it might have. This was a source of frustration and disillusionment throughout most of the movement's direct-action efforts, beginning with the sit-ins and eventually involving thousands of unconstitutional arrests. A history of direct action could be written around the two themes of unmet calls for federal intervention against violations of constitutional rights, and the related tendency of the movement to invoke the nation's fixation on violence to gain national legislative remedies.

The press and the public reflect one another, with constant mutual feedback. The violence syndrome in national perception of the move-ment reflects common faults of America's whole way of perceiving its public affairs.[10] Violence makes news; a folk outpouring of faith and be-lief in the best achievements of man's moral and philosophical thought —which was the heart of the movement—does not. And there is a journalistic expertise for ferreting out the human weakness in any enterprise, however noble, that is not compensated for by any techniques much above the sob-sister level for communicating that which is genuinely good. So by the time a reporter or a television camera got done with showing man's inhumanity to man in the volatile confrontations created by the movement, and finished exposing such flaws as the always glaring rivalries among Negro organizations, or the retaliatory anger or hate showing itself in an individual black face confronting in the flesh its owner's worst nightmare, there was little room left to tell of the beautiful and profound speech and music and intention that propelled the movement, especially in its early days, and probably even less ability in the audience to receive or demand such information. Meanwhile—and again, why might this be?—there was no artist there to communicate the higher meanings. James Baldwin came close to the real story; his natural idiom unfortunately seems to be acrimony, and he viewed the events mostly from afar and from a different culture.

So the nation by and large missed the deepest spiritual implications of the Negro movement in the South in the early 1960's. There was much talk about the conscience of the nation being stirred to action, and this was true. But what stirred it was not what the movement had set out to show. The demonstrations were originally designed to dramatize the injustice of segregation situations. (Sit-ins did so beautifully.) Soon, however, they seemed to seek merely to provoke rage at their affront to racist sensibilities (and there are instances when demonstrators deliberately taunted and goaded the beast of racist violence when it did not spring forth at once from their white antagonists), and it was this—the ensuing raw violence, a club on the head, a shot in the back—to which the conscience of the nation reacted. What this implies about what it was that bothered this national conscience, violence rather than injustice, is a matter not without ironic interest.

The freedom rides set both patterns—the fixation on violence and the failure of the federal government to protect constitutional rights—in full motion. In Anniston, Alabama, and Birmingham, white mobs attacked the Freedom Riders with no police interference. In Birmingham, the city police had been warned by the Justice Department to expect violence when the first bus arrived; they did not get to the bus station until ten minutes after it arrived. In Montgomery, some six hundred federal marshals were finally ordered out on May 22, 1961, after three days of mounting tensions, to prevent violence. But then when the

Freedom Riders went on to Jackson, Mississippi, and the Jackson police unveiled a police-state peace-keeping device of their own, simply locking up every Freedom Rider who arrived in town, the Justice Department did nothing.

Similar mass arrests in violation of constitutional rights were used effectively the next year in Albany. Thousands were marched to jail there in late 1961 and through the summer of 1962, as local police followed the lead Jackson had developed—arrests with such skill and efficiency that white violence was prevented and Negro goals denied. There was no federal intervention. The attorney general of the United States was among those who sent congratulations to Albany officials for preventing violence. A year after Albany's ordeal, a report from a SNCC worker on some renewed demonstrations caught the glow of what had been there in 1961 and 1962: "After the meeting I asked Marian Gaines when she was going to jail. Marian Gaines is eleven years old. 'Tomorrow,' she said. 'I couldn't go today on account of I had to go to music.' Her sister, Pat, had been jailed for picketing in the afternoon. Her brother had volunteered services for tomorrow. The ceremony of innocence had not been entirely drowned in Albany." If it had not, action at last taken by the Justice Department in the midst of these 1963 demonstrations probably did the trick. The action was against Negro demonstrators on the most ironic of grounds—interfering with the administration of federal justice.

The same patterns showed in the key direct-action developments that followed, a history that is told in the names of cities. After Albany came Birmingham in 1963. Again there was no federal protection of constitutional rights, but there was violence, mostly from the police. This and an ensuing outbreak of more than seven hundred demonstrations across the South set the nation moving toward enactment of the 1964 civil rights law, the turning point. The next decisive set of demonstrations was in early 1965 in Selma, Alabama—with television's best showing of racism's brutishness in a fast few minutes of film footage of Negro men, women, and children being tear-gassed, clubbed, and run over literally roughshod by Alabama's state troopers on horseback, and this brought the nation's most heartfelt response, thousands coming from every corner to join in protest. In the process three protesters were murdered. The 1965 Voting Rights Act was the result. The federal protection of marchers that finally came there was—in that campaign and for the movement generally—too late. Legislation to improve protection was finally introduced the following year, but then defeated as the conscience of the nation faltered.

The failure of federal protection in the early 1960's was a bitter pill. From the radio gangbuster days to kidnapings and espionage cases, the FBI in war and peace seemed to be enforcing other laws, with arrests as well as investigations. In those cases, of course, it had had the cooperation of the local police; certainly it hadn't had to police the local police, as would have been necessary in many civil rights cases in the South.

Failure to provide federal protection was especially bitter for the voter workers, for in the early VEP planning they had been led to expect full federal protection of rights and safety. In the context of the debate over voter registration versus direct action, this assurance seemed to mean that voter registration had a clear-cut advantage over direct action as a movement strategy. When the kind of protection expected was not forthcoming, disillusionment was doubly strong.

In the early days of the registration drive in southwest Georgia, a field report said that people were told to rely completely on the alertness of the Justice Department to protect their right to register. The report added: "The Justice Department is a magic phrase and in the deep South holds an unbelievable position of confidence, presently, in the minds of the oppressed." Not many months later, Jack Chatfield, a white SNCC worker in the same area, described disillusionment among Negroes about the federal government's power, the feeling that even it "can't negate Mr. Charlie's solid wall." What, he asked himself, about the nation, the sympathy of the world? And he answered: "What the Terrell County Negro does, he does on his own."

Civil rights organization leaders and VEP representatives met in early 1963 with Justice Department officials, including Burke Marshall, the assistant attorney general in charge of civil rights, to urge the need of better federal protection for the voting effort. Nearly a year of bitter experience, particularly in southwest Georgia, Mississippi, and Louisiana, was cited. A full day was spent in repeated urgings and repeated answerings that, in effect, the original pledge had not meant what it seemed to say. Frustrated from the day-long session, the civil rights leaders and VEP representatives discussed among themselves afterwards the possibility of a strategy that would put publicly the challenge they had just extended to the Justice Department privately. They conceived of an all-out registration drive by all civil rights organizations in one hard-core town where repression would be in full public view and full publicity focus. There, it was hoped, the issue of constitutional rights could be crystallized, and a change in government policy forced. As one of the strategists put it, the approach that had been used until then, of small cadres of civil rights workers slipping around in the hard-core area towns, working like an underground, was a good way to get killed. A show of force and highly publicized effort in such a town might make the government act before anyone was killed.

Greenwood

No immediate decision was made. But a short while later, on February 28, 1963, terrorism in one of the "slipping-around" projects in Mississippi almost resulted in the death of three workers. James Travis and Robert Moses of SNCC, and Randolph Blackwell, VEP field director, were fired on from a passing car just outside Greenwood.[11] Mr. Travis was wounded badly in the neck. The previously discussed plan for an all-out public showdown then was put into effect in Greenwood and Leflore County. Wiley Branton of VEP announced a "saturation campaign" to register Negroes there. At the time, Negroes of age to vote outnumbered whites 13,567 to 10,274. But registration of Negroes was 250, compared with 9,800 whites. The VEP voter effort had been begun in June 1962, by Sam Block of SNCC, a twenty-three-year-old Negro native of Mississippi. His earliest reports told of having to commute into the town because for a while he couldn't even find a place to live among frightened local Negroes, of being followed by police while he canvassed for voter registration, of being jailed several times, of being beaten by three whites, of being almost hit by a speeding truck while walking, of requesting protection from the Justice Department and not getting it.

The shooting came during one of those breakthroughs to which such "sneaking-around" voter efforts would build. On February 20, four Negro businesses near the voter registration project office had been burned, and on February 22 Mr. Block had been arrested on charges growing out of his statement that this was arson. On February 25, some 150 Negroes attended his trial and heard him refuse a suspended sentence on agreement he would stop his activities. On February 26 and 27, some 150 Negroes tried to register, the best result the voter effort had achieved. It was the next night that Mr. Travis was shot.

"The state of Mississippi," Mr. Branton's announcement said, "has repeatedly thrown down a gauntlet at the feet of would-be Negro voters, not only by the discriminatory practices of the registrar, but also by the economic pressures, threats, coercions, physical violence and death to Negroes seeking the right to vote. The time has come for us to pick up the gauntlet. Leflore County has elected itself as the testing ground for democracy and we are accordingly meeting the challenge there." Subsequently, during a mass meeting in Greenwood, Mr. Branton was to have the grim pleasure of pointing out, in reply to charges of local whites that he was an outside agitator, that the plantation owner for whom Greenwood and Leflore County are named, one Greenwood Leflore, happened to be his great-grandfather. ("That nigger," some townspeople are said to have responded, "ought not to be talking about things like that.")

Telegrams were sent from the VEP office to Governor Ross Barnett and Attorney General Kennedy saying that the registration drive would be attempted and that full protection of constitutional rights of registrants and civil rights workers would be expected. Records of a telephone conversation in which Mr. Branton informed Assistant Attorney General Burke Marshall of the plan show the difference in the respective approaches. It would be bad, Mr. Marshall kept saying, if the Negroes, faced with harassment, were to be turned down by the registrar when they applied to register. A hearing was pending on a suit which promised to force the registrar to accept Negroes. But if they should get discouraged during a campaign before the suit was finished, it might prove difficult after it was won to get them to try to register again. Mr. Branton kept saying he would expect the federal government to protect them against both harassment and against discouragement at the registrar's office *during* the campaign. There never seemed to be a meeting of minds in the conversation.

SCLC, NAACP, and CORE sent some workers into Greenwood and SNCC sent all its available Mississippi forces in. Here is how Frank Smith, SNCC worker in Holly Springs, Mississippi, recorded his reactions to being called to Greenwood:

You decided to take full advantage of your departure. First of all, you had to make people understand why you were leaving. Mr. Russell, a barber, was chief on your list. You went to him and explained everything. The speakers bureau goes out Sunday on schedule and you talk about voter registration and the shooting. Now, you have got to let the white folks know why you are leaving so you find a local "Tom" and explain the plan in detail. "I'm going to Greenwood because they shot my brother and I promised my God that I would take my body and stand it in the place where my brother fell." He was moved almost to the point of tears, and you knew you had gotten the point over. In a matter of days the "powers that be" would have gotten the message that every time one of us is hurt there shall be many more to take his place.

Everything seemed shaped toward a major turning point for voter registration—indeed, for the movement. The organizations were acting concertedly. The decision had been made to fight out in public the question of federal protection. Those involved were Southerners, oppressed against oppressors; volunteers from the North were not an important part of this campaign. The right to register to vote, far more fundamental than public accommodations, was the issue. On March 26, James Forman, executive secretary of SNCC, led a small delegation to the Greenwood courthouse to seek police protection against the continuing harassment of registration workers. They were threatened with a police dog and arrested. A large body of the Negro community then marched on the courthouse, some said to protest the arrest, others that they were merely moving together for protection in a registration attempt. Police met them, tried to turn them back. A police dog attacked and bit a Negro minister. The conflicting views of objective fact in such a struggle provide a rich study in human behavior—perhaps pathology. Greenwood city officials made it sound as if a mob had attacked the town; the Negro minister was somehow made to seem to have stuck his leg in the police dog's mouth—to gain, of course, publicity. Publicity there was—in terms the nation understood, indeed had come to expect: a snarling police dog, brutal police, violence, and marching Negroes. The main point of Greenwood was being lost in the clamor. The appearance of Negro comedian Dick Gregory, with his own flamboyant distraction of the news coverage, didn't help.

The fixation on violence had hardened. On March 1, two other SNCC workers had been fired on; on March 24, the COFO voter registration office had been set afire; on March 26, shotgun blasts had been fired into the home of a local Negro active in the movement.

On March 31, the Justice Department went into federal court with a petition for a restraining order against local officials. It not only sought protection of the right to register and vote, but demanded also that the local officials "release eight Negro voter registration workers from prison, refrain from further interference with a registration campaign and those taking part in it, and *permit Negroes to exercise their constitutional right to assemble for peaceful protest demonstrations and protect them from whites who might object.*[12]

It was the first and only time the Justice Department sought such protection for voter registration during the years leading up to the 1965 voter rights act, with one later exception. In June 1964, the FBI arrested three white men in Itta Bena, Mississippi, for interfering with voter registration workers. They were charged with conspiring to deprive citizens of their civil rights. Similar charges were brought *after* the fact of murder in several subsequent civil rights cases. And Greenwood was the only place where the Justice Department moved at all to protect constitutional rights as such, except for enforcing compliance with court orders, in the whole movement history from 1960 to 1966. But somehow, the importance of Greenwood seemed lost on the nation. Perhaps it was the lack of emotional simplicity, the clear cause-and-effect dimensions of such a situation as the sit-ins.

And on April 4 the federal government was able to retreat from its great advance without evoking the kind of national criticism that should have been forthcoming. The Justice Department agreed with local white officials to drop the request for an injunction on the basis of what seemed a promise that the local officials would guarantee safe registration so long as Negroes did not march to the courthouse. Among the terrible ironies was the import of the background story in the New York *Times,* which said that a major cause for compromise was the build-up of white anger in the area, which could have led to violence.[13] The threat of lawlessness, then, would rout the federal government in a showdown on the most basic right of American citizenship. This point, too, seemed largely lost on the nation, but not on the white and Negro principals in the showdown.

What chance there might have been for the meaning of Greenwood to sink in was lost in the ensuing eruption of the Birmingham demonstrations. And the Greenwood campaign lost its impetus, because it had been and was to continue true that the civil rights movement could not sustain more than one major campaign at a time. Dr. Martin Luther King, Jr., had not come to Greenwood. Some said it was because he was not invited. SNCC leaders, who dominated, had said there was no need for an invitation; the campaign was a joint venture from the beginning. Dr. King achieved in Birmingham what will probably turn out to be his greatest victory in the quest for effective national civil rights legislation.

But if there had been victory in Greenwood, the movement and American history might have been different. Solution of the basic, bedrock issues of voting and the administration of justice might have begun two years sooner than it did. The destructive aspects of Birmingham and Selma (and many other campaigns between) might have been lessened. And, probably most important, if the priorities had been thus rearranged, if voting and the administration of justice had been firmly established first, the other elements of civil rights—school desegregation, equal job opportunities, equal housing, equal access to public accommodations —might have been secured more quickly, and with less rancor among whites of the South and less "backlash" in the rest of the nation, and without the bitter disillusionment that was to come over many Negroes in the first two years of faltering enforcement of the Birmingham gains.

Another point was re-emphasized. In Greenwood, there was the whole basic constitutional issue and one police dog. The nation noticed the latter, and in Birmingham, Bull Connor unleashed a pack of dogs on defenseless demonstrators, and his fire hoses as well.

SNCC and the Negro people of Greenwood did not give up. The voter project remained a large one. By the end of July 1963, some 1,300 Negroes had attempted to register. An adding of insult to injury was the continued inability of anybody to find out whether any of them had been accepted.[14] In July of 1966, with the assistance of federal examiners, some 7,000 of the 13,500 eligible Negroes in Leflore County were registered to vote, compared with about the same number of whites.

The Freedom Summer

Out of Greenwood grew the next great adventure of the movement after Birmingham. This was the COFO (Council of Federated Organizations) Freedom Summer of 1964 in Mississippi, yet another approach to the growing art of attracting national attention to Southern civil rights problems and forcing reform. Violence was also a factor in its results.

COFO had been set up on paper by local leaders; it was seized on in 1962 by VEP as an umbrella group through which grants to all Mississippi civil rights organizations for voter registration might be made. Mississippi was the only state where four civil rights organizations were trying to do voter work at the same time. To avoid duplication of effort and to coordinate financing of them, the use of COFO was suggested by the late Medgar Evers, among others. The initial grant was $14,000 for August 1, 1962, to March 31, 1963, for work primarily in the Delta. Aaron Henry of Clarksdale, Negro druggist and state president of the NAACP, was named president of COFO, and Robert Moses, young Harvard-educated mathematics major from New York who had begun SNCC's highly dangerous civil rights efforts in Mississippi in 1961, was named director. In practice, most of the COFO voter registration projects were SNCC affairs, including Greenwood.

It is interesting to note the testimony given by Wiley Branton to the U.S. Commission on Civil Rights in Jackson, Mississippi, in 1965 regarding the atmosphere in which the COFO and VEP arrangement was born. He told of a meeting of all interested civil rights leaders in Clarksdale to set it up. The meeting lasted until after midnight. On leaving, six of the leaders were arrested a few blocks away by Clarksdale police for "loitering." Mr. Branton commented: "Well, I had practiced law for about eleven years before I went into this project, and I must admit I never heard of loitering in a moving automobile." The charges involved a forty-dollar fee for towing in the car. When the leaders were freed on bond, some of them went to nearby Indianola to help with voter activity and were promptly arrested for distributing handbills without a permit. The loitering charges were dropped in Clarksdale and the driver of the car was fined for hazardous driving. A 7:00 A.M. trial was set in Indianola. Arrangements were made in the courtroom for release on bond of those jailed, and postponement of the trial until they could get a local attorney. All seemed settled, Mr. Branton testified, "but then in the full presence of the chief of police and the judge, somebody came in with one of those aerosol insect bombs, walked over to where I was sitting and the defendants, and started spraying this thing in our faces with the loud statement, 'I have got to de-niggerize this,' and, of course, this brought a lot of laughs from the court . . . The judge did nothing about stopping this." Mr. Branton went on to testify that he had gone to great length to describe such incidents "because from there on out it appeared that we were subjected to this kind of harassment and intimidation every single week . . . Almost nobody could get out in an auto and drive anywhere without fear of being arrested for some trumped-up traffic violation, and in practically every instance the simple thing to do was to go ahead and pay the fine." [15]

It was in November 1963 that VEP ceased sending money to

Mississippi. The decision was made "reluctantly," Mr. Branton said in a letter to Mr. Moses and Mr. Henry. But more money had been spent with fewer results than in any other state, the letter said, and further spending there would take money away from projects in places where results could be obtained. The letter also noted the Justice Department's failure to obtain decrees in Mississippi voter suits.

While VEP was unworkable in Mississippi, other methods were not. Mr. Branton pointed out that in July 1963 the four civil rights organizations involved in VEP and two others formed two separate organizations, the Council for United Civil Rights Leadership, Inc., and the Committee for Welfare, Education, and Legal Defense, Inc. "Primarily because of the fact that I was already dealing with all of the civil rights groups, they asked me to serve as executive director of both groups . . . These separate corporations made grants to all of the civil rights groups and there were no restrictions as to the use of these funds, which included a substantial contribution for support of the mock elections in Mississippi."

Robert Moses, near the beginning of the VEP effort, had said in a December 1962 report that "we are powerless to register people in significant numbers anywhere in the state and will remain so until the power of the Citizens Councils over state politics is broken, the Department of Justice secures for Negroes across the board the right to register, or Negroes rise up en masse with an unsophisticated blatant demand for immediate registration to vote. Very likely all three will be necessary before a breakthrough can be obtained." The first two, of course, had not happened. Something approaching the third (though unsophisticated would not be the word) developed out of Greenwood and other frustrated Mississippi voter registration efforts. This phase began with an attempt in the summer of 1963 by unregistered Negroes in various movement centers, including Jackson, Hattiesburg, Clarksdale, Ruleville, Itta Bena, Greenwood, and Greenville, to vote in the August 6 primary elections. They proceeded on a section of Mississippi law, apparently intended for instances of clerical omission of registered voters, which said a citizen might present himself to vote even if not on voting rolls, submitting as he did an affidavit that he was qualified to vote. The idea apparently was developed by law students from Yale who were among a sprinkling of white volunteers in Mississippi during the summer and fall of 1963. (In 1962, a SNCC report on its over-all field program had said, "At this point it is too dangerous for whites to participate in the projects in Mississippi—too dangerous for them and too dangerous for the Negroes who would be working with them." The 1963 whites apparently had some hazardous run-ins with local whites, but in such a place as Hattiesburg, by summer's end, a Negro SNCC field worker was reporting that judging from experience with several who had been in and out, a full-time white worker there was feasible.)

"We hope that historians in some future time shall report that in 1963 the Negro in Mississippi cast his first vote for freedom," wrote the anonymous author of a proposal for the primary-crashing attempt. It was a well-organized affair in the several communities, with sample affidavits and directions to precinct polling places. State Attorney General Joe T. Patterson had announced in early August that Negroes making the attempt might be summarily arrested; nevertheless, a number elected to try. Here is a description of feeling from one young Negro in Greenwood, Billie Johnson:

I had fear in my heart because as soon as morning came, I had to face a big problem. That was going downtown and getting a beating. I know when the police see me they will hit me. I had it all in my mind how it was going to be: one would hit me on the head with a night stick, and the other would hit me in the mouth. Another was going to sic five or six dogs on me. I knew they were going to knock me down and kick me in the face. The moment came for me to go downtown. My mind was made up; I looked at the clock —quarter to nine. I was going at nine. If they whipped me for my freedom I would not mind. And all at once Sam Block came in and said the police said they would not arrest anyone. And my heart felt good then; I said "thank God" three times. Then we went downtown and we voted. Nobody bothered any of us. . . .

Of such was the adventure built. Martha Prescott of SNCC observed how many people were at the Union Grove Baptist Church on election morning ready to go to jail. "They were mostly old people, people with arthritis and things, that came to the church. Before we left the church we sang 'Is that freedom train a-coming?' One old man behind me on a cane said, 'Here's what hurts a man, if he's scared; but the trouble is, I ain't scared.'"

Between 500 and 700 "voted" in Greenwood; 26 tried in Ruleville, and three SNCC workers were arrested; 14 at Thornton and ten at Tchula and 30 at Canton tried and were refused, as were 430 in Jackson. None of the votes was deemed valid. "Two years ago," commented Stokely Carmichael of SNCC in his report on the activities, "we would have been shot for a stunt like this . . . As it was, reception from whites was polite at first. But hostile crowds gathered as Negroes continued going into the polls. There was no violence."

That fall, the better-known mock voting by unregistered Negroes for statewide offices was conducted, with Aaron Henry running for governor and Ed King, a white chaplain at Negro Tougaloo College, for lieutenant governor. Mr. Henry recalls that the originators of this episode were Al Lowenstein, a white volunteer who was later instrumental in recruiting for the Freedom Summer and still later emerged as a severe critic of the Freedom Democratic Party's performance at Atlantic City; Dave Dennis, director of CORE work in Mississippi; Robert Moses; and Annelle Ponder of SCLC. The original idea, Mr. Henry said, included elucidating problems to which the regular candidates weren't addressing themselves, and showing what Negro Mississippians might do if they had the vote. That 90,000 people voted in the mock election, with not all counties represented, indicated the degree of interest in democracy, and what movement methods could do for turning out a vote.

Out of all this—the voter effort, the participation of whites, the mock elections—came the massive Freedom Summer campaign and development of the Freedom Democratic Party (FDP). The Freedom Summer brought in a thousand or more white volunteers, mostly college students. (Such influxes of white volunteers had been discussed for at least two years. SNCC voter registration forces in southwest Georgia had a few year-round white workers from the start in 1962, and a small surge of college volunteers during the summer of 1963; CORE workers in Louisiana had at one time a plan for a statewide program of 1964 summer volunteers similar to Mississippi's, cutting back later to participation in one Mississippi congressional district and a scattering of white volunteers in some Louisiana counties. SCLC had similar 1964 plans for Alabama that didn't materialize.)

One of the lessons that had been learned from the 1963 freedom-vote adventure was that the nation and the FBI showed more concern about the fate of young white college students, especially if they were from prominent families, than about nameless Mississippi Negroes when intimidation and violence over voter registration occurred. This was a grim part of the rationale for the influx of white volunteers. The violence that did come that summer, the torture and beating to death of two white volunteers and one Negro SNCC worker ("black and white together") in Philadelphia, Mississippi, was possibly the most revolting of all in a long list of killings [16] that accompanied the movement's progress. It suggested a collaboration in hard-core areas between official and private-citizen harassment. Coming as it did so soon after the senseless violence that destroyed President Kennedy (and how much of hope in the nation and the South?), it was one more contributing factor to the nation's fixation on violence. The FBI turned over evidence to local authorities without results; federal charges of conspiring to violate the civil rights of the victims were involved in complicated legal maneuvering two and a half years later.

The Freedom Summer also brought to something of a climax a plexus of other concerns that had been part of the Mississippi voter registration effort. These included the emphasis on voter registration itself, and the concern with the problems of the poor. Freedom schools concentrated on dramatization of such things as deprivation of education, health problems, and lack of the basic stuffs of existence. Church, medical, legal, and other national interest groups became involved. The summer suggested forms the poverty program might have taken, and brought together the meaning of race and poverty as it also exists over much of the rest of the nation for any who wanted to see. And it brought about the largest political controversy that the movement was to develop—the consuming crisis of the radicalism which had been building up in the movement. This was the highly publicized, controversial attempt by the FDP to unseat the regular Mississippi delegation [17] at the 1964 Democratic National Convention, and its refusal of what many liberals considered a reasonable compromise of the issue.

By this time, there was the concept, among the youth-wing radicals mainly, of FDP not as merely a protest demonstration but as a separate political party. Later FDP was vying for the increasing number of Negroes finally becoming enfranchised by virtue of the 1965 Voting Rights Act. The FDP also conducted in 1965 an unsuccessful effort to unseat the Mississippi congressional delegation on the same rationale as its convention challenge, the contention that FDP elections for congressional candidates met legal requirements that those of the regular party failed to meet.

Despair and Discovery

The movement, which had used direct action as a substitute for the vote all the while it was pushing to gain the vote, came eventually, in

Selma, to depend on direct action to *get* the vote. Direct action and the voter effort were intertwined. The suggestions that movement energy be concentrated on the vote had not, whatever the intentions, diverted the movement from its radical path. The strange failure of the federal government to follow through on its promises and its normal duty to the voter effort surely contributed to the prolonging of dependence on the extreme remedy of direct action. Moreover, the revolution against the timetable of gradualism did not itself move fast enough. Despair came to many in the movement, and most of all to those who had worked in the voter effort.

Out of the Mississippi Freedom Summer and the FDP challenge at the 1964 Democratic Convention came awareness in the nation of the growing alienation and radicalism of the youth wing of the movement.[18] Serious questions were raised on the old bugaboo question of communist influence. A more pertinent question was whether racism, contagion of the virus they had fought, was a part of the young radicals' increasing anger. In the two years that followed, the split of the young radicals away from the rest of the movement grew, ending in their cry for black power—which seemed a renunciation of integration and non-violence and touched the ultimate question of the voter effort: Could democracy and self-government as evolved in America be made to do the work in the South that had been shaped by the movement? That shaping had been achieved at Birmingham and Selma. But the young radicals drew their inferences from Greenwood and Atlantic City.

Crucial to either view of movement history was the continuing work of registration. While the cry of black power captured attention in 1966 and 1967, the larger part of the energy of the movement in the South was still involved in voter registration and political activity, the hopeful but uncompleted work growing out of the victories. This perspective has all along been hard to keep. Not all of the South from 1962 to 1964 was a theater of guerrilla warfare where the Negro fought in vain for the right to vote, as the foregoing review of the high points might suggest. If a study of the first VEP must of necessity concentrate on its unproductive aspects, the real meaning of the project was in the numbers of Negroes who were able to register then, and the numbers more when the law was changed.

The 668,000 increase in Negro voters recorded between April 1962, and November 1964, brought the total of registered Negroes in the eleven states to 2,174,200, or 43.8 per cent of those eligible. During the first year under the new voting law, the halfway point was passed. The voter drives of 1966 and 1967 were digging deep into the population, reaching the poorest people, in whom alienation and despair had dwelt long before they were summed up in slogans. As the efforts to persuade these classes of Negroes to register and vote got under way, and as the effort to rid the South of racism continued, the challenge to democracy became obvious.

NOTES

1. Another favorite creative activity of the Southern political mind of then and more recent times was to think up epithets to fit the initials. "Niggers, Apes, Alligators, Coons, and Possums" was one contribution.

2. Alabama's injunction against operation of the NAACP in the state was finally voided by the Supreme Court during 1965. Whatever activity the organization had between 1956 and 1965 was in disguised form or through other organizations.

3. See *The Voices of Negro Protest in America* by W. Haywood Burns (London: Oxford University Press, 1963), pp. 13–14, for an excellent capsule history with the advantages and disadvantages of brevity. The National Association for the Advancement of Colored People was formed in 1909, an outgrowth of the Niagara Movement—which had been the first national-scale organization of Negro intellectuals seeking social change and offering alternatives to Booker T. Washington's accommodation-oriented leadership. The NAACP was thus the "young radical" organization of that earlier day. Among its first goals was complete enfranchisement of the Negro. The National Urban League, beginning in 1910, carried out a program of self-help and economic advancement for Negroes under such circumspect and "respectable" aegises as to gain support from some of the South's white-operated and segregated community-chest programs. It has tended since 1960 to speak in whatever idiom was being voiced by the rest of the movement, but its emphasis has continued to be economic self-help. This program was coming into its own in 1965 and 1966, with new law and new concern over poverty supporting it. The Southern Christian Leadership Conference, headed by Dr. Martin Luther King, Jr., was formed in 1957 as an outgrowth of the Montgomery bus boycott. The Congress of Racial Equality was organized in 1942 and, as did SCLC, developed direct action and much of the nonviolent philosophy. CORE operated in the Northern and border states until the sit-ins and freedom rides. The Student Nonviolent Coordinating Committee was formed in Raleigh, North Carolina, in April 1960, at a meeting sponsored by SCLC. The idea was to provide coordination of the student sit-ins, then sweeping across the South. At that first meeting, SNCC decided to exist independently of SCLC. (See Howard Zinn, *SNCC: The New Abolitionists* [Boston: Beacon Press, 1964], p. 34.) It was slow in developing form; as late as 1962, when SNCC workers had started the Albany Movement, it was still possible to describe it as a roving band of free-lance freedom fighters. Reaction of the NAACP to the newer groups and their new spirit in the 1960's could provide a case-study in the all-too-human emotional capacities of the organizations we create and live by. There was a great pride in the South's NAACP, part of it a pride of place

and of people. To such brave and faithful workers as Mrs. Ruby Hurley, the Southern director, and W. C. Patton, organizer of voter registration, the work and the South had become almost a matter of proprietorship. Their organization had its roots deep in the Negro middle class, or what passed for the middle class—the strongest people in Negro communities. The idea of leadership from the young, and later from the poorest, people was unacceptable. A strong tradition of virulent anti-communism, born of wary survival instinct as much as anything else, was also operative. When the sit-ins broke out, it was the Youth Councils of the NAACP that provided their backbone—out of all the middle-class, Negro-college respectability. But they never took credit, or were never allowed to take credit, and members were, in effect, driven out of the direct-action movement, or into the newer organizations. There was a crisis of dignity for the NAACP from the onset of the sit-ins; the new spirit threatened so much of power and pride. The NAACP was to become involved in direct action; it provided supportive services, but it never abandoned its old emphasis on operation within normal channels—court actions, political action. The NAACP Legal Defense and Educational Fund, Inc., a separate entity, was often the legal arm of direct action, sometimes reluctantly—with high costs of court action coming to it, and credit often to the other organizations. As between the Inc. Fund (as the legal branch of NAACP is called) and the NAACP proper, there was ever tension and jealousy. The strains of direct action intensified it. Through all of the direct-action revolution, the NAACP kept up harsh and disparaging criticism of the new organizations; if sometimes it was petty, often it was just, and always it was—given the old days and ways—humanly understandable. The figure of Roy Wilkins stands out as a symbol of all that was changed within the in-group world of Negro organizational hierarchies and personalities by the events of the 1960's. Assuming, when he did, top leadership of the NAACP, he would normally have been expected to be *the* Negro leader of his generation. Instead, Dr. Martin Luther King, Jr., if anyone, became that in the eyes of the contemporary world and probably history, and a long list of lesser heroes strode across the scene. Beyond the shrewdness and wisdom of such a man as Mr. Wilkins was the spirit in him that rose above bitterness at such a fate. The rivalries if not the complex cooperation of the organizations continued. In the Meredith March of the summer of 1966, the NAACP refused to sign a manifesto at its outset which included criticism of the Vietnam war; though the NAACP was instrumental in logistics of the march, it was, by vote of the younger organizations and some of their offshoots, excluded from the last day's victorious ceremony on the lawn of the Mississippi state capitol. Some understanding of the relationships of these organizations, often as touchy as international diplomacy, is essential to full understanding of movement history and of the South.

4. Gunnar Myrdal, *An American Dilemma* (New York: Harper and Row, 1962; originally published 1944), pp. 470–71. Far more study has been made of the impact of the movement on Negroes and segregationists than on the small number of white liberals and growing number of moderates. The distinction between the last two has often not been too clear. In the medieval mood of the 1950's, though, there was a fairly accurate litmus. If, to the larger happenings in the racial arena, like the school decision and Little Rock, your Southern white—especially if he was not involved in the events—responded by jumping back a pace or more into segregationism, he was a moderate. If he held firm, said this is right and will work, he was a liberal. Soon the moderates would catch up again. Not all the white liberals held firm on the sit-ins; the wise ones saw that not only were they right, but they had a constitutional basis at least partly assuring success. This marked the freeing of the white liberal, and he has moved fast and far from the description of him by

Myrdal. In direct-action dramas, white liberals—often through the state and local Councils on Human Relations, affiliated with the Southern Regional Council—worked behind the scenes, sometimes demonstrated, and were sympathizers and supporters. Sometimes they assumed the role of go-between, a difficult one as always, with risk of becoming despised and distrusted by both sides.

Some few white moderates of the South (and they seem to dominate the moderate Southern press) still seem to operate sometimes on the old fear of enraging the public, and still do a disservice to their fellow Southerners by praising in them presumed traits reflecting the old myths and hallucinations. This is not unlike the Nazi practice of praising German bucolic legend and splendor to help keep minds off the directions racism and the crushing of freedom took there. But a better part of the practice also survives, the appreciation and encouragement in public by white liberals of their fellow Southerners' real traits (humor, acceptance, and realism about the human condition, awareness of sin, knowledge of defeat, individualism, kinship with nature, and so on).

5. "The Southern Student Protest Movement, Winter 1960" published by the Southern Regional Council, February 25, 1960. A VEP field report recalls a forgotten episode of movement history that occurred in Tallahassee, Florida. The Reverend Charles K. Steele, a Negro of that city, and a friend of Dr. Martin Luther King, Jr.'s, observed the 1955–56 bus boycott in Montgomery, and went home to organize one in Tallahassee. In 1956, he formed an organization modeled after the Montgomery Improvement Association, held mass meetings every Sunday, raised money for legal costs, and "solidified the Negro community" in a bus boycott. Results were not spectacular; there were long court delays and finally a compromise which drew criticism of the Reverend Mr. Steele. Out of his organization, in 1959, there developed a Non-Partisan Voters League, which increased Negro registration from 1,200 to more than 5,000 in 1959 and 1960.

6. "During the early months of the Kennedy administration, civil rights leaders were informed that the administration would be pleased if, in addition to sponsoring freedom rides and sit-ins, the various civil rights organizations joined together and undertook a major Negro voter registration program in the Deep South," wrote Louis E. Lomax in *The Negro Revolt* (New York: Harper and Brothers, 1962), p. 232.

7. "Direct Action in the South," published by the Southern Regional Council, 1963, p. 10.

8. A widespread variant of the word "register" used not merely by many lower-class Negroes, but some of the middle and upper classes, too.

9. In a VEP "Statement of Research Aims and Methods," written in February 1963, it was pointed out that much of the unconventional research under way could not be evaluated quantitatively, "but the notion that social science is confined to quantitative findings is a recent one, and perhaps not an unrelenting tenet." The "valuable historical documents" contained in narrative reports from registration workers across the South are noted in the VEP's first annual report. It is interesting to see how narrative reporting came to dominate some of the research reporting. SNCC workers in Mississippi and southwest Georgia for many weeks were ignoring report forms calling for listings of the number of persons registered, for the good reason that they were unable to register any people. By the fall of 1962, staff workers at VEP were sending "this won't do" messages, and soon the suggestion was made that the SNCC workers write descriptions of what they were doing. The research statement included two other principles which have guided the authors: "As do any disciplines, the social sciences have developed problems which are largely intramural in their interest. All the issues of public policy are of interest to the social sciences; the re-

verse is neither obviously nor probably so. The VEP will not, therefore, seek to serve social science in such ways as the refinement of methodologies or the verification of statistical data." And: "The VEP supposes that increased political participation is a feasible means of bettering the living conditions of deprived groups. The implicit assumption is that the political process is a primary means by which the benefits of society are distributed. This assumption is, of course, basic to democratic theory."

10. This is not to disparage the work of the individual reporters whose coverage and interpretation of events contributed so much to national reaction to the movement, and to what awareness there was of the spiritual overtones. Such reporters were mainly from the national press. In the early years, Claude Sitton of the New York *Times* and Karl Fleming of *Newsweek* were outstanding. Not the least of their ability was in knowing where to be at the right time. They risked their lives more than once to give accurate accounts of crises and confrontations. With some notable exceptions, there was a paucity of Southern coverage of the biggest news and historical events in the nation during the early 1960's, going on right under the noses of countless city editors around the South. Neither the importance of the role of the national press nor the irresponsible failure of the largest part of the Southern press in the drama of the Southern movement has been fully acknowledged. The latter remains one of the more serious problems of emerging democracy in the South, and—so far as it reflects general conditions around the country—a national disgrace. The wire services, with their dependence on formula writing and their routinization of this great, continuing story, and with their business ties to racist publishers, seldom reported the story in its full dimensions and meaning. Most of all, they contributed to the fixation on violence, and the amoral tendency to view a profound moral crisis in the South in cliché perspective, so that it came to seem like a baseball game, complete with box scores of broken heads.

11. Mr. Blackwell was in Greenwood to discuss future plans of the VEP effort. The three left the voter registration office about 10:20 P.M. A light-colored 1962 Buick followed their car. They circled a block and pulled up behind the Buick. It had no license plate. When they got about ten miles out of Greenwood on Highway 82 toward Greenville, at about 10:30, the Buick passed them and a number of shots were fired. Mr. Travis was hit in the neck and shoulder. Subsequently two white men were arrested in connection with the shooting.

12. The New York *Times*, March 31, 1963. Italics added.

13. "The [Justice] Department reportedly was concerned over the threat of violence in Greenwood and the possibility that mass demonstrations might lead to a riot," reported the New York *Times*, April 5. "There is considerable evidence that an explosion has been averted here so far only because leaders of the Citizens Council have restrained the more emotional whites. The Council's members here include the city's business and professional leaders."

14. To the old, gradually lessening problem of unfriendly and uncommunicative keepers of such official records in various states has been added the new tendency of Southern state officials to disclaim any separation by race in the keeping of official records. A deputy sheriff in southwest Georgia, refusing to tell a SNCC worker the number of Negro voters in the county, maintained the voter records were not kept by race. "They're all mixed up together. That's how you want it, isn't it? All mixed up?" Some critics have said that if this were true, it was the only real integration going on in the South, and others have of course added that it is a shame the states can't do as well by people. This unavailability of official records has had a hampering effect on enforcement of all phases of the 1964 civil rights law. In the fall of 1965, the U.S. Office of Education was in the embarrassing position of actually not know-

ing how many Negro children were attending classes in formerly all-white schools. It was supposed to be enforcing the law on this. While the question of separate records rubs a raw place with Negroes, most in the civil rights effort would probably agree with a privately circulated memorandum by Carl Holman of the U.S. Commission on Civil Rights saying that as long as segregation exists in fact, there needs to be at least semi-private recording of it in official records. In late 1966, there were three different official policies regarding racial records among federal agencies.

15. *Hearings Before the United States Commission on Civil Rights*, Jackson, Mississippi, February 16–20, 1965, Vol. 1, "Voting," pp. 183–85. In his letter informing Mississippi civil rights leaders of the first grant to COFO, Mr. Branton had said: "The thought occurs to us that you should carry an item in your bookkeeping records known as 'harassment expense' and such items as fines and the unnecessary towing and storage charge and similar items should be charged to this account. . . ." The murder of three civil rights workers in Philadelphia, Mississippi, during the summer of 1964 followed their release from jail on a traffic charge.

16. See *New South*, November 1965, for a list of 85 slayings from 1955 to 1965. Most of the victims were on the side of civil rights.

17. Here is how a COFO handbill described what the convention challenge was all about:

> The Democratic National Convention is a very big meeting in August. It is a very important meeting because people in the Democratic Party choose the person they want to run for President of the United States. People in the Democratic Party from all over the country come together and talk. Mississippi sends a group of people to this meeting. This summer we are going to send a Freedom group to the national meeting. In order to choose the people that we want to go to the national meeting, we will have to have four kinds of meetings here in Mississippi . . . Why do we have the Mississippi Freedom Democratic Party? Because the Mississippi Democratic Party is only for a few people who have registered to vote under unfair voting laws.

18. For a detailed account of the youth wing and Freedom Summer, see "Encounter With the Future," by Pat Watters, published by the Southern Regional Council, Inc., 1965.

4)
The Negro Community and Politics

The entry of Negroes more fully into politics comes at a time when the American city, spilling over into amorphous suburbs and threatened with losing political coherence and identity, is beginning to take new directions. How much difference will Negro votes make? In many Southern cities Negroes have had a part in politics for decades. Yet it has been a crippled kind of participation, with limited results. In Atlanta, mayors have sometimes not had a clear majority of the white votes; they have won because of Negro votes. In Memphis, Nashville, Birmingham, Durham, and other cities, Negro votes have been crucial in the outcome of municipal elections and bond issues. But often this power to elect has been reflected relatively little in benefits for Negro communities. Caught in the employment and residential patterns of the segregated past, set at continuing disadvantage by inferior education and status of virtually every kind, Negroes have not been able to use even the seemingly equitable political process in a city such as Atlanta for equitable results. Votes have been, until now at least, an exceedingly weak instrument for assault upon inequities in the private as opposed to the public sector of communities; and often, in the face of strong resistance from segregation-minded whites, they have been of little use in the public sector.

It was not votes but law suits or federal regulations that desegregated most public buildings, schools, and transportation facilities. It was not principally votes but demonstrations that desegregated restaurants and hotels in those Southern communities where this was done before the Civil Rights Act of 1964. Even by 1967, in cities with Negro registrations of 30 and 40 per cent of the total, the votes had not yielded anything like equal or almost-equal schools in Negro areas, equal employment opportunities in city government, or equitable representation in governmental councils. Votes that had decided who would be mayor of Atlanta could not, or had not, altered the racial identification of clerks at city hall. Where Negroes had voted heavily, what they received for their votes usually was a more or less moderate political climate, more circumspect police conduct, and some access to city officials for the satisfaction of particular, limited requests for routine government services.[1] The Commission on Civil Rights study of "voting" and "non-voting" Southern counties in 1961 indicated little difference in street, water, sewage, street-light, and trash services for Negroes, whether they voted or not. Similar studies in Northern cities also have shown that major inequities remain. All of this suggests profound questions about whether the ballot truly will provide solutions to the most pressing problems in the cities.

Two new factors, having to do with Negro leadership and population percentages, actually tend toward a lessening of Negro political advantage. Urban Negro political organization in the past usually was limited to what a few principal Negro political leaders saw fit to establish and utilize. Even in Atlanta, with a large Negro middle class, the political leadership was small and fairly tight in discipline. In New Orleans, a very few Negro leaders guided the Negro community politically. This was the pattern in most Southern cities. But because of the sweep of the rights revolution, stimulating the leadership as well as the aspirations of Negro communities, old leaderships have been inundated by new activists. Unless some shift of circumstances returns the old-style city political machines, with all their mechanisms for control and discipline, the spread of leadership will continue, lessening the coherence of Negro political power. This change, coincidentally, comes at a time when many cities are experiencing a steady rise in the Negro percentage of population because of the movement of middle-class whites to the suburbs, and an influx of rural and small-town Negroes. In Memphis, Negroes are 37.1 per cent; in Birmingham, 39.7 per cent; in Charlotte, 28.0 per cent; in Jacksonville, 41.2 per cent; in Nashville, 37.9 per cent. This disproportion caused by artificial limits of cities' sizes is demonstrated in the instance of Atlanta, which in 1967 was 44 per cent Negro within the city limits but only 22 per cent Negro in the entire metropolitan area.[2] The prospect, however, is that in time Negro percentages of the populations of bigger cities will decline. The present high percentages were the result of slowness of territorial annexation, which lagged far behind the shift of population, racially, within the city limits. Annexations, though sometimes they will encounter increased race-inspired white opposition and possibly sometimes the opposition of Negroes who fear a dilution of their political power, are likely to catch up somewhat with this spread and decrease the Negro portion of cities' populations.

If politics has been an instrument of limited value for Negroes in the cities in the past, will it soon, then, be of even less value? Against the enormous problems which confront Negro communities throughout the South, such a prospect would be calamitous. All the federal legislation and moderation of whites' views may do relatively little to improve the substandard neighborhood school or to pave the street in front of a Negro's house. Conventional politics at the local level has not met these needs. It must be reinvigorated. This has to be done in two ways: by increasing the responsiveness of local government to people's pressing needs, as can be done by the reduction of white supremacist resistance; and by reinvigorating Negro communities with a new drawing out of their common people. We most need not a politics of administration but a politics of formative change and innovation.

Can the adaptive ability of Negroes, which sprang out of their historic position of disadvantage, now be applied to political opportunity? In the past, Negroes adapted to limited opportunity, to segregation, to complete exclusion; they adapted by means healthy and unhealthy, desirable and undesirable. But when the chance came, they often climbed up rapidly, and this repeatedly has surprised people who had thought Negro "traits" were unchangeable rather than temporary adaptations to brutal situations. The rural-county sheriff accustomed to seeing Negroes "in their place" was startled when thousands arrived at the courthouse to prove they really do want to vote. Often he truly had thought that, except for a "few troublemakers," they did not. He had mistaken necessary adaptation for acceptance, and "their nature." Politically,

Negroes in the big cities of the North adapted to the prevailing situations. Within a Chicago city machine, for instance, they built a Negro sub-machine. The limited value of such political adaptations becomes clear as other opportunities arise. Just as the civil rights movement devised various means of wrenching away from the social and economic adaptations of old, so new devices must be shaped now to break away from the old adaptations to political disadvantage, and the way of thinking that went with them. The forms the new adaptations should take are as indeterminate now as were the future forms of civil rights action at the outset of 1955, before the boycotts, the sit-ins, and the freedom rides (all of which were adaptations used with great success, especially after the 1950's), and the fill-the-jails and quarantine-Alabama devices (which were abortive). Regardless of what form the new political action takes, however, its course will be related to (and in part a reaction to) the political experience of the recent past, and the forms of the recent past. So a contemplation of Negroes' experience with those forms, which will be altered and supplemented but not replaced, is important. In Atlanta, we may see many trends and factors relevant to all the urban South.

Changes in Conventional Politics

As late as 1960, Negro political leadership in Atlanta was vested firmly in the hands of a small group who worked principally through the Atlanta Negro Voters League, an organization that meticulously maintained a Republican-Democratic balance in its leadership. In the nonpartisan municipal elections, party was of no consequence. In constant rapport with the moderate political combination that controlled the city government, the handful of Negroes who led the Voters League maintained a limited voice in city affairs; in turn, they made recommendations to the Negro electorate which prevailed on election day in Negro precincts. Atlanta had no machine in the traditional sense, with formalized organization into the precinct level and with patronage rewards for the politically faithful. It had a loose alliance of interests. For many years Negroes, most middle-class whites, and downtown business interests generally had been on the same side in city elections. Although Negroes frequently provided the victory margins of successful candidates for mayor and alderman, they nevertheless had little political leverage.

Often the challenger of Mayor William B. Hartsfield (who dominated city politics, with only one brief interruption, for twenty-five years) would be a segregationist who accused him of being maintained in office by the Negro "bloc vote"; or he would be, while himself campaigning among Negroes, nevertheless the beneficiary of all the strongly segregationist support and partially its captive. So Negroes had little choice, and little leverage. Many of their leaders, too, were swayed by money contributions from the mayor's side. The same circumstances frequently existed in races for the city council. The principal task of Negro political leaders, then, was not to make choices and obtain commitments but to marshal votes and periodically to make representations to the city administration on Negroes' behalf. They could do little more; any abstention from support of the Hartsfield type of leadership seemed likely only to elect someone less friendly.[3]

By 1961 the pattern had changed, partly as a result of an unpredictable, five-candidate election at the end of the Hartsfield era. Four of the five candidates for mayor sought Negro votes, with varying degrees of effort. The older Negro leadership endorsed Ivan Allen, Jr., a businessman who had the support of the retiring mayor and most of the downtown business leadership. But for the first time a new Negro political faction emerged behind another candidate, M. M. Smith, who had a legislative record with some appeal for Negroes. Other Negroes aligned themselves actively with other candidates. In the first primary, Negro votes were substantially divided. The tight hold of the older leadership was broken. The first primary established clearly that, given a real choice, Atlanta Negro voters and Negro leadership no longer would be a predictable "bloc." The "bloc" did re-emerge in the primary runoff, but only because the old circumstance had re-emerged: the runoff was between Ivan Allen and Lester Maddox, the one militant segregationist in the race, who had benefited from the big Atlanta segregationist vote that always had opposed the Hartsfield administration. Negroes voted overwhelmingly for Allen, who won by almost exactly this number of votes. White Atlanta, in short, even in 1961, had given half its votes to a man who preached the inherent inferiority of Negroes and defiance of the federal government and the Constitution as construed by the courts.[4]

Other Atlanta elections since then have shown the widening of Negro political leadership and a fading of old "bloc vote" patterns in certain circumstances. The decline in the importance of the Atlanta Negro

Voters League was evident in the 1965 municipal elections, and some politicians believed it would be worth less thereafter. It ceased to have the final word in determining (and reflecting) Negro political sentiment because, increasingly, Negroes had choices. Because high-level decision for the whole Negro community had died, the whole scope of political contact between politicians and Negro voters suddenly widened. Politicians no longer could simply rely upon an endorsement engineered with a few leaders of the Voters League. They began to go directly to the voters at the precinct level and under. Some white politicians were getting on personal terms with as many Negroes as had the established Negro leadership. Such contact is useful, of course, for more than vote-getting. More Negroes were finding access to governmental decision-making. A politician strolling and handshaking through the shops on Hunter Street might be petitioned informally by a store-owner for street or sidewalk repair, by a shopper for a new four-way stop light near her child's school, by a sports fan complaining about the prices of baseball tickets at the new municipal stadium. If he were adroit, of course, the politician would remember not only the petitions but the names of the store-owner and the sports fan, and the next time he would be calling the names. In short, the most useful ordinariness of conventional politics and representative government had set in. One reason it had was the destruction of the old, tightly drawn Negro leadership structure and thus the political unity of the Negro community.

In what was probably the last of elections in which the Atlanta Negro Voters League endorsement would be necessary to win Negro votes, one candidate for the Board of Aldermen in 1965 demonstrated a fact of importance for the future. He did not receive the Voters League endorsement, or the endorsement of the local Negro daily and weekly newspapers, principally because he was running against an incumbent who had taken care to mend his fences in the Negro community. But the challenger, a young Republican named Jack Sells, slipped under these traditional edifices of power and campaigned among the precinct managers and the people on the street. He won favorable introductions to church deacons, and then arranged invitations through them to address their congregations. He learned the names of influential Negroes in housing projects, and went to see them for help. He drew aid from Negro Republicans whom he had befriended in party meetings, and he berated his opponent for inaction on a pending measure against housing violations by slum landlords. In the end he lost in a close runoff election, but he won 48 per cent of the Negro votes against all the usual odds. It was certain proof that even an unknown white politician now could go over the heads of most of the important Negro power structures and do well. It was also suggested that, if elected, he could be held accountable by Negro voters at large, and not just by the Negro political leaders, for his promises.

A successful young white New Orleans politician noted in 1966 that the organizations of a number of ethnic groups in his city had been, in the past, the recipients of patronage. He was asked whether Negro organizations, with the emergence of a strong Negro vote, might not become heavy patronage dispensers in return for their endorsements, and thus become a force for disciplining and machine-molding the Negro community politically. He said he did not. It was already easy, he said, for white as well as Negro politicians to go over the heads of the Negro organization leaders and establish direct allegiances among Negroes. He had done so, he said, and he felt politicians could get by if necessary without the Negro organizations and endorsements.[5] It seemed significant that in both Atlanta and New Orleans, two Southern cities with a history of segregation and a present reality of large Negro voter registrations, the brightest and seemingly most promising younger white politicians in the mid-1960's were popular with Negro voters and maintained easy rapport with them. That kind of relationship seemed to discourage bossism extending downward from Negro organizational leaders acting as political middlemen.

Atlanta by this time had scores of Negro community organizations that played political roles of some importance. In the past most had been merely the devices by which the vote was organized for candidates favored by the top Negro leadership. Hereafter, it was clear, many would be individually important. In a city without a machine controlling precinct organizations by dispensing jobs and other favors, such a development pointed toward a working democracy. It also threatened, in a healthy way, the "bloc vote" patterns of the past.

Under the circumstances that had prevailed throughout the South in the past, there was a positive belief in the desirability of "bloc voting" on the part of most Negro leaders. In a study of Negro leadership in New Orleans, Daniel C. Thompson noted: "All Negro leaders interviewed, including those primarily interested in politics, agree that about the only way Negro voters can significantly influence political affairs in the city is by bloc voting." [6] Given the political atmosphere of a segregationist South, this conclusion probably was correct. It is just as easy, however, to conclude that in the future, as more opportunities for political trading appear, it will not be true.

Negroes running against whites in Atlanta generally have fared well with the Negro "bloc vote" only when they were people of prominence, had the backing of the Negro voter organizations, or were supported by city hall. In 1965 municipal elections, in fact, even an articulate young real estate man well known in the Negro community was unable to win overwhelming support there running against a white alderman regarded as acceptable though not especially liberal on racial matters. In a typical largely Negro precinct the alderman, Charles Leftwich, won 197 votes to 241 for his young Negro adversary, Eddie Billingsley. Such results have been seen on a number of occasions in Atlanta.

One effect of the widening of political leadership in this Southern city and the breakdown of the "bloc" when there was no reason for one, a phenomenon that already is becoming common, has been the use of conventional means to break down Negroes' disinterest in politics. Politics seemed irrelevant to Negroes in many locales partly because it *was* irrelevant. When it came to their own interests, Negroes had no real choices. The infinitesimal "differences" among white politicians often were like those which New Orleans confronted during the heyday of segregationist resistance to the federal government in the 1950's. Negro politicians there lined up variously behind candidates for governor who described themselves as "a hundred per cent" for segregation, "a thousand per cent" for segregation, and "a million per cent" for segregation. In fact, one Negro leader regarded as "militant" placed himself stoically behind the candidate who assured the Louisiana Association of Registrars of Voters that he was "a billion per cent" for segregation.[7]

When politicians establish real contact, however, and become both accessible and effective in their responses, the situation changes for many Negroes. They have a choice. Interest tends to grow. "I like to campaign down there," one white politician in Atlanta was saying of the Negro community in 1966. "Those people are *interested* in politics." Most of the Negroes he reached were, to be sure, not the poorest and most hopeless ones, the ones beneath the housing-project level; a big question remains about whether these can be reached in the same way. Many probably cannot, as many Negroes never were reached by the civil rights movement before communities were aroused by mass meetings for direct action. But conventional politics, when it works free of machine conformity and lack of choice for Negroes among candidates, can reach many more urban Negroes than it has in the urban examples of the past.[8]

Negro Political Organization

How have Negroes organized politically in such a circumstance as Atlanta's? One fairly typical community civic league is headed by a twenty-five-year-old high-school graduate who owns his own home and has a salaried job considered a good one. Lower middle-class home-owners predominate in his area. The civic league holds a rally, inviting most but not necessarily all the candidates. The executive committee subsequently chooses a slate to endorse, with the president having the most important word about who should be chosen. The voting in this community's two precincts, even so, is not thereafter a certainty. In 1965 elections, two white aldermen who were popular with Negroes won the league's endorsement and then received more than 85 per cent of the two precincts' votes, faring better than any other candidates. Several Negro candidates who had the local league's endorsement won more than 80 per cent. One white candidate who had the league's endorsement but not the approval of larger, city-wide Negro voter organizations received 65 per cent of the two precincts' votes. The differences in these percentages contradict a political generalization holding true in the recent past: that urban Negroes are not likely to split tickets or even vote in all races on the ticket. "Negroes in such areas [lower middle class] do more ticket-splitting than a lot of people think," one of the candidates said. Perhaps the strength of Negro political organization, heightening Negro interest, makes for more individual choosing rather than less.

Another kind of Negro organization exists in the housing projects, probably the most important centers of Negro political power in Atlanta because the concentration of people there makes it easier to turn out the votes on election day. In the area of one of these projects, a civic association covers twelve precincts, all of one state House district, and parts of two city wards. There are about 6,000 registered voters, a third of them in the housing project. If the association decides to support a candidate, it shows him its projected campaign expenses [with a 10 per cent overhead amount] and indicates his prorated share of the expenses.

A typical sum for an aldermanic candidate is $200. The ticket is drawn up before the candidates are asked to contribute.[9] On a few occasions a candidate has said he did not have the money to spare and this particular association has supported him anyway. The campaign fund provided, in a typical election, the full-time use of two telephones by workers for the ticket, the support of a daily news sheet distributed in the area, and the provision of eight or ten cars to take voters to the polls. Two leaders of the association devoted full time to the campaign for two to three months. Apparently the 10 per cent overhead sum provided what amounted to a very modest remuneration for their time. Why did they do it? The position makes them leaders. Simple community interest is apparently a big factor. Neither received any patronage rewards.

Half a dozen organizations such as these two can make or break a candidate for city-wide office. In lower-level campaigns, such as a race within one Georgia House district, they are even more important. A city's housing projects sometimes become a means of political control. A project manager may have strong influence with the chief political organizer within the project and with the official precinct manager, who conducts the election. Thus a line of power could run from a city's housing authority to the project managers to the political organizers to the precinct managers. The danger of such control is increased by the fact that in housing-project precincts an inadequate system of purging the names of voters who have moved may leave a big backlog of registrations for precinct workers to manipulate fraudulently. In such concentrated living circumstances, it is relatively easy to learn who has moved and left his registration in his old precinct. The figures for some Atlanta Negro precincts have indicated turnouts of more than 90 per cent, even though large numbers of their registrants have moved away. (Some, of course, return to vote after moving because they are familiar with their old precincts.) A political organizer who keeps close watch on his area through his block leaders may know exactly who has moved away, may ascertain that he did not move his registration, and may have someone else go "vote" him. This is, of course, as easy to do in predominantly white projects as in predominantly Negro projects, though in Atlanta there is less evidence of the practice in white projects.

Churches are still a big factor in Negro voting in most Southern cities.[10] The favors of some Negro clergymen in Atlanta may still be bought with "contributions" to the church, but the practice has declined sharply in recent years. The amounts of money involved vary enormously. A donation of $25 will secure the favors of some churches' ministers. On the upper end, one larger church is believed to have received $2,500 from an aldermanic candidate. The ability of a preacher to "deliver" is often questionable. On the other hand, the decision of one of the bribe-free leading ministers to support a candidate usually means that the members of that church will go heavily for him. A minister establishes a reputation in such matters; if he is not suspect, his personal influence can be enormous.

In all these political forms there is a certain distinctiveness. White areas of Atlanta do not have similar organizations as a rule, or similar immersion of churches in politics, and at election time candidates find it difficult to assemble white crowds for speeches. The Negro community of Atlanta, politically, is simply better organized, more interested, and likely to produce a better election-day turnout than does the white community. All of this contradicts the more general truth that Negroes are not experienced in politics in the South; in some places they are more experienced with organization than are whites.

Impact of the Votes

Why, then, has this vote not been more effective in eliminating inequities, at least those upon which city government directly touches? The answer has to do with the degree of resistance and the drag of the past. Over the years, mayors on occasion have been unable to muster half the white electorate. Mayor Ivan Allen won in a re-election landslide in 1965; but analysis revealed that even then he had received only 51 per cent of the white votes. (It is doubtful that he had more than half the white votes in his first race, in 1961.) So the main obstacle to obvious concessions to the Negro electorate seems clear. The shift of a relatively small additional part of the white electorate against the mayors usually would have been enough to defeat them. The same may be said of many aldermen over the years.

Thus Atlanta had Negro policemen as early as 1947, but they did not exercise general power to arrest whites until 1962. Perhaps that authority could have been given much earlier without political defeat for the mayor; but this surely cannot be taken for granted in a situation of such delicate balance. White-collar jobs in city hall were not available to Negroes, or jobs as firemen; and there was no integration of parks and swimming pools. The city moved along, basically bound in its place by a big force of segregationists and a middle force of white moderates who might desert to the segregationists in sizable numbers given what they considered a little too much provocation. What did the Negro votes do, then, for Negroes and for Atlanta?

They kept Atlanta from being Birmingham. When the issue was not truly integration but whether or not there would be law and moderation of racist tempers, Atlanta's strong moderate white leadership prevailed. But it would not have if there had not been a large bloc of Negro votes for moderate policies. Notwithstanding the fact that the city's newspapers and business and civic leaders offered moderate leadership most of the time, without Negro votes the moderates most likely would have been overwhelmed by that majority of whites who habitually voted against the city administration.

In Birmingham, meanwhile, few Negroes could vote. Moderate leadership was unsuccessful or non-existent for many years. Only with these conditions could a Bull Connor have been the city's leading political figure. This situation continued exactly until the time when a sizable Negro electorate first appeared in Birmingham, in 1963. Perhaps Atlanta would have been spared a Bull Connor anyway, but perhaps it would not have been, for all around it in Georgia in the 1940's and 1950's the racist fires were burning, often higher even than in Alabama, and Atlanta's moderates usually were the objects of the most venal political vituperation in the state.

As federal law has settled such matters as integration of private as well as public facilities, the race issue has been almost entirely removed from Atlanta politics. The city had arrived by 1967 at a threshold on which would be decided whether Negro votes could be truly effective in solving some of the main problems of Negroes. So had numerous cities all over the South and in fact, the nation. The stubbornness of some of these problems suggests that there is no easy solution even when the Negro electorate rises to 40 per cent of the whole. But with this much political muscle the main questions are how well the power will be used, how well the Negro community will be organized for action, and to what extent new means will be added to the old means of political action.

The old and traditional means, not yet fully exercised, already were proving their importance. Negroes' first real entry into conventional politics in Alabama resulted, even in 1963, in some fascinating unpublicized traditional-patronage activity. When a decision was made in Washington to add deputy marshals in Montgomery and Mobile, Orzell Billingsley, Jr., a leading Negro lawyer and politician in Birmingham, was asked for the names of Negroes he would recommend for the jobs. He consulted with local leaders in the two cities, made recommendations, and their choices were accepted. Also in 1963, the recommendations of the Alabama Democratic Conference, a Negro organization which had been established several years earlier at the behest of the Democratic National Committee representatives, were appointed as a Federal Housing Administration real estate appraiser and a post office employee-relations officer in Alabama. Such traditional patronage participation may not be the ideal form of advancement; but for Negroes it was a great improvement over all-white patronage control.

Non-Conventional Politics

Consider, as only one example of an area largely ignored by politics in the past, the urban slums. A typical large city may have a fairly good housing code and an apparatus to enforce it, and yet slums remain. Often the apparatus is oriented toward cleaning out slums primarily to reclaim the land for commercial and industrial purposes. Housing code inspectors are too few and frequently too little motivated to keep abreast of the problem, and procedures for forcing the slum landlords to comply are slow. In many cases, in fact, the city is not equipped with legal powers to reach the slum landlord who lives elsewhere. In any case, perhaps the slum landlords are aware that no big owner of numerous slum houses has yet gone to jail for repeated violation of the code; at worst, they face fines that are lighter than the profits they make because of inaction on repairs. The slum dwellers' deprivations today may even be greater than usual, because the owners are delaying repairs in the expectation of condemnation for urban renewal clearance; and when the condemnations come, the slum dwellers frequently are faced with hardships in finding new quarters they can afford and which do not add to their transportation and other running expenses. In such circumstances, ordinary political power can be of paramount value in moving the local government to firmer action.

But in local government, those who have power and influence beyond their votes get the most satisfying answers from government. If money and close personal ties to officials can get fairly swift results for the upper-middle class, what will do it for poor people, many of them altogether negative or apathetic about the usefulness of the political process? The rent strikes and the riots of the mid-1960's were two answers offered by the slums. Marches and picketing of city hall were others. It was becoming apparent that the controlled mass-protest devices of the civil rights movement were being shifted to problems of slums and urban poverty, even as violent forces threatened to intervene.

The new use of non-violent mass protest in the slums would require community organization, non-existent in most poverty-ridden places. There was growing interest in what had been done by Saul Alinsky's Industrial Areas Foundation. Mr. Alinsky, who began his work in the early 1940's in Chicago, had sought power for the poor and powerless. He created unity in incoherent communities by singling out a particular grievance or threat, agitating about it, and organizing people on this basis. Churches, business groups, and local block clubs helped in effect to create a community, and churches provided a large measure of the financing. With unity, the community went on to attack other problems. The means used were chosen to suit the peculiar natures of these communities. The all-important premise was that they must move for themselves through petitioning, endorsing candidates, picketing, and other methods.

Alinsky dealt initially with lower-middle-class white areas in the cities, but his approach was substantially duplicated, though not consciously, by the civil rights movement in rural, low-income Negro areas of the South. By 1967, their success in forming community coherence in such areas as Alabama's Black Belt and the Mississippi Delta was difficult to measure. It seemed likely that an extended experiment with community self-help organizations would spread, both in the cities and in the rural South, with the help not only of civil rights organizations but also of churches, foundations, new federal programs requiring local community initiative, and new responsiveness in city halls because of heavier political participation by urban Negroes.

All of this was related to a shifting in attitudes about conventional welfare approaches of the past. A large part of America, the remaining poor, simply had not been dislodged and moved out of poverty by the old welfare approaches and an expanding economy. It had not been lifted out of its lower depths by the availability of public education, by the fact that a booming economy was creating more jobs, by a dole to help people who were out of work, or by a welfare allowance for old people and destitute mothers with children. The third generation of many families was still on relief. An awareness of this failure seeped upward, to the top. The idea of participation by the poor in management of the federal poverty program was one potentially useful result. That program, initiated by President Johnson, did rest in part on a belief, not always acted upon, that the poor must participate in decisions about poverty and that they must be activated on their own behalf.

This new awareness enhanced prospects for more self-determination in sprawling, faceless, disorganized, often-exploited, always-lethargic urban slums and lower-middle-class ghettoes. The coming of the new self-help emphasis had striking parallels with the earlier coming of a new approach in the rights movement, dramatized in the Montgomery bus boycott of 1955 and brought to fruition with the birth of the sit-in movement in 1960 and the extension of the uses of direct action. Those were instances of mass self-help, reliant upon mass stirrings of the powerless. With these new approaches, the rights movement no longer rested its hopes simply upon the occasional use of the ballot and the courts, and infrequent negotiation of Negro leaders behind closed doors. The movement began to rely upon the creation of new forms of power to back up the traditional means. Now the negotiators had a mass force behind them which gave them something to negotiate with. This kind of widespread community arousal was exactly what the self-help efforts in the slums sought to create in the mid-1960's. Community coherence and self-propulsion were the chief objectives in each case. The slums already had learned from the rights movement.

What political ramifications are there for the city outside these areas? When a slum makes its claim for paved streets,[11] sidewalks, street lights, recreation areas, enforcement of housing codes, and decent schools, it only claims what the rest of the city already has been getting. The only immediate impact on the rest of the city, then, is a loss of some of the public funds that otherwise might pour into other areas. But there are long-term ramifications. The poorest might be expected to use new-found influence in favor of more property tax rather than more sales tax, or a city graduated income tax rather than a uniform increase in sewer charges. We might expect a push for rent controls, more public housing, and less advance industrial zoning of lower-income residential areas before pressing shortages of lower-income housing are met.

It will continue to be easier, however, to move a community into action to obtain the paving of a street or the enforcement of a housing code than to oppose a given kind of tax. The latter is the kind of issue which a middle-class citizen, relatively comfortable about the matter of streets, sidewalks, and schools, may be able to turn to; it is unlikely that a poverty-ridden area will exercise itself much about these broader issues as long as it must contend with garbage dumped on vacant lots nearby and the lack of a good roof on a house. One may guess, then, that the influence of even an aroused poor neighborhood upon these bigger issues will be less than its influence upon what affects it down the block. The idea of a nationwide political coalition of the poor, especially one arising from a network of local self-help organizations in poor areas, seems much less tenable than the idea that hundreds of thousands of small local organizations can effect changes of their immediate situations by local means.[12] A "proletarian politics," as reflected in some of the mid-1960's proposals, seems unworkable. The poor in our country are an unstable political entity, always shifting in membership and location and inevitably unstable in organization and devotion to long-term programs. The poor may be effective in smaller groups for specific, visible, local ends; but a national party of the poor is a shaky concept indeed. No one wants to fight for the values of poverty, for the "way of life" of the poor, or for the right to be poor. The mere achievement of a modicum of material success removes a man from the constituency of the poor and that constituency's main interests. Enactment of a guaranteed annual wage, for instance, might undermine the whole program of a nationwide "proletarian" political formation; and such legislation probably would be the product of economic forces entirely apart from that formation.

The Negro Community

In the meantime, rising expectations had brought us to convulsion in the urban ghettoes. There the nation had had riots not simply because of squalor, want, and human misery; chaos was upon us partly because these circumstances had remained at a time when hope had been aroused even among many of the hopeless. Expectations outran the productive machine, or at least the apparatuses of distribution, economic and political. And so we were at a flash point.

For Negro slum dwellers, because there was genuine social disintegration, there was a lack of effective social control. Martin Luther King, Jr., could go to Chicago to become a rallying point because Negro political leadership there had been so ineffective against monstrous problems that it had lost the confidence of many people.[13] The Chicago situation was a typical one for Negroes in the big cities. There, the Negro masses were touched less than their Southern counterparts by such great binding forces as churches, fraternal organizations including most of a community's leadership, and a generally recognized hierarchy of local Negro leadership. They also lacked conservative forces, which sometimes held back the progress of Southern Negroes but which also served for effective social control and guidance: an influential middle class which, though small, was very much *within* the Negro community. In the South, because of more rigid segregationist pressures, the middle class was unable to slip out of the Negro community and escape into the white world; in the North, it frequently did.

The lack of effective community organization in the non-Southern ghettoes was a logical result of transplanting the Southern Negro community organization. The Northern ghetto was the Southern Negro community with most of its debilitations but without its cohesive and conservative forces, and with an additional cause for embitterment: the fact that many Negroes had come here from the land of Jim Crow as if traveling to the Promised Land. The more cohesive, recognized Negro leadership in the South had been the creature of white supremacist rule as only the South had known it. So it is misleading to say, as often is said, that Northern *de facto* segregation was the same in its effect as the old, complete, and legal segregation of the South. These two worlds of segregation were not simply different sides of the same coin. Only the Southern version produced some sense of identity and even unity, however weak, on the Negro side of the tracks; some substantial knowledge of why a Negro's lot was as it was, and often a sturdy ability to cope with the situation because of that knowledge. In the South, this awareness often has been a sustaining force for individuals.

Robert Coles, a psychiatrist who studied children involved in school desegregation, quoted the grandmother of a Negro child who was among the first to integrate New Orleans schools. She was asked whether the pressures the Negro children faced might also have been faced by some of the whites who befriended them, some of whom were persecuted, for resisting the mob. "Yes," she said, "we is all the same under God, so we has the same problems; but colored folk has special ones, too. It's the same, but it's different." Coles noted that skin color, at least, affords a Negro some measure of definition as a person, some visible reason for why he faces what he faces. "We may not have anything," the grandmother said, "but at least we know why." [14] Negroes of Northern ghettoes, though they still have their color, presumably had left the land of white supremacy and they were less likely to know the why of their individual deprivations and inabilities. A riot is a collective aberration, but it is a collective expression of individual frustration. That individual frustration might be greater in a Northern place where the walls could not be so easily seen. The result of being stopped by unseen barriers could not be so easily explained, and a man's anger could not so easily be focused upon something that was removable by orderly process.

Negro Community Structure and the Middle Class

The structure of the Negro community is all-important as we consider how effective Southern Negro political and social action may be. But it is also significant for what it tells of the Southern Negroes who have moved into Northern ghettoes. We can only select a few aspects for consideration here. They reflect the Voter Education Project's empirical findings in efforts to deal with and to shore up local Negro leaderships throughout the South. The VEP director and all of its field men during a three-year span were Negro Southerners. This seems worth noting inasmuch as the authors of this book grounded in the VEP's work and research, white Southerners, have become increasingly aware of the fact that hardly any Southerners, and hardly any non-Southerners, can easily see all of a single bi-racial Southern community. They cannot, because they are not both white and Negro. In a sense, to borrow from James W. Silver's phrase in *Mississippi: The Closed Society*, all the South has been two closed societies, each closed to the other except for narrow meeting places. A white reporter or researcher with the best of credentials, instincts, and intentions is unlikely to plumb the subtleties and essences of the Negro community in a Southern town or county *as a Negro sees it*; and a Negro project worker with the best of credentials, instincts, and intentions cannot easily measure and comprehend the nuances and perspectives of the white community in a Southern town or county, *as a white may see it*. This is one of the more inhuman, and more subtle, legacies of segregation.

The Negro field secretaries of VEP sometimes reported great difficulty in establishing real rapport and exchange with local Negro leaders, many of whom, confronted by the outside "race man," adopted roles and disguises that became so predictable as to be easily categorized. White reporters knew the same experience from contact with scores of unsophisticated small-town mayors, police chiefs, and other white leaders, who adopted their own easily-predicted roles and disguises for the visitor. The good field secretary and the good reporter know how to discount for such factors, with tired resolve. But it is at least rare for a Negro Southerner to know just how and where to weigh the nuances when the spokesmen are white, and for the white Southerner to know how and where to do the same when the spokesmen are Negro. Perhaps an even greater factor is the simple one of perspective: which town do you see when you go to McComb, Mississippi; which do you "identify" with, and which affords you more familiarities and acceptances? The authors make their assessments here with a strong awareness of their limitations as whites of the white closed society, and especially conscious that most whites who have written with sensitivity and insight about the South have nevertheless ignored the peculiar perspective of the Negro South; they have virtually ignored half the South except as it affected the other half.

In *The Mind of the South*, W. J. Cash was concerned about the Negro mainly as an agent affecting the behavior and personality of the whites. V. O. Key, in *Southern Politics*, was concerned about the Negro only as an agent upon which white politicians acted. Both wrote about *the white South as affected by the Negro*. Another perspective entirely was that of William Faulkner. He was concerned with the Negro, most often, as an individual, as another human being rather than as part of a peculiar culture within another peculiar culture. It was principally Lillian Smith who went further in exploring the Negro's South, and the Negro himself in it, before the years of the rights movement. With the coming of the movement, writing about the South began to focus more often upon the Negro's predicament. Even then most of this came from outside the movement rather than from within it, from whites rather than from Negroes. The writings of Dr. King; SNCC, *The New Aboli-*

tionists, by Howard Zinn (Boston: Beacon Press, 1964); *Echo in My Soul* by Septima Poinsette Clark (New York: E. P. Dutton, 1962); *The Free Men* by John Ehle (New York: Harper and Row, 1965); *Freedom Summer* by Sally Belfrage (New York: Viking Press, 1965); *Letters From Mississippi*, edited by Elizabeth Sutherland (New York: McGraw-Hill, 1965); *Our Faces, Our Words*, by Lillian Smith (New York: W. W. Norton, 1964); and magazine articles by Margaret Long are outstanding. Dr. King, Dr. Zinn, Mrs. Clark, Miss Belfrage, Miss Sutherland, and Miss Long write from experience of participation in the movement. Of all these authors, only Dr. King and Mrs. Clark are Negro.

In several Southern cities, Negro community leadership has been studied by application of some of the methods used by Floyd Hunter in *The Community Power Structure: A Study of Decision Makers* (Chapel Hill: University of North Carolina Press, 1953). The use of the power structure concept as an analytical tool tends to exaggerate an already too prevalent belief among Negro intellectuals in the existence of a rigid white elite which governs large matters and small. In part, this prevalence is due to the frequent Negro sense of powerlessness and a concomitant belief that power must lie with a disciplined elite somewhere, rational in its purpose and methods. When the homes of civil rights leaders were bombed in 1965 in Charlotte, a surprise to most people familiar with that city's racial moderation, an important figure in the rights movement immediately arrived at an easy explanation: "They were pushing too hard." The Negroes had been pushing against the local power structure. So the comment suggested retaliation by the white power structure—retaliation through use of bombers and burners. The power elite, in other words, controlled all, even the hoodlums. Another able Negro intellectual was saying at the same time that the Georgia gubernatorial campaign had not yet shaped up because "*they* haven't picked a man yet." When *they* did, the outcome would be certain, he indicated. In New Orleans, the Negro leadership undertook a study of how it might best bring its influence to bear upon the power structure there; the study began with the stated assumption that Negroes had moved the power structure in Atlanta, as indicated by Floyd Hunter's study. (Atlanta was the unnamed "regional city" of Hunter's book.) Thus there was a study of *how to use* a disciplined power structure that was now *assumed* to exist, in almost finite form. One study of recent years was actually a manual for human relations groups, suggesting how they might use the disciplined, highly organized power structure that was assumed to exist.[15] Professor Hunter had taken some care to note that the power structure (in Atlanta) was not monolithic, rigid, constant, and all-encompassing. Some of those who have used his study as an avenue to conclusions beyond it have been less careful about qualifying the original propositions.

Community Power Structure [16] implies great diminution of the importance we ordinarily attach to political life. By its stress upon an elite largely beyond the reach of democratic control it implies that votes have relatively very little power. This kind of analysis of power has, certainly, some validity. But what is grossly wrong is the inference that in most cities the structure is disciplined, is involved in a wide range of issues, is consistent, and is rational. Such suppositions are a reflection of the "they" psychological-conspiracy syndrome.

From Negro intellectuals' viewpoint, there may be further distortion. Upper-level Negro leadership in a city such as Atlanta is more competent at social analysis, in a general way, than its white counterpart. It is more intellectually inclined; even its businessman element, significantly a smaller portion than in the white leadership, frequently is at home with the terminology of social dynamics and with such studies as Hunter's. This Negro leadership has spent a lifetime looking for explanations of phenomena that press upon it but of which many whites are simply oblivious. Its white counterpart did not find the structure of the community its chief problem, and so it has not been obsessed with it.

An important result of this difference in familiarity with social analysis is that Negroes tend to look for rational and thoughtful motive behind a particular white community action when, in fact, such an action may have been taken without reference to any of the factors the Negroes thought must have governed them. Thus, Negroes may think the power structure decided a certain outcome of events because there has been that outcome, and because it has a certain effect which is believed to be in keeping with what the power structure would want. In reality, this conclusion by Negroes may be attributing entirely too much to the power structure not only in power but also in comprehension of certain social dynamics. What the Negro leadership, with greater familiarity in that field, may see, the white leadership may not.

After all, one of the great clues to the success of Dr. King and the student wing of the rights movement in its earlier days was the small-town (and even big-town) lack of comprehension of many factors involved in social engineering. Bull Connor could not have behaved more perfectly for Dr. King's purposes (principally, national legislation and policy) than he did in Birmingham. Much of the white South has been clearly predictable in its responses, and so anyone who could predict them was in a position to maintain the initiative. The rights movement, by contrast, was in no way predictable by the Bull Connors or better men because they simply had never thought about, or thought through, the uses and structures of power involved. They did not even understand their own, and its bases, and they could not defend it therefore. The rights movement, however, had arrived at some profound insights in such matters.

Understanding of the dynamics of the Negro community begins with recognition of the aspect that makes it most different from the white community: the stifling of its middle class. Negro communities, it often has been said, are short of middle-class people. In 1960, 8 per cent of the Negroes in the South were in white-collar occupations: professional and technical men and women, officials, managers, teachers, sales personnel, or self-employed businessmen. Even in Durham, noted for the size and leadership of its middle class, the proportion was only 15 per cent. Yet there is more to be said. In entirely rural areas, for instance, class lines are frequently obscure and the white community may have as little middle class, in the urban sense, as the Negro community. It was not shortage of a middle class so much as the crippling of the middle class that was the paramount factor in Negro community structure and leadership. In a rural area where relative prosperity rather than role makes a white or a Negro farmer middle-class, only the Negro farmer was kept off the county school board, off the sheriff's force, off the agricultural acreage-allotment committees. More importantly, perhaps, only he had been kept off the board of directors of the town bank where he did business. He had not been a participant in the economic, political, and social power of his community, notwithstanding his otherwise middle-class status. In the towns and cities, the middle-class Negro was deprived in the same way. So in many important ways, he could not really be called middle class. The effects of these deprivations upon leadership have been profound.

Consider the impact upon teachers. A study of Negro leadership in New Orleans noted that the city had 1,600 Negro public school teachers, the biggest element in that Negro community's middle class.

On the face of it, 1,600 college-educated, relatively prosperous Negroes should stimulate all phases of Negro community leadership. Yet few public school teachers had played important roles in community life outside their professions. The local NAACP and CORE organizations could have been staging areas for large bodies of intelligent teachers, well-organized and harnessed for attacks on all kinds of community problems. But they were not. Teachers played, the study showed, a "relatively weak role." [17]

Teachers feared participation. And because white officials did not want them to "agitate," they did not always have the trust of other Negroes whom they might have led. Thus the biggest potential source of Negro community leadership in New Orleans, as in most other large cities, was crippled by the system. A number of reasons were apparent: they were dependent upon the white officials who were their superiors, and subject to state laws making it almost impossible for them to identify themselves with organizations concerned with racial relations. They also were less dependent upon the Negro community and so less inclined to identify their specific self-interest with its general well-being. They were predominantly women, and although women often are socially and culturally dominant in Negro society, relatively few of these best-educated women have evinced a strong activist's interest in advancement of rights. Thus the biggest potential source of Negro community leadership in New Orleans was crippled.

In 1965, Dr. L. S. Alexander, executive secretary of the all-Negro Mississippi Teachers Association, told the Commission on Civil Rights that there had been "very little response" when teachers were urged at association meetings to register to vote. He said their fears of dismissal if they did register were justified and the situation, even then, did not seem to be improving. In Mississippi, he said, there were 667 Negro teachers with master's degrees and 7,460 with bachelor's degrees.[18] It is obvious what a force this would have been if it had been active for civil rights in a state where educated Negro leadership was almost unbelievably limited.

A somber example of the crippling of many Negro school professionals and its consequent injury to students is found in a VEP report from a rural south Georgia county. There, a Negro principal made especially subservient by ruthless local white supremacy reduced the teaching of civics and government because it was in these classes that embarrassing questions most often were asked. The same principal acted with hostility, from the outset, toward voter registration workers who had arrived in the community. A student leader restrained his own involvement with voter registration because, eventually, he hoped to obtain the principal's recommendation for entrance to a college he already had chosen. He feared antagonizing the principal. The basketball coach, no doubt responsive to the principal, informed members of his squad that he would drop them if they became too friendly with the local registration workers of the Student Nonviolent Coordinating Committee. Teachers themselves did not dare to register. The mother of a student who had been involved in a small local demonstration was fired from her job in the school lunchroom. No one can say how deep was the impact of all this suppression, created by school professionals who were themselves crippled by the force of higher authority. A perceptive young male teacher in another school nearby, who was rapidly becoming an alcoholic apparently because of despair arising from a similar situation in his school, said of the students there: "We are killing them every day." In many such schools all over the South, a segment of Negro middle-class leadership became at times actually anti-leadership insofar as the community's interests were concerned.

Even the most unsophisticated Negroes in rural Southern communities have been aware of the toll taken of teachers and principals. While they sometimes showed compassion for their school people during the wrenching experiences of the 1960's, they also often ignored them. In Lee County, Georgia, a principal was disturbed by the coming of young registration workers who undoubtedly would bring upon him more pressure from his white superiors. (A principal often was, to the white supremacist, a man who could control or should have been able to control his community.) The principal told a Parent-Teacher Association meeting of the terribly disturbing events brought to his campus by the registration workers: he told of their distributing registration leaflets, of their standing too close to the high-school girls on the campus, and so on. Then one of the registration workers rose and stated their case. The Negro audience gave the "outsider" registration worker stormy applause and cheers. That was all. That was the community's verdict. The principal was not publicly scorned, rebuked, and humiliated there. But his position was understood, and his effort at leadership on behalf of his white superiors was simply ignored. There is an old spiritual that says, "I been 'buked and I been scorned." Perhaps in a community where most Negroes have been rebuked and scorned,

there is an added measure of tolerance for those among them who in
other societies might be considered worthy, at a given moment, of
rebuke and scorn.

Teachers on college and university faculties sometimes have responded in an altogether different manner. In Atlanta and other larger
cities, they frequently have taken leading roles in civil rights matters.
But they, too, in many places have been subject to repressions cor-
responding to those faced by public school teachers. This has been
especially true in the case of state-supported schools. But it also has
existed in many private colleges that depend in part upon local white
support or upon Negro church hierarchies that are relatively conservative in outlook. A number of Negro college presidents became job
casualties in the rights revolution because they did not "keep the students in line." The threat of dismissal was certainly real in the case of
those at the head of Negro colleges in the hard-resistance states.

What of the lawyers? As late as the end of World War II, only one
Negro lawyer was practicing in New Orleans and there were only three
in all of Louisiana. When the rights movement swept over Mississippi
in 1963, only four Negro lawyers were practicing in the state. In this
aspect of middle-class Negro life, shortage is the most prominent fact.
Still, an impressive number of the Negro practicing attorneys in the
South have played prominent roles of leadership. In the 1940's, when
their number was even smaller, a few lawyers such as Austin T. Walden
of Atlanta were carrying the fight against some of the most oppressive
instruments of white supremacy. Mr. Walden successfully fought a
court battle to remove inequality in pay for Negro teachers in Georgia.
He fought the Democratic white primary in the courts, and in one case
assisted a white prosecutor in a Ku Klux Klan case. For many years he
played a major political role as leader of Georgia's Negro Democrats.
Mr. Walden was practicing in Georgia courts at a time when neither
judges nor lawyers could bring themselves to call him "mister." It is one
of those bad jokes of an ugly social system that although they could not
call him "mister" they could call him "colonel." "Colonel Walden"
lived to become "Judge Walden," by appointment of Mayor Ivan Allen,
Jr., to a part-time municipal judgeship as his career ended. There were
other notable stories of bold service by Negro lawyers in the all-white
courts when segregation was stringent. Some Negro lawyers braved the
inflammatory atmospheres of disturbed small towns to defend Negroes
charged with murder and rape. Later, as the movement of the 1950's

and 1960's began, numerous Negro lawyers took leading roles. In Mississippi at one point, three of the four active Negro lawyers were heavily involved in rights cases, leading one to comment that their normal practice was being sorely neglected but first things should come first.

Many of the demands made upon Wiley Branton, director of the Voter Education Project, were in themselves evidence of how thin was the Negro legal profession across the South. Mr. Branton's duties were primarily executive; yet, because he was a lawyer and one with demonstrated success in Southern courts, he was repeatedly called upon for legal aid when voter projects encountered difficulties. "I frequently went to the rescue because I knew about the incidents first and there was no one else to call on," he said. Often there simply was no lawyer on the scene to whom Negroes might turn in any matter involving the civil rights movement.[19] The effectiveness of a number of Negro lawyers in Southern courts also had another dimension: For many white people, to see a Negro attorney standing alone in the presumably cool and dispassionate atmosphere of a court, winning a case against white adversaries, was an object lesson, just as it must have been when Thurgood Marshall was repeatedly winning over the band of defenders which white state governments retained at substantial expense and usually called "great constitutional lawyers." The notion of inherent Negro inferiority must have suffered at least a few momentary lapses in those courtrooms.

But the Negro legal profession, too, was subject to stifling effects. The effect simply of not having regular contact with other lawyers, since they were excluded from white bar associations and professional social life, probably has been substantial. Law is not practiced in a vacuum; exchange with fellow professionals is essential to it. Then, too, the Negro candidate for admission to the bar or admission to practice in certain courts had to be passed upon by all-white official boards. Scores on bar examinations are confidential. But one Negro candidate for admission to the bar in Georgia, who had been active in desegregation efforts, was surprised one day when a lawyer for the state commented on his bar examination score. The systematic exclusion of Negroes from the judicial system, from judges to clerks and bailiffs, and the occupancy of these positions by many whites positively hostile to Negro aspirations, obviously has had a serious effect upon the professional life of many Negro lawyers.

The doctors and dentists often have been the most prosperous members of Negro communities, but their professions have given them some peculiar limitations. One doctor who helped as he could with civil rights activities was described as a man who would do any task assigned to him but who was too busy professionally to undertake high leadership. That has often been a common position of the doctors most sensitive to their communities' needs. Others, of course, have virtually withdrawn themselves from any involvement, being relatively prosperous and comfortable. Many arrived at points of decision as to how involved they could become in view of their need to use the white-controlled hospitals and other medical facilities. Southern Negro doctors (but not dentists), like Negro teachers and lawyers, often had been dependent in the end upon the tolerance of white fellow professionals and hospital administrators.

Within a white supremacist system, Negro politicians were excluded from officeholding, and so they usually could be only the middlemen for white politicians seeking the Negro votes that existed. Frequently, too, their support was dictated only by money or the hope of a few claims upon low-level menial jobs for relatives or friends. This was the Negro politics of the past.

The same forces that affected Negro political leadership have come to bear upon members of the Negro middle class ranging from farmers dependent upon bank loans to store-owners dependent upon supplies, police protection, and credit. An arresting fact about the difference between white and Negro community leadership is this: businessmen have constituted the largest occupational group in the white leadership, and ministers have been the largest among Negroes.[20] The explanation is obvious: ministers usually were, at least potentially, the most independent figures in the Negro community, barring only the undertakers (who also were notable in leadership in Negro rights causes in scores of small towns). Virtually all other occupations brought middle-class Negroes into crippling situations.

This was one of the more irrational results of a situation created by an ostensibly conservative white society. By enforcing a system that stifled the Negro middle class, it did two things which any conservative society should be determined not to do: it created a discontented middle class, a most revolutionary social force; and it made masses of Negroes distrust their own more conservative leaders, increasing the chance that the masses would turn from these leaders directly to more radical forces or simply to more radical, more detached patterns of thought which would be receptive to radical leadership. When the students went to Mississippi in 1964, some were the radicals which this situation invited. Others, probably a majority, were there in reality to become a substitute middle class: to do those things which a healthy Negro middle class already might have done by way of organizing Negro communities to claim their rightful place, and to try to do little more. Establishing little libraries and health centers where there were none, conducting voter registration efforts, organizing communities into civic councils, the workers of SNCC and CORE were in essence a substitute bourgeoisie in the uniforms of the proletariat. Perhaps white Mississippi can be thankful for them on that ground alone; they became a focal point for orderly action in a place where rising discontent and distress might easily have exploded. The psychological duress of all the forces acting upon middle-class Negroes must not be ignored or underestimated. Serious mistakes could be made in the future, on the part of the federal government, for instance, if it ignored the psychological duress borne by the Negro middle class.

Categorical psychological statements about middle-class Negroes are, of course, dangerous and subject to the error of all expansive generalities. But the middle class might be considered in the light of what the psychiatrist Robert Coles has said, consciously oversimplifying for the sake of an important point. Of many Negro Southerners, especially in rural areas, he observed: "I think their self-contempt is real, and also a childlike capacity to be rather easily frightened or contentious with one another, all coming from their childlike position in this country. ('Boy,' do this or that.) On the other hand, the same people who are scared of the Klan and secretly wish they were white, hence display contempt of their own leaders, can also show anger, defiance, bravery, and a sudden unexplainable ability to transcend themselves . . . Many of the Negroes I know, the ones who seem most alert, unafraid, and effective, are also divided inside themselves and with one another, and fearful and all the rest. What enables them to 'get with it' is that a crisis or a very real social event or situation brings out the strengths in them." [21]

The strength of many Negroes in crises that have torn them out of themselves and their workaday lives always has been a powerful source of wonderment and irrepressible admiration among those who have closely watched, evaluated, and written about the rights movement in the South. Time after time, men and women intimately acquainted with very real daily prospects of death and personal humiliation have risen to extraordinary heights of courage and resolve in the South's confrontations. These inner strengths have welled up in people who did not themselves know they possessed them, and surely no commentary on the debilitations left by the white supremacist system can ignore the obvious legacy, also, of great powers of endurance, of strong souls, and of an almost fatalistic bravery in the midst of justifiable fear. The small heroes have been mainly unsung, but there have been many Curtis Bryants in the South.

Curtis Bryant, a barber and railroad worker, was president of the NAACP chapter in McComb, Pike County, Mississippi, when that area went through crisis. For a time, the Klan and an equally extremist organization called the Americans for the Preservation of the White Race were dominant in McComb. Bombings and burnings were frequent before a band of white citizens took hold in remarkable fashion and reversed the tide. In the spring of 1964, in the midst of the town's bleakest period, a Negro field secretary of the VEP went to see Curtis Bryant in McComb about voter registration. When he arrived, he found Klan leaflets had been distributed throughout the area. Bryant's barber shop had been bombed. A cross had been burned on his lawn. His family had received threats and obscene telephone calls. As VEP field secretary John Due and another visitor, Robert Moses of SNCC, settled in the modest Bryant home to spend the night, Bryant himself took out his shotgun. Others, obviously, would know he had visitors. The visitors went to sleep. Bryant sat guarding the house until 4:30 A.M. Then a friend, one of a group who had watched protectively over the Bryants during their ordeal, relieved him and guarded the house through the hours of dawn. The next day Due and Moses went to a Negro church, where the meeting began with a mournful and somehow perfectly right old hymn of release from self-reliance, "Leaning on the Everlasting Arms." Then Due and Moses talked to the congregation. They had a federal government that was concerned about their needs, Due said, but it needed hard information on which to act. They must help him gather information about intimidation and denial of their right to vote. Moses told them, too, about what Negroes were doing elsewhere in Mississippi; about the Mississippi Advisory Committee, composed of white and

Negro Mississippians, helping the U.S. Commission on Civil Rights. Those in McComb, too, must help. The congregation sat silently. There was, Due reported later, a "stone wall of fear" between those who lived in McComb and those who only came to visit. When the talks ended, only two people came forward in response to the plea for information. They were a slight teen-age girl and her younger sister, who wanted to give Due a statement about the dismissal of their father from his job because the Klan had threatened his employer.

In the midst of such fear, of a kind that bound McComb's Negroes even in the presence of other Negroes who had come to share their risks and try to help, Curtis Bryant went on resolutely day after day, under threat, doing his work for civil rights. Eventually affidavits were obtained. Still later, McComb's Negroes were able to register freely, and shortly they became such a substantial force of voters that they could not be ignored. In a later time, when he no longer had to sit with a shotgun in his own home at night, Bryant was calling upon mayors in Pike County, still prodding the community to abide by the law and treat Negroes fairly. Bryant's courage was known to few. His was a story repeated many times throughout the South. One cannot ignore the depths of strength that emerged in hundreds of unsung leaders out of the Negro communities.

Who knows, even now, about the Negro leadership of Plaquemines Parish, Louisiana? In that parish (county), Leander Perez, Sr., the leading Louisiana white supremacist, combined methods of suppression and paternalism to eliminate Negroes as a political factor over a span of four decades. Even Perez' tiny white opposition, harried and sometimes bloodied, had cause to fear exercising the right of assembly. In 1965, the leader of that almost-underground opposition, sought out by one of the authors, said he could not get some of his principal allies to attend a political meeting because of fear of Perez. Rights workers from nearby New Orleans feared to enter the county at all at night. In this county, which was America's closest approximation of a full-scale totalitarian dictatorship, Negroes might have been expected not to stir at all when federal examiners were sent in under the Voting Rights Act of 1965. But in the first weeks of their presence, some 1,200 Negroes, in grim little bands from tiny communities all over the parish, went to the post office at Buras to stand in line under the eyes of prying deputies to signify their intentions to vote. No parish-wide Negro organization was known to exist, and no affiliate of a national civil rights organization.

Every Negro knew that he might be harassed for being there. But somewhere a hidden force stirred Plaquemines's Negroes to register heavily. There was leadership, hidden, but there.

But the debilitations of the Negro middle class still have to be reckoned with. One of the by-products of the Voter Education Project was the result of its search for local community leadership all over the South to help with voter registration. We are accustomed to speaking of the South as one great entity. It has been mercilessly studied and scrutinized as a region unto itself. This suggests the existence of a kind of region-wide familiarity with all its resources, peculiarities, and people. But the voter project, in search of an informal chain of local leadership, came hard upon the fact that within the Negro subculture there has been little region-wide or even state-wide solidarity, or even contact of leadership. Who are the Negro leaders of Decatur, Alabama, and what are the sources of their influence? One sitting in Atlanta cannot simply pick up the phone, call the Decatur Chamber of Commerce or the Decatur newspaper, and find out. The white leadership may be closely related to certain business and community institutions, but the Negro leadership is much less predictably so.

One field worker for the VEP, after experiences of discovery with hundreds of Decaturs all over the South, suggested that if he now were going into a strange Negro community to organize a project, he would proceed this way: He would go first to the "independents," the undertaker, the grocers, the preachers. Then he would go to the school principal. ("In some cases you can go to the principal, ask who his enemies are, and you have the leaders.") Having made contact with these, he would assume that he had discovered the principal community leaders. He would assume, too, that the Negro church was at the center of the community because "the church belongs to the folks." He would regard the deacons of churches ("because they're the preacher's men") as very important to anything he undertook. Finally, he would assume that for action, a strong outside stimulus probably would be necessary to break what frequently was a local paralysis.

Another field worker who had had the same experience of discovering unknown Negro community leaderships suggested this approach for organizing a campaign, such as a voter registration drive: "I would start by seeing the upper-middle-class people who are usually regarded as leaders of the community. I would do this mainly to neutralize them. They usually do not oppose having the job done—they want it done, but they don't want to be embarrassed if someone else does it and they are left out. After seeing them, I would find people prepared to work hard for recognition. Then I'd try to wed the two together and monitor the group."

In both evaluations there is a judgment that the middle-class leadership, where it exists, cannot be ignored and yet often is paralyzed. If it is not to provide the leadership itself, it at least should not be hostile. One reason most of the student grass-roots stirrings in Mississippi in 1964 were short-lived was that many projects were undertaken with a disdain for local Negro middle-class leadership. The antagonism that consequently developed between older (and frequently moribund) NAACP branches around the state and the Johnny-come-lately student projects was costly.

Leadership in Southern Negro communities often is deceptive. (The word "deceptive" is appropriate in several ways; since slavery days deception has been a necessary requisite for leadership in many areas if it was to survive.) Voter registration workers frequently found that the real leaders were not the people in places of position. An elderly woman of no title and with no organizational support might be highly influential simply because she was noted as a kind of personal problem-solver. Sometimes such a person, because of her effectiveness in small matters and the trust consequently built, could be a key figure in efforts to persuade people to register to vote in a difficult area. In Tennessee a man who was an officer of the local NAACP branch and president of the local voter league was highly influential; a VEP field worker concluded, however, that the main source of his influence was not his occupancy of these offices, but the fact that he operated a well-stocked food market in the Negro community, had a liberal credit policy, and was constantly in personal contact with large numbers of customers.[22] "This man's influence, because of his location and work, had a very positive effect on the voter registration campaigns," the field worker reported. White people sometimes are leaders of Negroes for exactly the same reason. In one very small Georgia town, a white store operator who sincerely befriends Negro customers, treats them well, and encourages them to vote has been repeatedly elected mayor because of their votes. One suspects that if a local NAACP officer were pitted politically against this mayor, friendship and personal considerations, in a Southern world more attuned than most to the personal and the small courtesies and amenities, would prevail over official position in the Negro community.

In 1967 political opportunity summoned all the ingenuity demonstrated by the civil rights movement in breaking through the old paralysis. It had been a paralysis of Negroes, and perhaps more importantly a paralysis of many whites who did not like the system they lived with but who somehow could not move themselves to do much about it. Negro ingenuity, through the marches and the sit-ins and through the ability to create an entirely new set of dynamics in Southern communities and in the nation, had shaken the white paralysis. But the white paralysis lingered in part, and there was perpetual drag as white leaders waited to be forced to do that which they knew they ought to do. In short, they still left the initiative to Negroes, and soon it was the Negroes who were defining the issues, and even the terms of the exchange, and who thus were shaping the destiny of the South. Racial roles had been reversed. Within a decade much of the leadership of the South—that part of it which was determining the region's destiny—shifted from white to Negro. The initiative, by default, had been left almost entirely with Negroes by the mid-1960's. Whether they would hold it was uncertain. Their own paralysis of leadership, broken by the innovations of the rights movement, also lingered in part. We could not know how well the Negro middle class would be able to overcome its debilitations, how well it would be supplemented by discovery and employment of other kinds of leadership, and to what extent both would find the means needed for the activation of Negroes and for the release and revival of whites.

NOTES

1. In the first phase of heavy Negro voting in Birmingham, which came after the mass demonstrations of 1963, a similar limitation of impact could be seen. Paul Good wrote in December 1965 that in Birmingham the Negro "is as far removed as ever from the seat of power." WHITE and COLORED signs had been removed from city hall restrooms, he noted, but one had to ask around for a key. At the public library, the restrooms had simply been locked and left closed. There were no Negro policemen. No real progress had been made on employment within the city government. (See Paul Good, "Birmingham Two Years Later," *The Reporter*, December 2, 1965.) While accepting the main import of this analysis, we would add that there had been one very important result of the new Negro voting: the new admin-

istration of Mayor Albert Boutwell was not the diehard segregationist administration in which Eugene "Bull" Connor had been the chief leader. It was a "moderate" administration, although in a way it was paralyzed by the standoff between Negroes seeking gains and segregationists opposing them. Most of those being elected to the city council by this time were winning on the strength of the Negro vote. A logical conclusion was that the Boutwell administration was merely transitional and that more real Negro gains would come as white supremacist opposition continued to be undercut by such forces as the Civil Rights Act of 1964 and continuing Negro registration. In short, though one might expect a temporary reaction to set in and slow Negro gains, one could not conclude from the situation in December 1965 that political power of the conventional kind would not be effective for Birmingham Negroes.

Durham offers an interesting case study. William R. Keech, in an unpublished doctoral dissertation at the University of Wisconsin, made a detailed analysis of Negro gains in Durham, which had a population of 78,000 in 1960, 37 per cent of it non-white. Negroes have voted freely in Durham for many years. After 1935 they exercised their influence principally through the Durham Committee on Negro Affairs, one of the most effective Negro political organizations in the South. The DCNA was formed primarily to end a corrupt ward-heeling system of delivering Negro votes. It has been noted for its honesty, its system of submitting endorsements to its members in open meetings for approval or rejection, and for its remarkable success in shepherding Negro votes on election day. In bond-issue votes, the DCNA recommendation was the one that prevailed in the city-wide vote 90 per cent of the time between 1946 and 1965. The Negro vote could have changed the outcome in more than half of these referenda. Since 1945, 40 of the 52 candidates endorsed by the DCNA in Durham general elections had won. A shift of Negro votes would have reversed the outcomes of two-thirds of the mayoralty races in that period.

This powerful leverage, however, yielded mixed results. Keech concluded that, in the years of much strong white resistance and a general adherence of the South to segregation, there were "severe limits on what [could] be achieved by the Negro vote." He concluded that it did not effect any change in the strictly private sector, such as private housing; did not secure the integration of such facilities as parks, libraries, and schools; and perhaps played only a small role in developing public accommodations and gaining jobs for Negroes. Where Negro votes *did* have effect, he concluded, was in bringing more equitable distribution of funds for public facilities such as parks and street lights, opening municipal jobs, and halting police brutality. It was particularly effective in bond issues, in assuring equitable distribution of the public facilities to be built. In one case it resulted in a commitment for integration of an industrial school to be built by bond funds. Keech suggested that the vote was least effective on matters "very visible and salient to the rest of the community as a whole, not to speak of being unpopular," such as the opening of employment in business establishments. From this we may conclude that in Durham, as elsewhere, the strength of what might be called the white resistance vote was so great that on many matters not even a powerful, well-organized Negro vote was able to overcome it on the scales used by politicians. Even progressive Durham, as with a number of other cities in the South, was held in check politically by that resistance force. None of this, however, is cause for denigrating the value of the vote. Durham simply had too much vote hardening on the other side.

2. The presence of Negroes in Atlanta's state legislature had one immediate effect upon annexation considerations. When the legislators were asked to approve a refer-

endum under which Sandy Springs, a suburban and mainly conservative community of about 25,000 people, might be annexed to Atlanta, Negroes among the legislators withheld approval until their colleagues accepted a similar referendum for the Adamsville suburb, largely Negro. The possibility of such tit-for-tat annexations, keeping the racial ratio of the city about the same, was extremely limited, however. Negro politicians' attitudes about further mainly-white annexations seemed flexible. The city's first Negro alderman, in fact, made the most dire of all threats against white suburbs in the event they did not eventually enter the city. In March 1966, the alderman, Q. V. Williamson, suggested that if Negroes became a majority within the city limits, as they would under current trends, they could use their political power to force annexations by cutting off municipal services bought by residents outside the city, such as water. The import of his remarks seemed to be that he as one Negro politician might be willing to use extreme measures to see that Negroes did not dominate the city or have the whole residential property tax bill to pay. Negro leadership in Atlanta generally went along with a prevailing view among the white moderate-liberal leadership that a heavy Negro majority within the city could hurt it economically and lead to less rather than more integration.

3. A remarkably similar pattern existed in New Orleans and, in fact, in many Southern cities. New Orleans' Mayor deLesseps Morrison had the same reputation as did Hartsfield as a racial moderate, fought by segregationists, aided by Negro votes. But what Negroes obtained for their support there, too, was limited. "He would just come talk to Negroes about all the great expressways he was going to build and what a great city we were making," a New Orleans Negro leader said. "Hell, Negroes couldn't even get jobs working on those expressways." (Interview with the authors.)

Two other factors seemed to limit Negroes' gains in New Orleans. They were not as unified and as well organized as Atlanta Negroes. And they probably suffered from the fact that Morrison wanted to be governor of Louisiana, whereas Hartsfield never sought a political coloration that would make him acceptable to the entire electorate of Georgia. Year after year, New Orleans Negroes were forced to sacrifice immediate objectives and withhold pressures in the interest of Morrison's political future. Since he never won election as governor, the sacrifice was abortive. As a lesson in political strategy for Negroes, it underscores the fact that a local politician may be unresponsive to the needs of his immediate electorate if he has his eye on a different kind of electorate.

Hartsfield's successor, Ivan Allen, Jr., was asked in 1966 whether he might seek Georgia's governorship in the future. "You can't properly do the things the mayor of Atlanta needs to do and at the same time appeal to Georgia voters at large," he said.

4. There was no question of white ignorance of Mr. Maddox's views, which were widely known. "I think it's against the will of God to mix our races, to amalgamate our races," he had said. ". . . If you think about the leaders among the Negro groups at this time you'll seldom ever find one that's not a mulatto." He declined to disavow the Ku Klux Klan. In his restaurant, he distributed a different kind of KKK sticker for automobiles. It said: "Kan the Kennedy Klan." He had been badly defeated in races against Hartsfield in 1957 and Allen in 1961, an interviewer noted. He had won "the majority of the white votes," he replied, and "beat everybody but Martin Luther King." (See "The Segs," by Reese Cleghorn, *Esquire,* January 1964.)

5. Interview with the authors.

6. Daniel C. Thompson, *The Negro Leadership Class* (Englewood Cliffs, New

Jersey: Prentice-Hall, Inc., 1963), p. 114. Also on bloc voting, see Henry Holloway, "The Negro and the Vote: The Case of Texas," *Journal of Politics*, August 1961, pp. 538–540, and Hugh Douglas Price, *The Negro and Southern Politics* (New York: New York University Press, 1957), p. 74.

7. Thompson, p. 115.

8. James Q. Wilson has written that in the past the only political mechanism by which urban poor whites and Negroes fared relatively well was the machine, and it is collapsing. Negroes are emerging at a time when the whole "lower-class style of politics—the politics of friendships, trades, patronage, and neighborhood localism—is falling into disrepute," he has said. (See Wilson, "The Negro in Politics," *Daedalus*, fall 1965, p. 964.) Wilson and Edward C. Banfield have noted that in a machine city such as Chicago, Negro sub-machines have provided approximately a prorata share of Negro representation within the machine. Within the Richard Daley machine there was the Negro machine of Congressman William L. Dawson, maintaining its power by the usual means of exchanging jobs, favors, and protection for votes. In that they receive about as much of this kind of attention as their numbers would merit, Negroes in a machine city in one sense benefit from the existence of the machine. Without it, they might not get their share of the smaller favors. But Banfield and Wilson noted that Dawson's men would not propose anything of importance without clearing it with Daley. See Banfield and Wilson, *City Politics* (Cambridge, Massachusetts: Harvard University Press, 1964), pp. 304–306. The other side of this story, of course, is that though the machine may provide a type of equity, its discipline and responsiveness to the boss stifle the kind of truly big change that Negroes' circumstances in Chicago demand. Implicit in Dr. King's manner of moving into the Chicago slums in 1966 was the idea that the machine was part of the problem.

9. Negro political organizations, of course, sometimes give rather than receive political funds. In Birmingham in 1965, during a municipal campaign, the chief Negro political organization financed its own canvassing for the candidates it supported. In effect, that amounted to contributions to them, since in the wards affected they were relieved of the usual costs of canvassing. The same Negro organization gave $5,000 to help finance a television appearance of President Johnson during the 1964 campaign.

10. The reason for this is the continuing centrality of the church in Negro community life. See Thompson, pp. 34–35. For a commentary on undesirable aspects of this, see Joseph R. Washington, *Black Religion* (Boston: Beacon Press, 1964).

11. Such matters as street paving often are not as simple as they seem. Thus more is required than mere pressure upon a city construction department to get the job done in a slum. In many cities, streets are paved only by assessing owners of adjacent property for the costs, and this frequently means that landlords, white and Negro, will not assent. In Atlanta and Durham, both of which have powerful Negro electorates, some Negro areas remain without paved streets because of the assessment system. If residents of more prosperous residential areas have paid for the paving of their streets, is it equitable for the city to pave streets in the slums without such assessments? In 1966, the mayor of Atlanta was privately saying that somehow this job must be done even though some whites who had paid for their own streets were bound to see injustice in it.

12. A nationwide network of community organizations in the poorer areas might emerge as a major political force nationally, some spokesmen for the "New Left" said in the mid-sixties. In the summer of 1965, James Forman, then executive director of SNCC, said in an interview with the authors: "We're forming new coalitions

within the country . . . Two years from now people are going to wake up and discover it." A central part of it, he said, would be local community organizations exerting not only a national influence in concert with each other but also local pressure upon party organizations and for better local government services. Others of the student left were even more specific about the idea of tying together the community organizations for national action.

13. The effect of Negro leadership's powerlessness was noted in the New Orleans study. Professor Thompson observed that Negro interviewees often commented affirmatively about Negro leadership when talking to the study's white interviewers but commented very negatively about it when talking to Negro interviewers. It was as if they were embarrassed, in a very personal way, about the powerlessness of their leadership.

14. Robert Coles, "It's the Same, But It's Different," *Daedalus*, fall 1965, pp. 1108–1110. See also Coles, *Children of Crisis* (Boston: Little, Brown, 1967).

15. See A *Manual of Intergroup Relations*, John Dean and Alex Rosen (Chicago: University of Chicago Press, 1955), and a commentary about it, James B. McKee, "Community Power and Strategies in Race Relations: Some Critical Observations," Social Problems Series, Vol. 6, published by Michigan State University, Institute for Community Development and Services, 1960–61 Reprint Series.

16. Although the weighing of a community's "influentials" and their impact was pioneered by the Lynds in *Middletown* (New York: Harcourt, Brace & World) in 1928 and James West's *Plainville, USA* (New York: New York University Press), which followed in 1945, it is Hunter's study that most often has been taken as a model for studies in Negro communities. That is why it is singled out here.

17. Thompson, p. 46.

18. *U.S. Commission on Civil Rights*, Jackson, Vol. 1, p. 218. A voter registration worker's report from Holly Springs, on the edge of the Mississippi Delta, told where many teachers stood even when they did become involved. Holly Springs was a relatively moderate Mississippi town and so its teachers would have felt vastly more freedom than those in many other places. The registration worker reported: "In the Voters League [here], it is the teachers, city businessmen, and the ministers who are the conservatives. The farmers, both owners and tenants, and the students, are the militant element."

19. Mr. Branton was well qualified for this work, in several ways. His Arkansas background and his legal work among white law enforcement and court officials had given him very useful comprehension of the workings of rural law, and in his appearance he could be easily mistaken for white. Once, when two young voter registration workers were jailed in one of the plantation counties of south Georgia, Mr. Branton called the sheriff, put on his best drawl and good-old-boy informality, and greeted him like an old friend. "Sheriff," he said, "this is old Wiley Branton up here in Atlanta. Lawyer, you know. Been down there a few times." The sheriff responded cordially, apparently assuming he should remember the white lawyer from Atlanta. Mr. Branton went on to say he understood the sheriff had picked up two boys. He wanted to get them out, he said, because the mother of one of them worked for him. Familiar with that tableau because he had responded often to white lawyers' interventions on behalf of white ladies' maids, the sheriff said: "You can get the black one out for twenty-five dollars. But you'll have to pay seventy-five for this white one." Shortly, the money was paid and the two registration workers were released.

20. See Tilman Cothran and William Philips, Jr., "Negro Leadership in a Crisis Situation," *Phylon*, summer 1961, pp. 107–118.

21. Robert Coles, interview with the authors.

22. Perhaps this man, in singlehanded fashion, was a substitute for the kind of community inner organization that is taken for granted in most of the white community. "The Negro communities now need a rapid development of inner organization . . ." Leslie W. Dunbar has said, "They are woefully short of capital . . . They are short of their own welfare institutions, such as orphanages and homes for the aged. They are short on their own credit unions, charitable foundations, recreation centers, and just about everything. To say this presents us with questions that confuse. The civil rights movement has proclaimed the goal of integration, not the goal of communal development." One of these questions, he said, is this: "Does the Negro community need another white social worker as much as it needs, as a small business loan, the money his or her education cost?" Dunbar, A *Republic of Equals* (Ann Arbor: The University of Michigan Press, 1966), pp. 121–123.

5)

The Struggle—
Fear and Apathy

In 1964, at the end of the first Voter Education Project, after two years of concerted effort, only one of the eleven states of the South had as high a percentage of eligible Negroes registered to vote as its percentage of eligible whites registered. And that state was Texas, where Mexicans—who have their own internal and external difficulties with gaining access to the ballot—are classified as white. The comparison was 57.7 per cent of eligible Negroes, and 53.2 per cent of eligible "whites." The only state where the averages were reasonably close—an indication of some degree of equal access—was Tennessee, 69.4 per cent of Negroes, 72.9 per cent of whites. In Virginia, the percentages were 45.7 of Negroes, 55.9 of whites, an indication of the degree to which both races were discouraged from voting. States with fairly close comparisons of Negro and white eligibles registered, respectively, were Arkansas, 54.4 and 71.7, and Florida, 63.7 and 84.0. North Carolina's comparison was marked by the high percentage of whites registered, 92.5, compared with 46.8 per cent of Negroes. Georgia had 44 per cent of eligible Negroes registered, and 74.5 per cent of eligible whites; South Carolina, 38.8 and 78.5; Louisiana, 32 and 80.4; Alabama, 23 and 70.7; Mississippi, worst of all, only 6 per cent of eligible Negroes and 70 per cent of eligible whites.

VEP records and voter workers during the 1962–64 drives talked of "hard-core resistance" areas, and of "easy" areas. Probably no two Negro leaders would agree exactly on which parts of the South were one, which were the other. The time-honored observation that high Negro population in ratio to white almost invariably meant severe repression of Negroes was applicable. Another way to gauge roughly the geographical distribution of resistance was to look at a map of the South that shows the Black Belt, that trailing of the South's once most fertile land where the plantations flourished, where most slaves were, and where later the harvest of sorrow continued in high percentages of impoverished Negro population and high incidence of racial animosity.

Mrs. Bernice C. Johnson and Miss Doris Nelson, of the Alabama State Coordinating Association for Registering and Voting, prepared a report on their impressions of conditions in a sweep of Alabama counties in June 1963. It is interesting for what it shows of diversity—at least in the views of these voter workers—in a state generally considered bad all over, and for what it shows of the varieties of voter registration problems. In one county, it was not hard to qualify, but hard to convince voters of this. In another, no meeting was held because the man supposed to set it up had three threats on his life by the Ku Klux Klan. Police were alerted to pick up the car of the visiting registration workers. In another county, it was not hard to qualify, but a local leader said, "The people in general will not do anything that they feel will aggravate the white man because the Negroes of this county have no jobs to offer their fellow men and they depend upon the white man for their income." In another county, the man supposed to set up a meeting went on his vacation without bothering to tell anyone. In another, the meeting had to be moved to bigger quarters to accommodate a crowd of young adults "eager to improve their community . . ." In a county with little organization, leaders were school teachers, afraid for their jobs. In another, Negroes had helped elect the incumbent mayor and sheriff, and were treated with "more respect."

There was "good" in the worst states, just as there was bad in the best. Some places were better than others, but in virtually none were things the way they should have been. This was the main import of the voter figures.

The voter campaigns from 1962 to 1964 were generally of two kinds

—those that mainly battled white resistance, and those whose chief problem was called "apathy," for want of a better term. SNCC's work was almost entirely in areas of bad resistance. CORE was in bad territory mostly, but in some easier areas, too, as was SCLC, whose voter work was less. The NAACP was across all the South, good, bad, and in-between.[1]

Local groups, some affiliated with the national organizations, some independent, were mainstays of nearly all the voter drives. The preponderance of the first VEP research and experience strongly showed that where it was possible to register people, the best results were usually obtained from locally organized and staffed drives. The reasons for this seemed so obvious to most Negro leaders that they were surprised anyone would ask about it. Intimate knowledge of conditions, psychology, and people, was involved, they said, and a natural enough inclination among the people to trust and respond to leaders they had long known. Negroes in Southern communities speak of the "come-here" and "been-here" people. The "been-heres" have to stay on and live with the problems a special campaign might develop, not the least of which, usually, involved local whites.

How It Was Done

In hard and easy areas alike, the essentials of the work were much the same. As many people as possible—preferably volunteers, though sometimes there was pay—went out door-to-door canvassing, asking if people were registered, urging those not registered to register, or asking them to come to voter registration meetings. Meetings were held regularly, in the spirit of direct action's mass meetings, to create interest, provide instruction and, in the hard-core areas, to keep up courage.

A CORE campaign in Tallahassee, Florida, began with one worker, Mrs. Patricia Due, speaking in churches and calling on leaders. An integrated steering committee helped get an office and funds to run it, and set policy. Volunteers, mostly white and Negro college students, spoke every night at every kind of meeting, from labor union to lodge hall, and canvassed every day at houses and bars, poolrooms and barbershops. Teachers, businessmen, and other leaders were drawn in and did canvassing on an organized precinct and block basis. All civil rights groups, various church groups, some unions, and the Negro business league cooperated. Car pools carried registrants to and from the courthouse. From all this, registration was increased from 5,576 to 6,349 between November 1963 and April 1964. This was not considered unsubstantial.

The Chatham County Crusade for Voters, headed by Hosea Williams, registered 2,000 Negroes in three months, 5,000 in less than a year in the Savannah (Georgia) area. Hired workers [2] canvassed and set up block leaders in thirty-two areas. They compiled 20,000 names and addresses; a telephone committee, using phones rented from a collection agency, tried to call them all. A courthouse worker took names and phone numbers of all unregistered Negroes who came in on other business; she also served as watchdog over irregularities by the registrars. Negro businesses, organizations, schools and PTAs, churches, and youth groups cooperated.

Memphis, long the best-organized city for Negro voting in the South, did things like sending three workers to the courthouse to urge auto license-plate buyers to register. Of 5,182 such contacts, 1,472 registered and 800 who had registered before reported their change of address to prevent being disqualified.

These were the kinds of campaigns possible where resistance was not strong. But there were failures in such places, too. "Much paper work, little registration," was a VEP field worker's appraisal of efforts in New Orleans in 1963. It might have been made about many other communities. Shreveport was notorious for an inability, somehow, to get voter work organized. If any civil rights activity might have had a chance against the repression there, it was the voter work.

Cities imposed their own special conditions. The All Citizens Registration Committee of Atlanta, a generally successful effort, concentrated much attention on public housing projects. Fifteen block-workers could reach 1,207 families in two projects. Mobility of Negro population in cities was a special problem. In Knoxville, the NAACP exerted as much effort getting registered people to report changes of address as to getting unregistered ones to register.

The methods of organization were a study in buried abilities of people largely blocked from other expressions of creativity. Reflections of Madison Avenue (buttons, bumper stickers, posters) glittered, and people improvised—there were barkeepers who wouldn't sell drinks to the unregistered, businessmen who wouldn't hire them, pool-hall owners who said, "If you're old enough to play, you're old enough to vote."

"Stop begging, start voting," said a bumper sticker. "Don't talk politics in here unless you're registered to vote," said a poster. Churches across the South had "our church record of registered voters," and schools put gold stars by the names of children who badgered their parents into registering.

Handbills were a special study. They almost invariably hammered at the practical advantages. "Your vote is your ticket to freedom. . . . Your vote can help you get paved streets, better playgrounds and schools, better housing, better jobs, freedom and equality." Nearly always, paved streets were a goal—and sewers, garbage collection, parks. Even in relatively advanced Miami, a handbill of 1963 listed better street lights and sidewalks along with jobs, housing, schools, and "equal opportunities for your children." By the spring of 1964, a new one included non-segregated housing and better integrated schools. The earlier one had said, "Freedom Now," the spring one, "Complete Freedom Now." A postcard-sized handbill in New Orleans in late 1965 emphasized how easy registration had become. "Show who you are, where you live, and for how long. There's no excuse for you." It showed a startled "voter too lazy to even vote" being poked in the chest by "LBJ's powerful voting rights bill."

Methodology presented never-ceasing items of interest: "He is the man who gets all the gossip and is probably one of the most effective people in the barber's chair and in our organization. Once he gets a customer in the chair he rarely lets them go without first getting a promise that they will register to vote in the near future." And: "I went up to the county with Mr. Alexander on May 12, which was the second Sunday. I was asked to teach a Sunday school lesson, which I readily accepted. After Sunday school I was able to talk with some of the people who wanted to work with a church [voter] project. . . ." And: "To aid us in getting about in these areas, the students have collected six or seven bicycles. We are in the process of following up on 300 or so names of persons contacted. . . ."

In Tallahassee, a bus was chartered and picked up people at their regular stops to go to the registrar's. In Miami, workers boarded regular buses to announce cars were waiting at a certain stop to take people to register. In Roanoke, a tobacco union collected fifty cents from members for a pool to pay poll taxes of the needy, and in Norfolk a poll tax lay-away plan was instituted. Contests among churches, civic groups, volunteers, and social clubs were numerous—an effort, pertinent later, to draw into the voter drive the energies middle-class Negroes put into their organizations. A Huntsville, Alabama, group sent letters to all registered Negroes urging each to sign up five more. Atlanta borrowed the idea of block parties from the white middle class to use in housing projects. "Snatching folks off the street" was a common technique. And from a North Carolina town: "Our group has come up with several plans. Probably you would like to hear about one of them. In the . . . homecoming parade Saturday, we will have a float stressing the vote-register theme. On the front platform will be a casket. The large sign on the side of the float will read, 'This man doesn't vote. He's dead. What's your excuse?' "

The suffering of the movement in the worst areas was used to motivate people in the less difficult ones. "If you would go with me to the Deep South and see what Negroes go through just to try to vote," cried a speaker in Winston-Salem, North Carolina, "you'd be first in line to register here." "It is silly to condemn Wallace or talk about how they beat and murder Negroes in the South if you are just a talker," said a handbill of the All Citizens Registration Committee of Northern Virginia, pointing out that in 1964 Negroes were running for office in Tuskegee, Alabama, but not in Virginia.

Negro ambulances were used in Birmingham to haul registrants. A Charlottesville, Virginia, group reported good results from a "wino" block captain, paid by the jug. In McIntosh County, Georgia (where voting age is eighteen), the school principal served on the registration board, and required seniors to register. An NAACP poster said, "I can't vote because I'm a jackass" (depicting one), and some communities paraded a real one with the sign. In Atlanta, workers attended civic meetings and proposed voter registration each time complaints came up about city or county services. In New Orleans, a middle-class Negro subdivision was won over when a petition against a nearby trailer camp, incomplete drainage, and gravel streets got nowhere without registered voters.

The staple of the work was canvassing. A report from the SNCC unit in the Twentieth Senatorial District of Arkansas indicated the degree of dedication that could go into the job. It told of high-school students canvassing church and PTA meetings, cafés, cotton fields, and from house-to-house every afternoon and night and all day Saturday and Sunday. "We do not canvass on Fridays," the report added, "because it will make us late for our Friday night mass meeting. We go around announcing our meeting . . . instead." "Most of the people are farmers," said another report from the same area, "and we spend a lot of our time on these plantations . . . The biggest problem we found was not trying to get the people to register but to build up their interest in voting, because a number of those that bought poll taxes from us seem to have been buying them just to help us in the voter registration campaign rather than for future benefit." [3]

To know such things about a people was surely a part of the inspiration of the work. To play upon the themes closest to the good hearts of such people became the art of voter registration workers. "God holds you accountable to improve things for your children," Hosea Williams could cry to a church audience in rural Bryan County, Georgia, sure of the several responsive chords he struck. But more than one conscientious voter worker wrote in the VEP reports of the tricky moral problem involved in using these intimate and, indeed, sacred beliefs of Negro Southerners to motivate them to vote. The voter workers tried to avoid cynical manipulation, and they had to keep reassuring themselves that the vote was a valid and viable goal—that they were not calling forth the best in the people in vain.

There were quiet little dramas of grandeur. At the voter headquarters in Merry's Market in Jackson, Tennessee, the lady in charge refused to spend precious money on a wastebasket. She used paper sacks—but not the store's. Each morning she brought one from home, with the wrinkles all creased out. A report from a VEP field worker told of sitting in the shade outside a Negro funeral home in a small town in South Carolina, and discussing with the leader of the voter drive there how he might spend the money sent for his drive. This leader had used old tablets for report forms, and canvassers were all volunteers, and not a cent had been expended.

Miss Elizabeth Wyckoff, a white SNCC worker, caught the feeling of the voter effort at its best in her little story of how the Reverend Samuel Wells of Albany, Georgia, had always kept a ledger in past registration efforts, dating back to the 1940's, of all the names of all the people on the streets, along with assignments, names of street captains, and the like. "I believe," she wrote, "the job could be more 'efficiently' handled with a file of index cards. But this is the system which Reverend Wells had evolved on his own in earlier drives. And a look at the old book in which the records for those were kept inspires the greatest reverence for the patience and persistence with which the long effort was made and the laborious entries were set down. I have felt it would be only confusing to try to introduce a change, as well as impertinent. Also, I notice in my co-workers a spirit of reverence for 'The Book,' so like those in which church records are kept, and an interest in setting things down in their best and clearest hand, which would never be extended to a set of 3-by-5s."

What came of all this? One would almost feel that every unregistered Negro must have been asked at least twice to register. Some individual projects obtained remarkable results. From the fall of 1963 to the spring of 1964, registration increased in Raleigh, North Carolina, from one Negro for every 7.4 white voters to one for every 4.9, close to the population ratio of one Negro for every 3.86 whites. The Miami voter effort was something of a case study. One CORE worker, Weldon J. Rougeau, was able to organize most of the Negro community into a drive and get help from various liberal white groups. He also got help from the city's bi-racial advisory committee in putting Negro registrars in the neighborhoods and at night. Canvassing pinpointed the non-registered; they were peppered with 125,000 leaflets, 1,000 posters, and 1,550 placards. There were car pools and phone committees. Nearly 6,000 new voters were registered between July and October, 1963, and another 2,700 in two weeks the following spring.

There were other campaigns of marked success. Among them were: Jacksonville, Florida, where 75 per cent of Negroes were reported registered, a gain of 10,000 made during the course of two drives. Petersburg, Virginia: 1,250 of a goal of 1,500 between December 1963, and May 1964, and August through October 1964. Rome, Georgia: 2,690 from September 1962 through September 1964, bringing total Negro registration to 73 per cent of the potential. Atlanta: 32,000 between April 1962 and September 1964. The history of Memphis' Negro registration was particularly notable. From 1952 to 1961 it increased from 7,000 to 76,000. By November 1964 it had reached 93,358, one-third of the total vote. Other notable successes were in Nashville (Tennessee), Birmingham (Alabama), Charlotte, Richmond, Portsmouth, Norfolk, and Lynchburg (Virginia), and Macon (Georgia). It is no coincidence that these were all fairly sizable cities. Access to registration was usually better in cities, and most of these campaigns were of the NAACP local-organization variety.

In the areas outside cities, there was a good degree of success generally in Arkansas and in South Carolina. The state-wide organization created by VEP in South Carolina obviously represented, as did those which had already existed in one form or another in the other Southern states, a potential force in politics as well as voter registration.

The figures in the middle of the bell-shaped curve of results, even in the easier areas, were less encouraging. A breakdown of a month's registration by the Peninsula Coordinating Committee of Newport News, Virginia, showed:

Number of homes assigned: 450. Number of persons contacted: 262. Ineligible (can't read, write): 6. Not interested: 39. Physically unable: 2. Promised to register: 185. Registered: 30. Not contacted: 188. Not at home: 109. Moved: 45. Ill or in hospital: 8. Out of town: 6. Wrong address: 9. Refused to answer door: 3.

This was the drudgery, the dreariness and the heartbreak of the voter effort. What happened to 155 of the 185 who promised to go down?

Trouble at the Registrars'

The traditional administrative barriers entered into the equation, even in the easier areas. Alabama, Mississippi, and Virginia had both poll taxes and qualification tests during the 1962–64 drives. Georgia, North Carolina, South Carolina, and Louisiana had tests only. Arkansas and Texas had poll taxes only, leaving only Tennessee and Florida with none of these hindrances.

Alabama registration offices were open only on the first and third Mondays of each month. Some of North Carolina's were open only during the three weeks before an election. If there was no election in a given year, there was no registration. Qualification tests, even if administered impeccably, normally operated to discourage registration of a class in the South that had been systematically short-changed on education. In Atlanta, a worker noted that many people who proudly showed they could sign their names balked at going to the registrar for fear of being embarrassed by the revelation they could write nothing else. Much energy of the movement was consumed in all areas in instructions on how to fill out the test forms, the straightforward ones as well as the tricky. When they were not administered fairly, they could be as devastating as bombs. The court records of the numerous Justice Department suits were filled with instances of Negroes' being turned down en masse while whites, illiterate or not, never were. A miscalculation by one day of his age could disqualify a Negro college graduate, or mispronunciation of one word in an oral "interpretation" of the Constitution.

A late 1963 court order applying to Dallas County (Selma), Alabama, ordered registrars to "cease rejecting applicants for errors or omissions in the questionnaire when other answers or information reveal that the applicant is qualified, and to cease using the questionnaire as an examination or test, unless the registrars present to the court and propose to use a definite set of standards for the grading of questionnaires. . . ." Questions that were on a Louisiana test in 1963 ranged from "The President is elected —(a) by the Congress; (b) by the direct vote of the people; (c) by the people through electors" to such unanswerable riddles as "Limits are placed on the right to vote by the— (a) national government; (b) state; (c) courts" and "Our constitution has been changed— (a) by the President; (b) by the Congress and the people; (c) by the Supreme Court."

An application in use in Mississippi included 17 personal identification questions, a requirement for copying and reasonable interpretation of any section of the Mississippi constitution, and an essay on "Your understanding of the duties and obligations of citizenship under a constitutional form of government."

One of the better moments of all the voter effort years came in February 1965, when, before a national television audience, a registrar from a Mississippi county where no Negroes were registered was handed a copy of the state's constitution and asked by a U.S. Commission on Civil Rights member to interpret section 182. He began, "Well, it means that the power to tax corporations, their property, shall never be surrendered or abridged by any contract. And—"

The commissioner said, "I didn't ask you to read it—I asked you to interpret it."

The registrar then declined to answer the question, on ground of "pressure being put on me before a committee like this."

"On the ground it may incriminate you?" he was asked.

"That's right," he answered.[4]

Slowdowns were common. Separate tables would be assigned whites and Negroes. If a line of Negroes were waiting for the Negro table, a white might go in ahead of them, use the empty white table, and leave. In Anniston, Alabama, a report said the white table was larger, and Negroes were not allowed in the room when a white was using it. Another variation was to seat four Negroes at a table, and make three wait until the slowest had finished, while others waited outside in line. These methods were particularly effective when coupled with the one or two day a month registration periods.

Purges, the removal from voter lists of persons deemed no longer qualified, were often lopsided. In four Louisiana parishes between 1961 and 1963, some 3,500 Negro voters were dropped from the rolls, 90 per cent of those registered, compared with 30 per cent of whites.

In one north Florida county, the registrar didn't bother with any of these refinements, and didn't close his office when Negro applicants appeared. He simply sat with his legs stretched out across the doorway. Negroes didn't break through them.

Then there were the poll taxes. Even where not a part of the worst resistance, the utter complexity of laws and regulations around them was a deterrent. This and their cost struck hardest at Negroes, traditionally the least educated, poorest people. The United States Supreme Court outlawed poll taxes for state elections in March 1966. They had previously been outlawed in federal elections by amendment of the U.S. Constitution. Many whites had become as impatient with them as Negroes, aware that in such a state as Virginia they disenfranchised whites almost as effectively as Negroes, and that in other states they were no longer stopping all Negroes.

In the worst areas, voter workers took these administrative blocks as normal, and remarked on them mainly when the registrars seemed to be applying them in a particularly nasty way. "Of course the lady in the office is very rude," said an SCLC report. A report from a Mississippi town stated without comment: "She said she didn't have time to give the Negroes voting applications to fill out, but she did have time to give white people fishing licenses." Such encounters had to take into account the sensitiveness of some Negro personalities. Frank Smith of SNCC wrote of a friend in Holly Springs, Mississippi, who paid his poll tax in early January 1963, but got a receipt dated December 1962. "He went back down and the lady told him that it was just the slip of the pen. He was very happy about it because he's kind of shy and couldn't have been expected to put up much of a fight if his rights had been violated."

"Many persons," wrote Ronnie Moore from Louisiana in July 1963, "refused to participate because of discouragement, fear, ignorance, and apathy. We can overcome the complacency, but Lord help us overcome the registrar, because the federal government is moving too damn slow."

In at least one instance, he did overcome the registrar. The one in Iberville Parish, in June 1963, announced that all 2,700 registered Negroes would have to come to the office and verify their registration or be dropped. After 500 persons showed up in a five-day period, the registrar announced it would be all right for them just to call up.

In some areas, there seemed to be reliance on the administrative procedures—without blatantly discriminatory application of forms and the like—to hold Negro voting down. The words of J. Love Hutchison of Quincy, Florida, quoted in the St. Petersburg *Times,* described one of the better attitudes: "I don't go out in the street and grab them around the neck and drag them in here. But I defy any civil rights commission or anybody else to prove that I've . . . set up any barriers." The easier states of the 1962–1964 period allowed neighborhood registration, and some—Tennessee, North Carolina, Florida, Texas—allowed night registration and Negro personnel to accept applications.[5] These were not mere conveniences; they alleviated problems deep in the roots of so-called apathy.

"Apathy"

"Apathy" was too easy a catchword. Negroes themselves could be most harsh in invoking it; the word recurred in all manner of VEP reports. Even after the great spirit and results of the Birmingham demonstrations in the spring of 1963, a report from there in November of that year cited "apathy and illiteracy" as the "number one problems." What were the ingredients of "apathy"? Bill Hansen of SNCC, quoted in the Memphis *Commercial-Appeal,* described what was wrong in many places in a comment he made about the Arkansas "Delta" (along the Mississippi): "Negroes were fragmented by the culture of segregation. . . . These people don't realize how to get together or what they can accomplish with their votes if they do get together." People who should have been registered, college graduates, professionals, were ashamed to admit that they never had bothered, or previously had been afraid to register. A middle-class home was visited at the time of the March on Washington by voter workers in High Point, North Carolina; there were pictures of three presidents on the wall, but the family didn't know how to go about registering to vote.

"Apathy," wrote Miss Dorothy Dawson,[6] a white worker with the

National Student Association who headed a special SNCC-NSA project in Raleigh, North Carolina, back in 1962, "has frequently been used to describe the reasons why Negroes do not register when encouraged to do so, but the term is inadequate to describe all the factors influencing Negro attitudes on politics. When a Negro in Raleigh asks why should he bother to vote, his question is not caused by apathy. Rather he wants to know, justifiably, how his vote will benefit his own life . . . With virtually no choice in candidates, with fear that any Negro who runs for office is in league with the white power structure and unconcerned about their own welfare, with no awareness of political issues and how they might affect social and economic changes, they maintain the attitude that politics is white folks' business. Beyond this, many Negroes have a general fear of legal matters, since the law has always meant going to jail or paying taxes, and thus they fear the legal technicalities of registration—taking an oath, signing one's name, and questions about jobs, home, family, etc. . . . What results can be expected from total Negro participation in politics? This is not an irrelevant question since it is the question asked by the so-called apathetic Negro." She went on, in this remarkably perceptive report, to answer the question, saying full Negro voting would lead to small changes toward token desegregation —about the shape of things in the best of Southern locales as late as 1967. "The changes which are needed, however, are not toward token desegregation so much as toward the improvement of the conditions facing all lower socio-economic classes in our country."

There was apathy in the hardest of resistance areas. And to understand "apathy" in its fullest meanings was to know that once all the South was totally resistant to the Negro vote, and that still none of the South was free of some form of resistance, and that just as the worst resistance of 1962–64 cast its shadow on areas where things were easier, so the memory and the shadow of all the past resistance would be some part of "apathy" in 1962–64, and, probably, for some time to come. For a century and more, violence and intimidation had been leaving their marks. Even when there was no imminent danger of violence or subtle reprisal, Negroes could not be sure. Damaged psyches and phantom fears were often found by registration workers after the direct threat was gone; violence and intimidation not just last year but twenty years ago take their toll. The theme runs constant in workers' reports from Black Belt counties.

From a wrinkled old matriarch, refusing to register and asked whether she wanted always to be a slave: "I was born a slave, I've been a slave for seventy-eight years, and I reckon I'll die one. White folks is white folks, no matter how you take 'em."

From a worker who had talked to a woman in her home: "She'd been down since January with the flus and if she went to the meeting next Wednesday it might turn into the eight-days pneumonia, and that will kill you. She then went down an amazing list of the diseases she could get if she went to a meeting. It's amazing what forms fear will take."

"I tell them about the Fayette County story," wrote SNCC's Carver Neblett in southwest Georgia. "Then they start saying yussa and nossa, you sho' is right, boss, etc. No matter what you say, they still say yussa." Jack Chatfield from the same area remarked: "Sawhorse Sam looks at the registration form like I were offering him heroin from the great big unknown kingdom of the East. 'I don't think I'm interested in it.'"

Apathy was not simple. A report from Albany told of a "talkative old lady [who] was eating scrambled eggs and offered us some, but she would never agree to go down and register—they'd have to drag her down. Besides, she'd had a stroke and couldn't make it downtown, even if we carried her. When Grady asked her name, she said she didn't have one. He said she could go down to the courthouse and they'd give her one, and then she could register. She was very talkative and not hostile—just adamant and very tenacious, like we were on the other side, or something. I suppose this is the way many people regard us— especially when there's a white in the group—and it's difficult for them to understand our purpose."

When the Civil Rights Commission held hearings in Mississippi in 1965, Negroes from Washington County were asked why Negro registration was not better there. Washington's registrar administered the difficult state test without discrimination. The police chief of the county seat, Greenville, was noted for his fairness. The local newspaper, published by Hodding Carter, Jr., was regarded as fair, and white community leaders met with Negroes to talk about local problems. Yet only 12 per cent of the Negro adults were registered in 1960. The great difficulty of the state registration test, even when fairly administered, was one obvious explanation.

But James Carter, Negro operator of a Greenville dry-cleaning business, related others: "Sometimes what happens to your neighbor affect you. Now there are eighty-two counties in Mississippi. And even though Washington County might seem a little liberal in their registration and voting . . . there is other adjoining counties. When even though one county might be liberal, in another county, when they hear what happened in the other counties, it keeps that county in fear, too. But it is not on account of the law enforcement or people who are in control of the voter registration. It is a matter of the mind in the people." [7]

None of these considerations should detract from the fact of bravery, anger, defiance, and swift, unexplainable ability to transcend themselves that have so often marked Negroes' behavior in the movement. In fact, it should underscore that bravery; for among the great obstacles many a black man (and perhaps every black man in a white society) has had to overcome is the barrier within himself. One of Dr. Martin Luther King's main assistants, the Reverend James Bevel, has described the two phases that many Negro registrants or demonstrators go through. First is the time of "picking up one's soul," when a man decides he is going to register or march, despite the chance that he may be killed. He has begun to move, even though in fear. The second state Mr. Bevel calls the time of "walking with one's soul." In this phase, a man has forgotten his original fears and is moving with less consciousness of any danger, real or unreal, which he had had to set aside, repeatedly, in the earlier phase.[8]

Fear

Often it seemed to be a matter of pushing the fear back, repressing it. Miss Joyce Barrett told of a spark of hope in her long-running efforts to interest a prestigious group of seemingly apathetic middle-class matrons in the voter work of Albany. One of them finally admitted she was afraid she would lose her job if she canvassed. "It was the first time anyone would admit fear." The Hattiesburg, Mississippi, "Voice of the Movement" had an essay on fear by Jim Campbell in August 1963, which asked: "How can you tell a man that he is afraid? The hardest thing to see is your own fear because we, somehow, managed to convince ourselves first and most lastingly that, 'I am not afraid; it's just that I don't want to get mixed up in that . . .'"

In the areas of strong resistance, the fear was the center of the struggle. "That prohibitive kind of fear which binds the minds of the people here, especially the Negroes," the reports said. "The same appalling, nebulous fear . . ."

Miss Penny Patch of SNCC, one of the first young white women to attempt voter registration work in the hard-core areas, wrote in 1962: "As far as voter registration in the counties is concerned, the local people who work with it can never forget that their lives, homes, families, churches, are in jeopardy . . . And this is, too, all part and parcel of the lifetime of conscious or subconscious worry that is part of most Southern Negroes. It is difficult to speak with authority though. I can learn from observations and from my friends, but I, myself, again only experience, as I have all my life, momentary flashes of fear." Hers was the norm of American experience. What the Negro Southerner has known is abnormal—that special kind of fear born of helplessness and awareness of swift, savage power over him, unrestrained. Other lands in this century know such fear; many people through history lived with such fear. The history of the free world has been a history of escaping it.[9]

"Honey," an older Negro woman told a fresh-faced young white collegian come to the town of Dawson, in Terrell County in southwest Georgia, to work on voter registration, "this has always been a *hard* place."

The fear worked on local whites, too. Its silencing of dissent is a sad, familiar history,[10] but a report from Mississippi in 1963 suggests how it also influenced men to overt action against their will. A white businessman had prosecuted a Negro man on trumped-up charges after he had registered to vote. The white man told SNCC workers how he regretted its being this particular Negro, because they were friends, and his own children had been fed at the Negro's table and had played in his yard. The VEP report went on: "He said Jeff must have been misled. He said Jeff had taken sides with Communism and went down and registered. He said what he [the white man] did he was forced to do. They made him do it. He said, 'Of course, I don't blame the colored people, if it just was left up with me I would treat everybody right, never harm a colored person, but I was forced to do what I did . . .' "[11]

One must understand about the fear. A young Mississippi Negro woman was testifying before the Civil Rights Commission about going to the courthouse to register:

COMMISSIONER ROBERT S. RANKIN—Do you agree with your father it's better to go one by one than for a group to go down?

MISS CAIN—Well, I agree maybe more than one by one, but I wouldn't—

COMMISSIONER RANKIN—You would like to have had somebody with you; is that right?

MISS CAIN—Well, I wasn't alone because I had prayed, and I believed that Somebody was with me. That's why I had the courage that I had when I went there.[12]

Economic Intimidation

To understand this more fully is to know the details of the worst forms of white resistance. One of the civil rights organizations finally evolved a standardized form for checking off excuses of Negroes for not registering. It was a catalogue of the ingredients of apathy: "Feel votes of Negroes not counted. Thinks politics are un-Christian.[13] Just not interested. Don't have the time to discuss voting. Feel the politicians are going to do whatever they want, regardless of votes cast. Too busy engaged in personal affairs. Feels Negroes should not become involved. Must consult with someone else. Fear of being embarrassed at the registrar's office. Wants time to think it over. Feel poll tax should be abolished. Don't like the way things are carried out. Been advised not to register. Satisfied with things as they are."

But at the head of the list was "fear of economic pressure." This, in a land which blocked Negroes from most avenues to money-making, was a particularly cruel weapon. It was also among the very most effective. There are, in fact, as many ways of exerting economic intimidation or retaliation against voting as there are of having economic power. "If you can afford to vote, you don't need a loan," said a Citizens Council usurer to Negroes in one Mississippi county.

"It is literally understood," Ralph Allen wrote from southwest Georgia in April 1963, "that anyone who works for a white man in Terrell County and registers to vote can expect to lose his job." Jack Chatfield mused, of the wife of a man so threatened, "She is an old lady. If her husband, who is old, loses his scant salary, where will she be? On one day of the year she will be at the polls. The other 364 are not accounted for."

Political jobs, including teaching, were especially jeopardized. A white man who wanted Sampson Wright to resign as treasurer of the Terrell County voter drive reminded Mr. Wright that he had "hoped" him get his job as school bus driver ($100 a month), and that he could "hope" him lose it. Mr. Wright refused to be intimidated. And not all teachers were. They joined their pupils in the Birmingham marches; in Selma, a brave line of them risked their jobs to try to register.

A Terrell County report told of how "Mr. Agnew James is having trouble with his gas man. The man came to his home and took his [butane storage] tank away. Others in the county have said that they will not let him have a tank. . . ." A little known factor in such intimidation was the manipulation of various informal (and likely illegal) credit arrangements common between Southern whites and Negroes.[14] A white merchant sells to a Negro on credit, and requires him to sign a check for the amount of the principal and interest on a bank where the Negro has no checking account. Then if he should default, the merchant has him prosecuted for writing a bad check, a jailable offense. This use of police and court powers as collection agencies for private business was easily adapted to voter intimidation. A man tried to register, and a merchant had him prosecuted for the alleged bad check.

The economic powers of government were also used. One has only to consider the large influence in daily life of local, state, and national government, and to remember that in the South these all were in the hands of whites, and often white racists, to imagine the possibilities. The willingness of Negroes to believe out of past experience the worst about such all-white governments was a contributing factor. There were rumors in almost every area covered by VEP that registering to vote could result in the cutting off of welfare checks or other government aid. Jack Chatfield told, in December 1962, of a lady in Terrell County, Georgia, who received an old-age pension. She didn't know whether it was from the state, county, or federal government, but "she was afraid of losing the check given to her by some unknown source. All she knew was this: the white man gives and the white man takes away."

Economic intimidation was, of course, intimately related to the poverty of Negroes in the South. These were the poorest people of the poorest area of the nation. The voter workers saw what this meant, in big things and small. A report from a small Mississippi town told of Mrs. Anderson, owner of a little grocery shop, who said that the children weren't coming in to buy cookies. "And when the kids aren't buying their cookies, you know things are bad." They were worst in the rural South, where year by year mechanization and federal surplus programs rendered more and more Negro field hands and sharecroppers obsolete. Charles McLaurin of SNCC wrote from Ruleville, Mississippi, in late 1962: "This has been a very dry year and the cotton picking machine did most of the cotton picking, this meant that there were very little to be picked by hand. So most of the people had nothing to do and made no money, some of the ones that had said they would not go down to register for fear of reprisals. During this month, most of the people that had not made any money went to the boss to borrow money and some of the bosses was all mad because of the voter registration drive. The bank would not loan money to people that had tried to register, or if anyone in their family had attempted. The Negroes was getting mad."

The psychological and financial intricacies of sharecropping (as complex as international banking) are drearily familiar.[15] Aside from whatever the basic injustices of the system, the greatest complaint seems to have been the powerlessness of the sharecropper, particularly the Negro one. He often was not allowed to see the totaling up of expenditures and profits, let alone question the final rendering. Or he had to accept the landowner's word for weights of cotton, and the price a crop brought. The late George Mitchell of the Southern Regional Council was fond of saying that a standard contract for sharecroppers would be one of the saving possibilities of the South. At best, share-cropping had been the barest of eked-out existences. Even this was taken away.

Movement elements, including young radicals, attempted in 1965 to organize the cotton-pickers in the Mississippi Delta. It was a protest demonstration against the law of supply and demand, and merely has-tened automation. The AFL-CIO talked of organizing the relatively few men who drove tractors. The young radicals, they complained, didn't seem interested in anything actually capable of producing results. But the radicals, whether they knew it or not, were protesting something else—the end of agrarianism, which had come at last to the South. With all its evils, and particularly its evil-doing to Negroes, it was pref-erable to the next stop for the sharecroppers—the city slums. The values of a new era were involved—the prestige of having useful work to do, the privilege of living on the land. Many sharecroppers and field hands, because of that desperate Southern way of attempting kindness in an unkind social system, were allowed to stay on the land after they were no longer needed. But when they tried to register to vote, the kindness often ended; they were evicted, as were others still useful but easily replaced. This was common during the 1962–64 drives; it was increasingly so in subsequent years.

The VEP reports abounded in details of the poverty. At about the time America was discovering the statistics of poverty in such works as Michael Harrington's *The Other America*, the voter workers were confronting some of its most cruel American reality.[16] They told of the ragged children, the neighborhoods where an outhouse was a high standard, the people caught in nightmare mazes of credit and installment buying, of charcoal in a bucket used to light and heat a house where the electricity had been cut off for non-payment of the bill. They described the farmlands and little towns that had become reservations for the very old and very young, left behind in the mass exodus to the cities. (Good intentions of parents to send for the young'uns were often blighted by what they discovered in the promised lands to which they migrated. Rosie, a fourth-grader, was described in one report. She lived with her older sister, twenty-three, and her little brother, and five nephews and nieces. Some days she spent the whole day hungry. Her mother sent her a dollar from New York for Christmas. Other parents at Christmastime would tell the children Santa Claus was sick, and he would be by to see them when he got well.)

Charles McLaurin told, in December 1962, of "things I notice while in Indianola, Mississippi: People who must come to Indianola to sign up for [federal free food] commodities had to stand out in the cold, below freezing temperatures, while two or three went in to tell the history of their lives. There was space enough inside for the people to sit or stand out of the cold. If a white person brought 'his Negroes' down, he could carry them in and the others would have to stand out there all day. Then some of them had to come back day after day. The process is very slow and painful." In the winter of 1962 and 1963, several counties tightened requirements, and cut back on items dispensed. Negroes had to get "responsible persons" to countersign applications and, as a VEP report said, "due to the voter registration drive . . . the 'responsible people' are not particularly inclined to favors for the Negro." Sunflower County, home of Senator James Eastland, engaged in this. Leflore County (Greenwood) went a step farther. It stopped the free-food program altogether in December 1962. Though it was stoutly denied by officials, the voter registration effort apparently had tipped the scales in favor of those who generally oppose such largesse in such communities. The opposition is usually led by merchants. Planters, whose laborers are fed free in off-season, tend to favor this particular form of socialism. This is, of course, up to a point. In Washington County (Greenville), the county board of supervisors refused a year-round food distribution program. "The program would benefit primarily Negroes and land-owners feel they would have more difficulty in getting spring labor if commodities were not cut off in March," reported the *Delta Democrat-Times*.

At any rate, the 1962–63 cutoff came after the voter effort had begun to get troublesome. It did not result in "widespread starvation," a VEP report said, but it added to an already tense situation and a hard winter for Negroes. This was in the background of the Greenwood voter pro-test campaign. The voter workers began to bring food and provisions in from the rest of the country. There was at least one arrest (in Clarks-dale) of SNCC workers on grounds that medicines in one truckload of provisions were "dangerous drugs." The COFO headquarters set up a center to distribute food and clothing, and this kept up for a period of months, even after Leflore County was given its choice of resuming its program or letting the federal government resume it, and chose the former. Even the act of accepting the COFO food was opposed by the whites, a number of bitter reports said. Some plantation workers were threatened with eviction if they dared it.

An affidavit at the time said:

I, . . . age 26, have six children, age ranging from 10 years to one year. On the evening of the 19th February, 1963, I informed Mrs. H. [for whom she worked as a domestic servant] that I wanted to take time off on the 20th February, 1963, to go to Wesley Methodist church to get some of the food for the children and I. She told me that I couldn't go because she had to go to Greenville, Mississippi. She also told me that the food was poisoned. At this point, I informed her how bad my children needed food and clothing. I was making only $18 per week, and out of this amount I have to pay my house rent, grocery bills, and hospital bills. On the morning of February 20, 1963, Mrs. H. came for me to go to work. At this time I told her that I was going down to get the food, and she told me not to return to work. I am now unemployed. But today I went down to the circuit clerk's office and made my first attempt to register to vote.

The COFO food distribution was keyed in to voter registration. "The food is identified in the minds of everyone as food for those who want to be free, and the minimum requirement for freedom is identified as registering to vote." Such a program of direct aid was never attempted on a large scale again by the movement anywhere, but involvement in economic problems increased.

Economic intimidation worked best on those who had something to lose, however small their stake in the good American life. For those who could not be hurt much more than they already were, the vote was held out as hope. History is full of examples of the folly of offering such hope falsely to people so desperate. "Look at a case like this man, Mr. Meeks, who is thirty-seven years old," cried Samuel Block in a Greenwood report in January 1963. "His wife is thirty-three years old, and they have eleven children, age ranging from seventeen down to eight months. Seven of the children are school age, and not one is attending school because they have no money, no food, no clothes, and no wood to keep warm by . . . The house they are living in have no paper or nothing on the walls and you can look at the ground through the floor and if you are not careful you will step in one of those holes and break your leg or ankle. And they now want to go register."

Police Intimidation

Not all the intimidation and reprisal, of course, was economic. The registration process itself was often the scene of traumatic confrontation. From Americus, Georgia, Sammy Mahone, then a junior in high school, told of being cursed by a deputy registrar in Leesburg as he helped an elderly lady with her application. She became frightened, and left without finishing, muttering of how they used to hang Negroes. He remonstrated with the man, and the man raised his fist. "Then I said, you mean to tell me you'd hit a kid like me? Then he said, yeah, because you got no business here. These people here ain't your concern. Then I said, I think they're my concern. I am a citizen and a Negro and I have every right to be here in this building. Then [the deputy registrar] turned and walked out the door and said, 'You ain't nothing.' "

The Southern county courthouse is the dwelling place not only of the registrar, but also the sheriff and his deputies, the court officials; usually city police station and its jail. All could be turned against the voter effort. Sometimes it was a matter of not offering the law's protection the county jail is attached or nearby, and somewhere close will be the against lawlessness. But worse was the use of police and court powers themselves to thwart registration. Police surveillance of voter head-quarters and personnel was common. Reports told of "stake-outs" on offices, workers followed, questionings of workers or those who helped them, such as landladies; opened mail, "stool pigeons," telephone taps.[17] The offices would be raided and ransacked. CORE workers in Monroe, Louisiana, in January 1964, reported: "The chief [of police] expressed enough interest in our records to make us sneak them out of town the next day. They have the bus station completely covered, so we had someone drive us to Alexandria where we got the bus for Baton Rouge."

Police cars in towns and state troopers on highways got behind known movement cars and trailed them, and made arrests for crossing the center line, weaving, and the like—or for more serious offenses, some real, some trumped up.[18] Often voter workers were arrested on the strange charge of distributing handbills; ordinances required permission from police for this exercise of free speech. Such arrests occurred in Indianola, Mississippi, the first day Negroes were brought from Rule-ville to try to register. Despite it, they went on in the courthouse. A report told how it took all day to get twenty-six people processed and how they loaded into their bus to go back home and then were stopped a mile outside town. "The bus with all the people had to go back to town. The driver of the bus was put in jail for having a bus the same color as the county's school bus. He was charged $30. The people took up money and got him out of jail . . . That night a mass meeting was held in Williams Chapel . . . We let the people talk about what had happened that day and we sang freedom songs. This we felt would help them forget the fear of being stopped. . . ."

Fifty-eight Negroes were arrested in Itta Bena, Mississippi, in June 1963, when they marched out of a voter meeting in a church into which smoke bombs had been tossed by terrorists. They had planned to ask for police protection. In the little town of Mileston, near Tchula, Missis-sippi, between Jackson and Greenwood, on the night of May 9, 1963, the home of Hartman Turnbow was attacked with a Molotov cocktail. When Mr. Turnbow, with his wife and child, tried to run out of the house, whites from a car opened fire at them. He fired back. The next morning, sheriff's deputies arrived and arrested Mr. Turnbow and Robert Moses and three other voter workers on the scene. The charge: arson. A few days before, Mr. Turnbow had been the first Negro to try to register in a voter campaign. He and others at the courthouse had been photographed by a deputy sheriff. The sheriff's department said the fire bombing was an attempt to revive the voter drive, that the story of whites shooting and missing was "fantastic." The charges were dropped when a federal suit was filed in Jackson. Mr. Moses, however, was fined fifty dollars for interfering with investigation of the fire by taking pictures of the damage.

In Americus, Georgia, on October 3, 1963, the most serious charge to be made against voter workers was lodged against four young men— John Perdew, Don Harris, and Ralph Allen of SNCC, and Zev Aeloney of CORE. (All but Mr. Harris were white.) The voter campaign in Americus had escalated to direct action, with more than 300 demonstrators arrested, and into scenes of near violence as white and Negro crowds faced each other in the close, oppressive night heat. The four were charged with attempting to incite insurrection, a crime which under the Georgia law carried the death penalty. The case was one of the earliest to attract national attention to such misuse of the apparatus of law enforcement against the basic law of the nation. Press coverage included criticism of the conditions in the jail where the four were held under exorbitant bonds pending trial. Representing the four were nationally prominent defense attorneys, including Morris Abram of New York, president of the American Jewish Committee and former Atlanta resident who had previously won the case against Georgia's political malapportionment. The defense was successful in setting aside the disgraceful charges.[19]

Among those pondering the logic and law argued by the defense in the case was Warren Fortson, the county attorney and brother of Georgia Secretary of State Ben Fortson. He later emerged as an advocate of sanity in various racial crises in Americus. Soon, he was no longer welcomed as Sunday-school teacher, club leader, and the like, nor his wife as a social leader. They finally moved from the town, their lives threatened.

On January 10, 1963, in Helena, Arkansas, two SNCC workers were arrested while seated in an automobile talking with a Negro minister. The charge: *planning* to disturb the peace.

Voter work, like direct action, produced many stories of whites' being thrown into cells with local prisoners with the word that here were "nigger-lovers," the jailers then ignoring the ensuing beatings. The jailing and beating of registration workers in Winona, Mississippi, on Sunday, June 9, 1963, became famous through the retelling by Mrs.

Fannie Lou Hamer at the 1964 Democratic National Convention. The arrest occurred at a lunch counter in an interstate bus terminal when Negroes, returning from a voter registration workshop in Charleston, South Carolina, sought service at the rest stop. A state trooper and local police made the arrests, according to the accounts of the Negroes. When one of the Negroes protested they were obliged by law to be served, one of the arresting officers said, "There ain't no damn law." Six went to jail: Rosemary Freeman, Euvester Simpson, June Johnson, Annelle Ponder, Mrs. Hamer, and James West. Lawrence Guyot, later to be chairman of FDP, apparently came to investigate, was jailed and beaten, too. Mr. West, in a report entitled "Things That Happened to Me in Jail," said: "They put me in a cell and made two of the fellas in jail beat me for about 30 minutes, and then knocked me out." Miss Ponder and Mrs. Hamer described their ordeal in an interview with VEP staff members the day after their release from the jail. A tape recording of what they said ("It was the mos' horrifyin' experience I ever had in my life . . ." "They really wanted me to say 'yes sir,' you know. And that's one thing I wouldn't say . . .") is transcribed in Appendix I.

Their remarks made clear that the role each had played in voter registration in Mississippi had cost them much in the brutality of treatment. They also showed how far along the movement was by then in distrust of and disgust with the FBI in "investigations" of such incidents. The episode was one of the touchstones to which the young radicals frequently referred in explaining their subsequent alienation and revulsion regarding all of America. Mrs. Hamer and Mr. Guyot went on to their respective roles as leaders of the Freedom Democratic Party. One of the hardest-line black power adherents of 1966 would take off his shirt and show the scars of similar beatings he received in Mississippi. But how explain the human difference in the response to the same brutal forces in the Southern experience? Miss Ponder, sweet of spirit, her beautiful black face filled with sadness, went on with her work in community education for SCLC, no more angry-seeming, or bitter, or denunciatory than her calm words were the day after she got out of the Winona jail (her intonations then were like those of the chorus in a Greek tragedy—anguish and compassion in the stark recitation of events). In 1966, as in 1963, her faith, as was Mrs. Hamer's, was in the Negro people, in what might develop out of a small amount of help to them in the tradition of "picking up one's soul."

One reason the national press didn't converge on Winona was that the arrests occurred on the eve of Governor Wallace's stand in the door at the desegregation of the University of Alabama. Most of the reporters who were then the nation's main contact with what happened in Southern civil rights struggles were in a motel room in Tuscaloosa when the first word of Winona came in. "We ought to be there instead of here," one of them said. But they weren't. The theatrics of that day, with the federal government following a script that sadly underestimated the potency of demagoguery, were a boon to Wallace's political future. His shabby stand, displayed on TV and front pages, was followed by a rash of racist violence over the South, including the murder of Medgar Evers. The executive secretary of the Mississippi NAACP, long a leader in voter efforts and other civil rights fights, was shot in the back in his own yard on June 12. Byron de la Beckwith of Greenwood was arrested and tried twice, both trials resulting in divided juries.

"Somethin'," cried Mrs. Hamer, "got to break." [20]

An affidavit published by the Inter-Citizens Committee of Birmingham described an incident of the kind that didn't get famous from a telling before a national television audience. It was signed by Bennie J. Luchion of SCLC, a frail young man of some musical talent.

One day in July, 1963, I was canvassing for voter registration in [a small Alabama town], and was picked up along with about five others and taken to the city hall . . . The police chief . . . tried to make me say who I was and where I was from, but I would not say. He stomped on my toes and kicked my shins, but still I would not say. Then he got out a brand new [electric cattle] prod [21] and applied it to me several times, but I took it. I began to get weaker and dizzy, but I tried to take it. Then when he put it to my genitals, I said to him, "What about your God?" He stopped, but he threatened to put the Klan on me. We were not released til dark, and for about two days I was in a daze as a result of the prod treatment given me by the police chief.

Not all police and sheriff's departments in the hard-core areas, of course, were so bad. Some did their duty against the worst of odds.[22] But over-all, local law enforcement was unable to cope with hard-core resistance at its fiercest, including private terrorism.

Private Violence

The torture and murder of James E. Chaney, Negro, and Andrew Goodman and Michael H. Schwerner, whites, COFO Freedom Summer workers, in Philadelphia, Mississippi, in June 1964 was the most sensational, most publicly noted episode in the long, amazingly quiet history of unhampered (if not police-helped) private violence. The Mississippi Freedom Summer alone produced 35 shooting incidents with 3 persons injured; 30 homes and other buildings bombed; 35 churches burned; 80 persons beaten; 3 other murders. A few other examples: Three churches were burned in southwest Georgia shortly after the voter effort started in 1962. "This action of perhaps a dozen men, the inaction of 4,000, clumped the voter registration drive a sound blow to the skull," reported Jack Chatfield. Preachers cited the burnings as reason for not letting other churches be used for voter meetings. The people retreated in terror. Money was collected nationally to rebuild two of the churches and white people of Sasser financed rebuilding of a third.

Robert Moses complained in 1962 to the president of the U.S. Fidelity and Guaranty Company, in Baltimore, of the cancellation of a $2,000 fire insurance policy on the Williams Chapel Church in Ruleville after it had begun to be used for voter registration meetings. The cancellation, his letter said, was the act of a local agency. It was a five-year policy in its third year. Pointing out that a city tax exemption and free water to the church had also been cut off, he said in the letter: "The thought occurred to me that [the company] would not want to be used to help coerce minority people who seek to exercise constitutional rights." A supporting letter was sent by Clarence Mitchell of the NAACP. A reply to Mr. Mitchell from a senior executive vice-president of the insurance company said, "We believe that our policy was validly cancelled pursuant to terms and that insurance, even if application were to be made to an agent of our company, would not meet our normal underwriting standards." Such cancellations were not uncommon in the hard-core areas. The Williams Chapel, an arc-shaped old building, was subsequently fire-bombed, but not destroyed.

After the fire-bomb attempt on Mr. Turnbow's home in Mileston in 1963, these events were reported in the same area: a dynamite bomb was tossed into another home, landing on the bed of a young girl without going off; two white volunteers were beaten; a Negro minister was forced into the car of two white men and his life threatened; a newly built community center was set afire and a car fire-bombed (its rusted hulk was still sitting there a year later). Of more than 8,000 voting age Negroes in that county (Holmes), 41 were registered.

The terror took grotesque forms, strange little dramas of the hunted and fearful. A Negro taxi driver in one town allowed his cab to be used by the movement, hauling applicants, carrying messages. He received a warning from friends that a man charged but not convicted in a civil rights murder planned to kill him if the opportunity came. There was no way for him to know if it were true. But finally he gave up his cab, and worked as the janitor of the voter registration office.

The recital becomes dreary. In April 1963, Ralph Allen, driving a Negro woman home from a Terrell County (Georgia) registration attempt, was stopped by two whites, a man and his son, who beat him and kicked him when he crumpled to the ground. (Those trained in nonviolence would fall at the first blow and lie in a fetus position, knees drawn to chest, hands wrapped about the skull. It helped to prevent serious injury.) On Sunday, January 9, 1966, when the voting rights law was six months old, Vernon Dahmer of Hattiesburg, Mississippi, spoke on the local radio. As chairman of a new Negro registration campaign, he offered to collect the money for poll taxes from Negroes and pay at the courthouse. That night his home and grocery store were fire-bombed. He was fatally burned, and his wife and daughter required hospital care. Two sons and an elderly aunt in the house escaped serious injury. He staggered out of his burning home and fired a shotgun at a car driving away. There were subsequent arrests of white men. Mr. Dahmer made a deathbed statement: "I've been trying to get people to register to vote. People who don't vote are deadbeats on the state. I figure a man needs to do his own thinking. At one time I didn't think so, but I have changed my mind. What happened to us can happen to anybody, white or black."

Fixing the Blame

The white South, with schizophrenic ability to produce delightful, subtle people, highly likable, while at the same time engaged in the crushing of human personality and, with cold, almost machinelike cruelty, the crushing of freedom, rationalizes itself, saying to itself, "There are many Souths." There are, and there is not much, in truth, that the state of Tennessee can do about the kind of psychopathic politics the state of Alabama engages itself in. The little that decent officials might do—disavowing the demagogues and refusing interstate, regional dealings with them—is not attempted. The low level of education of the country-town whites, these left-out, left-behind Americans, is another time-honored explanation and excuse. The chief of police in a little piney-woods crossroads town, where the wealth is owned in forest tracts by paper mills or in plantations by the rich who come down occasionally to kill birds, cannot be thought of in the same terms as the chief of police of even a similar-size town (let alone a city) in an area of healthful economy and self-satisfied mediocrity. Ignoramuses and psychopaths are attracted to the low-paid police and jailer and executioner jobs everywhere; in benighted areas of the South, the tendency is merely exaggerated. The line between the law and lawlessness is blurred in such places anyway, and the normal restraining forces on them, the men of minor affairs who control little towns, are in not much better intellectual or psychological condition. One despairs of democracy's ever healing in such places, even with the help of Negro votes and leaders. But they were only the worst showings of the ravages of racism. A Negro lady in Terrell County felt the elusiveness of fixing blame. It was the bad whites, she said. Who were the bad whites? "I don't know who they are. The bad ones, they're sneaky. There are bad ones, though."

How far apart in belief and conditioning and perception of reality and value systems were the whites in power and the Negroes against whom the power was used. The gulf showed in the occasional little exploratory encounters between them, little efforts to talk to each other. Often the voter workers would call on the mayors of the towns to tell them what they were up to. "He said he didn't mind my being in town as long as I didn't agitate," Charles Cobb reported of a discussion with one mayor. "Beyond a vague reference to Albany, he didn't define what he meant by 'agitate.' At this point the mayor realized that I didn't speak with a Southern accent, and he asked me where I was from. I told him Massachusetts, and he told me that he had spent a couple of weeks up North visiting Boston, New York, Philadelphia, and Washington, D.C. He suggested that I go back to Massachusetts and straighten it out, and 'leave Mississippi alone.' He asked me if I honestly believed that the Negroes in Mississippi were worse off than those in the North. I told him that I did, and began to tell of incidents of terror, denials, harassments, and intimidations. When I got to the Emmett Till case, he said that Till had propositioned and made 'lewd advances' to the woman involved, and although he didn't agree with the resulting violence he wasn't going to condemn the men who did it. He commented on the Ruleville shootings by saying that it had been done by Negroes . . . I asked the mayor about economic reprisals against Negroes trying to exercise their constitutional rights, and he said . . . in [his county] no economic pressures were applied to prevent Negroes from registering to vote. He asked me if I had heard of any intimidation or discrimination in [the town]. I told him no; of the forty to fifty Negroes [out of several thousand eligible] registered to vote . . . none seemed to have any complaints to make. The mayor told me that I wouldn't, either, and if I did hear of any, to tell him about it. 'The nigras here live in peace and harmony with the whites.' I left the mayor to mull on the idea that Negroes might be suppressed rather than happy."

The mayor of Ruleville liked to tell people that Memorial Day was started in Mississippi, and the Order of the Eastern Star, and how there were more churches per capita in the state than any other, and how the Mississippi crime rate had been the lowest in the nation in 1964.

There must have been in the occasional casual contacts with the whites a desire in the voter workers—as in the nation—to find deep down somewhere that it really wasn't so, what they saw every day in the determination that Negroes should not vote, and a desperate effort to undo what this knowledge was doing to them, personally. One of the gentlest of the voter workers wrote of his personal reaction to a federal court's [23] freeing of a white policeman charged with shooting a voter registration applicant:

I personally didn't understand myself the day of the trial . . . The case had been presented to the jury and it seemed they were just begging for somebody to give them an excuse to acquit the man. The judge did. He emphasized "under the color of law" and "without reasonable doubt." He said that even if the man did it, it must have been done under the color of the law. The sap sucker did it and nobody in that darn court thought otherwise. The judge more than anyone else, even the poor [defense attorney] who didn't have a case and knew it. [The defendant] got up in that chair and lied his tail off and nobody said a mumbling word.

I looked at the jury and then at [the defendant] and then at the judge sitting up there in his robe and I was disturbed within me. All within me twisted and turned. My guts bubbled. I hated that man, not the system that produced him, not [the defendant] or the jury, but that man in his black robe of shame.

I said it over and over. If I were violent I would have tried to do harm to that man's physical body. I left that room and walked the streets . . . for half-an-hour, and every white face I saw I said to myself, "I hate it."

Man, I was afraid of myself; I did not understand what was happening, and supposed that it was only happening to me. We were all in bad shape, I later found out when I told this to the group. I called a special meeting and spilled the beans. I felt much better and understood what was happening much better after we all got in there and struggled with these issues.

This had been a development of continued frustration at the throne of justice all over Mississippi, in Louisiana, the school case in Virginia . . . and all the Albany cases, the most immediate ones on voter registration and the hundreds on civil liberties and civil rights. Here was the skunk sitting on them. I saw him sitting in that room representing the stench of death across the South which must take somebody with it before it goes. He represented all that I hate about the system of segregation, and it is men like him who rob us all, black and white, of the living we have fought for, and die and live to fight again for. As you can sense, I have not quite gotten over it as yet; I'm trying hard. . . .

NOTES

1. All four organizations were in Mississippi under the COFO arrangement. CORE and, to a lesser extent, SCLC and NAACP were in Louisiana; SNCC and SCLC made little bridgeheads into Alabama's Black Belt; SNCC was in southwest Georgia. The NAACP was virtually alone among the national organizations in Tennessee and Texas, and directed drives also in the other states. SCLC worked in a few places in Tennessee, Florida, Georgia, South Carolina, North Carolina, and Virginia. Similarly, SNCC had a few projects in Arkansas, South Carolina, and North Carolina, and CORE in Florida, including its resistant northern half, South Carolina, and North Carolina. The Urban League conducted a survey of Negro registration in Winston-Salem, North Carolina, and did some voter work in Fort Worth, Texas; Richmond, Virginia; and Louisville, Kentucky. Some of the larger local organizations outside the hard-core areas were: Voters of Texas Enlist (VOTE), an arm of the Texas coalition working mainly in east Texas; the statewide program of the Arkansas Voter Project; the Davidson County Independent Political Council in Nashville, Tennessee; the All Citizens Registration Committee in Atlanta, and a statewide organization of the same name, if not effectiveness; a Bibb County (Georgia) organization; and the Chatham County Crusade for Voters in Savannah, Georgia; the South Carolina Voter Education Project, a state-

wide organization, and a local group in Charleston; the Durham Committee on Negro affairs, the Citizens Committee of Wilson County, and local groups in Hatfield County, Warren County, Asheville, Winston-Salem, and Charlotte, and a joint project in Raleigh by the American Friends Service Committee and National Student Association, all in North Carolina; the Virginia Voters League, a statewide effort, the All Citizens Registration Committee of Northern Virginia, the Tidewater Voter Project in Norfolk, the Peninsula Coordinating Committee in Newport News, the Crusade for Voters in Richmond and local groups in Nansemond County, Suffolk, Portsmouth, Lynchburg, and Richmond, all in Virginia. Some of these had ties with the national organizations or heavy influence from their local affiliates.

2. J. H. Calhoun, an Atlanta Negro leader, in one of his reports in 1963 told of points upon which he said he and Randolph Blackwell, then VEP field director, agreed regarding registration efforts. One was that registration workers should *not* be paid. There isn't enough money, Mr. Calhoun said, and it discourages volunteers.

3. The only registration requirement in Arkansas at that time, apart from age and residence requirements, was payment of a poll tax. Voter workers spoke of "selling" the poll taxes, and people "buying" them to describe the process of registration.

4. *U.S. Commission on Civil Rights*, Jackson, Vol. 1, p. 78.

5. Fulton County in Georgia later was to allow night registration in Negro neighborhoods by Negro deputy registrars with good results, particularly in the Atlanta area.

6. She was later to become Mrs. Robb Burlage of Washington, D.C.

7. *U.S. Commission on Civil Rights*, Jackson, Vol. 1, p. 194.

8. Object lessons in intimidation lost some of the old power. In Quincy, Florida, Negro and white registration workers drove together and later ate together in a Negro restaurant. They were asked by police to leave the restaurant, and put in separate patrol cars and driven to the police station. No charges were made, and they were finally released. A crowd of some two hundred Negroes gathered. Mrs. Patricia Due of CORE, in charge of the drive, said the incident was a breakthrough in arousing interest in voting. A report from Hugh T. Love of CORE on Brownsville, Tennessee (Haywood County), in the western part of the state, gives insight: "Just a few years ago, Negroes of Brownsville lived in constant fear of the white man. A Negro dared not try to register to vote, or complain at city hall about unjust treatment. Vigilantes and Ku Klux Klansmen kept a veil of fear over the minds of Brownsville Negroes. But as the years went on and the new Negro sprang up, the clutches of fear began to loosen and the eyes of the Negro began to open. Brownsville Negroes began to retaliate. They started demonstrations to protest unjust treatment. Though not as successful as they should have been, these demonstrations told the Klansmen and vigilantes that fear no longer ruled the minds of the new Negro. There has been some opposition toward Negroes who have tried to register, but usually it is only a threat from some white man about what he is going to do to 'John' if he registers."

9. A wise Negro Southerner, an educator, said there is, even in the safest places, always a little touch of awareness, wariness. When you drive into the rural areas of the South, he said, it is strong, constant. You make mental balances—deciding whether an objective is worth the amount of risk and fear it entails. Civil rights workers talk of the fear, of the ways they overcame it, or learned to live with it. Some have war-front psychology about going into dangerous areas—the feeling that "it won't happen to me." One of the last reports received by VEP from southwest Georgia, in 1964, from two young men of the area, Sammy Mahone and Sammy Rushin, began: "There are still the same fears that have been imbedded in the

Negroes' minds for the past hundred years here, fear of losing their jobs, their credit, or fear of bodily harm to them which has happened before."

10. See C. Vann Woodward, *The Burden of Southern History* (Baton Rouge: Louisiana State University Press, 1960), particularly Chapter Eight; Silver, Chapter One. In "The Tragedy of Southern Leadership, 1820–1860," a paper read before the Fifth Annual Civil War Conference at Gettysburg College, Professor Silver said of the pre–Civil War days: "As it gained in power, the Southern majority protected itself by ruthlessly suppressing minority dissent within the section. When expedient, Southern rights associations and vigilance committees made their appearance. The threat of violence was usually sufficient and by 1860 thousands of moderate Southerners had departed from their native land or had acquiesced in helpless silence. This is not to say that a reign of terror prevailed in the immediate ante-bellum South but waves of pathological fear did sweep across the land whenever a crisis developed. The chief intellectual exercise of the time consisted of super-patriotic exhortations. . . ." The parallel in the ten years after 1954 was all too obvious, though less widespread and concerted. Woodward has noted a parallel, too, between the South's sudden destruction of dissent on slavery with the nation's clamp-down in the 1940's on criticism of capitalism and examination of its abuses, pointing out that in both instances there was unprecedented ferment and dissent just before the crackdowns.

11. A motel-keeper in a little Alabama town insisted on knowing the business connection of two newspaper reporters checking in late at night. His manner was enormously friendly; he was obviously a decent, harmless man. But he kept insisting. Finally, they asked why he wanted to know so much. "They want to know," he said in almost a whisper. "Who?" "The Klan. They won't bother y'all when they find out who you work for. But they'll bother me if I don't find out."

12. *U.S. Commission on Civil Rights,* Jackson, Vol. 1, p. 30.

13. This notion, perhaps tied to separation of church and state, crops up in various parts of the South, usually part of the credo of conservative Negro ministers. In 1966, it was being expressed by Jehovah's Witnesses Negro churches in several areas.

14. The widespread abuses of installment credit—reaching high into the middle class and far beyond the South—is another problem. At its rawest in the South, such abuse amounted to highway robbery. Automobile dealers figured frequently in the VEP reports as particularly adept. One report—out of Mississippi and based on the victim's version of things—went into the intricacies:

A Negro sharecropper bought a three-year-old car for $1,000 plus $500 carrying charge. He paid $1,370, and then missed one payment. The dealer seized the car, and without the owner's consent, repaired it while it was being held. The repair bill was $400. The white man with whom the Negro sharecropped refused to help him pay the car out, but bought him another, with money from the sharecropper's expected earnings, for $565. Thus the sharecropper lost his previous investment; his own money spent by the landowner would have saved it. The implication was that the landowner was in cahoots with the car dealer. The hapless sharecropper missed a payment on the second car, had it seized, and another $167 worth of repairs charged against him without his permission. He went to a finance company and borrowed money to get his car back, this at the usual high interest rates. Now he owed three different people for his one car, which was absolutely necessary transportation. On the way home, the "repaired" car broke down. It cost him another $25 to get it running again.

15. See James Agee, *Let Us Now Praise Famous Men* (Boston: Houghton-Mifflin

Co., 1941 and 1960). Also: Charles S. Johnson, Edwin R. Embree, W. W. Alexander, *The Collapse of Cotton Tenancy* (Chapel Hill: University of North Carolina Press, 1935).

16. The reports showed a particular loathing for the exploiters of the poor people and the swindlers who preyed on them. In a southwest Georgia report, one man was described who had paid installments for years every crop time, to come finally to own his own farm. But the white lady he had paid kept delaying bringing him the deed. And the next thing he knew, a white man came saying he had bought the land from the lady, and to get off. Such stories, repeated in countless variations through the reports, were unverified. This one may or may not have been true; it is a class of thing that did happen, and that is the main point. Hatred for a particular white or all whites by Negro Southerners is not in such a context difficult to imagine. The miracle was that there was not more, or that it was not more overt. Intimate and emotional knowledge of such things in the South was a driving force in the voter effort; this was its logic. To offer the vote to the most oppressed victims of the South's inequities was to enter their world. In the process, the vote, all of democratic theory, and perils to democracy were revealed.

17. There is something especially appalling about the reports and indications one sees (e.g., envelopes from a hard-core area are opened when the letters arrive) of tampering within the U.S. Post Office. Albany workers complained of phone-tapping, with a lot of clicking and whirring on the line. One of the authors of this book had the experience in Albany once, amid the usual clicking and whirring of a tapped phone, of having a voice cut in and curse him, apparently in criticism of the story he was dictating to his paper over long distance.

18. Part of this problem in the hard-core area was the lack of Negro lawyers or whites willing to take such cases. The 1964 Freedom Summer brought in volunteer lawyers from over the nation, giving badly needed representation for Negroes and civil rights clients, and forcing the white lawyers and white-run courts to more professional standards, if not to the rather basic responsibility of their profession, the defense of unpopular clients. The NAACP Legal Defense and Educational Fund, Inc., had all along worked in Mississippi. After 1964, it and the Lawyers Constitutional Defense Committee (which after notable work during the Freedom Summer became an arm of the American Civil Liberties Union) continued the work in Mississippi and other under-represented parts of the Black Belt. The Lawyers Committee for Civil Rights Under Law came into Mississippi during 1964 more as missionaries to the Mississippi bar than anything else, but subsequently developed a program similar to the other groups. The National Lawyers Guild was in Mississippi during 1964, and was in and out subsequently.

19. Americus, through 1965, was to remain restive. During SCLC demonstrations in 1965, a white man was shot to death. Two Negro men were charged in the death, one sentenced to life imprisonment, the other to five years. Out of the 1963 efforts, Negro voters increased from 300 to 600, and some intangible inroads were made against the fear: "I went down to register and my knees were shaking and I could hardly sign my name," a middle-aged Negro woman told a reporter. "But it was all right, and maybe now I can get up the nerve to vote."

20. The first mention of Mrs. Hamer was in a Ruleville report of December 3, 1962. It told of her being thrown off her plantation home for trying to register. "She is a very good singer and she can do most anything. While on the plantation she did all the book work for the boss man. She knew all the people on the place and they respect her and we feel that she will play a big part in getting people from the plantation to register." A January 1963 report told of her going to Indianola to see how

she did on the voter test. "Mrs. Hamer returned with joy in her eyes. She had passed."

21. These are battery-operated devices that produce a skin-searing electrical charge. Normally, they are used to steer cattle in slaughter houses. Their use on human beings—widespread among police in the hard-core South—is among racist indecencies closest to the concentration camp mentality.

22. Occasionally one finds, as when three Negroes were peppered with birdshot outside a voter registration office in Canton, Mississippi, in June 1963, arrests of white terrorists. A local paper told of arrests of a gang of young whites charged with vandalizing Negro churches where voter meetings were held in East Feliciana Parish, Louisiana: "Breaking a case usually gives an officer a feeling of pride and accomplishment but there was considerably less of such feeling in this case because the officer . . . determined that the culprits included his two sons. . . ."

23. Such testimony as this one from the VEP reports offers as valuable insight as exists into the souring of idealism and belief in America among the young radicals. When one knows that the judge in question was one of several ardent segregationists appointed by the Kennedy administration, it becomes easier to understand how liberals emerge as the source and target of much of the radical anger.

6)

The Struggle—
Jacob's Ladder

An exchange between the Reverend Theodore M. Hesburgh, president of Notre Dame and a member of the U.S. Commission on Civil Rights, and Dr. James W. Prothro of the University of North Carolina during the 1965 Commission hearings in Jackson, Mississippi, is suggestive of how difficult it was for America to grasp the meaning of the worst resistance in the South. Dr. Prothro, a political scientist who had done extensive research on Negro voting in the South,[1] had been explaining a study he had conducted for the commission on Negro teacher attitudes in four Mississippi counties.

COMMISSIONER HESBURGH—The thought has been crossing my mind that having had the opportunity of living under a dictatorship for three years at one point in my life when I was studying abroad, I find that fear in this society was perhaps the most corrosive element in the whole society.

And reading your report, it just crossed my mind that if this report were written about Nazi Germany or Fascist Italy or Communist Russia, it might make more sense.

I find it very hard to understand for a rather superior group in our society, teachers, whom we assume are more sophisticated . . . I find it hard to understand, I want to ask you this professional question: How can people who have such fear as expressed in a thing like this—asked if he would vote, he counts on help coming from the outside. Asked if he believes he will ever vote in the county, he says, "Not unless we get some help, outside pressure, protection. If I decide to vote I go down there and they might bomb my house. If I register they might do anything. I don't trust the law officials. I trust them about as much as I trust a mad dog." How can people who have this mentality expressed over and over possibly do a good job of raising future citizens?

DR. PROTHRO—It must be very difficult . . . I agree with you it is very difficult to imagine some of these counties existing in the United States.

COMMISSIONER HESBURGH—I must say I couldn't expect worse of some of the worst countries I know of. I mean this kind of attitude of citizens living within this country. And—

DR. PROTHRO—I think it is, sir, a local totalitarian system.

COMMISSIONER HESBURGH—But it seems to me that it creates an almost psychopathic situation for teachers who are supposed to bring youngsters up in a spirit of freedom in this county, and to try to give them some sense of free expression, responsibility of citizenship, a sense for law and order, some idea of the beauty of life that might be achieved through personal expression.

If the teachers themselves feel a complete lack of personal expression, even the most fundamental citizenship such as voting, it seems to me it will create for us a whole generation of youngsters who leave school with a kind of psychopathic fear that is not only unworthy of any kind of society, but most unworthy of the kind of society we profess in the United States. Do you agree with that?

DR. PROTHRO—I have the same concern. Yes sir . . ." [2]

Concerted Terror

There were not in the South—as one might have imagined from the outpourings of outrage—any mass executions; there were no systematized police machines of torture and brainwashing, not even any fully efficient police-state spying. The latter was in rudimentary stages; perhaps the old Southern failing of inefficiency entered in. That it did not go further (it did not, yet again, happen here) was surely in part due to all the telling about it, the freedom there was to tell of it, a strength still in the national will and institutions for freedom to stand a hard test. For in the South of the 1950's and first half of the 1960's, in the hard-core areas, Americans breathed as strongly as ever in the nation's history the stale, deadly air of tyranny—indeed, of totalitarianism. James W. Silver's book, *Mississippi: The Closed Society*, was the gravest warning. The danger was not confined to the state about which he wrote, though it was probably greatest there. It was, as his scholarship so well noted, a converging of old threads in Southern culture, long spun out and acknowledged, a repeat in a sense of the South's own nineteenth-century version of tyranny, the savage destruction of dissent and traditions of freedom in the build-up to the Civil War. But the danger seemed somehow more sinister in its mid-twentieth-century manifestations. Maybe this was only because humanity had crawled back deeper into the staleness of the cave of tyranny during the years since the Civil War, had explored its furthest reaches; men knew about Buchenwald this time.

As one goes over the mass of reports, official testimony and other documents of the denial of democracy in the hard-core areas, it is not so much the individual acts, the patterns repeating themselves in many places, over many years, that chills. It is the feel of concertedness that comes, the realization that not this individual registrar, or that sheriff, or just the Klan or the Citizens Councils but whole towns, whole counties —whole societies as controlled by whites—were involved. That was the frightening realization, the intellectual version of the fear. Southerners so involved would never, of course, have conceded that it was denial of democracy. Even by 1965, in the savagery of Selma, with all that the movement had said and done by then, the majority of white Southerners still seemed unaware that democracy was what the struggle was all about. Such blindness is terrifying, too. The South in the 1950's and early 1960's partook of the guilt of our age, the same sort of guilt that Germans of the Nazi era stand convicted of—the inability to perceive evil. The evil was not as great; racism had not gone to such lengths. But to muffle evil, the very evil to which you stand in silent accessory, as Hannah Arendt tried to say in *Eichmann in Jerusalem, A Report on the Banality of Evil* (New York: Viking Press, 1963), is at the crux of the dilemma of the modern world. To most whites in the hard-core areas, whether they battled the Negroes back or acquiesced in others' doing it without ever giving the matter a thought, the voter effort was not different from all the other unseemliness the movement had stirred up. It was just niggers trying to shove in where they didn't belong, where they had no right to be.

When it was most deadly, the resistance had as its organizational mode the Citizens Councils. These thrived mainly in the hard-core areas, mainly Mississippi, Alabama, and Louisiana. The most frightening thing about them was what they sought—respectability. "White Citizens Councils," wrote Samuel DuBois Cook in 1964, "sought, first of all, . . . a good public 'image.' To a significant degree, they were successful. Composed of prominent and responsible citizens—bankers, businessmen, public officials, and other politicians; doctors, lawyers , and other members of the upper and middle class, as well as farmers, laborers, and similar 'God fearing' ordinary people, councils represented the 'power structure' or 'establishment' of local communities and states. Indeed membership was a 'status symbol.'" [3] Again, it should be emphasized, this was not true of all Southern areas.

It was when respectable coercion began to crumble—in Mississippi during the Freedom Summer of 1964 and with the successful desegregation of public schools—that the uglier organizational forms, the Klans, the Americans for the Preservation of the White Race, the lynch mobs, and the free-lance shotgun and fire-bomb murderers emerged at high noon in the worst areas for a final showdown. Their full emergence signaled the defeat of the Citizens Council strategy. For these others had been in the shadows all the while; their violence, which the councils claimed to eschew, had been going on all the while. But the councils saw violence, or the constant threat of it, as just one of many weapons of terror (their preference probably economic coercion), and not the reason for existence. By the end of 1965, the councils seemed dormant, and the Klan was being investigated by the House Un-American Activities Committee—the remnants of the old regime dying not with any dignity or glory, but appropriately, before klieg lights, in a last-act scene from the theater of the absurd. The scene was the least reassuring of a number of disturbing phenomena in the South and the nation, however, to those who genuinely cherish freedom. The John Birch Society, meanwhile, seemed the most likely next organizational mode for the resistance, or for those of it who had not overnight become apostles of opportunistic racial moderation.

At any rate, the different aspects of the terror that we have described one by one seldom came one by one. In the worst areas, it was concerted, a galvanized, organized onslaught of total community resources against the voter effort. This is the explanation, the setting for references to the voter effort as guerrilla warfare, the forces working for democracy as an underground. Medgar W. Evers, the Mississippi leader who was murdered by a shot in the back, had described in 1955 the way Citizens Councils combatted democracy. He cited Humphreys County, where "the employer would have a [voters] list and if he found this person's name . . . he'd say, 'We can't employ you until you get your name off this list.' By this method they knocked down registration (from 126 Negroes) to about 90 names, and they started getting down to the hard-core and other types of pressures were used. They'd come tell them, 'You've lived in this community for a long time and if you want to stay here in peace, you'd better get your name off this list.' After they started making personal visits, the Negroes gave in to the extent that there are now only 35 left." [4]

The order was reversed in Ruleville in 1962. The voter program was proving effective. "This," said a report, "the Citizens Council knew. Then the intimidation started. The shooting and arrests and other harassments weren't enough to stop the people because they had lost enough fear to continue their efforts. Then came the firings and economic reprisals. This was the breaking point in Ruleville. We had to turn our efforts from voter registration to relocating families and finding funds to sustain people and get them back on [government food] commodities."

It could be like a barrage. "Negro voter applicants and civil rights workers are constantly intimidated, harassed, arrested, prosecuted, and subjected to constant economic, political, and physical reprisal by private citizens, public officials, and sometimes by businesses," said a report from CORE in Louisiana in October 1964. Earlier that year, Ronnie Moore had cited closed registrar offices, firing of school bus drivers and book mobile librarians and others, delay of a canning company to let contracts, and jailings in the state. The "worst parish of all" was described: "Our only contact is under constant harassment by the local busters, and the KKK is very active." Another parish, Leander Perez' Plaquemines, saw CORE give up a just-begun voter effort in the spring of 1964 when "Perez began cracking down." The opposition was overwhelming and "quite hazardous to say the least." A swamp prison awaited civil rights workers, its horrors including poisonous snakes all about.

In Georgia, the fate of one man in a Terrell County community who was among the first to work with the voter effort is illustrative. Whites refused to weigh corn he wanted to buy for his hogs. Whites wanted him to swear out a warrant and publish a statement in the local paper against SNCC workers. The white owner of a gas station made him sit when no other cars were there for half an hour before selling him gas. The mayor instructed his Negro hired hands not to go near his house. The man had said when SNCC first came, "Go to every house." The people would respond. Now he said, "There's nair a man in Bronwood with me." In Selma, Alabama, the Citizens Council advertised for members in the local newspaper on the promise it would prevent voter registration of Negroes, among other disturbances. There were two years of mounting, concerted opposition to the voter drive in the city before it finally exploded.

One of the natural consequences of the concerted action was increasing Negro anger and retaliation. It is perhaps easier to forgive and love with redemptive non-violent grace the lone individual bent on your destruction than it is to do so for a whole society.

In the fall of 1963, the Reverend Joseph Carter of West Feliciana Parish, Louisiana, refused to be bluffed out of registering and sued the parish for $100,000 on the issue. Finally, with the Justice Department looking on, crosses burning, a white mob standing with hands joined before the front door of the courthouse, he got in the back door to become the first Negro registered there since 1902. A few other Negroes followed his brave example, and there were beatings and threats and more cross burnings. Pleading for federal protection which didn't come, Ronnie Moore described the parish as an armed camp, saying, "Negroes have vowed to shoot on sight any white face which appears on their property after dark."

"Fear," began a CORE report in September 1964, "seems to be the greatest disadvantage of conducting a voter registration drive in Jonesboro . . ." In 1965, the Deacons for Defense and Justice, the first organized self-defense unit of Negroes in the South, were fighting the forces behind the fear there and in other Louisiana parishes. The same idea and imitations sprang up over the Black Belt.

Strategy Against Fear

The civil rights organizations, going into these worst of the hard-core counties, some where no Negroes had registered since Reconstruction, were well aware that the fear was what they had most to fight, and the very real terrorism behind it. "You cannot," wrote Jack Chatfield of SNCC in southwest Georgia, "come around and break a world in two. You cannot forget the force of two hundred years." But this is what they set out to do—in Mississippi, Alabama, Louisiana, southwest Georgia, and the other areas of resistance. They might be, as two CORE workers in Louisiana were, arrested the first night they got to a town and be taken to the city limits and told "never to return on penalty of death, or something like that." In this case they sent another worker, posing as an insurance salesman.

The "atrocities" likely to occur in a rural campaign will cause the urban people to turn out in indignation, said one of the earliest 1962 voter proposals. Said another: "Whatever the apparent procedure, purging or inflating of voting lists, economic warfare, police brutality, etc., all attempts to nullify the right to vote among Negroes have aimed at psychological enslavement which has increased in effectiveness throughout the years. The Student Nonviolent Coordinating Committee intends to deal with this grand historical strategy on the same level which causes it to be effective. We propose to engage in a battle for minds." A year later, the language and expectations were more modest: "Many of the registration work activities in Mississippi are the same as those in southwest Georgia; especially similar is the need for tedious canvassing—a job which is not just leafleting, but spending hours with potential registrants convincing them that being a citizen is worth risking one's life for. Similar, too, is the need to deal with harassment calmly and patiently as part of the day's work."

The early proposal for southwest Georgia discussed selection of specific counties as part of the strategy against fear. Albany was chosen because it was the most advanced town in the area, a crossroads, a symbol for miles around. Lee and Terrell counties, nearby, were chosen for the opposite reason; they were among the worst around. Terrell, with 48 of 8,500 Negroes registered in 1962 (compared with 2,810 of 4,700 whites), had been the subject of the first "victorious" suit brought by the Justice Department under the 1957 Civil Rights Act. County officials had been enjoined from interfering with voter rights. "Terrible Terrell." It and Lee "must be obliterated as symbols," wrote Charles Sherrod, leader of the SNCC southwest Georgia voter project. Worse than either of these was Baker County, nearby. Bad Baker. No hope in Baker. "It would," wrote Sherrod, "be the last symbol to smash down. . . ."

It was to be a long road. "Baker beckons," he wrote a year later, in 1963. In July 1965 an Associated Press story told of two Negroes, who had been directing a voter registration picket line, being beat up by whites in front of the Baker County courthouse in Newton. One of them was Charles Sherrod. He had finally gotten there. A year and a half after the Voting Rights Act, Baker and surrounding counties were still considered hard-core territory. Like other counties in the area, Baker had for years been given over to hunting-plantation holdings of wealthy Southerners and Northerners. Mr. Sherrod was still there in 1967, married to a young woman of Baker County. A gentle man, he never attained the national attention that such a figure as Robert Moses did. (Moses was so dismayed by it, he changed his name to Parris and left Mississippi.)

Two items in the VEP reports tell much about Mr. Sherrod. One is a discussion he wrote of his torment at having to enforce discipline—"the attempt to respect the human dignity of people with whom you work on the one hand, and the attempt to get work done effectively against over-whelming odds on the other." The other item was a report describing how some Negro teen-age boys took one of the precious, broken-down old cars so vital to Mr. Sherrod's work out on a joy ride and turned over four times, demolishing the car. Policemen brought the news to him and asked him if he wanted to swear out a warrant for arrest of the kids. Charles Sherrod shook his head immediately, sadly—no.

"Now this is not to say that after Baker falls, there will be no more violence," his 1963 report went on. "I am speaking of solidified images in the minds of people down in this section of the country. There will be no more 'unbearable Baker.' People would not be afraid to go through there from miles around."

The fear dictated another necessity with ramifications for the future, the emphasis on youth. It was a youthful movement everywhere, but in some of the hard-core areas, it was almost exclusively so, and later the older leaders were to resent this, and assert new authority. In 1962, in Mississippi, Robert Moses wrote, "We can't count on adults. Very few who 'have the time' and are economically independent of the white man are willing to join the struggle, and are not afraid of the tremen-dous pressure they will face. This leaves the young people to be the organizers, the agents of social and political change. . . . They operate at extreme disadvantage; they suffer from the most backward educa-tional system in the United States;[5] they very seldom are free to work in their own home towns because of the pressures brought to bear on their parents and/or their relatives . . . They have little knowledge of procedures and skills involved in writing newsletters, press releases, reports, etc., so their ability to analyze and report on their activities is limited; they do not have a functioning adult structure to provide a framework for their operations. Such structures as exist are usually paper organizations with no active program . . . capable of implementing. It is a sign of hope that we have been able to find young people to shoulder the responsibility for carrying out the voting drive. They are the seeds of change. . . ."

Part of the strategy against fear also was that the voter effort was interracial, from the beginning in all but Mississippi, and there, of course, later. And this in areas where the sight of a Negro and white on equal footing walking together—let alone living in the same house together—was a violence-provoking affront to most whites. "We have for some time now been in and out of these counties, black and white together," wrote Charles Sherrod. "Many of the people are so afraid that they will not open the door to us, but that is the price of fear. These same people who are afraid when we come, black and white together, are afraid when we come just black. But images are prone to be re-enforced and generalized; we hope this will happen. They will somehow get used to seeing black and white together as they have become used to the separation of the groups. Then too, there is the idea that as products of the system, the Negro in the South has been trained to react in a certain way to a white man. This is well known. The question is what psychological basis is there for believing that told by a white man to go register, the Southern Negro would go? . . . Our opinion is that we can fight the system with every justifiable instrument at our disposal." [6]

Mass meetings were important in the strategy. They meant more than pep rallies. They were an exercise in construction of group attitudes and in group therapy. "It is here," said a report, "that we hold soul searching sessions. It is repeated over and over again that it is not shameful to admit fear, but rather a sign of maturity—the first step. This is done in the group and each person understands in time (intellectually or by personal identification and acceptance of being free to admit the developed fears from their youth) . . . The acknowledgement of fear, separation, and inaction among the Negro population becomes the first step to courage, unity, and action." There was at the meetings an attempt to "relate the relevance of the Christian gospel" to which the people were "usually highly sensitive." Here, too, registration was first broached—rather than in the personal confrontations of canvassing. "We come together in a group," Mr. Sherrod wrote, "and there we lay before the people the reasons that voter registration is the most important activity in their community today . . . They come out slow and hesitantly. They are not pushed. Later, the people who continually come to the meetings are questioned individually if necessary and then pulled out in the meeting [to tell specific fears of registering]. This is a very sensitive point of development for the community." The meetings were held in such places as "St. Peter's Rock Baptist Church" (Pine Bluff, Arkansas) and "Old Piney Grove Baptist Church" (Lee County, Georgia). A list of the church names would be a glossary of folk poetry.

One report described a voter mass meeting in Albany during the period of its despair, following the failures of all its many fervent direct-action mass meetings. It opened with singing by students and two hundred adults, the songs led by seven- and nine-year-old girls. One couldn't see them, so small they were behind the rostrum, but they were certainly heard. "Ain't gonna let nobody turn me round." Then:

Deacon Bruner got up to speak for Terrell and the audience hushed. Teen-age boys leaned forward and old women urged the soft-spoken and shy deacon on, "Take your time, son." "We're with you, son." Agnew James spoke for Lee County and gave one of the tightest and most moving statements I've ever heard him make. People stood for him as he came forward, giving him a type of respect that only the battle-worn can get. The people of Albany knew the kind of leaders they were listening to . . . Then Don Harris led Mama Dolly [7] through a standing crowd up to the platform. Standing tiny and straight, she told the audience to stand up as mothers and fathers for what they believed . . . Those Albany people sang "We Shall Overcome" longer and harder than they had in a long time.

The other methods were the same as in the easier areas—yet with a difference. Voter registration classes would emphasize ways to overcome trickery. Or they might consist, as Jack Chatfield reported from southwest Georgia, of a worker reading the U.S. Constitution to people to prove to them they had the right to register. Canvassing was far more time-consuming, workers "often spending afternoons with one or two individuals getting to know them and creating the feelings of trust and confidence which are the necessary first steps for registrants. And then going back again and again until the person will finally come to a meeting or citizenship class or go to the registrar," as one report put it. Canvassing involved doing chores—cutting wood, even ironing—for the reluctant, involving delicate decisions as to whether an afternoon's work would win a housewife to mass meeting attendance.

There was always a flavor, a style to the work. Frank Smith of SNCC, who liked to write about himself in the third person, was proud of his "speaker's bureau" in Holly Springs, Mississippi. "Smith," he wrote, "used a gradual, depth approach to the community. On Sunday morning, he would disperse all of the speakers to the churches and then he would choose a church. After the speech and sermon, Smith would go home with one of the members of the church, have dinner, and have the member show him around the county and to some of the 'most likely' persons. This was very effective for it reached the point where Smith could walk downtown on Saturday and all the people would know or have heard about him which saved him some of the problems of explanation." Of course, he noted, "it did not take the sheriff and police force long to discover that Smith was in town, too."

The need to get influential people into these hard-pressed voter drives was crucial. They were needed to encourage and reassure the average run of people. Frank O'Neal spoke his joy, after many visits, of getting three important families to a meeting in Lee County. "This is typical of the slow stages by which we work. A few more visits, a few more meetings, and we may expect a few more registered voters." There were continued contacts with such organizations as the Negro units of the American Legion and the Masons, the quilting clubs, the mission societies, the PTAs.

Communication was ever a problem in the rural areas. In southwest Georgia, an elaborate grapevine for announcing meetings, news, and the like was set up on the school buses that went to all the reaches of the counties. The voter effort seldom got the publicity that direct action did. But it developed some little mimeographed community newspapers, performing—for the first time in many Negro communities—all the functions of a responsible press.

The voter workers came to recognize almost predictable cycles in the development of a program. Charles Sherrod wrote in April 1963: "Lee and Terrell are doing better. Sumter is booming. We have begun this pace in the counties before but it seems that every time, some violent reaction from the white community unfurls to slow down our activity. I hope that this time we will have reached the point at which the people will register in spite of apparent dangers. And so, possibly, when the word is heard to run for cover, they will stand together." Robert Moses had written in February of that same year, after violence had slowed down Mississippi drives:

We know this plateau by now; we have had to crawl over it in McComb City, Amite and Walthall Counties, Hattiesburg, Greenwood, and Ruleville; you dig into yourself and the community and prepare to wage psychological warfare; you combat your own fears about beatings, shootings, and possible mob violence; you stymie by your own physical presence, the anxious fear of the Negro community seeded across town from paneled pine and white sunken sink [of the white community] to windy kitchen floors and rusty old stoves [of the Negro community], that maybe you *did* come only to boil and bubble and then burst, out of sight and sound; you organize, pound by pound, small bands of people who gradually focus in the eyes of Negroes and whites as people tied up in that mess; you create a small striking force capable of moving out when the time comes, which it must, whether we help it or not.

Here is how Charles McLaurin described the cycle as it operated in Ruleville:

The people was having a good time singing freedom songs, the little children could be heard singing, "Ain't going to let nobody turn me round," and "We Shall Overcome." Everybody was talking about Freedom.

And then:

The shooting. On the night of September 10, 1962, about 8 or 8:30, three shots were fired into the home of Mr. Joe McDonald, the house where we were staying. The car that the shots were fired from went on and fired several shots into the Sissons' home that hit two young girls who was there to get ready to start school. The FBI men that came didn't seem to be looking for the person or persons that did the shooting, instead they asked the people if we were asking them for money. And if they thought we did the shooting. The FBI did more to frighten people than to help them.

The community after the shooting died. We could not get a person to come to the meetings, they would not let us come into their homes, they were afraid to be seen in our presence, or to let us write letters to their homes. They said if we had not come to Ruleville, all this wouldn't have happened. So most everybody in the community was down on us and we had to do something to get them on our side, so we went from house to house asking them about everyday problems, we would carry them to the store downtown, help pick cotton and cut wood . . . [This and assistance in getting government surplus food soon restored confidence, and Mr. McLaurin closed his report:] More and more people are coming by to talk to us, so you see we are not only voter registration workers but lawyers, welfare workers, preachers, and anything the people need. All this helps us to work with them and when we work with them, they will work with us (meaning go down and register plus helping their friends down). . . .[8]

Heroes

The fight against fear had known its moments of small success from the beginning. In Ruleville, five people were found willing to try to register the very first week. When meetings were held in the Terrell County tent in 1962, after the churches were burned, forty people were willing to come. Ralph Allen returned to Terrell after a year's absence in the spring of 1963 and wrote of a new "tone of feeling." There had been harassment all year, a bombing of headquarters in the fall, but in February of 1964 Negroes dared to picket in Dawson, the county seat, urging the vote. There was "cursing, steaming, blowing" from the whites, but "they took it." In the spring of that year, 1964, 238 Negroes voted and helped defeat a school superintendent they were against, and almost beat their old enemy, the sheriff. A report said, "Terrell is now a place of much hope." Such progress was repeated across the Black Belt.

In one of the 1963 reports from Alabama was a snapshot. In the slightly tilted perspective of amateur photography, it showed nine Negroes in a formal pose, three rows, the two in the front row kneeling—a big-shouldered young man with a small rain-hat on, an attractive young woman holding a file folder. Three older men wearing farmer's clothes were on the next row, and a young woman in what looks like her Sunday best. On the third row were two more men in farmer's clothes flanking a tall young man in a white shirt wearing a necktie. In ink with the picture was a note: "This is one of the pictures I took before we went down. (Front row left to right): James Austin, Mrs. Colia Lafayette. (Second row, l., r.): Monroe Pettway, Mrs. Nancy Brown, Hazzel McLeod, Timothy Miles. (Third row, l., r.): Clinton Pettway, Lonnie Brown, Frank Holloway." Six of them, accompanied by Mrs. Lafayette and Mr. Holloway from the Selma SNCC office, were the first Negroes in fifty years to dare to attempt to register to vote in Wilcox County, Alabama, where Negroes outnumbered whites, and no Negroes were registered. Their faces in the snapshot (just "before we went down") reflected the solemnity, and danger, and dignity of their under-taking.

When they got to the courthouse, they talked to the circuit clerk, the probate judge, and a former sheriff. None of these gentlemen could say where the registrar might be, or when his office might be open. They went back home to Gee's Bend, determined to try again. The report said: "A Mr. Brown, native of the county, a young Korean War veteran, emerged as the leader who had started voter education classes. He is very dynamic." He was the young man of the white shirt and tie in the snapshot. The report quoted him as saying, "I'm going to die one of these days anyway, so I might as well die for something worth-while." Three years later, he was a candidate in the same area for the state senate of Alabama, unsuccessful that first time, but nevertheless a candidate, and alive.

Frank Holloway in February 1963 described the first visit of Selma workers to Gee's Bend (also called Boykin), an all-Negro town in Wilcox County, fifty-one miles from Selma. Thirty men in their work clothes were present at a meeting in a little church. There was some talk of danger that whites would break it up, but they were "there and singing." They had come to discuss a crisis over the Negro high school. They had been told by someone, presumably white school officials, that they would have to raise money to fix up the old school building. These were Negroes who earned about twenty dollars a week. The report said, "After having discussed the problem, they all agreed that they wanted their children to get an education, and therefore they agreed to tax themselves $25 for the year. This would be paid by September." Then they discussed voter registration. Ten volunteered to try. Others walked out at mention of the subject. "Many of the men present appeared to be unable to read or write, but most of them had the freedom spirit." Wilma Dykeman and James Stokely, in *Seeds of Southern Change: The Life of Will Alexander*, discussed the Gee's Bend area as an example of primitive living conditions discovered during the New Deal that shocked the nation. Mr. Holloway's report said:

This area up until [the 1930's] was the most backward area in Alabama, and probably the United States. The Negroes in Gee's Bend were living in the most primitive style. They knew nothing of running water, gas, or electricity, or automation in any form. They were not [able] to come out of Gee's Bend. They were born, they lived, and they died in Gee's Bend. . . . It seems that all [actually, it is nearly all] of the Negroes in Gee's Bend are named Pettway. In fact, Gee's Bend also used to be known as Pettway Bend [after the owner of the land]. During this time the Negroes . . . did not live in houses, but they actually lived in little primitive huts. The federal government became aware of this situation and went into Gee's Bend and built a few houses, barns, etc. The Negro farmers were given 40 years to pay back the federal government. The situation today in Gee's Bend isn't much better. It is still a very backward place. Very few of the Negroes come out. Most of the children do not attend school, because they have to work in the field . . . Most of the people know very little about what goes on outside Gee's Bend.

Its population was 700 in 1965. Dr. Martin Luther King, Jr., during the Selma campaign in 1965, traveled to Gee's Bend and spoke in a little church there lighted by a naked bulb, heated by a pot-bellied stove. Tears rolled down his cheeks as he looked out at the people and told them: "I came over here to Gee's Bend to tell you, you are *somebody.* You may not know the difference between 'you does' and 'you don't,' but you are as good as any white person in Wilcox County." The old ladies with head scarves knotted in front nodded, and said, "It's so. It's so." In 1966, voter registration for many had been achieved, a "movement" organization existed, and "self-help" programs were under way.

Mr. Anderson T. Thomas had worked on a plantation near Ruleville most of his life, for thirty years. In January 1963 he told of a thing that happened to him: "I have worked for Mr. L. all this time and he never said a thing about nothing I did. We would talk and things seemed to be swell between us." But on November 29 his wife had applied to register to vote. In several conversations, the plantation owner's son urged him to have his wife go back and take her name off the rolls of those applying to register. Otherwise, the family would have to leave the plantation. "At this time," Mr. Thomas said, "thinking of my family and how they would live, I asked my wife to go down and take her name off the book, but she would not do it. Later I began to wonder why it was so important to take a name off the books. Why would a man I have worked for almost all my life make so much noise about a person going to register? Then one of the fellows came to my house and explained things to me. I then apologized to my wife for having asked her to withdraw her name." The next time the owner's son came, Mr. Thomas told him no, even though the owner's son promised him anything he wanted if he would do that one thing. Six months later, Mr. Thomas and his family were destitute.

There were many other nameless heroes. Some of the names are told in the VEP reports. Agnew James, who was president of the Lee County movement in Georgia and lost his job and many of his friends and had his home shot into; James Mays, who lost his teaching job and finally had to move to Mississippi, working for the National Share-croppers Fund, though his family had one of the largest farms in Lee County; Wilbert Henderson, who was the man who had all the pressure put on him in Bronwood to renounce the voter effort, but said he "would never do a thing like that, because I know what you are doing is right"; Mr. and Mrs. Joe McDonald of Ruleville, who took the SNCC workers into their home and then had bullets fired into it. "Many times the mayor told Mr. Joe to get us out of his house or he would have real trouble," a report said, "but Mr. Joe stood his ground, and after losing his job hauling laborers, he would not put us out, plus he would speak up for us."

Interviews by one of the authors with upwards of a hundred of the young people in Selma during the height of the voter demonstrations there brought from virtually every one of them the same answer to the question, "What do you want out of all this?" It was the single word, "Freedom." And what was freedom? Almost to a boy and girl (and some were as young as seven and eight), they began listing the ingredients of opportunity: decent schooling and housing; better jobs for their parents. Few of them ventured into abstractions. Della Simpson, fourteen, a ninth-grader, slender and tall, had marched out of the church in nearby Marion, Alabama, on the night in February 1965 when state troopers beat the marchers back into the church and a Negro demonstrator was shot to death. She was one of those hit by the troopers' clubs. "I didn't think it would happen to me," she said. "But I would do it again." What did the movement mean to her? "There are many poor people who need help. I want to help them out—maybe build a children's home for orphans. I live in a community where there are lots of poor people. They need clothes and food. In the winter they walk around barefooted."

And there were many other brave people. Sam Block's report in October 1963 on the first mass meeting in Belzoni, Mississippi, said: "Present was Reverend Lee's wife who told me that she was so glad to know that we had finally made it back to Belzoni, Mississippi, to carry on where her husband had left off. I realized that . . . her husband was killed in Belzoni because of being active in voter registration activities back in 1956, and nothing had been done about the killing in those many years." An old man, eighty-six or eighty-seven years old, at the same meeting, told him, "If you are here to stay, we are with you, not behind you, but with you all the way."

The Fear Overcome

The two outstanding facts about the worst resistance of the 1962–64 voter effort were these—how very bad the resistance really was, and how, nevertheless, the fear by many was overcome. The resistance and the fear were still out in the open in the voter efforts of 1966 and 1967. Apathy, in the deeper meanings we have explored, remained. An answering anger and threat of retaliatory violence brooded. And the way that the fear was overcome points one way toward fuller citizenship and selfhood for all Negro Southerners.

A voter registration meeting, one more of the many, was held on the night of July 25, 1962, at the Mount Olive Baptist Church in Sasser, Georgia, in Terrell County.[9] The church was wooden and small, with three tiers of wooden benches which looked, some of them, handmade, and the floor was unfinished pine. Behind the pulpit was a painting of Jesus, and a framed photograph of some local Negro patriarch, bearded and old-fashioned, and on the wall to the left of the pulpit hung a calendar with a picture of President Kennedy large on it, and small around him, pictures of all the previous presidents of the United States. Charles Sherrod, a thin-faced, sensitive, brown-skinned young man, sat at the piano, hitting bass notes randomly as the crowd slowly came in. A big Negro man in overalls sat to the right of the pulpit near the front with his head resting on his big farmer's hand, the other hand thrust across the top of the pew ahead. Two other men were on a front row, and behind them were a young woman in a sleeveless black blouse and yellow skirt, and an adolescent girl, and a little girl with pigtails. As the rows slowly, in near silence, filled, an old woman settled herself down with a blanket around her shoulders on this summer's night, a straw cap on her head. There were middle-aged men and women, some in family groups, and young men and women, and teenagers and children, a sparse little grouping, not half filling the church, perhaps thirty in all when the meeting started. The crowd was smaller than usual, Mr. Sherrod said. It was never very large, but it was smaller than usual because there had been a warning from the whites that the meeting would be broken up tonight. Heat lightning flashed in the dark out the open window.

They began their meeting with the song, "Pass Me Not O Gentle Savior," and they said the Lord's Prayer. A car horn blew outside. A few more Negroes continued coming in. The young white woman with SNCC, Miss Penelope Patch, eighteen, a Swarthmore student from New Jersey, came in, blonde, baby-faced. Mr. Sherrod led them in reciting, "The Lord is my shepherd . . . Yea, though I walk through the valley of the shadow of death, I will fear no evil . . ." A car door slammed outside. Others slammed. Mr. Sherrod began another Bible passage. He stopped it, and said in a quiet voice, "They are standing just outside now. If they come in, I'm going to read this over again." The voices of the whites out there could be heard. "And whom," Mr. Sherrod read, "He called among them, He also justified . . . He also glorified . . . If God be for us, who will be against us? . . ." Ralph Allen, another white on the SNCC staff, came in almost running, found a place, sat down, breathing hard.

Then about fifteen white men of Sasser moved into the rear of the church, and stood across the back, one in a deputy's uniform, a Terrell County patch on the shoulder. The church was silent. "If God be for us, who will be against us?" Mr. Sherrod's soft voice almost sang the words, and went on, apparently improvising: "Who is he that condemneth? . . . We are counted as sheep for the slaughter . . ." Then he began praying: "Into Thy hand do we commend our minds and souls and our lives every day . . ." The sheriff of Terrell County, back there in the back, seventy-one years old, round-shaped and rough looking, not in uniform, wearing glasses, closed his eyes and bowed his head.

"We've been abused so long," Mr. Sherrod's prayer went on, and the Negroes grunted and murmured assent in the pauses. "We've been down so long." Amen. "All we want is for our white brothers to understand that Thou who made us, made us all . . ." Uh-huh. "And in Thy sight, we are all equal . . ." Uh-huh. Amen. "Forgive us for evil in our hearts. Forgive us for pride to look at others and say they sin . . . We aren't praying for safety from the storms of life. We are praying for strength to go through the storms of life . . ." Amen. "And, oh Lord, we pray for love . . ." Uh-huh. Amen. "The love that allows us to stand up to our adversaries and love them despite the evil they do to us. . . ."

Then he led them in the Lord's Prayer, and then, with the whites all in their silent row still standing behind, the Negroes began to sing, faces calmer now, voices weak at first, but gaining strength: "We are climbin' Jacob's lad-der," with a slow, heavy beat. They sang several verses, "Ev'ry round goes high-er, high-er . . . Climbers, climbing Jacob's ladder . . . Sinner, do you love my Jesus? . . . If you love Him, why not serve Him," and in the midst of it, the whites turned and walked out of the church to stand about outside, and the singing, with none looking back to see that they were gone, suddenly rang out louder, faster— victorious: "Rise! Shine! Give God your glory, glory! . . ."

Lucius Holloway, chairman of the Terrell County voter drive, began presiding, and when the sheriff, Z. T. (Zeke) Mathews, and another sheriff, Fred Chappell of nearby Sumter County, and two Terrell deputies,[10] one with a side-arm on his belt and one brandishing a two-foot-long flashlight, re-entered the church, heavy-footed on the wooden floor, Brother Holloway told them, "Everybody is welcome. This is a voter registration meeting . . ."

Sheriff Mathews said, "I have great respect for a religious organization. But my people are disturbed—they're getting disturbed about these secret meetings . . ."

Then followed an incredible performance by the whites, with Sheriff Mathews standing before three white newspaper reporters [11] on the front row, justifying to them why it was necessary to look in on the meeting. People of the town, he said, were upset. They wanted to know what might be going on in these meetings. He was here investigating because he was afraid, he said, that otherwise there might be violence.

"We are," Sheriff Mathews said, "a little fed up with this registering business. Negras down here have been happy for a hundred years, and now this has started. We want our colored people to live like they've been living. There was never any trouble before all this started. It's caused great dislike between colored and white."

The deputies demanded names of Negroes in attendance, and wrote them down. One of the deputies called out, asking if any "outsiders" were needed to get Negroes registered in Terrell County. There was silence. Finally one voice said, "Yes."

Sheriff Mathews told Ralph Allen, "Ralph, I'm going to have to ask you to stay out of this county until this thing quiets. I can't protect you."

"There's not a nigger here that needs help from somebody from Massachusetts to register and vote," one of the deputies said to Mr. Allen, staring at him with great hostility, the hate stare. They smirked at Miss Patch. "Who's she over there?" "She's one of the coordinators."

A deputy, taking the name of an older Negro man, pointed to the whites and said, "They'll be gone week after next. You'll still be here."

Sheriff Mathews talked most of all. He told of his benefactions to Negroes. "I never turned one down in my life. I've tried to help 'em. I've helped more colored people than any man in the South."

The talk kept up, developing arguments about technicalities of registration procedure, and more rough talk from the whites, the whites dispersed around the church, confronting little groups of the Negroes. The Negroes began humming, as the white men kept haranguing them, the movement's "We Shall Overcome." The sheriff was up front talking when the humming became words, "We shall overcome some day," and the whites retreated then, to the back of the church, the song continuing.

"Some of these niggers down here," one of the deputies said, going up the aisle, "had just as soon vote for Khrushchev or Castro. . . ."

"I'm on my way to Freedom Land," they sang next, with hand claps. Then they conducted their meeting with the local whites—six citizens having joined the law officers—standing in the rear. Various workers gave reports, including James Mays, who told of progress in Lee County, of how voting would help make peace on earth and good will toward men here in America. A story was told of a beating, another of a poor family with many children and no work for the father. Finally the whites moved on out, back into the yard.

The little crowd in the church stood and joined hands in a circle and sang, "We shall overcome . . ." Fear had come back into the church. Now they had to walk out of it into the Southern night, where the whites were waiting. But the song grew stronger, and very loud on the verse, "We are not afraid . . ."

Mr. Sherrod prayed once more, loud enough to be heard by the whites outside the door: "As we come to the close of this meeting, we thank Thee. Hear our white brothers trying to understand themselves, explain themselves. May we be able to communicate to them what we are trying to do. Which is not to destroy, but to build a community where all can live in self-respect and human dignity." The Negroes all the while hummed, "We shall overcome" in the background, still in their circle, the little girl in pigtails looking up at the adults holding her hands.

There was no violence that night to the little band.[12] A few nights later, their church, with Jesus and the American presidents on the walls, along with two other churches, was burned to the ground. But there was never any question in anyone's mind who had won there, and that was the way the South was won. Eventually it might be the way the gains of victory would be consolidated.

NOTES

1. See *Negroes and the New Southern Politics* by Donald R. Matthews and Dr. Prothro (New York: Harcourt, Brace & World, Inc., 1966).

2. *U.S. Commission on Civil Rights*, Jackson, Vol. 1, pp. 211–212.

3. "Political Movements and Organizations," in the *Journal of Politics*, February 1964, p. 155.

4. Margaret Price, "The Negro Voter in the South," published by the Southern Regional Council, 1957, p. 12.

5. Here in its entirety is a report from such a youngster in Greenwood: "I canvassed, while I was canvassing we discussed that the problems of some of the Negro race are afraid and do not understand their rights as being citizens simply because all their lives they have been taught that the Negro race isn't as good as any other race in the South which in most cases that's true."

6. The mind of the movement, with such stark realism in its idealism, and especially the youthful wing's, could be the subject of a great study. The courageous struggle to be black and white together where it was most dangerous gave way, when it became less dangerous, to something close to "if you're white, get back, get back . . ." A southwest Georgia report from a white worker in 1962 said: "The power structure (political and economic leaders, newspapers, sheriffs) say that they have nothing against Negroes registering; it's just that the good white citizens ain't used ta havin' white and colored mix . . . As a SNCC worker, the only contact I've had with whites have been hostile ones. On the top of their minds is the accusation that we're down here just to have sexual relations with Negroes. They get this point across in many ways—none of which bears repetition." The old Southern truth that sexual terror and guilt are at the base of segregation winds its way through the voter reports. Liaisons of staunch segregationist whites with Negroes are apparently still common gossip in the Black Belt, judging from the reports. One told of the reception at a Negro church service of a Negro woman known to live with a white man. The worker reporting was a Northern Negro: "What surprised me about [her] presence was that she was accepted with so little surface consternation, although careful observation reveals that she is handled in much the same way in which the simple-minded and the drunks are dealt with." He added: "I am convinced that if we could understand the complexities of such relations as these, we could understand

the mind of the South." A part of it, anyhow, and of that of all humanity, one might add.

7. "Mama Dolly" Raines was the Negro woman with whom voter workers in Lee County lived. A December 1962 report spoke of her attendance at a voter meeting where she "spoke most movingly of her new fervor in the cause." Another report from a young Northern white woman told of coming down with the flu and being taken to Mama Dolly's "where I slept and drank sassafras tea."

8. Reading Mr. McLaurin's reports of obviously deep-felt belief in his work and enthusiasm lends pathos to the description of him as withdrawn and hard to get along with by COFO white volunteers in Ruleville in 1964. The antagonisms between the summer volunteers and old COFO hands were a sad part of the Freedom Summer. The contrast, observed in 1964 by one of the authors, between Mr. Mc-Laurin's handling of a voter registration meeting and the same task undertaken by the white volunteers was the difference between a virtuoso and earnest beginning students. He was the man who usually filled in for Robert Moses as director of COFO when the latter was out of the state.

9. In *Nobody Knows My Name* (New York: Dell Publishing Company, 1963, originally published in 1961), James Baldwin speaks of the Southern night. "In the Southern night, everything seems possible, the most private, unspeakable longings . . ." Here are notes by one of the authors on the landscape leading into Terrell County, in the afternoon's prelude to the Southern night: Small town along way. Brick post office. White bank-looking building. "Closed." Sheds over sidewalks, gallery at second floor. "Super Store." Countryside: pecan tree with big limb with nuts in green clusters, swaying in shower breeze, and touching the ground. Greens of foliage pushed down in heat. Trees, green, tossing. Limb curving down, a section of leaves missing, then a burst of leaves at end, waving over black tar of road twisting ahead with center line of dashes like drops of sweat dribbling around little curves and on out of sight. Sand and light reds of roadside clay lift up to haze-heat of air to blue of sky like heated metal, sun yellow and hard and fierce . . . Sunset with great circle of red full at horizon sending not streaks, but crimson coloring over all of upward spiraling clouds. Field of stunted corn, brown and burned. Watermelon truck pulled up at closed filling station. Sawmill. Negroes in dirty work clothes. Rural roadside: three boys on stick horses galloping up one side of road; Negro boy about same age on his stick horse in yard on other side of road. Birds, continuous noise. Gnats . . .

10. Chief Deputy M. E. Mathews and Deputy R. M. Dunaway. They figured frequently in the Terrell voter reports.

11. They were Claude Sitton of the New York *Times*, Bill Shipp of the Atlanta *Constitution*, and Pat Watters, then of the Atlanta *Journal*. Sheriff Mathews stuck out his hand, introduced himself genially. When Mr. Sitton identified his paper, the sheriff muttered something about "Yankee newspapermen." "I'm a Georgian, sir," Mr. Sitton replied. "And an American. Just like you." The sheriff was rueful about the whole thing afterward. He confided to Jack Chatfield: "When those newspapers got a hold of me they made me sound like Uncle Remus." He had, Chatfield commented, "been backed off by the fatal combination of press and federal action." Harassment of voter workers was considerably lessened, he said. A federal suit based on the incident was dropped in late 1963 on the promise of the county officials not to interfere with voter registration. They were already under federal court injunction not to do so at the time of the church incident.

12. A tire of the reporters' car had been flattened outside. Such was their state

that they didn't notice it until the car was out of the churchyard and halfway up a little dirt road, surrounded by dark fields, toward the highway. Two carloads of the Negroes stopped with them and stood around them as they changed the tire. A white drove by, laughing. The reporters' car followed a car containing Miss Patch and several of the Negroes back to Albany. A carload of whites followed them, their license plate bent so that the numbers couldn't be seen. Sand, it was discovered the next day, had been poured in the gas tank of the reporters' rented car. Mr. Sherrod, a year later, had to stop a minute to recollect the events of the evening. It had been a part, merely, of the norm of his everyday life.

7)

Field Report—
Telling It Like It Was

The large file of regular narrative field reports of voter registration workers in VEP projects constitutes a unique contribution to the literature of American history. What follows are excerpts selected almost at random from some five thousand or more pages of such material. The attempt has been not only to pull out some of the more dramatic, or apt, or particularly colorful narratives, but also to give a representative feel of the whole of these files. In this way, it is hoped that the flavor, spirit, and reality of the movement during these years will be conveyed.

There has been no effort to edit or clean up the excerpts. It is therefore appropriate to remind the reader that they were written often under the most stressful of conditions, and that while some indicate less than adequate education, others more nearly reflect momentary inattention to details of grammar and punctuation. They were written to convey information (and, certainly, often feeling), not as finished compositions. As often is the case with such writing, there is probably more communication in them than in most prose consciously set down for print.

From Carver "Chico" Neblett, Southwest Georgia Project, fall 1962—
How does one get it across to the people that we are not alone, when

all round them white men are killing and getting away? Not only getting away, but also in many cases being promoted . . . These men were not punished, and the Negroes know it. How do you push a meeting when they tell you, "I might be killed, my house may be burned, I may be fired from my job, etc." I came back with the FBI being down here . . .

From Charles M. Sherrod, project coordinator, Southwest Georgia Voter Registration Project, December 1962—

Since our last report, 13 meetings have been held in the three counties of our area: In Sumter on the Thursday nights of Nov. 15, 22, 29, and Dec. 6, in Terrell on Wednesdays Nov. 14, 21, 28, and Dec. 5, in Lee on Saturdays Nov. 10, 17, 24, and Dec. 1 and 8. The meetings are at present absolutely essential to the program and every effort is made that they should be attended not only by the project coordinator and the staff working in the particular county, but by the staff from other counties and from Albany.

Our faithful friend the Rev. Samuel B. Wells of East Albany never fails to drive out, which helps us provide transportation for those citizens of Albany who wish to accompany us . . .

The importance of this "outside" attendance can hardly be over-stressed as a morale-builder. The sense that "we are not alone" is important, and so is the practical usefulness of the sharing of experience . . .

We are hoping to change the emphasis of the meetings slightly. In the early days their primary purpose was to enhearten the wavering, to encourage the unregistered voters who attended to move on from the first crucial step of summoning up the courage to come, to the decisive step of going to the courthouse and making the effort to register. The sense of fellowship, the heartening influence of the prayers, the songs, the scripture readings, the tales of hardship bravely borne, all these must stay with us. But by now a large proportion of the local attendance at any mass meeting is made up of people who have already registered.

In the context of the legitimate emotion of the meeting, they should be given more than the simple instructions and exhortations concerning the registration procedure, and the exchanges of information on progress in the counties, which have been the bulk of the content of the meetings to date.

From Penny Patch, Student Nonviolent Coordinating Committee, Albany, Georgia, December, 8, 1962—

It is now five o'clock in the morning and the cocks are crowing. You know, Southwest Georgia is very, very, beautiful. It just needs a little bit of fixing. . . .

The role of the white student in the "hard-core" South has come under serious question. People say: "White students increase the fear of the Negroes, the rage of the whites, the amount of harassment." All of this is true, to some extent. Fear in the Negro is there anyway and they deal with it every day of their lives. A whole lifetime is spent in ever present awareness of the white. (I cannot generalize and say that this is true without exception, but I think that almost everyone has some of it in him. It involves always being careful and not missing a step.) . . . Yet, this *can't* turn into black against white, and with the lack of white Southerners to help for the moment, the white Northern student has a valuable role. We've got to deal with the enragement of the whites, though. We have to make an effort to see their feelings and somehow to comprehend the centuries of indoctrination that lie behind them. Someone once said to me: "When they see Negro and white together it is as though way deep down inside of them two broken ribs are grating together." A great many of the harassments that we experienced this summer dealt with this. Threatening phone calls almost always referred to "that white girl" or "white boys." It seems to be a feeling of betrayal. Encounters with police or local whites have the same "tone." On the other hand, harassments, beatings, shootings occur with non-integrated groups. Witness Mississippi, witness Southwest Georgia before last summer . . .

From Charles M. Sherrod, Southwest Georgia Project, December 1962—

We have placed almost total allegiance to the group in the areas of strategy and practice. In the group the individual finds the strength he cannot or rather does not see outside of its jurisdiction. One of the reasons the white man with the segregationist attitude has been somewhat successful in blocking the black man in the past has much to do with the effectiveness of isolation . . .

From Jack Chatfield, Southwest Georgia Project, December 1962—

Talked to one ancient man on the porch of his home, and he said, "Looks like they tried to scare some of those fellows away, but it weren't no spo't." He was speaking of the fellows in the movement, whom he said he had seen "on the television." We told him they wouldn't pull no spo't with us either.

He told us he was from Florida and has lived in north Georgia. "I said 'Yas' and 'No' down Florida . . . and north too. . . ."

Southwest Georgia is "Yassuh" country.

He was an intelligent man and his hands were scarred hideously. I suspect his intelligence was scarred too.

"And after all that," he said, "three dollar a day."

Somewhere in Bronwood, in a house with a green roof, there is a blind man who wants us to talk to him. . . .

Faith Molsaert, Southwest Georgia Project—

Right now, it's a big step if people, instead of complaining to themselves of harassments, tell us. But *some day, they won't even need the students.*

SNCC Field Report, Southwest Georgia Project—

Willie May, 18, had planned to attend a segregated movie in Americus with her boyfriend. When we told her about Freedom and how she would be paying the owner of this establishment to keep the movie segregated, she changed her mind and decided to attend the Lee County Mass Meeting instead. . . .

Jack Chatfield, Southwest Georgia Project, December 1962—

It is shocking upon consideration that the night air above the red roads of the colored section is not filled with furtive hymns of plot and overthrow, of philosophy and abstract design. Since September (the registration drive began officially in January and reached a height during the torrid summer), I have not heard report of a single unofficial gathering of citizens whose discussion topic was: "What can be done?" There are no doubt countless dinner conversations, but nothing which remotely approaches a loose "organization" or "conspiracy" of any sort.

As for Mrs. Silas, whom we recommended contact Mr. Henderson about getting transportation to the tent in Sasser, she "ain't seen him." As for Mr. Henderson, whom we recommended contact Mrs. Silas (who was "interested" in attending a voter registration meeting with Mr. Henderson), he "ain't seen her."

As for Mrs. Nelson, whom we recommended speak to Deacon Green (who had recently attended his first meeting), she "ain't spoke to him."

As for Deacon Green whom we recommended contact Mrs. Nelson (who shared his fears), he "sho' ain't stopped by."

Sometimes, under the weight of the awful impotence I have encountered spasmodically, you find yourself hollering, "How the hell do you make them move? Where is the courage, where is the wisdom? Why don't they move?"

Ten o'clock and you have resolved that they have failed; eleven o'clock and you have resolved that you have failed. Twelve o'clock and you don't know a damn thing. . . .

Ruleville and Sunflower County, Mississippi, January 4–12, 1963, by Charles McLaurin—

On January 4, 1963, we made it back to Ruleville, that night we went to the home of Mrs. Bessie Lee Green, who lives in Ruleville. She have attempted to register and have attended most of the meetings. She did not make enough money picking or chopping cotton to carry her through the winter, she have bills to pay on her stove water lights and gas and an addition to her house. Mrs. Green have a daughter that have a small child sometime the child don't have milk to drink. Her daughter's husband don't have a steady job he is 23 years of age and have not tried to register because he feel the person he is working for would fire him. Mrs. Green needs $260 or she will not have a stove to cook on and the lumber company could take her bathroom fixtures . . .

On January 5, we went from door to door trying to find people to go down to register, we found three persons who said they would go down Monday January 7th.

On Sunday, January 6, 1963 the Ruleville Christian Citizenship Club met, there were 19 persons present. This group is made up of people who have gone to Indianola and took the test, at this meeting was Mrs. Irean Johnson chairman of the group and one of the four persons to pass the voters test. Each member said they would try to get at least two new persons to come to the meeting, the meetings are open to everyone. We played the record (Freedom In The Air), and talked about it.

January 7th we helped needy persons fill out COFO Welfare and Relief applications, those people need help other than commodities and the small Welfare checks that they receive. COFO is giving clothes, shoes, to them, this will inable the people to use money that they would buy clothes with to pay bills and other needed items.

Tuesday, January 8, 1963, we did not take the three people down to register because they wanted to wait and see if others would go from the meeting that night. In the meeting four more said they would go down Thursday January 10th. So on the 9th we gave out some of the clothing we had for the people. Thursday night we attended a mass meeting in Shaw, Mississippi. Rev. James Bevel gave a class on Voter Registration, there was about 50 to 75 people there. Meetings will be held in Shaw every Thursday night.

We are going to Drew, Miss. Wednesday January 16, to start canvassing. On Sunday January 13, one of us will go to church in Drew, this way we meet some of the leading people.

From Reginald Robinson of SNCC, Orangeburg, South Carolina, January 6–12, 1963—

In my first report I said the NAACP was the only vocal group here. In this report you will see how vocal they are. They given me nothing but the run around this time, but they have been vocal. What happen was I had to see the committee of the committee, that speaks for the committee, and can't say anything until the committee meets. Well, on with this weeks report . . .

From a letter to Chicago friends of SNCC from Robert Moses in Greenwood, Mississippi, early 1963—

This is a new dimension for a voting program in Mississippi: Negroes have been herded to the polls before by white people, but have never stood en masse in protest at the white seat of power in the iceberg of Mississippi politics. Negroes who couldn't read and write stood in line to tell the registrar they still wanted to vote, that they didn't have the chance to go to school when they were small and anyway Mr. John Jones can't read and write either and *he* votes. We don't know this plateau at all. We were relieved at the absence of immediate violence at the court house, but who knows what's to come next . . .

Mrs. Vera Pigee, Clarksdale, Mississippi, January 16–23, 1963—

I carried 20 or more to the Circuit Clerk Office here in Coahoma County, 17 was processed, however, I don't know if they passed the literary test or not but I will know in the next 30 days.

The reason the 3 out of 20 didn't get to take the test was because the Clerk deputy only processed (1) one at a time, by this way the time ran out before they got a chance . . . the room she used can seat 20.

I have also seen [the] Circuit Clerk let people who are not Negroes put their name on the book without taking the test.

Fear plays a part also, some women say if they try to register their husband will lose their job, they will lose theirs, their children are teachers and will [lose] their job . . .

Frank Smith, Holly Springs, Mississippi, January 4–15, 1963—
After returning to Mississippi from the retreat, we found things to be in reasonably good shape. I think we were beginning to shake off the effect of the "Ole Miss" crisis and become our normal selves again. . . .

On Sunday it was raining and muddy and our Speaker's Bureau didn't get out. I went to the County to see Mr. Pegues and got stuck. Man what a predicament, scared to ask anyone to give me a push and damned sure I was not going to walk from out there. My partner, Beamon, and I had a pushing good time.

From Reginald Robinson, Orangeburg, South Carolina, January 1963—
Friday 11, January, 1963—Most of today I have been putting all of the notes from interviews together. I called Mrs. Rackely about 5:30. She had talked with Mr. Earl Middleton and he did not know of a place in which I would work out of, and he told her he want to see me. Mrs. Rackely went on to say she had about three more place to call . . . Went to see Mr. Earl Middleton. We talked about what I had been doing all week. Mr. Middleton said the reason I was being sent from person to person and could not get their support was, because they want the credit of anything done in Orangeburg. They [NAACP] does not like for anybody coming in using the local chapter. The local chapter here in Orangeburg will not work with another group; because they have there own project. The only help you can get is from the people as individuals not as the NAACP. Middleton told me I could get anything I needed to work with. I asked him for a map of the city or county. He gave me a map broken down by ward & precinct. There was a list made of all the registered Negro sometime back. I asked Middleton if I could have a copy. Middleton said "he was told by one of the NAACP heads not to let me have this list." He also said he did not understand why I could not have a copy, and that if I come back to see him Monday, he would have a copy for me. This is when I left, because I had taken as much as I could. I knew now the only way I was going to get anything was to make my own group, and the hell with these people.

From Mrs. Colia Lafayette, Selma, Alabama, February 1963—

The people from Browns, Ala., have to drive 18 miles into town to attend the voter classes. Five of the people from Browns have been trying to register since 1956. They are Mrs. Rebecca Anderson, Mrs. Lillian Tean Kimbrough, mother of 13, Mrs. Ethel Washington, 76, had six sons to serve at the same time during World War II, Mr. Eddie Griffin . . . and Mr. Gus Tabb.

From Jack Chatfield, Southwest Georgia Project—

We strolled round the colored section, and at one point during the afternoon we were buzzed by a pick-up; he turned around and buzzed us again at about 50 miles per hour. My lungs runneth over with dust. There was a colored boy in the front seat with him, admirably demonstrating, I believe, "the white man's" total lack of comprehension in the area of Negro affairs.

We had been told by Mr. Henderson that Les Holly, a blind man, wanted us to stop by. We stopped by.

Les Holly was sitting on a tiny porch on the front of his home, surrounded by all appearances by a retinue of relatives or visitors. Chico introduced himself and I did the same. A lady whom I took to be his wife or daughter repeated, "This is Mr. Chatfield."

I was holding Mr. Holly's hand and he asked, "Is this Chatfield?"

He said that he wanted us to stop back, so that he could sit and talk with us for a long spell. I was in love with this guy: his eyes, shielded with dark glasses, were facing in our general direction; he became the symbol of the human tragedy, this waste of human lives, and it was as though he had been waiting for us a very long time—and the wait was not for someone who could lift him out of the tragedy, but who would understand it. He is over the hill—blind, ancient, surrounded by cackling kin; it was as if we were the only ones who would know him.

These are the times when the man is reduced, in human terms, to the myth, the legend. But in human terms—so that he is saved from destruction.

"I wish I could have seen you before my sight went," he said. His sight had gone in August of this year.

I said that sight did not matter, and I told him that we would sit and read the constitution of the United States together. He smiled.

"The radio said all Chatfield would say was the fourth constitution. He wouldn't tell 'em anything except the fourth constitution."

He was talking about the fourteenth amendment, which Holly's whole life has been a violation of.

So now in Bronwood, there is Les Holly, who has been waiting a long time, who perhaps up until Saturday was happy with the myth, and who now we shall have to make happy with the reality, which is tough.

From Lafayette Surney, Greenville, Mississippi, February 18–22, 1963—

This week I have been working on commodities in Washington county for the needed people in the county.

We carried about 28 people down to make a registration attempt. Miss Smith, who is 77 years old, went to the Circuit Clerk office to make a registration attempt. She went up to the registrar and told him that she couldn't read or write and would like to register. The registrar told her that she would have to fill out the application, because it was the law. Then she said okay and walk out.

This week about 50 or 60 people have been in to get food and clothes. We will continue to give out commodities next week and try to get more registration attempt.

From Ida Holland, Greenwood, Mississippi, February 1963, on food distribution by COFO—

Some of them had walked from as far as 20 miles to get here. Some were so cold they could hardly talk. Others were without proper clothes and shoes. Some didn't believe; it was "too good to be true." I asked the people if they would like to vote. Some didn't know what voting was. Others couldn't read or write. Some said no, but the majority said yes.

From Essie Lee Marks of Greenwood, another helper—

On Feb. 20, we distributed more food and we didn't get to everyone. There were hundreds who didn't receive anything and really needed it. We just didn't have enough food and clothing to get around to everyone.

The people were very nice and attentive when we told them, we just couldn't get to them.

On Feb. 21, we went to the church and sorted the clothes and shoes into sizes. On Feb. 22, we started distributing the clothes and shoes to the needy people. These people were in bad shape. Some of them didn't have shoes on. They were wearing raggedy dirty old clothes. Most of the ladies had on men pants, big shoes, and some type of rag on their head.

We gave all the clothes out to these people. Still there were many more who needed things badly. We need more clothes for these children. Lots of them are out of school on account of no clothes and shoes. These children are between the ages of six and fourteen years of age.

From James Austin, Selma, Alabama, February 1963—

On January 22, 1963, I started my first class with only one student, on January 24 I had two students, January 29, I had four students and January 31 I had six students. Starting the month of February, the students began to come in more and more. February 5 I had six students and February 14, I had 14 students. I am also sending the names of students to go down Monday 24 of February and registrated. They are as following: Charles Mazey, Sadia Mitchell, Eddie Griffin, Gus Tabb, Rebecca Anderson.

From Frank Smith, Holly Springs, February 1963—

Saw Mr. Pegues Tuesday, January 15, and gave him some forms for our welfare relief program. He said, "I think you ought to give these to Reverend Echols he would be a better person." He offered the excuse he had to do business and didn't want to become involved. He said he was scared for his wife and family.

Mrs. Loullen asked me for some names and addresses because she said that she knew that she was going to be "messed with." She is a great lady. She carries people down to register, tries to get them welfare and just worries them to death if they don't. She is a valuable person or asset. Boy does she live in the country, when it rains, the only way we can communicate is by mail.

Mr. Ingram took a family the other day that had been put out. The man didn't have any place to stay and Ingram provided him one.

From Wallace Harvey, Greenwood, Mississippi—

On off time from my job, one day in August I met two young men, they were strangers to me. Then and there I noticed something different about these two men. They introduced themselves and told me things about their movement, and I had that feeling of intellect. I was empressed with that extra boost. I saw the green light on and that means go, and I have been going since.

I started that week working on Voters Registration. It was hard to get my people to cooperate. The first and most important was fear. When questioned, 7 out of 10 of the people stated they had not worked since cotton time. . . .

Coahoma County, Mississippi, Branch NAACP, February 26, 1963, Aaron Henry, president—

The Clarksdale Police Department has the task of explaining the death of a Negro prisoner in the City Hall. The attitudes and actions, by both the Clarksdale Police Department and the City Administration, against Negroes all along, makes a thorough investigation in this death necessary by both local and federal authorities.

It appears the most sure remedy to this kind of treatment is a sustained "Registration to Vote Drive." We must be willing to go, time and time again, to the Circuit Clerk's office and offer to register, regardless of how many times we are denied the right to register; most of our problems can be cleared up with the vote.

We can vote for decent treatment of Negro Prisoners by voting for a Mayor and City Commissioners that will not tolerate abuse of prisoners. The chief of police and all other policemen are employees of the city administration. We can vote for better and fair law enforcement by voting in men and women who will administer the law fairly without regard to race or creed.

We can vote for employment by voting into office and administration those that will secure industry which will employ *all of the unemployed* and not just industry that will employ the *white unemployed.*

We can vote for a better school system—one that will obey the laws of the nation—by voting in a city administration that will respect the law of the nation. We can vote for better streets and lights in Negro neighborhoods by voting in men that can be fair in their administration if the popular vote will support them.

We can vote for the right to vote by supporting men who will not make it so difficult for Negroes to become registered voters. The vote will help tremendously in our struggle to gain dignity, respect, and employment from the downtown merchants. In the meantime we must rely on the boycott. Let us plan now to wear our old clothes for Easter. Those items we cannot do without, let us purchase them on this side of the railroad track or go into other communities to purchase them. The NAACP is still supplying transportation to Memphis, Helena, Arkansas, and other cities where more courtesy and employment are available to Negroes.

The votes will, in time, help the local press refrain from its continued discourtesy in refusing to refer, in print, to adult Negroes with courtesy titles. The personnel of the local press is really sympathetic to our cause for freedom. They disagree with many of our methods, which is understandable, none of them being Negroes . . .

The Negro is not without fault in this whole affair. Citizenship schools have been set up to help the Negro improve himself in every facet of livelihood. These schools are under the direction of Mrs. Vera M. Pigee, and are held every Monday and Tuesday night, from 6:00–8:00 P.M. The schools are conducted at: Chapel Hill Baptist Church, Rayford Chapel Baptist Church, Silent Grove Baptist Church, Pigee's Beauty Salon, and Johnson's Sandwich Shop. All citizens are invited and encouraged to attend these schools to effect self betterment in every facet of life.

From Carver Neblett, Southwest Georgia Project, early 1963—

I have been after Joe to register for almost a month now. His excuse has been that I work out of town. And that he is off from work at 6:00. When I heard that he was off from work Monday, December 24, I jumped on him with all four feet. Joe has been coming to meetings for the past month.

I predict that when Mr. Holly, Bronwood, Mrs. Beasley, Parrot school teacher who plans to register against the county superintendent's will, and Joe registers, maybe we will start a few of the more reluctant people such as Mr. Henderson, Mrs. Silas, Mrs. Collier, Etc., to thinking and maybe coming to meetings. WE SHALL OVERCOME . . .

From Jack Chatfield, Southwest Georgia Project—

In Bronwood, Les Holly (blind) listened while I read the thirty questions on the illiteracy test, and while I read him the new leaflet. He told us, in interim periods, that Dawson and Newton, Georgia, were, for their size, the worst towns in the country for brutality to Negroes (ref. Atlanta *Constitution* article this summer).

"How many have you got so far?" he asked us.

We answered that over a hundred had gone down.

"Maybe if you keep on you can get a thousand," he said.

From Elizabeth Wyckoff, Albany, Georgia—

East Albany is largely a working class area, and many of its residents are fairly recent immigrants from the adjacent rural areas, and still have relatives there. While it is apparently true that in Albany itself simply applying for registration does not expose one to reprisals, and the registrars, both at City Hall and the Court House, are not overtly obstructive, many East Albany residents are convinced that it is dangerous to attempt to register. Others believe that voting is futile. Still others are (often rightly) uncertain that their degree of literacy is sufficient to pass the test, and almost equally alarmed at the prospect of the test for illiterates. Only a few of these people react positively to the suggestion of attending citizenship school . . . The area has been canvassed several times in the last few years, so that most of the unregistered voters are people who have at some time been urged to "become first-class citizens," and have decided against it, whether consciously, or by procrastination. They are therefore harder to persuade than those not unearthed before, to whom the idea is a new one . . .

There is also in the area a hard core of registered voters. These are those who have served Rev. Wells as street and block workers in the past, and besides these one meets, again and again, even on blocks where it may be that no one else is registered, people who look one in the eye and say firmly that they have been registered "ever since the colored could vote." These are the people on whom we must build.

From Charles Sherrod, Southwest Georgia Project, February 1963—

Terrell,—As you know, a white policeman was summoned before the throne of justice in the presence of people of the counties around. We have been talking about this case and the possibilities of his conviction for some time. The people had built their hopes up high. Actually, they were prepared to see him eaten by the lions. He was to be a sacrifice of appeasement. They wanted to see his blood. They came to Americus, Georgia, each day of the week during the period in which the trial was to come up. From each county they came, Terrell, Lee, Dougherty, and Sumter. On Wednesday night, they turned out to the mass meeting at Sasser, on Thursday they turned out to the meeting in Sumter, and on Saturday after the acquittal ruling was made they turned out in large numbers at Lee County. They were broken in spirit but they made us feel ashamed that we were all so despondent, not openly, but the people love us and though they respect their leaders, they love and understand us as they do children for we are what they hope their children will become (they don't know do they). The meeting in the tent on Wednesday night after the decision of the court was the most inspirational of my memory. Some of the people went up to such an emotional pitch that they arose together when it was suggested by one lady about fifty that we march on Dawson's City Hall. Of course, the opinion was respected and treated with consideration, and then we moved on to the issue at hand.

It was amazing how some of the people with whom we work have not been discouraged by this defeat in our opinion. They said that it was a victory even to have been able to get the policeman to stand in judgment before a judge and jury . . .

We were told by John Martin, an attorney of the Justice Department, that the case of the United States vs. Z. T. Mathews may not come up in court. This was again very disappointing to us. The people need to see blood. This is bad but they must have a victory in the courts. A white man must be punished for doing harm to a black man, a white man with a badge on must bow to justice. And this is different. The officials in Terrell think that they can put on a badge and do anything they like and the black men of this section think that the badge is magic too. Anybody wearing a badge can do anything. It's about time that these sons learn that they stand under the judgment of the same badge that they wear. Anyway, Martin of the Justice Department told us that the county officials did not want to go to the court but rather wanted a settlement out of the courts.

From Leflore County, Greenwood, Mississippi, Report of Registration Campaign by Mrs. Monetta Hancock, Reporter—

On February 26, 1963, we accompanied large numbers of people to the county court house of Greenwood, Mississippi, to register to become qualified voters of Mississippi.

I arrived about 15 minutes until 10:00 with a small group. I was accompanying John H. Ball who is leader of the Voting Committee. At the time I arrived, I was told that at least 49 people had already taken the test. New people were coming in to register also. I took some of their names and John Ball was taking some of their names too . . .

After about an hour or so the jailer and a prisoner came out with a buffer to buff the floor where these people were standing. Because of this, the people had to move and scatter about. After he buffed the area where the people were standing, he came over where they were standing in the beginning. So, I decided to follow the people and stand in line with them. After a while the prisoner came back to where we were standing. I asked the boy if we moved over this time would he be through this time? He came closer to me and told me, "Look, lady, I'm not doing this on my own. I am doing this because they (the jailor) told me to do this. They don't want you all to vote; but you all stick right here." I told him thank you and proceeded to tell John Ball about this incident. He said that he was already aware of what was going on. So the floor was being buffed all while we were there.

From John O'Neal, Lee County, Georgia, March 6, 1963—

Mr. C. . . . deserves some comment. [He] is 25 years old, married and has one child. He himself has experienced quite a bit of difficulty in his attempts to register. He has gone down about four times and each time has been unable to complete the process because of . . . [the official in charge]—sometimes he sick or absent for some other reason and sometimes he's just plain cantankerous.

[Mr. C.] has personally been responsible for getting at least ten or twelve people to go down, however, including his wife and three other ladies whose husbands live and work on the plantation. He is important because of the fact that so many people in exactly the same position refuse to cooperate because of their positions—being directly dependent on a white man's judgment of his worth. There ought to be some way to provide for the economic security of people in such positions. They could be fired for simply leaning on the wrong tree.

Mr. C. is a very effective worker and is very persuasive. I worry sometimes if his enthusiasm might not override his better judgment. He has invited us to his home several times which is situated right in the middle of the plantation in plain view of everyone. His home is one of several places that Negroes are permitted to use in order that the guests of the plantation can see how well the good negras are treated down heah. This favor is also a symbol of the high status that the dog trainer occupies on a sports ranch. (The place is owned by a North Carolina textile manufacturer who vacations there three months out of the year. There are 11,000 acres in the place, which is used primarily for bird hunting.) If we become too regular as visitors, surely our presence, even all Black, will be noticed and our identity already is too well known to remain secret to inquisitive Brothers. If [Mr. C.] is fired or hurt in any way, the Plantation types will quickly turn back to their shriveled existence with no more than a mournful host of "I told you so's." Many of the gains that we are beginning to make in this area would be lost.

From Cleveland Banks, Leflore County, Mississippi—

On March 26, 1963, about 50 people went to Wesley Chapel to go down town [Greenwood] and register. We walked down Howard, and went by the city hall to talk to Chief Lary about some protection. Before going to the courthouse. Instead of talking to Chief Lary, Mayor Simpson was standing in the door of the city hall, he told us to get out, but no one moved, he gave two minutes to leave, still no one moved, then he stepped back inside the door and told the policeman with the dog to come out, he came out and repeated what the mayor had said "You have two minutes to leave." If not he was going to let go of the dog. The people started moving backward after the policeman let the dog have some slack in his lease he snapped at the people. Bob said "I would like to see Chief Lary." The dog tore his trousers from the cuff to the knee. Jim Forman said "Let's leave and go to the courthouse." Jim had taken several pictures of the policeman with the dog, and the policeman tried to take the camera. McLaurin took the camera from Jim and ran with it. The police picked up Jim and Bob at the post office and arrested them. After they had picked up Jim and Bob the people formed in small groups and some came to the courthouse and the others went back to the church . . .

From Charles Sherrod, Southwest Georgia Project—

But we are having a couple of problems here with the young girls' parents. At least one parent has told his three children that it would be impossible for them to continue to work with us. The young girls told us that all kinds of allegations had been made—we were teaching them immoral codes of ethics and practices of the same. The girls who work with us are the best looking and brightest at the high school and junior high in Albany. But they are picking us out as "boy friends" and so on. Although the opinion of this particular father is wrong, we have run into the problem of boy-girl relations, yea, sexual relations. This is a hell of a problem! It meets us squarely every day so much so that it is our idea now to ask the help of the young girls who work with and swing those hips so unmercifully before us. They must understand what could happen if some mishap should occur among us and many of the girls are under seventeen—jailbait summa cum laude. We elected to call a meeting and ask for their help. We would call their attention to our codes and call their attention to the many ways in which they frustrate them, pointing out further that they do so with cold and calculated forethought. Finally, we intend to start them to making reports for the week, also. This will help them and us . . .

From Jack Chatfield, Southwest Georgia Project—

Chico and I had returned, though, to Mr. Les Holly's house and had finally (I was personally extremely hesitant) broached the subject of "the meetin's." Mr. Holly said that he wanted to go, but in the tone of voice that a man uses to tell you that he wants to take in some—any—movie (this is usually the tone one encounters, at any rate) . . .

From Prathia Hall, Southwest Georgia Project, February 23–March 8, 1963—

Rev. Wells never ceases to amaze me. But when he showed up last Saturday at our 7:30 AM canvass meeting with Mrs. Otis Holloway the dean of Women at Albany State, I just stared. Mrs. Holloway is a friend of McCree Harris'—Rutha's sister. She was willing to risk her job to help us. She promised to help us by doing some research on voting statistics and voting rights on the political structure of this area. Already Rev. Wells had her making phone calls for canvassers and registrants.

The technique of sending canvassers down in front of City Hall to "snatch folks off the streets" and taking them in to register was extremely good. It served its purpose for voter registration and also served to physically and psychologically confront people with the movement—a type of direct action. We might well have been picketing. Some people were frightened to death—like the woman who pushed me away as she ducked into a store to avoid giving me her name which I asked her for when she hastily told me she had been registered for years. I don't know, some I believe, and some I don't. Some were quiet about their fear and sheepishly hauled their excuses out of moth balls. And, of course, other people were willing: they were either already convinced or were just on the border line. I found two such people. As a group we found 15 who more than anything else, needed an invitation.

From Mrs. Colia Lafayette, Selma, Alabama, April 1963—

Cleophus Hobbs [a youth leader] . . . said he just had to keep up with us because if we had not come to town he probably would have gotten his boys to rob a bank or something.

Letter from Louise G. Wilson, Winston-Salem, North Carolina, May 28, 1964—

Dear Mrs. Whitaker: It is finished! Alas, but we all were so sad. Our last night of work was a tearful one. The young people had become so interested in the work, and I had become so attached to them—(they all called me "Mom" both white and colored). You can imagine the look on some of the faces when we were out on the street and someone (especially the white kids) would holler, "Mom, stop up here." We all went out to dinner together, including the registrar, on our last night. I had waited to send the last report in hoping that I could make a report on our plans for election day.

We had hoped one of the candidates would give us $125 for a week of campaigning for votes. Our Negro candidates are *too poor*—the white one will have *nothing* to do with CORE and NAACP. However, you will note we plan to have a "GET OUT AND VOTE" project in the evenings and on election day. Everyone is to bring a picnic basket and we shall start at 5:30 A.M. and work until 6:00 P.M. We shall surely let you know our results.

From Prathia Hall, Terrell County, Georgia—

As we left she went to the yard to chop wood. Chico offered to help her sometime. She took him up on it immediately and we spent the next half hour watching Chico chop wood. She still wouldn't agree to go to meeting though.

She said she had to iron. Faith and I just didn't have the time to do her ironing for her. Maybe next time we will, if we think it will work.

From Jack Chatfield, Southwest Georgia Project, April 1963—

Spoke to one man—the blind man whose erstwhile determination to register and vote seems to have sputtered out.

From Ruby Tyler of Biloxi, Mississippi, NAACP—

Three out of every five people contacted actually has no intention of registering, and merely says so to get rid of the worker. Especially when a worker abolishes all their excuses. We have had as many as 15 people which say they would go and when the driver comes, they're sick, or have to go to work and maybe five will go. Our only tactic has been to get the block worker to go with the driver when the person sees the worker, they're usually ashamed not to go. This has worked fairly well for us. We still have a large percentage of people who feel there is no need to register. My only suggestion is, instead of an annual drive, try and keep the program before the public . . .

From Charles Sherrod, Southwest Georgia Project, March 10, 1963—

As you can see when you go through the reports, some of the ideas which we have had for a long time are beginning to materialize. Let us take the idea that the most effective way to organize communities in this area is to widen the identification of "community." In essence, this idea is directly in opposition to the development of the community as the tradition of the system of segregation had dictated in this area. It (the system of segregation) has called for rigid control of the mobility of the person in accord with color, of course. It operates in the attitude of persons located in one geographical to another geographical area. In practical terms, for example, the people in Albany have been afraid to go to Terrell County; the people in Terrell are afraid to go to Leesburg; the people in Sumter County feel that the people in Leesburg and Dawson are the victims of merciless situations in everyday life, and the people are therefore afraid to associate freely at any time of day or night. In Albany it has always been hard to get people to take us to either of these places, until now . . .

This sense of the "new community" has given birth to other ideas. Take for an example, the idea of Mr. Vinson Collier—he proposes that we instigate a loan association. He proposes to have five base members to begin with. Each base member would earn four shares and no more at five dollars per share. This accumulative one hundred dollars would be the capital on which the association would operate initially. The loan system would operate on this wise—one could borrow five dollars every two weeks, the interest would be fifty cents and the insurance or dues would be twenty-five cents. An additional one-dollar and twenty-five cents could be given toward a share of stock. The interest would be shared with the stockholders at the end of the year. This is the idea of a man who hardly has a high school education. This is, as you know, the general arrangement made by any credit union but this idea is original because it came out of this man. His wife works with us in our Voter Registration drive and this is his contribution to the drive. Of course he does other things for us; he is an auto-mechanic and does work on our cars for free . . .

From Lee County, Georgia, spring 1963—

One agriculture teacher registered last week, whatever that may mean. That is sort of like seeing a flying saucer in Lee County.

The teachers were really stumped at having to face their own students (some of whom were registered) as if they themselves were students, and at being asked things like, "Don't you feel any responsibility for what goes on over at that school?" . . . We can now use the students as a sort of reserve weapon.

From Joyce Barrett, Albany, Georgia, March 1963—

We ran into a gang leader from North Albany, James Knighton, who said that his boys were ready for action. They want to demonstrate and canvass. Eddie thinks he's bull-jiving and he may be right.

SNCC Report, local worker, Greenwood, Mississippi, March 1963—

One thing here in this city of Greenwood, the older people are a bad influence on the younger people. On Tuesday, I went canvassing and talked to some. About six out of seven are afraid of the white man.

John Due of VEP staff, field report—

Mr. Robinson, by his very own words, is typical of a growing number of Negroes, although to me few in number, who in their early 50's are now willing to die. They have "Uncle Tommed" enough now that their children are out of school.

From Weldon Rougeau of CORE, Dade County, Florida, September 2, 1963—

Preparations for a county-wide voter registration drive involving most community organizations began on July 8 and initial steps were taken to contact leaders from the Negro and white communities at that time.

The intensified portion of the drive is scheduled to last until October 5, when the registration books are expected to close for the November 4 election. Our goal is to get at least 40,000 as the number of registered Negroes in the county.

Our areas of concentration are North Miami Beach, Opa-Locka,

Liberty City, Brown's Sub, Downtown Miami, Coconut Grove, Richmond Heights, Goulds, Perrine, and Homestead. My main purpose in each community has been to get existing organizations to get active and begin assuming the responsibilities for engineering their phase of the drive in their community.

The organizations contacted to help generate an adult-youth effort are the League of Women Voters, the National Conference of Christians and Jews, the B'nai B'rith youth organization, the American Jewish Committee, the Greater Miami Council of Churches, the Florida Labor Council, CORE, NAACP, Community Relations Council of Dade County, The Women's International League for Peace, and several other organizations from the community. Each pledged to help in whichever way it could.

In many ways this is not an opportune time for a registration drive due to the lack of political appeal in the upcoming election. However, I still believe that with a concerted effort we can obtain significant results. I hope we are able to have a banner drive.

The people have been very receptive towards the drive but rather apprehensive about working. This is the time when they feel the students should do the hard work. However, I remain very optimistic about the results of the drive. I guess when one is committed to this line of duty, optimism must be prevalent for encouragement . . .

From Atlanta, August 1, 1963—

I, Rev. Fred C. Bennette, attended another meeting at Allen Temple . . . This was the fourth attempt to organize the section . . . known as the near Westside . . . There were approximately six persons present. It was suggested that the meeting be recessed in hopes that more would attend the next one.

From Carl Arnold, Hattiesburg, Mississippi, September 1963—

They come by the office and I sit down with them and we go over the voter registration form together and then I go down and stand beside them as they take the test. Determination is the thing that makes them go down, and the thing that overcomes their fear of not being able to handle the questions on the form. You know to be patient with them; you have to coach them and when their fear of the written form causes them to panic and fall into a state of indecision and confusion, you have to lead them out.

From Jack Chatfield, Southwest Georgia Project—

We never got to Bronwood, though we planned to go. Chico was typing and I walked to Deacon Green's store to arouse discontent, much like opening a safe with your teeth. (The book reads, "The Negro's social misery, heretofore a kind of paralytic disability, is in this mid-century being tapped and directed into victory after countless victory.")

I said "Hi" and Deacon Green said "*Hi*" and I said, "'Bout meetin' time" and Deacon Green said, "'Fraid I cain't make it around tonight" and I fished around for change for to buy me a soda for to give me time to gather my defense. No change. "Why not, Deacon?"

"'Fraid I jest cain't make it round tonight."

Actually, what had preceded all this is interesting: An insurance man had called me into the store by name (I was waiting for him to conclude his business) and when I came in I saw that he was eating a Baby Ruth and not selling insurance at all, so I said, "Did you call me?"

"You don't have to be afraid to come in just because I'm here," he said.

I said I was merely waiting for him to finish his business, which was a half-truth (I'm tremendously self-conscious around whites).

At any rate, he was a New Yorker who joined the Air Force and was sent South and learned Karate and twenty-eight ways of killing a man with the nipples of your breasts, shorn of hair; learned that justice for all men was okay stuff and why not justice for the colored man? because that was okay stuff, too; had outsold every insurance man in the state of Georgia, had killed the enemy in Guam (1957, which must have been a war this county never knew it was fighting) with piano wire thrice or more and was prepared to show me with string how it was done. I declined the gambit, feigned fatigue, but he succeeded in getting the string around my ersatz neck (forefinger) and we pranced around in a little murderer-murdered game for a while. He had defused bombs at Turner that Cyrus Citizen would never know existed and had run down a Yugoslavian spy with a fire truck after watching him toss a napalm bomb into the cockpit of an airplane that Alvin Average would never know existed ("I meant to kill him. That was orders").

He excused himself after a time, and John O'Neal and Eddie Brown happened by from Lee and I excused myself.

It had been an exhilarating afternoon . . . .

From Weldon Rougeau, Dade County, Florida—

The month of September proved to be a productive one for voter registration here. Through a community effort, we were able to add 5,593 persons on the registration rolls.

The highlight of the drive was from September 16 to September 28. During that time, we registered 5,567 persons. Of that total approximately 100 were whites.

Registration was conducted in eleven predominately Negro areas which had sub-stations placed in them by the county for the convenience of the people living in these areas . . .

These locations were opened from Monday to Saturday, from 8:00 A.M. to 5:00 P.M., with the exception of Tuesdays and Thursdays when they remained open until 9:00 P.M. The turnouts on Tuesdays and Thursdays were very heavy despite rain in some areas.

The personnel for these sub-stations came from the eleven areas and were hired by the county. They were all Negroes who were registered voters. In most instances, there was representation of the two major political parties.

The task of getting the sub-stations was not an easy one. Initially, there was considerable opposition because of the nature of the registration drive which was supposed to be in the Negro areas only. Only after I brought the matter up at a meeting with the Catholic Bishop of the Diocese of South Florida did the leadership of the county begin to seriously consider rendering this service to the community.

Several members of the Community Relations Board [official biracial committee] took the matter before the County Manager. He was very receptive towards this and asked that preferential locations for registration sub-stations be submitted to him by the Board. I was asked to name the locations for this and after I had consulted with residents and leaders I submitted a list of locations for the books to be placed . . .

Again, there was the omnipresent problem of getting the organizations in the Negro community to take an active part in the drive. We were given too many promises from the recognized giants in the community. A few organizations did get members to work with us, but the number from these organizations was not representative of the active membership in them.

The organizations that helped were: The National Conference of

Christians and Jews, the B'nai B'rith Youth Organization, the Boy Scouts (Goulds), CORE, the League of Women Voters, the Florida Labor Council, several local organizations both youth and adult, and countless individuals who were not direct representatives of organizations . . .

In conducting our drive, we were given publicity by the two Negro newspapers, a Negro radio station, and several nightclubs in the county who constantly announced where the registration sub-stations were, the times they were open, and the qualifications for one to register.

In following our publicity phase of our drive, we also had persons to go into churches on Sundays and make announcements about the registration drive and the need for a good showing to insure our getting the books again at a subsequent date or pre-election period. We also had persons going to theaters and making announcements and appealing for help with the drive.

We were able to get the principals of all the schools in these areas to send memorandums to the parents, make daily announcements about the location of the books in the community, and also instruct the leaders of the student organizations to help in the distribution of leaflets, canvassing, and office work. About 50 of each student body participated in one way or another.

Several weeks before the acquisition of the books, we had persons canvass each area we were anticipating having the books. The information gathered was whether the persons of voting age were registered, their name and address, and telephone number if they had one. We also informed them that there was a possibility of getting the books in their community and if we were successful, we would inform them of the location, times, and give them transportation to the sub-station if they did not have any.

When we were officially notified that the books would be in the areas we had selected, we had leaflets, posters, and placards printed with the 11 locations, times for registering, qualifications, and reasons why one should register. We distributed over 125,000 leaflets, 1,000 posters, and 1,550 placards. This proved to be very effective in notifying the people we had contacted while canvassing.

Money continues to be a problem here. CORE does not get enough from VEP to amply meet the needs of Dade County when there are so many other areas with vociferous opposition confronting our staff in trying to perform their duties. Therefore, I hope you will be able to include more money or enough money to meet the necessary needs of

Dade County—a county with a population of over one million people. Respectfully submitted this 10th day of October, 1963.

Field Report, September 1963, Ronnie Moore—

The Congress of Racial Equality has 15 task force workers and two field secretaries working on voter registration in Louisiana, covering seven parishes; namely, West Baton Rouge, St. Helena, Iberville, Tangipahoa, East Feliciana, West Feliciana, and Pointe Coupee . . .

We are aiming at registering 1,550 people in the named parishes by October 31, 1963. The number is based on imagination and optimism . . .

IBERVILLE—Voter registration has not been its very best, but we anticipate better results for October. We have 12 Negro candidates seeking election to office of sheriff, police jury, coroner, parish Democratic committee, constable, justice of peace, and state Democratic central committee. CORE has workers in 7 of the 9 wards, and SCLC is working in the remaining two wards, since Major Johns is running for state representative . . .

We have set a quota of 900 as our October voter registration goal. PRAY FOR US.

ST. HELENA—The story is about the same. The registrar is still turning Negroes down 4-1. Community interest in voter registration is still good. Negroes are still attempting to register. However, because the registrar in this parish . . . and others like him, have used the (LR-1) application form to turn down 90% of the persons denied registration, we anticipate the federal government's filing a suit in the next few days against the use of the LR-1 forms as a test. On the basis of numerous complaints filed by CORE, this suit was possible, so say federal officials. Ha! Ha! Nevertheless, we are sitting tight, waiting for the suit to get to court . . .

POINTE COUPEE—From the standpoint of cooperation of leaders, this is a good parish . . . The registrar is nice but a wizard at turning Negroes down in large numbers. However, we shall continue to work in the same areas with the hope that the recent racial and political developments will give the local people the shot they need to overcome apathy.

WEST BATON ROUGE—Voter registration is moving without interference from the white power structure. We anticipate registering large numbers when we overcome the large degree of apathy and illiteracy.

WEST FELICIANA—September has been a month of canvassing and

setting up and conducting clinics. We have had persons in large numbers attending clinics and I think I didn't include the number of clinic participants: 85–115. People are waiting until later October before attempting to register, because of "sweet potato" contracts with the all-white canning company . . .

Only the naked eye can convince you of the economic problems in housing, education, and political attitude of the local people. I invite you to come to Louisiana and see Hardwood, of this parish.

EAST FELICIANA—As indicated in the past, intimidation by parish officials continues to hinder voter registration efforts. The registrar is worse than the registrar in St. Helena because he is turning Negroes down in larger proportions . . .

At voter registration rallies, policemen and sheriff deputies stand guard in cars around the area. Negroes fear both political and economic reprisals if they attempt to register and vote. However, we still canvass on plantations, back woods, and dusty roads in Wilson, La., Clinton, La., and Jackson, La., and throughout the parish.

TANGIPAHOA—Voter registration is still rough because the registrar is still turning Negroes down in large numbers. Community interest is good. Local voters leagues are active with CORE in sending lines of Negroes to the registrar's office daily, so reports CORE worker Galway Kinnell.

CONCLUSION—At one time I thought that some parishes were better than others. I still believe this to some extent. Nevertheless, when you look at the total situation, in one parish we find apathy, in another fear, and yet another illiteracy. In every parish it is discrimination by nature in the Louisiana voter registration system, but from one registrar to another discrimination varies.

In short, we are doing our best, but unless this damn system is obliterated, the task of developing the Negro voting potential in Louisiana is a lost cause.

From Dickie Flowers, regarding arrests in Indianola, Mississippi, October 1963—

The jail was the filthiest one I ever been in. The floor was dirty, the bathtub was in bad shape, and there was a split pipe in the tank of the commode. There was a hole in the floor and clothes were filthy, the mattresses raggedy with half the cotton on the floor under the bed. No water to drink unless we wanted to drink from the bathtub. We had to eat from tin pans which were rusted. There were 18 of us in that bad place, and we were obliged to share 4 bunks . . . Although there were 8 beds, there were only 4 mattresses, so we had to put the mattress on the floor in order for a maximum number of us to sleep at one time.

From Roy Shields, Jr., Southwest Georgia—

I plan to get up and talk to some night clubbers tonight . . . I plan to speak in a few churches tomorrow . . .

From Lee County, Georgia, worker—

We are broke and hungry, going day by day with no more than one meal, and sometimes nothing. I have been spending all my subsistence money for the last seven weeks on nothing but needs in the field . . .

From All Citizens Registration Committee, Atlanta, November 4, 1963—

There is no registration progress yet at Herndon Homes [a public housing project]. Mrs. Burnette, the tenant association president, received the material sent out . . . No registration committee was ever organized and, of the two women who were going to help Mrs. Burnette, one moved and one had illness in the family. Mrs. Burnette herself had an accident and was hospitalized. She is currently recuperating on crutches . . . Mrs. Burnette was not sure whether the official registration list supplied by ACRC could be utilized as it was very inaccurate . . . A subsequent phone call . . . revealed that they would be able to bring the list up to date (a change of 100 tenants). They intend to send out questionnaires to the new tenants to find out if they are registered.

From W. C. Patton, March 1964—

In Atlanta, Texas, we had the sad experience of having one of our prize winners return his check because he was afraid to cash it over the signature of the NAACP. We are trying to adjust this by having him endorse the check and return it to us and we, in turn, will send him a postal money order.

From Ronnie Moore, Plaquemines Parish, Louisiana, April 1964—

CORE has been active in the parish for a period of two months. Due to a mass rally held in New Orleans, Perez began cracking down on the Negro community. Up to that time, contacts had been made to start a voter registration clinic at a Catholic Church. Since Perez's intimidation, the Negro Community has withdrawn and activity has been at a standstill. I would say that in this parish, official and unofficial opposition is great and quite hazardous, to say the least.

Report from Albany, Georgia, late 1964—

[Albany is] much used and misused . . . a place of goodbyes . . .

Much of the tiredness and bitter feeling causes people to waste much time and energy. The threshold of frustration in Albany is very low. Much of this frustration is manifested by a growing feeling of nationalism, not only among "movement people" but "block boys" as well. [One local leader] projects increasingly his own frustrations in the form of blackness. It is not uncommon for him to quote Malcolm X or other Muslim leaders he has met in New York. Increasingly too he seems to be losing confidence in the philosophy of nonviolence.

Unsigned report, Louisiana CORE, fall 1964—

Unless there are immediate aggressive and affirmative steps taken by the federal government to eradicate the numerous impediments faced by Negroes in their efforts to become registered voters in the state and to obliterate the pattern of discrimination embedded in the Louisiana voter registration system by prejudiced registrars, CORE and other civil rights groups will go nearly bankrupt in trying to keep Negroes applying for registration. The constant and numerous denials of Negro applicants creates an enormous amount of apathy in the Negro community.

Discrimination is just one part of the problem. Negro voter applicants and civil rights workers are constantly intimidated, harassed, arrested, prosecuted, and subjected to constant economic, political, and physical reprisal by private citizens, public officials and sometimes by businesses.

The following is from a sixty-page report by John Due, then a field worker for VEP. In April 1964 he traveled through rural Mississippi gathering affidavits and evidence on voter registration harassment for presentation before the U.S. Commission on Civil Rights in Natchez. He was accompanied on the latter part of the trip by Miss Emma Bell of the COFO office in Jackson. The two were arrested after running a road block at the scene of an accident, Mr. Due being under the impression he was not supposed to stop.

They let Emma sit in the car. When we entered the lighted room, only Sheriff Daniel Jones was there. I wondered to myself where the other two men were who had been with the sheriff down the highway when he had first searched the car. Jones was looking through my legal pads, one for Pike County, the other for Amite County. Also in his possession were statements and affidavits, and also the COFO materials concerning intimidation and brutality in Southwest Mississippi. He also asked for whom I worked, and I repeated the same story but being a little more explicit that I had been researching the "economic conditions" in Amite County, knowing where my notes were going to lead him. By that time, Butler had demanded my billfold and spent much time going through my cards. He found my membership card to the Florida Bar, my NAACP membership card, and my CORE membership card and threw them to the sheriff, saying, "that communist organization."

The sheriff took my Florida Bar card and asked me if I was an attorney. I said yes. He then said, "Well, attorney, what good is being a lawyer doing you now?" I admitted that it was not doing me much good. Sheriff Jones went briefly through my report on Amite County and said, "Well, we don't want Bobby Kennedy down here, so I will give these papers all back to you nice and pretty." I don't think he noticed where he had been involved in [two of the affidavits].

The state trooper then motioned the sheriff into another room and discussed something about which I could not hear. The sheriff then came out, took my papers and placed them in his safe. The trooper then left. After I had been charged with reckless driving and failure to stop for an emergency vehicle, the sheriff then said that my cash bond was $100, and asked whether I wanted the trial in the morning or in the afternoon on Wednesday. I chose the afternoon. He then said for me to be there at 3 P.M., warning me that he wanted me to be there.

I was free. I got in the car, and Emma drove off. She drove past the place where Lewis Allen was shot, which I really didn't care to see at that time; and she searched for the road that would lead out of Liberty other than the highway toward McComb. It had been two years since she had been in the area, and she couldn't find it. We drove back into the main part of Liberty and went past the courthouse into the highway toward McComb. It was now after 1 A.M., and it seemed that no one was stirring. Emma drove slowly, both of us keeping close eyes to the side of the road. About 15 miles away from Liberty, we drove past a building behind which a state trooper was parked. About six or seven miles away from McComb, lights of a car approached us from behind. We were traveling only about 40 mph. The car passed us, and with our bright lights shining into it, we could see six tall men sitting ramrod-straight—who seemed to be farmer types—all of them wearing wide-brim hats. Emma in about a mile turned off from the highway onto a county road which leads to Magnolia, Mississippi. From Magnolia, we entered McComb from the side. Emma said that if we had gone farther on the highway, they probably would have met us at an underpass where the highway divided with no place to turn around.

As we drove into McComb, we passed a . . . gasoline station, at which Mr. C. C. Bryant had said earlier that he does not like to do business because he believed that the owner was a member of the Klan. There were several cars of people gathered at the station, but we did not tarry there in order to determine whether Mr. Bryant's belief was true or not.

Emma then dropped me off by the Negro hotel. I told her to return at 6 A.M. I wanted to be out of Amite County before the sheriff would get to his office. Also, we had to get all the information as soon as we could out of Wilkinson County and get to Natchez, Mississippi, so that I could report . . . about the sheriff stealing my papers.

I had a very restless night; however, I was dressed and ready to go when Emma came by. I decided not to take the most direct route to Centreville and Woodville, Wilkinson County, which was by Liberty, Amite County; but rather, we drove south out of the way and then took the county road to Centreville. One pick-up truck followed our car for about five miles, but it went on to Liberty when we turned off into a very rugged county road that finally led into Centreville.

We soon reached the home of Mother O'Quinn, 94 years old, but seemed to be in her 70's. When we introduced ourselves, she invited us in her half-lighted living room. We explained to her why we were there. She understood and was eager to cooperate. The daughter-in-law . . . who we were looking for was in Florida; so we decided to take her statement.

Her own son was shot-gunned one dark night as he was coming into his driveway, over five years ago. [His son], Clarence O'Quinn, who had made his home in Florida and was teaching, came to Centreville to live and comfort his grandmother. Around the first of April of this year, he came home and told her that [a] chief of police had beaten him. She asked what happened. Clarence said that he was only going in the post office and was on the steps when the chief approached him without any explanation or cause and said, "You damn uppity nigger, you think you own the town," and began to beat O'Quinn. Clarence asked his grandmother what he should do. She said, "You have a life worth living; you should not throw it away. You have no rights and privileges here." She told him to get all his things and leave Centreville that day. Clarence did leave Centreville that day to save his life and is presently living in Florida.

In this work, I had been objective, not emotionally involved with the particular person, but tears came to my eyes as Emma and I turned to leave. I had almost become used to stories of beatings and "mysterious shotgunnings." I had not become used to a grandmother telling her grandson to leave her—in order to live—because he had no rights and privileges. I suddenly remembered the hot argument I had with a high school chum back in 1951. He had volunteered for the Air Force rather than waiting to be drafted in the infantry. He argued that he did not want to die in Korea fighting people of his color, when here in the United States he was not even treated as a human being. I do not remember the counter arguments I used, but whatever they were, they are implicit in the activity of Emma and I trying to get statements before the Mississippi Advisory Committee to the United States Civil Rights Commission; but moist eyes belied the same old frustrations felt by my old high school chum.

Emma and I then went to the O'Quinn's restaurant in Centreville to see her daughter who might be able to tell us about the Walker killing a la Lewis Allen in Woodville a few miles away. Although Mrs. Ida O'Quinn was in Florida, her daughter was there managing the restaurant. She was able to direct us only to the address of his mother-in-law, who could tell us nothing. She was only able to give us a vague direction to his former residence, which was supposed to be on the way to Natchez near Woodville. We didn't find the house, but rather than spending any more time, I decided that we should go on to Natchez. I didn't want to miss my appointment with Courtney Siceloff of the U.S. Civil Rights Commission. I wanted to tell him what happened, hoping the USCRC would procure my papers by a court order.

It was a relief to arrive in Natchez. Emma didn't understand my feelings because the very reason the hearing was being held in Natchez is that most of the known cases of brutalities and beatings have occurred in Natchez. After a while, we finally arrived at the funeral home of Mr.

Archie Curtis, the place where I was to meet Siceloff. Curtis is a Negro who seemed to be in his 50's. He has an Adenauer-type face resulting from having recently suffered from a stroke. It had not incapacitated him except to require him to speak slowly and to write slowly. He welcomed us into his private study. Although it was already planned that he appear before the Advisory Committee, he told us what had happened to him. One night in March of this year, he received a telephone call for him to pick up a body. He and his assistant, Willie Jackson, took the hearse wagon and drove in the direction of the given address. He said to Jackson, "We must have the wrong address" because they were in a deserted area when a car drove up behind them and they were ordered to stop. Curtis told me that six armed men in hoods got out of their car, and one of them demanded from him his NAACP membership card. Curtis told them that he had no NAACP card (it so happened that his new one had not yet arrived). They proceeded to beat him and his assistant. He begged them to stop beating him, telling them that he had had a stroke, but they continued until they were tired of it and then left him and his assistant in the street. This same "trick" happened to another Negro funeral director, George West. Mr. Curtis is actually not active in any NAACP but has been active with Natchez Negro Business League which has been urging Negroes to register. Their success which would arouse the KKK to be excited is that only about 200 Negroes are registered.

Mr. Siceloff arrived, and while eating a lunch brought by Emma, I told him what happened. He expressed a great concern about my papers because now in jeopardy were all the people I talked with, being that they were in the possession of the sheriff, Daniel Jones . . . Rather than forfeiting or even getting consent that I could forfeit the bond, I decided to return to Liberty and appear for the trial and stand mute; but at the same time, I believed that I should present a written demand for my papers.

Upon the advice of Mr. Wiley Branton, I asked Mr. Siceloff to be a witness or ascertain whether a member of the FBI would be present. Siceloff was willing but said that he had to call Washington to make sure that they were on notice. As it was after 2:00 and the trial was at 3:00, Emma and I left Natchez.

When we arrived in Liberty, I already felt like a martyr. I had solemnly prepared written motions, such as, appearance to stand mute, demand for papers, and request for an attorney and a jury trial. I gave copies to Emma, putting them in an envelope which she hid. I anticipated that they would deny that I ever presented the motions.

When I arrived in the office of Sheriff Jones, a quite sullen deputy sheriff was waiting for me. Soon, I heard the voice of Mr. Siceloff, and I felt as if the U.S. Marines had arrived. Mr. Siceloff identified himself and expressed an interest in the papers which Sheriff Jones had. The sheriff, in a surprised voice, said, well, he was going to give the papers back anyway. I had information which was useful for his investigation, he said. We all then went up to the Justice of Peace's office.

The Justice of Peace was an elderly man who seemed almost gentle. After reading the accusation, he asked me for my plea and I told him that I stood mute and explained what that meant. Sheriff Jones interfered, saying that in Mississippi, there is no such plea, that *nolo contendere* took the place of "standing mute." I admitted that I was not all that familiar with Mississippi law except that it was a common-law state, and "standing mute" is part of the common law. I then presented the written motions and the demand for my papers. I may have made a mistake, but I proceeded to explain my action on account of the fact that the sheriff had taken my papers without my consent. Sheriff Jones exclaimed that he was going to return my papers regardless of whether I plead guilty or not guilty; so he hurriedly went downstairs and restored to me my papers.

I then pleaded "guilty" after a long pause of thinking. It seemed unreasonable to fight both the traffic case and the sheriff's action. I decided to fight Mississippi's methods of dealing with traffic violations another day. The Justice of Peace then gave a statement about the seriousness of what I had done and that the maximum sentence included 30 days; but because I was so "reasonable and fair," so said the Justice of Peace, I was fined $50 for both charges and $19 for the cost of court. After paying the fine, we all left. Soon Emma and I were leaving Liberty.

The day before, Monday afternoon, I had planned to go on Tuesday to Port Gibson, Claiborne County. COFO had a contact there who could probably lead us to persons who probably could make an appearance for the committee or at least give us some signed statements; but it was already 4 P.M., and we were reluctant to be driving after sunset. Siceloff had offered to give us his car because of the belief that our enemy now knew our car. We planned to stay in McComb Tuesday night, and Port Gibson was too far away. We decided therefore, to go only to Bude, which was only 30 miles away from McComb.

Bude is in Franklin County, which is comprised mostly of the Homochitto National Forest. COFO had received a newspaper account dated in March of this year picturing the Negro club, the "Horseshoe Circle," owned by a Mr. John Clark, to be demolished in front by dynamite. The picture shows the stone front demolished by, again, "unknown persons." When we arrived there, we talked to Mrs. Clark, who was obviously afraid and who did not give us a statement. Other than that, she was friendly, and we took our leave . . .

When we arrived in McComb, Mississippi, we revisited Mr. C. C. Bryant and Mr. Willie Thompson, seeing that the affidavits which he had would be notarized and sought to assure them that a carload of people from McComb would come to Natchez. Mr. Willie Thompson said that at least he and Mr. Bryant's brother would drive to Natchez. Emma then dropped me off by the hotel I stayed the night before, and she then drove to her home.

Around 6:30 Wednesday morning, Emma and I left McComb going to Liberty to pick up Evelina Tobias. We again wanted to be out of Liberty before too many people stirred around. We then remembered that we had procured no real information about the Lewis Allen killing of February of this year. During the excitement evolving around my situation, we had relied upon the Jackson COFO office to follow through in reaching Mrs. Allen in Louisiana. Emma called her and told her as I had promised, that we would pay for her expenses if she would come to Natchez, but Mrs. Allen told her that she didn't want to have anything to do with Mississippi. However, we still had hopes that she might come.

After we picked up Evelina Tobias, she told us about how the Sunday before, a high school boy by the name of John Harris was beaten by the Klan. Evelina knew where the family lives, so we went there to talk to them. They lived in the town of Gloster, 12 miles west of Liberty on a small farm. In reaching their home, we had to pass the homes of Sheriff Jones and the deceased Lewis Allen. Both of them had been neighbors. We turned into the driveway of the Harris' home, and Evelina went to the door and brought to the car Mrs. Lillie M. Harris, the mother of John Harris. I told her what we were doing and asked her what happened to her son. She said that on Sunday, April 19, her son, the members of the family, and members of the choir were coming home from church when hoodlum whites, without their hoods, drove up in their car and stopped, ordered John Harris to come to them and proceeded to assault him with the blunt end of their pistols. He screamed for his mother and then begged for them to kill him. Without hearing more, I asked her whether she and her son would go with me to the hearing in Natchez. She said yes, and in a short while we had picked up her son, who wore a cap to cover the stitches on his head wounds. We then picked up Mr. Franklin Robinson at Mr. Westly's farm, and finally reached Natchez about 11 A.M.

When we arrived at the place of the hearing at the Natchez Post Office, Mr. Siceloff asked us to return later because members of the Mississippi Advisory Committee were having a preliminary discussion. We went to a Negro restaurant, and while there I met Mr. Archie Curtis, who notarized my affidavit that I witnessed personally the signatures on the signed statements I had in my possession. He also brought with him a man . . . [who] had somebody for me to see. I told Emma to take everybody on down to the U.S. Post Office, and that I would be there later.

Even Mr. Curtis could not come because it was a secret hiding place, and with him already having been beaten, he could be beaten again in order to tell the Klan where the place was. [The man] brought me to the place, and as I entered a bedroom, there was lying on the bed a young Negro of about 25 years of age. (Whereas only *this* person is in *immediate* danger as distinguished from the other persons who gave me their statements, and who are in probable danger only, I shall not expose this person's name.)

He had worked as a general handyman for a white farmer. On April 13 of this year, on a Sunday night, he was in the barn. He was trying the ignition because the truck had not been starting. He just happened to turn around and stared in the barrel of a shotgun. A man in a black hood holding the gun said, "Get out, boy." The Negro pushed the gun out of the window and quickly rolled the window up. He turned around to roll the window up on the other side of the truck and looked into the barrel of a rifle. This man also in a black hood told him, "You better do as he says." Each of them got to the side of him and began marching him to the back of the barn. As soon as he came to the edge where he could see the back of the barn, he said about six more men in hoods were all armed with guns. One man said, "We have been waiting for this a long time." He immediately pushed the two by his side together and turned, sprinting toward the house. He was able to get one side of the barn between him and them for awhile, but he had at least 50 yards to reach the porch of the house. He ran screaming for Mrs. X (the owner of the farm), and had attained about 20 yards when he received a shot in his shoulder and back. The force of the bullets spun him slightly around when he was dropped by a shot in his leg.

Mrs. X ran out screaming, "What is the matter, what is the matter?" She saw that he was covered with blood. She told him to "play" like he was dead, and she ran and got a raincoat to cover him up with. With both of them straining together, they were able to get him on the floor of a car and she drove him to the hospital.

Why did this happen? He is the only Negro in Kingston who has been registered and he has been voting since 1960. Whites have made pointed remarks about this, his voting being a common known fact. Because of this, he has acquired a personal debt of more than $435 medical expenses incidental to four bullet wounds.

I then returned to the hearing of the Advisory Committee. While the hearing was in session, I saw now that there remained only one more hurdle—to get my witnesses back safely in Liberty and McComb, and then get back to Jackson. Courtney Siceloff was worried about this. So was William Taylor, the General Counsel to the U.S. Civil Rights Commission, who was there with the Advisory Committee. We also were worried about retaliation by the Klan against these people.

When we first had arrived in Natchez and when my party first got out of the car, I noticed how we attracted the attention of curious people, such as the white attendant, who in the service station next to the bus station "studied" us and then made a phone call and talked to someone while still "studying" us.

On my return to the post office and when I went back to the car to get the cross out [a charred Ku Klux Klan cross picked up as evidence], and as I carried the cross down the block across the street, going to the hearing room, I deliberately avoided looking into the face of the same attendant or other white persons standing about. I left the cross outside the door of the hearing room, not wanting to take it in. I felt that it might just interrupt the proceedings.

Pretty soon two carloads of men drove up to the post office, disembarking their passengers. Although there were a few thin high school youths and a thin man about 40 in a business suit, the most of them were husky white men in their 20's and 30's wearing tight levis and khakis, western hats, string ties, and sunglasses. One wore sun-mirrored glasses which he wore throughout the hearing, and sat in the front row easily frightening the members of the Committee. However, most of them were in good spirits, even joked about the cross standing in the doorway. When they first came to the door, they hesitated when they were confronted by the scene of an integrated panel presided over by the Negro, [Dr. A. B.] Britton. Not wishing them to be standing by the door because of my example, I pointed to vacant seats. They nonchalantly took their seats, even next to Negroes—some preferring to cluster together and some preferring to sit in the front row, as did the one with mirrored sunglasses.

They remained quiet, but they were still an ominous group by their mere presence. One of them got a pad out and as each witness would identify himself, the "cowboy" would busily write down the person's name, address, etc. I received a hidden joy to see the members of the committee become a little unnerved. I was glad the Klan was there because that was exactly what we wanted to show the committee, and eventually the American people, fear and intimidation produced by the Klan. Only Dr. Britton, although wet with beads of perspiration on his forehead—which I cannot blame only because of all the stuffiness of the hearing room—seemed brave when he dryly stopped the proceedings. He indicated that the committee noticed the presence of new people who had just arrived. He explained the purpose of the committee and indicated that if any of them had any information to present, such as being injured by violations of their civil rights, etc., the committee would hear them.

In a few minutes, I saw Attorney William Taylor abruptly leave and then return. Dr. Britton then called a short recess and asked everyone to leave. I then saw the local police come into the room. At first I thought he was after my charred cross, but I learned later that Taylor had received a bomb warning.

After my people from Pike and Amite Counties testified, I presented my statements and explained to them why some of them were not notarized. I also produced the charred cross, since some of the members of the committee had never seen one.

For the closed session, Dr. Britton asked everyone except the witnesses and their families to leave. After a short recess, the closed session was called and more testimonies were taken.

By this time, Robert Moses and his wife had made their appearance. Dr. Britton acknowledged their presence and asked Bob whether he had anything to say. Bob then gave a run-down of all the cases and killings and brutalities which had been reported to COFO and demonstrated the need for federal protection in the area. Dr. Britton then asked Bob a leading question about the kind of people doing violence. Bob told the Committee that these people believe that the U.S. Government is an illegal government and that their actions are a response to their beliefs.

It was now after 4 P.M., and by an unspoken unanimous agreement, it was decided that we terminate the hearing so that everyone would be able to get home before dark. Because my people had to go to Liberty, Amite County, and McComb, Pike County, I was able to persuade Dr. Britton, with his carload of committee members, and Courtney Siceloff, both of whom were going to Jackson, to go out of the way and go as far as Bude, Franklin County, following us. This would leave only about 30 miles for us to go, but this 30 miles was all in Amite County. Robert Moses and his wife were also in a car. It was clear that a caravan of five cars was attracting attention; but at a very slow pace, we finally reached Bude and waved goodbye to Dr. Britton and Siceloff, who continued on their way to Jackson. Mr. Robinson, who was in my car, offered that I should go only as far as Mr. Westly's farm and that he would take Miss Tobias and the Harrises home. I appreciated that, realizing that my black car was well known in Liberty, and it would be safer if they were in Mr. Robinson's car. We reached Mr. Westly's home and I said good-bye to these good people of Amite and Wilkinson Counties. I was glad that I had given to Mr. Taylor of the USCRC the names and addresses of persons I brought to the hearing.

Our caravan of three cars went by an out-of-the-way country road until we were about six miles from McComb, and then we said goodbye to Mr. Thompson and Mr. C. C. Bryant who drove their car on to McComb. . . .

When I had paid the cash bond to Sheriff Daniel Jones the Monday night before, I asked the sheriff whether I could speak to him frankly. I had already seen an "Impeach Earl Warren" pamphlet on his desk. He said that he always intends to speak frankly. I then said that I was interested in Mississippi and the rest of the South being better places for all the people, both black and white. The sheriff rejoined, not in an angry tone of voice, that that was his duty—to make his county a safe place for all the people. He said he has been surely taxed by the outside agitators—

who are bent to break the law and stir up people, and that he intends to enforce the law. He mentioned Bob Moses. He then produced the well-known picture of Martin Luther King [Jr.] sitting with a couple of so-called Communists at a Highlander Folk School meeting. He said that "this is the type of people we are dealing with." He then looked at me and said, "I don't know how you are tied up with this. I think you are just brainwashed. I advise you, I am not ordering you or warning you, I am just advising you to leave Amite County and not come back."

Therefore, Bob's statement before the Advisory Committee is indeed true. I believe that the sheriff was actually sincere in believing that the civil rights movement is a Communist conspiracy. But so was the KKK sincere in the belief that in the 1870's the Scalawags and the Carpet-baggers were raping the South. But how can this justify the murder of innocent Negroes?

One night in February of this year, Mr. Lewis Allen had just got out of his truck when obviously he found himself in trouble. It seems that he was trying to run and get under the truck when he was shot from both sides by deer shot and buck shot. His face was so indistinguishable that at his funeral the casket was shut.

He had signed an affidavit, with a copy filed with the COFO office, that he had witnessed the murder of another Negro, Mr. Herbert Lee.

Mrs. Lewis Allen was arrested by Sheriff Daniel Jones for the killing of her husband and was subsequently released. Robert Moses came to the funeral. His assistant, Dave Dennis of CORE, cried without shame before a gathering of New York area attorneys.

Such, as this report indicates, is the war against "communism."

Unsigned Louisiana CORE Report, fall 1964—

Complaints on discrimination in applying the Louisiana voter registration laws and in defiance of the voting section of the new civil rights law are filed daily with the Federal Bureau of Investigation and the Justice Department. No action of a strong affirmative nature is ever taken. However, we shall push on, and on, and on.

8)

Federal Action and
a Crisis in the Courts

When John F. Kennedy campaigned for president in 1960, he conveyed an unmistakable commitment to action on many fronts, including civil rights. He seemed to differ from the Eisenhower administration more in spirit and attitude than in direction. Richard Nixon, fairly or not, bore the burden of the administration's attitude of executive aloofness in the field of civil rights. President Eisenhower had never said whether he approved or disapproved of the Supreme Court's school desegregation decision of 1954; he had tenaciously maintained a hands-off policy insofar as the entire trend of court decisions on race was concerned. Against pleas from civil rights leaders and others to place the moral force of the presidency behind the court's decisions, he held fast. Under his presidency, the first two civil rights bills since 1875 were passed by Congress, but his own role in bringing this about was limited. The Eisenhower Justice Department, given substantial powers in the voting field by the 1957 act, allowed a year to pass before bringing the first suit under that act.

During the campaign of 1960, Mr. Kennedy underscored the importance of voting as the foundation of all other rights. He stressed that vigorous executive action, rather than new legislation, was needed in the civil rights field. His initiative in telephoning Mrs. Martin Luther King when Dr. King was in jail in Georgia and the well-publicized telephone efforts of Robert Kennedy to secure Dr. King's release were, in the context of the campaign, a calculated and unmistakable suggestion that a Kennedy victory would mean that the presidency would indeed forcefully commit itself to the furtherance of the civil rights cause. Consistent with the message that all of this conveyed, President Kennedy did in fact move very early toward stronger executive involvement. The appointment of his brother as attorney general brought his own personal prestige into the administration of the department that would have the chief role in policy formation on civil rights. The relationship between the attorney general and the President, in turn, gave Robert Kennedy a freedom and authority for action which another attorney general would have lacked. With the Kennedys, the country for the first time gained a definable executive policy on civil rights.[1] One reason was that for the first time there could be little doubt the President and his chief agent in the field of civil rights were of one accord and were committed to action.

It quickly became clear also that there would be no early drive for rights legislation and that the Justice Department would attempt to exercise fully, within its limitations, the provisions of the 1957 and 1960 Civil Rights Act related to voting.[2] The civil rights section of the department, which had been elevated to division status by the 1957 act, was enlarged. It now had some priorities, and its status was enhanced by the selection of Burke Marshall, a respected corporation lawyer, as its director. The highest levels of the Justice Department in general, in fact, were filled by lawyers of distinction, most notably including, besides Marshall, Archibald Cox, Byron White, and Nicholas Katzenbach. This was a strong team.

The Civil Rights Act of 1957 had created the Commission on Civil Rights, which began to gather vitally needed information on voting practices. (It also gathered facts on many other racial matters, of course, and within the federal establishment it shortly became an influence for stronger federal action in the field.) Most important, the 1957 act had authorized the attorney general for the first time to initiate legal actions against practices that denied the vote because of race. The chief flaw in that part of the act lay in the fact that it was evaded when, confronted by federal legal action as individual officials, registrars simply resigned and registration boards were abolished. Since this kind of evasion of the law was second nature to those Southern politicians who had been eluding federal court decisions and federal law for decades, the flaw was great. The Civil Rights Act of 1960 corrected it by enabling the attorney general to proceed not simply against individual registrars but against the states themselves. The new law also required that voting records be preserved for twenty-two months, and made subject to inspection by Justice Department representatives. Finally, it provided that if federal courts found a pattern of discrimination in a given locality, a federal judge could name a federal referee to handle registration.

The Eisenhower administration had filed only six suits under the 1957 and 1960 acts' authority for the attorney general to initiate voting suits. The Kennedy administration immediately moved for more. By May of 1963, thirty-seven suits had been filed, eleven in Mississippi and the rest in Georgia, Louisiana, Alabama, and Tennessee. Burke Marshall's staff had personally gone into rural areas and cities all over the South painstakingly gathering evidence needed.[3] The division's *modus operandi* and some of the reasons for it were soon clear: It would generally forgo criminal prosecutions, and in civil actions it would seek broad injunctions under which large numbers of Negroes (rather than a lone individual here and there) would be placed on the voter rolls. The decision against criminal prosecutions was motivated in large part by the knowledge that, even in the federal courts, it would be difficult to persuade Southern juries to convict. Further, the criminal laws related to the denial of the vote had substantial weaknesses that might make convictions difficult to obtain before any jury. And, of course, such prosecutions would tie up attorneys who otherwise might be working on civil cases intended to achieve broad injunctions that might immediately end discrimination against thousands of Negroes.

This was the reasoning that governed the Justice Department's most important actions in the voting rights field from the outset of the Kennedy administration. It was an optimistic strategy. Marshall himself was hopeful that it would achieve widespread breakthroughs in the South. It did not. There were, to be sure, a few big local gains, notably through court orders that applied to Macon, Bullock, Montgomery, and Jefferson counties in Alabama and Washington, Bienville and Jackson parishes in Louisiana.[4] But Justice strategy and effort had embodied the administration's principal push in the voting rights field, and in that context the result after three years was a massive failure, one with many profound implications.

Marshall himself, a meticulous and circumspect man, subsequently acknowledged the failure. It was underscored in 1963, when the Commission on Civil Rights reported: "After five years of federal litigation [since the 1957 act], it is fair to conclude that case-by-case proceedings, helpful as they have been in isolated localities, have not provided a prompt or adequate remedy for widespread discriminatory denials of the right to vote." [5] Harold Fleming, former executive director of the Southern Regional Council and later executive vice-president of the Potomac Institute in Washington, wrote in 1965: "The lawyers in the Civil Rights Division have worked untiringly since 1961 to overcome voting discrimination against Negroes. That so much time and effort went to waste because of inadequate legal tools is an incalculable loss to the nation." [6] And in 1964, Mr. Marshall wrote: "The federal government has demonstrated a seeming inability to make significant advances, in seven years' time, since the 1957 law, in making the right to vote real for Negroes in Mississippi, large parts of Alabama and Louisiana, and in scattered counties in other states."

One of the ramifications is suggested in the confidential letter which Wiley Branton, director of the Voter Education Project, sent jointly on November 12, 1963, to Aaron Henry, state president of the Mississippi NAACP and president of the Conference of Federated Organizations (COFO), and Robert Moses of SNCC, who had worked at length on voter registration in Mississippi. In informing them that VEP was cutting off funds for the Mississippi registration program except for a nominal amount, Mr. Branton noted that use of the money elsewhere could put more names on the voter rolls. He added: "Of almost equal significance to our decision is the fact that the Justice Department has failed to get any meaningful decrees from any of the voter suits which have been filed in Mississippi and we know that until and unless favorable decrees are rendered and then vigorously imposed, we will not be able to get many people registered successfully. We are also very concerned about the failure of the federal government to protect the people who have sought to register and vote or who are working actively in getting others to register . . ." Mr. Branton added his appreciation of "the thousands of people who have constantly braved . . . insults and harassment, intimidation and violence" in voter registration efforts without federal protection. But Mississippi was not again to receive large sums under the VEP's first three-year program. The fact that this difficult decision was made underscores the seriousness of the federal failure. In this stage in the life of the rights movement in the South, the elements of the movement that were most inclined toward direct action such as picketing and marching had consistently set these aside over long periods of time for the arduous task of voter registration. In fact, because of federal tax considerations, no workers engaged in voter registration with money from VEP could be involved in direct action. The months of work in Mississippi preceding VEP's decision (as well as the massive thrust into Mississippi in the summer of 1964) were largely without demonstrations of any kind except for quiet lines forming at courthouses. Voter registration and citizenship education had taken precedence over all other rights activities in some of the most repressive areas of the South, over an extended span of time. Often it was the young people of SNCC and other organizations who, to frightened people in weathered shacks beside rutted dirt roads, were explaining that despite the local whites' hostility the federal government was interested in them and would open the way for voting. "I have found . . . that talk of Washington and 'federal power' sometimes falls on dead ears," a young worker in southwest Georgia had reported in December 1962. "There is the most nebulous conception of government, or . . . really a disbelief in the government's real power." He and others were often the unofficial messengers telling people that the federal government was for them, would help them, and was stronger than the local white supremacists. Yet the inference of years of federal effort was that, in fact, in many places the white supremacists were indeed stronger. Specifically, the federal effort had failed in the areas where resistance was strongest. The Commission on Civil Rights noted that the Justice Department policy, significantly, had been successful in one state, Tennessee, where there had been little state resistance.[7] In the states where discrimination was worst, the policies were least successful. Since all of this became oppressively evident at a time when millions of Negroes had risen to new heights of expectation, it unquestionably added dangerously to bitter frustrations and hostility toward government itself. Eventually (an appropriate word for even the span of two or three years, considering the pace of advancing aspirations for freedom, once aroused), the federal government did assert its superiority with the Voting Rights Act of 1965. But, before then, how much bitter seed had been sown, shortly to produce new seedlings of anarchy and bitterness?

Certainly the Justice Department should not be singled out as the villain of that scenario. Those chiefly responsible were the defiant representatives of white supremacy, whether they were courtly senators in Washington resisting at every step the simple application of constitutional demands and the normal processes of the courts, or whether they were sheriffs with billy clubs. But it must be noted that while many a student worker was in the cotton fields explaining that the government in Washington was superior to the sheriff at the courthouse and justice would be done, Burke Marshall was writing that a chief difficulty simply was that civil rights workers in the South did not understand the federal system and were engendering hostility toward the federal government.[8] No doubt the latter was true, in a sense; yet in the earlier days of the registration movement in the South, it was true only as a by-product of the notable lack of success in bringing many federal officials to do what could have been done.

The Justice Department action had rested upon a decision to rely upon civil rather than criminal actions in the courts, to trust in the power of persuasion, to keep the FBI away from the kind of apprehension and arrest actions that it constantly engaged in when bank robberies or auto thefts were involved, and to refrain from legal action unless there was prospect for victory. Further, the strategy rested upon more than a modicum of faith that Southern federal judges, no matter how chosen, would act with reasonable dispatch, reasonable attention to the facts presented, and reasonable commitment to the established tradition of honoring the binding legal precedents enunciated by higher courts. In retrospect, too, one is struck by the department's willingness to accept the jury discrimination within Southern federal courts as well as in Southern state courts. No real effort was made to correct even the biased federal grand jury lists in the South, although United States attorneys in those areas, answerable to the Justice Department and appointed by the President, seemingly could have accomplished this without great difficulty. On the books, this discrimination had been prohibited for eighty years, by Title 18, Section 243, of the United States Codes. Since the administration had chosen litigation in Southern courts for its principal thrust in civil rights, the failure to desegregrate federal juries is startling.[9]

The Southern Judges

Setting aside for the moment the courses which the administration rejected or ignored, consider what happened with its litigation, and why. The Southern judges who were called upon to bear the unusually heavy judicial burden that these cases embodied were a widely divergent lot. We need cite the performance of only a few to suggest the extent to which the courts failed to apply the law expeditiously and fairly in voter registration and other civil rights cases. Consider District Judges William Harold Cox and Sidney C. Mize of Mississippi, J. Robert Elliott and Frank M. Scarlett of Georgia, and E. Gordon West of Louisiana.[10]

Judge Cox, a college roommate of Senator Eastland's (and the first of President Kennedy's judicial appointments in the South), in one outburst likened some Negroes seeking the vote to "chimpanzees" who "ought to be in the movies rather than being registered to vote." Judge Cox consistently opposed the government on voter registration suits and was almost as consistently reversed by the U.S. Court of Appeals for the Fifth Circuit, the appellate court for most of the Deep South. The Fifth Circuit court emerged as the strong steadying hand for law in the South, but it was not sufficiently superhuman to prevent enormous delays and notable temporary aberrations while matters were lodged before certain district courts. In many cases, these district court departures, even though reversed, were perfect proof of the dictum that "justice delayed is justice denied." If a man were denied the right to vote in one election and then another and then another as his case was being unnecessarily delayed in the courts, he was being denied exercises of his rights which could never be recovered, no matter what the ultimate outcome of the case.

One of Judge Cox's most notable performances was in a suit involving voter discrimination in Clarke County, Mississippi, which for thirty years had permitted no Negroes to vote. A Justice Department suit filed on July 6, 1961, when there had been no Negroes on voting lists in Clarke although there were 3,000 in the county, alleged arbitrary denial of the right to vote. Judge Cox moved to block the government from the outset. Although the 1960 Civil Rights Act gave the government the right to inspect public voting records, he refused to permit this. Months were consumed in appeals before the government attorneys could in-

PERA Body OK's Change In Investing

The Public Employes Retirement Association board approved changes in its investment policy Friday, including purchase of growth stocks as recommended by a consulting firm.

The board also hired Andrew Montoya as engineer and supervisor of the PERA's, new $4.4 million, five-story office building nearing completion adjacent to the Capitol. Montoya will start at $720 monthly salary.

The board decided to ask for bids for janitorial services for the structure, which is scheduled for use by state agencies in January.

Board members also will ask the State Finance Board next month for permission to spend approximately $105,000 to operate the new office building from January through June 1968. There was no appropriation for this by the legislature.

The $105,000 will come from rentals which during the period are expected to total . . .

Sugar Crop

HAVANA (AP) — The worst drought in years is threatening the sugar harvest in Cubas' largest producing province of Oriente in the east, the Communist party newspaper Granma reported Friday. It announced the 1968 harvest will begin the first two weeks in November, earlier than ever. The harvest carries over into 1968.

"The party and harvest organizations, faced with this situation, have directed greater efforts at all levels to compensate in quality in sugar yield to offset possible decreases in cane volume," Granma said.

The newspaper reported that up to Sept. 30 Oriente received only 25 inches of rain, compared with more than 26 inches in 1962, which it called the previous driest year of recent times.

This may not sound like much of a drought to dry land farmers in the United States, but it is in Cuba, where rainfall in the cane fields averages from 35 to 55 inches a year.

Cuba earns about 80 per cent of its foreign exchange from the sugar crop. The 1968 goal was believed to have been reduced from 8 million metric tons to about 7½ million although no figures have been announced.

This year's goal was 7½ million tons, but the harvest that began last Nov. 22 was 6.1 million tons. Of this, Oriente Province produced more than two milli . . .

Damage in the year ending June 30, 1967, totaled some $6,236,000. In the previous fiscal year it totaled some $6,555,000 the figures show.

Only one of the 168 fire departments in the state which received State Fire Protection Fund monies did not estimate total loss, and that was the Albuquerque department, which normally doesn't.

While damage was less, however, more fires were actually reported. The total was 11,442, compared to 9,539 the previous year. Residential fires were most frequent, with grass fires second.

LEGAL ADVERTISEMENT

STATE OF NEW MEXICO
COUNTY OF SANTA FE
IN THE PROBATE COURT
IN THE MATTER OF THE ESTATE OF GILBERT FREDERICK
No. 3884
NOTICE OF APPOINTMENT
OF ADMINISTRATRIX

Notice is hereby given that the undersigned was on the 23rd day of Oct., 1967, appointed Administratrix of the Estate of GILBERT FREDERICK TRUJILLO, deceased, by the Probate Court in and for the County of Santa Fe State of New Mexico.

All persons having claims against said estate are hereby notified to file the same with the Clerk of the above named Court within six months of the date hereof, or the same will be forever barred.

Signed and posted this 23rd day of Oct., 1967.

CHARLOTTE L. TRUJILLO
Administratrix of the Estate of Gilbert Frederick Trujillo, deceased
(Legal No. 4572, Pub. Oct. 28, Nov. 4, 11, 18, 1967)

Ralph McGill UM 10/28/67

On a Book of the South and the Blacks

A newly - published book, "Climbing Jacob's Ladder," opens with a scene in a tiny town in Terrell County, Georgia. It sets the mood of a whole region in that time.

It was a hot July night in 1962.

The Rev. Charles Sherrod, young and thin - faced, led a quiet group of rural Negroes into the Mount Olive Baptist Church. It was a plain, plank structure. A picture of Jesus hung over the pulpit. On one of the walls was a calendar with President Kennedy's picture. About it were pictures of other American presidents.

Fifteen white men, four of them deputy sheriffs, came in and stood at the back of the church in stony silence.

The young minister said a prayer: "If God be for us, who will be against us? Into Thy hands we commend our souls and our lives every day . . "

A hymn was sung:
"We are climbing Jacob's ladder —
Every round goes
Higher, higher . ."

There was then an announcement that everyone was welcome to what was to be a voter registration meeting.

The sheriff of Terrell County came forward, a man in his seventies. He explained, almost gently, how happy Negroes were in the county. "We want our colored people to live like they've been living," he said. "There never was any trouble before all this started . . "

The 15 white men came forward as he talked and stood looking hard at the congregation. When the sheriff finished, they all left.

A few nights later three small Negro churches in Terrell County were burned — including Mount Olive with its pictures of President Kennedy and other presidents before him.

At the very end of this book is a table of voter registration in the South — 1962, 1964, 1966. On the night of the voter rally in the Mount Olive Church, later to be burned, 1,344,519 Negro voters were registered in 11 Southern states. In 1964 the total was 2,074,461. In 1966 it was 2,620,359.

Every round of Jacob's ladder does indeed go higher, higher.

Authors of the book, an important one, are South Carolina-born Pat Watters, a good journalist, but for some years now the director of information for the Southern Regional Council; and Georgia-born Reese Cleghorn, associate editor of The Atlanta Journal. Watters and Cleghorn, with very consider-able skill, mixed into the necessary statistics the many stories of human beings. These include experiences of torture and bombings in various jails for the crime of trying to register to vote. One might say there also are murder mysteries in the book, since somehow law enforcement officers not always were able to arrest those responsible for killings. And when they did make arrests they must have got the wrong men because the juries, sometimes grinning and smirking, found them not guilty. The book is dedicated to 13 men, black and white, who are the known killed in the effort to bring voting and basic citizenship rights to persons long denied.

The book is compassionate even as it indicts. The old sheriff, for example, who wanted everything to stay the way it was, was himself not really too different from some Southern senators who never sought to help their states solve their problems. Instead, from the Olympian peak in Washington, they were too often inflammatory and appealed to the worst in their region.

"Climbing Jacob's Ladder" is a fine book — disturbing, yet not without hope. It is a necessary book for those who want to know.

spect the records. A full year passed before government attorneys could even get a hearing date set for one initial motion.

The local registrar testified that whites registered for each other and took no tests. Under questioning about what he did if Negroes appeared, he said: ". . . I would always just tell them that I wasn't going to refuse them the opportunity to register but then I would just like for us to consider this matter, that due to the fact that they were having trouble in other parts of the country and that we folks here in Mississippi, white and colored, were getting along together and they were our friends and we were their friends and we weren't going to have trouble either way, and then I just suggested to them that they go back home and consider this matter and think it over and come back later."

Early in 1961 the names of five Negroes strangely had been placed on the voting list, which also was the list for jurors. They did not know they were registered, nor did they know about it when they were "called" to jury duty in 1961 and did not show up to serve. The registrar, A. L. Ramsey, later testified that they had been added to the list because a Negro was to be tried in the murder of a white man and the courts had been reversing convictions when no Negroes were on the jury lists.

The addition of these five Negroes ostensibly to the jury list was quite clear in its intent. But Judge Cox found that act extremely significant for other reasons. When he finally ruled in the voter case, he held that 1,500 white persons had been illegally registered but that the registrar also had been illegally registering Negroes. In that context, he noted these five on the voting list. The federal attorneys had sought a finding of a "pattern or practice of discrimination" against Negroes in particular, because this would be grounds for appointment of a federal voting referee; Judge Cox ruled that no such pattern or practice existed in Clarke County. This incredible finding subsequently was reversed by the Court of Appeals, which called it "clearly erroneous." Undaunted, Judge Cox still refused to find a pattern of practice of discrimination; instead, he withdrew his earlier finding and exercised his claimed prerogative not to decide the matter. This necessitated another appeal. In the meantime, the judge decided that a perjury charge should be pressed against two Negro witnesses he felt were lying. The Federal Bureau of Investigation looked into the facts of the matter, after which the Justice Department advised the judge that there was no basis for prosecution. The judge insisted. Eventually the acting attorney general, Nicholas Katzenbach, instructed the United States attorney in the case, Robert Hauberg, that the cases were not to be prosecuted and that he should not prepare or sign any indictments which the grand jury might issue in these cases. Judge Cox ordered Hauberg to ignore this order and when he refused the judge ordered him held in contempt of court. He also ordered Katzenbach to show cause why he himself should not be held in contempt. On January 25, 1965, the Court of Appeals reversed the contempt order. Thus, four years after the case had been filed, Judge Cox was still tangling with the government attorneys and refusing to recognize any pattern or practice of voter discrimination.

On other occasions he wrote to voter registrars criticizing the Justice Department for bringing voter actions. He issued an injunction restraining CORE from encouraging Negroes to use a bus terminal in McComb, Mississippi, on grounds that CORE had publicized its intent to desegregate the terminal for the purpose, in the judge's opinion, of "provoking the tempers of the community . . . and to taunt and tantalize the community." At one point he used contempt hearings to harass a Negro attorney, R. Jess Brown, of Jackson, Mississippi. In a study of the judge's actions in that instance, Professor Alexander R. Bickel of the Yale Law School commented that the judge had abused his power "after the fashion of a two-bit sheriff." Professor Bickel urged the Judiciary Committee of the U.S. House of Representatives to consider bringing articles of impeachment against him.[11]

The difficulties which some Southern jurists had in properly discharging their duties are suggested by the anthropological nostrums to which they clung. Judge Sidney Mize of Mississippi, a Roosevelt appointee, commented in one school desegregation case that "the learning traits which are characteristic of Negro children do differ to an educationally significant degree from those which are typical of white pupils. . . ." He said that "differences between Caucasians and Negroes are genetically determined and cannot be changed materially by environment. . . ."[12] Judge Frank Scarlett of Georgia, a Truman appointee, found in a school case that there were substantial differences between Negroes' and whites' learning capacities and these are "attributable in large part to hereditary factors. . . ." Integration, he said, would cause "intergroup tensions and conflicts" which would interfere with the educational process.[13] Contentions of this kind, which he permitted to be raised, had so clearly been rejected by the Supreme Court that rights attorneys offered no rebuttal to them. The never-say-die Citizens

Councils for some months afterward held this to be evidence that these contentions of inferiority had been irrefutable and were new elements. The councils spread the word across the South that the subsequent anti-integration ruling by Judge Scarlett had set the country on a course of reversal of the Supreme Court's 1954 decision. It was, of course, not the Supreme Court but Judge Scarlett who was reversed.

Not only were government and civil rights lawyers up against judges who still asserted the inherent inferiority of Negroes as a factor in desegregation cases; they also were up against some who felt it proper, a decade after the Supreme Court's school ruling, to base decisions upon the premise that the ruling was wrong and to state why. Judge West in Louisiana, a Kennedy appointee, called the Supreme Court's decision "one of the truly regrettable decisions of all time" and said the trouble that resulted had been caused by the "agitation of outsiders." [14] In one of his more noteworthy civil rights decisions, he refused to order the voting registrar of East Feliciana Parish to open his office after it had been closed for six months. He reasoned that since a three-judge federal court had ordered the registrars in twenty-one counties to stop using certain discriminatory voter registration requirements, the East Feliciana Parish registrar would have no "usable criteria" now for registration if he opened his door again. By this reasoning, presumably, any of the registrars could have closed their offices indefinitely simply because a non-discrimination order had been issued.[15]

During the turmoil in Albany, Georgia, in 1962 and 1963, the performance of Judge J. Robert Elliott was such a classic case of delaying that the federal courts were for all practical purposes closed as a place of remedy. The result was an extended denial of rights and greater turmoil for the community. Judge Elliott, an old ally of the Talmadge family and an appointee of President Kennedy's, in two Albany cases delayed decision until nine months after a hearing had been held. His decisions later were reversed by the Fifth Circuit Court of Appeals. Before his appointment, Judge Elliott had been a leading defender of segregation laws and practices that denied Negroes the vote.[16]

To be sure, a large number of federal judges in the South were not subject to such criticisms. They recognized the binding nature of higher court rulings and did not arbitrarily influence justice by delays or captious requirements. But some of the most obstructive judges happened to be in the areas of greatest struggle. Sometimes young voter registration workers found themselves trying earnestly to explain the action of these judges to local Negroes in such a way that some faith in judicial processes would be maintained. Faith Holsaert, one of SNCC's southwest Georgia workers, told of going to a meeting in the tiny community of Sasser, in Terrell County, where Negroes were ruthlessly suppressed through a sheriff's constabulary as well as through private action. "I went over Judge Elliott's decision . . ." she reported later. "Outlined what a class action is, why Elliott didn't consider this a class action. . . ." But to many of the local Negroes, these cases were heart-breaking lessons that meant only that the white man was still in the saddle. After a federal court freed one sheriff's deputy in a brutality case involving the denial of constitutional rights, a frustrated young registra-tion worker wrote: "If one ever had the naïve hope that the system had disappeared, the federal court hearing . . . has made quite plain the fact that the system is quite alive, and fostered by some of the ablest minds around. Thanks, men, for bringing me back in touch with real-ity."

Registration workers in the Black Belt reported a common saying among Negroes about the most ruthless whites: "They can do it and get away with it." Part of the mission assumed by some of these workers was to persuade the Negroes that this was not true and that they must take some risks to gain their rights. But as the courts continued to fail in some of these places, disillusionment grew, searing bitterness into minds that had tried to fight it down in others. All of this helped build the frustration that increasingly soured local Negroes and embittered and drove away some of the best elements of the idealistic young people's movement of the early 1960's, at considerable cost to the nation. The later turn of SNCC toward rejection of its white allies and a plunge into an obscurantist and almost narcissistic search for "Negritude" and iso-lated black power was one direct, tragic result. The SNCC leaders who took that part of the movement into this new direction were those who had worked the toughest Black Belt counties of the South, and there had been schooled in the rawest injustice.

What good judges could do was amply illustrated by the no-nonsense performances of such men as Judge Frank M. Johnson in Alabama. Judge Johnson, a native of Winston County in Alabama, had been a friend of George Wallace's at the University of Alabama Law School. A Republican, he was appointed to the federal bench by President Eisen-hower. It was Judge Johnson who issued the strongest orders on school desegregation in Alabama; enjoined the Ku Klux Klan from interfering with Freedom Riders in 1961; ordered police protection for the Selma-to-Montgomery marchers in 1965 and dissolved Governor Wallace's ban on the march; and drew effective voter discrimination and jury selection orders that established principles later to become guidelines for other courts. In the Macon County voter case most notably, Judge Johnson issued the kind of order which the Justice Department had fondly hoped for when it determined to make civil suits in the voting field the main objective of its litigation in the South. In this case, involving the home county of Tuskegee Institute, Judge Johnson ordered the local registrars to certify all Negroes whose literacy was equivalent to that of the least literate white who had been registered. He also ordered the registrar's board to give him a monthly report of its progress. Since the board previously sometimes had kept Negroes waiting in line for days outside locked doors and had even taken two days to test one Negro, this monthly report requirement was a kind of assurance against continuing recalcitrance. It embodied, too, the kind of administrative function that a Southern federal court sometimes had to assume in order simply to assure that its ruling would not be subverted by subterfuge. A judge hostile to higher court rulings, who wanted at best only to do as much as had to be done in order to seem to meet the issue before him, was not likely to use such effective techniques.

Another jurist who entertained no specious, legalistic evasion and acted with dispatch was Chief Judge Bryan Simpson of the Middle District of Florida, sitting in Jacksonville. Judge Simpson's firm hand during the turmoil at St. Augustine in 1964 must be contrasted with the performance of Judge Elliott during the Albany crisis. Each city, fully segregated and fully resistant, was the site of demonstrations led by Martin Luther King, the chief difference being that in Albany the local police did maintain a sort of order.

It has been said that Judge Simpson excelled all others in "his speed in enforcing the law and in his willingness to embark on new legal territory to protect Negro rights." [17] Demonstrations in the nation's oldest city had been met with extraordinary violence and callousness on the part of local law officers. The Ku Klux Klan was rampant. Sheriff L. O. Davis' answer to the problem was to ban the night marches being conducted by Dr. King and local leaders. When civil rights lawyers went to court seeking to end the ban and to remedy conditions in the local jail, Judge Simpson took only ten days to rule. He found in favor of the demonstrators on all counts. Establishing that the sheriff's force included a convicted felon and a number of members of a Klan front organization, the judge severely lectured the sheriff. He held that the marchers were entitled to police protection and had not received it. He continued step by step to follow events in St. Augustine, knocking down first one evasion and then another. He issued an extraordinarily inclusive injunction against intimidation and coercion and applied it not only to named defendants but also to "any other person to whom notice or knowledge of this order may come." Two ardent segregationists shortly were held in contempt for violation of the order; one, an unpaid deputy sheriff, was ordered off the sheriff's force, an action that moved Senator J. Strom Thurmond of South Carolina, ever a champion of white supremacy, to cry "judicial dictatorship." But soon the violent ones in St. Augustine saw that the hoodlum element simply was not going to prevail. Without the presence of federal troops or marshals, St. Augustine was brought into orderly compliance with the law. If every district judge in the South had taken Judge Simpson's determined approach, voting rights might have been extended without such a great wrenching of the federal system as there was; and rights workers trying to move fearful Negroes out of their shacks and their depths might not have had to endure the brutal harassment that was so constant. At one point in the proceedings, when Judge Simpson asked why one band of armed hoodlums on the scene of conflict was not arrested or identified or even disarmed, he was told the reason was that no law had been violated at that moment. "I can't believe that the State has no authority to seize weapons in that kind of situation," he said. When another official offered the same explanation, he replied: "The law isn't that big a boob." [18]

But repeatedly in the South even the federal courts allowed the law to be a boob. The Fifth Circuit Court of Appeals, despite clear divisions among its own nine members, performed a service of rectification that made it the most important court in the country except for the Supreme Court itself. As some district judges erred and delayed and employed a wide variety of dilatory tactics, the Fifth increasingly bore down with extraordinary measures to effectuate its own and Supreme Court decisions. At times it even was forced to resort to mandamus, prohibition, and injunction orders binding the district court judges themselves, a process that the Court of Appeals pointed out made the district judges litigants in the cases before them; the Fifth noted that such procedures were in order, as the Supreme Court had held, in extraordinary cases of lower-court disruption of normal processes.

Chief Judge Elbert Tuttle of the Fifth Circuit Court of Appeals, an Eisenhower appointee and former chairman of the Republican Party in Georgia, led the way. Many of the civil rights cases were handled by three-judge panels, a normal procedure in the Court of Appeals. Judge Tuttle chose the panels. With him most frequently in taking positions sustaining the letter and spirit of high-court rulings in the mid-1960's were Judges John Minor Wisdom of Louisiana, Richard T. Rives of Alabama, and John R. Brown of Texas. Judge Homer Thornberry of Texas (appointed by President Johnson in 1965) was frequently identified with the Tuttle-Wisdom-Rives-Brown contingent. Consistently on the other side were Ben F. Cameron of Mississippi, who died in 1964, and Walter P. Gewin of Alabama (a Kennedy appointee). The positions taken by Judges Griffin Bell of Georgia (also a Kennedy appointee), J. P. Coleman of Mississippi (a Johnson appointee), Warren L. Jones of Florida, and Joseph C. Hutcheson of Texas (who became incapacitated in 1963 and was replaced by Judge Thornberry) were more mixed.

Judge Tuttle's selection of the three-judge panels inspired an extraordinary criticism of him in 1964 by Judge Cameron. In a dissenting opinion, he referred to the Tuttle-Wisdom-Rives-Brown contingent as "The Four" who dominated the panels. The criticism underscored the importance of Judge Tuttle's use of his power to choose the panels. The history of the civil rights revolution in the South might have been very different but for this force within the Fifth Circuit. Without it, there would have been much more delay and circumvention, with a resultant increase in frustrations, tensions, and explosive situations as Negroes sought elsewhere the relief they could not find in the federal courts. This could have altered the entire tone and thrust of the rights revolution in the South and thus in the country. Democratic process would have been the loser.

Many of the judges who tried to lead the federal courts into that destructive avenue were appointed by the Kennedy administration. In addition to the Court of Appeals judges just cited, this was true of District Judges Cox in Mississippi, Elliott in Georgia, E. Gordon West and Frank B. Ellis in Louisiana, and Clarence W. Allgood in Alabama. Other choices, too, might have been stronger, but these alone made the Kennedy record on judicial appointments a dismal one indeed. Democratic presidents traditionally have chosen Southern judges largely on the basis of the recommendations from Democratic senators of the states affected. Republican presidents have had the advantage of being free of this pressure in the South. Republican organizations during the Eisenhower era were, in fact, rebels within the South, since they were cast politically against the entrenched, Democratic organizations. Thus President Eisenhower was able to choose, without alienating Southern Democratic congressional powers, such men as Elbert Tuttle and Frank Johnson in Alabama, both Republicans, who steadfastly worked, without delay, within the confines of precedent and higher court decisions.

The Southern Veto and Federal Power Unused

Even given the limitations imposed upon all Democratic presidents within this realm, did the Kennedy administration have to yield so much? The Kennedys bowed, as others had been doing for almost a hundred years, to the Southern veto in Washington. They had alternatives. Perhaps they could not have chosen ideally suited judges for the Southern bench; yet they need not have chosen some of those they did. Others might have been suggested by the senators if they had been forced to bargain, and the results might have been at least somewhat better. Further, there was one clear option which the Kennedy administration chose not to exercise: federal judges may be temporarily assigned from one area to another to fill vacancies. In the Little Rock school case at the time of the disturbances, the judge (Ronald N. Davies) was from North Dakota; he had been assigned to that district in the absence of a permanent judge. No doubt there would have been howls if the Justice Department had rotated judges from elsewhere (including elsewhere within the South) into vacancies in the Southern District of Georgia (Elliott) and the Southern District of Mississippi (Cox), but the effects could have been salutary. In those two districts alone, the resultant change in judicial process in rights cases might have had an enormous effect in preventing the frustration, bitterness, black nationalism, and general alienation which later appeared strong among Black Belt rights workers and local Negroes. Others felt frustration, too. Many capable white and Negro attorneys, members of the Democratic Party, noted for their moderation and willingness to support the Constitution in the South, were passed over in the appointments. Their loss pointed up a dilemma for members of the bar in the South. If they took racial cases and became identified as controversial, judgeships and other federal plums were withheld from them.

How weak was the law with which these judges, and the Justice Department and civil rights lawyers, had to work? Somehow the same laws and the same statutory authority seemed to grow stronger as time passed. At first, for instance, the Justice Department maintained fervently that FBI agents had none but investigative authority in civil rights cases in the South. Rights workers were beaten in the presence of FBI agents without arrests. FBI agents worked closely with local law officers who often were parties to the violence and intimidation against Negroes, a fact which did untold damage to trust in the FBI and even in the federal government as a whole.

One of the worst examples of this was in Selma, Alabama, in 1963, when a Negro voter registration effort was under way against the heaviest opposition. This was in a county which had refused to allow Negroes to register. On October 7, a "Freedom Day" was declared by registration workers, and Negroes lining up at the courthouse had to run a gantlet of Colonel Al Lingo's state troopers, local officers bossed by Sheriff Jim Clark, and a photographer, whose picture-taking, they knew, could cost them their jobs. Sheriff Clark, who was to win notoriety as white supremacy's strong-arm man in the county during demonstrations there in 1965, not only kept the registration organizers harassed but arrested three of them on the steps of a federal building. While this elemental invasion of their rights was taking place, actually on federal property, four FBI agents and two Justice Department lawyers were on the scene. They intervened in no way. Nor was there any other effective federal action against a stand of resistance by local officials which was an obvious violation of federal statutes.[19]

There was a request for federal marshals in Selma in 1963 to prevent this kind of suppression of rights. If it had been answered, Selma might have never seen the massive onslaught in 1965 led by Dr. King in an effort to force the necessary federal action. (Even then, when peaceful demonstrators were beaten at the Edmund Pettus Bridge by state troopers and members of the sheriff's posse, there was no prosecution by the federal government.) Similarly, marshals were unsuccessfully requested in Greenwood, Mississippi, in early 1963 in the face of heavy official opposition and a reign of terror by local hoodlums during voter registration efforts there. If that call had been answered, the big push of rights forces against Greenwood later in 1963 might never have occurred.

By 1966 the FBI was taking steps which it had seemed to regard as impossible earlier, greatly expanding its operations in the South, sometimes taking a more detached position in regard to local police, and working on rights cases with a greater evident commitment. At times as many as 2,500 of its 6,000 agents were working on civil rights matters, seemingly not an improper distribution for a leading problem in enforcement of law and the Constitution. By February of 1966, the Bureau had increased the number of agents in the South almost 100 per cent within two years. A subtle change apparently was being effected: just as agents once had looked toward good work in countering espionage as perhaps the best avenue for promotion, so now it was possible to look also toward good work in civil rights cases (which once had seemed to be regarded by many agents as just a nuisance and an inconvenience). Some commendations were being handed out to encourage this good work. All of this seemed to indicate that the FBI, tragically lethargic in earlier years on civil rights matters in the South, had been stirred somewhat by criticism or higher authority or both to move more professionally. (The FBI, it sometimes is forgotten, operates under the authority of the attorney general of the United States.)

While the Southern veto thus had even seemed to be influencing policy in the FBI, it also was playing a powerful role in other areas of the federal government. Why was there a Judge Cox sitting in Mississippi, having been appointed by a President Kennedy? At the time Judge Cox was appointed in 1961, Mr. Kennedy had more than seventy federal court appointments awaiting clearance by the Judiciary Committee of the U.S. Senate, headed by Senator James Eastland of Mississippi. Why was the Civil Rights Division of the Justice Department a relatively small division within the department even at the peak of civil rights legal involvement by the federal government? Why was no strengthening of the voter laws proposed by the Kennedy administration until 1962, though the need for them clearly had been established and legislative proposals had been outlined much earlier by the U.S. Commission on Civil Rights? In each case, the answer was Southern congressional power. The administration had to deal with the chairman of the Senate Judiciary Committee, and with the other powerful Southern figures, such as Senator Richard B. Russell, key figure on the Appropriations Committee and chairman of the Armed Services Committee, and Senator Harry F. Byrd, chairman of the Finance Committee. Was it really necessary, in order to attain Senate approval for the appointment of Thurgood Marshall (a leading Negro civil rights lawyer) to a federal judgeship in New York, to appoint a Harold Cox in Mississippi? And was it a good course, in order to gain approval of other important legislation, to delay a full-scale battle with Southern forces over new rights legislation? Such considerations are familiar enough to those who know Washington. But they were never publicly mentioned by administration spokesmen. Consequently, the legal philosophy and rationale which administration spokesmen used to explain the government's passivity in a wide range of civil rights matters often had a hollow ring. Talk about legal philosophy was no good substitute for talk about the real obstacle, which was fear of Southern power.

In the matter of protecting voter registration workers and bringing local officials into some recognition of the higher authority of the courts and national government, the Justice Department had at its disposal several weapons. Title 18, sections 241 and 242, of the U.S. Criminal Code, left by the Reconstruction era, was the potentially most useful. Section 241 outlaws conspiracies to "injure, oppress, threaten, or intimidate any citizen in the free exercise of any right . . . secured . . . by the Constitution and laws of the United States. . . ." The courts specifically had held that this section was applicable to actions by state officials or private individuals that prevented voting in federal elections. By court construal, it also apparently covered discrimination by state officials in state and local elections. Section 242 applies to state or local officials or anyone acting in concert with them. It states: "Whoever, under color of any law . . . willfully subjects . . . any inhabitant of any state . . . to the deprivation of any rights, privileges, or immunities secured or protected by the Constitution and laws of the United States" is subject to prosecution.

These sections were seldom used. One of the scores of occasions on which they could have been and were not was in Albany, Georgia, in 1961. In enforcing segregation of bus terminal facilities by police power, for instance, officials there were acting "under color of law" against citizens exercising their constitutional rights. No action was taken by federal officials, just as none was taken in many other violations—at Selma, Americus, Birmingham, Danville, and Greenwood, to name only some. In some of these situations, local officials "under color of law" were illegally arresting thousands of Negroes. Ironically, although officials at Albany were spared criminal prosecutions, the Justice Department moved to prosecute nine leaders and participants in the Albany movement after the picketing of a white grocer whose role on a federal jury had angered Negroes. One of those prosecuted, Slater King, earlier had pleaded for federal action when he and others had been jailed; when his pregnant wife had been beaten by a deputy and lost her baby; and when his brother, a lawyer, had been battered in the face by the local sheriff. In each case, he had pleaded in vain.

The first federal arrest, on complaint, under Section 241 anywhere in the South during these years came on June 26, 1964, the kind of action for which there had been no arrests despite repeated well-grounded complaints in the previous years. The FBI arrested three white men for interfering with voter registration workers in Itta Bena, Mississippi. Thus at that time, late in the struggle, the Justice Department seemed to be doing exactly what it often had indicated it could not do.

As for the federal exercise of police power when necessary for the maintenance of order, this, too, was provided for in national law. Section 333 of Title 10 of the U.S. Code authorizes the President to "take such measures as he considers necessary to suppress, in a state, any insurrection, domestic violence, unlawful combination, or conspiracy if it . . . opposes or obstructs the execution of the laws of the United States or impedes the course of justice under those laws." The Justice Department cited this section when it intervened with federal forces in Montgomery, Alabama, in May 1961; at Oxford, Mississippi, in September 1962; and in Tuscaloosa, Alabama, in June 1963. In each of these cases, the federal forces were used, against the wishes of state officials, not to assume general local police powers in any comprehensive way but solely to enforce a particular federal court order, as authorized in the portion of Section 333 quoted above. Another portion of that section is even broader, and it provides more authority than the Justice Department has ever chosen to exercise in the modern civil rights struggle in the South. It authorizes use of federal force to suppress insurrection, violence, conspiracy, or unlawful combination in a state "if any part or class of its people is deprived of a right, privilege, immunity, or protection named in the Constitution . . . and the constituted authorities of that state are unable, fail, or refuse to protect that right . . ." That section would justify intrusion of federal forces against the wishes of a state's officials and even in the absence of a federal court order to enforce. But the Justice Department regarded use of this particular authority as undermining law enforcement at the local level. The argument was that this would alter the federal system in practice. The counter argument is simply that areas where use of such authority was justified were, in effect, outlaw counties insofar as the Constitution is concerned, and temporary federal assumption of police powers there would have been no real alteration of the federal system, because officials of these areas had tried to place themselves outside the federal system in violation of the Constitution.

On this point, the Notre Dame Conference on Congressional Civil Rights Legislation said in 1963:

The evil of [voting] discrimination is confined . . . to certain communities of the Deep South where the constitutional prohibition against voting discrimination is openly flouted and efforts to obtain or to exercise voting rights are met by acts of intimidation, harassment, and physical violence, sanctioned and sometimes even participated in by local authorities and law enforcement officers. These are, and should rationally be regarded as, outlaw communities . . . New and more refined legislative remedies are not required to reach this blatant disregard of rights. To contain and disarm lawlessness, a clear federal presence is required at the first outbreaks. We think the Attorney General has the power, in the face of determined lawlessness supported by an acquiescent or conspiratorial community, to send federal marshals and agents of the Federal Bureau of Investigation for on-the-spot protection of the exercise of federal rights. Such marshals and federal agents should be deployed in accord with principals and with authority adequate to deal with all anticipated exigencies, including authority and instructions to enforce compliance with federal law and to make arrests for violations.

This condition does not pose an issue of federalism. Federalism is a system of divided power among governments, and governments are instruments whose whole purpose is to establish an order of law. In these outlaw communities where citizenship rights are flagrantly destroyed, there is no law to respect.

A similar point was made on June 30, 1964, in a statement by twenty-seven law professors of Columbia, Harvard, New York University, Pennsylvania, and Yale:

Surely there is reason to believe that violence and combination are now so hindering the execution of the laws of Mississippi and of the United States as to deny to the Negroes of Mississippi rights secured by the Constitution and laws of the United States. . . . [There] can be no question but that the provisions of (10 USCA 333) subsection (2) fit the circumstances precisely. Violence, combination, and conspiracy in Mississippi are unquestionably obstructing the execution of the civil rights laws of the United States—the provisions, that is, of Sections 1981 and 1983 of Title 42 and the provisions of the Acts of 1957 and 1960 with respect to voting rights.

The Southern Regional Council, citing these statements by legal authorities, noted in a 1964 report: "The question of federal police intervention in Mississippi, and the extent and kind of it, is, in other words, not one of *power to act*, but of policy." [20]

Repeatedly, Justice Department and other administration officials stressed the desire to avoid creating anything approximating a national police force, a judgment probably concurred in by the overwhelming majority of Americans. The FBI, under J. Edgar Hoover, has been careful to avoid expansion in that direction in spite of frequent demands upon it to utilize enforcement powers that would make it something of a national police force. Robert F. Kennedy cited aversion to a national police establishment in justifying much of the Justice Department's thinking on civil rights problems during his tenure as attorney general.

In the foreword to a book by Burke Marshall, *Federalism and Civil Rights*, Mr. Kennedy wrote in mid-1964 that there was clear federal responsibility to send U.S. marshals and troops to Oxford for the integration of the University of Mississippi in September 1962 and to Montgomery for the Freedom Rides in May 1961, but not for sending such forces to Birmingham in May 1963 during the demonstrations and riots there or to Mississippi in 1964 when civil rights workers were under siege and three were murdered without effective state action against the perpetrators of violence. For the federal government to undertake police protection of civil rights workers "would lead inevitably to creation of a national police force," he wrote.

Probably the whole question was cast in the wrong terms—by civil rights forces demanding protection for all workers pressing for constitutional rights in dangerous areas, and by the government officials responding to that broad demand. For federal forces to try to provide escort, clear the path, and arrest and prosecute obstructionists for civil rights workers all over the South would have required, surely, a broad assumption of local police powers. The federal failure was not, however, a failure to create a national police force, a development which would have chilled many civil-libertarians. The real failure, obscured by discussion of protection in these terms, was the failure to act with full decisiveness with the powers and forces that existed: to enforce existing federal statutes, and to defend, by *some direct means,* the exercise of undisputed federal rights.

In Albany in 1961 and 1962, the Justice Department never consented to seek a broad injunction that would order all local parties, official and unofficial, to stop interfering with the exercise of constitutional rights. Yet during the Greenwood voter registration push of 1963, it did exactly that, at least within the narrower field of voting rights. Then, as if to repent, it traded away that forward position in a compromise that was defensible only if peace and the status quo were the objectives: it agreed not to press the suit if Greenwood would release those who had been arrested. (It did not even require that the local charges be dropped, and they were not.) The kind of injunction involved here was the kind that Judge Bryan Simpson subsequently issued, of his own volition and not at Justice Department request, for St. Augustine. In that situation the injunction broke the defiance and effectuated the law. (In St. Augustine, the judge ordered police to protect rather than interfere with orderly marchers. In Albany, the police had arrested masses of orderly marchers.) Why did the Justice Department fail to pursue such obviously effective injunctions in the countless conflicts from Virginia to Arkansas and down to the Gulf of Mexico? Notwithstanding all the elaborate answers which the Justice Department produced, most of them in the language of constitutional construction and executive propriety, the true answer was to be found in the remaining power of southern white supremacy in Washington.

Mere Justice

The caliber of the judges and of the jurors sometimes has been invoked as an explanation of inaction. Especially was this true in the case of criminal charges. The department may have been correct in its judgment that criminal convictions were unlikely in the Southern federal courts, but was this good reason not to seek any? Anyone familiar with the mystique which a racist Southern sheriff can build around himself, often resting upon his success in defiance and "keeping the niggers down," is aware of how quickly his bravado may be drained when he is in real trouble. It may be that a sheriff indicted and later acquitted of a federal criminal charge would be temporarily a hero; but suppose he were faced with the prospect of inexorable prosecution for his federal criminal violations, frequent necessity to be under the personal strain that would result, frequent requirements to spend days in court away from his home town, frequent explorations of his uglier deeds by tough-minded federal lawyers—would this have no salubrious effects on the sheriff at hand and on other sheriffs? To the more violence-prone part of his community, he might be a hero anew each time, for a while. But to the middle-class, business-oriented, church-oriented part of his community, the unavoidable awareness of his true nature and the embarrassment for the community (undoubtedly in search of new industry at that very moment) likely would far outweigh, in due course, the delight of the strutting, slack-jawed hoodlums. One of the authors, visiting Philadelphia, Mississippi, concluded that the sight of the local sheriff, Lawrence Rainey, spread across the pages of national publications, jaw full of a plug of Red Man as he sat in federal court in connection with the murder of three civil rights workers, had had something of a traumatic effect upon the middle-class citizenry of the town. It had become necessary to deny that a man just like this existed; the denial might be an almost hysterical mass cursing of the national press for distortion, but underneath the denial was an agonizing new awareness of a community force that previously could be unseen if one did not wish to see it.

One problem was that in Washington a lawyer's judgment was applied to what was essentially not a lawyer's job. The Justice Department had been made the chief planner and executor of federal policy on civil rights. For such a function to be thrust upon a body of lawyers was in itself questionable, for an all-lawyer team is hardly one to excel in innovation and flexibility. Inevitably, too, such conventional lawyers' considerations as whether a conviction might be obtained took precedence over the proposition that where an offense has been committed and there is substantial evidence against the known perpetrators, there should be prosecution, no matter what the government's appraisal of the prospective jurors. Perhaps to arrest a police chief on the street as he committed an illegal act would not result in a conviction by his home-state peers; but if, for instance, he were aspiring to a better police job off in Nashville, the prospect of such a besmirching might be sufficient to persuade him to mend his ways. And the knowledge that the police chief down the road had been arrested that way only the day before might be just the persuader necessary to produce a more law-abiding attitude.

With amazing consistency, bitter-end places which have suffered the trauma of racial demonstrations in the South have found ultimately that simple compliance with the law was not very difficult after all, and some residents of such places then have begun to wonder why they ever had to go through all the damaging nonsense. The recurrent truth is that lawlessness (of the hoodlum variety or of the official-resistance variety) prevails only when it seems to have a chance—when the forces of law and order appear irresolute, as President Eisenhower did before he eventually moved on Little Rock, as the Kennedy administration did before it finally took hold with last-minute determination and boldness at Oxford, and as many Southern police forces have until the flashpoint has been reached and they have had to stop winking and assert their authority in their communities.

One wonders what good effects might now have resulted if the Justice Department had doggedly pressed criminal charges against key officials scattered about the South as they self-righteously violated federal law, and at the same time had moved with executive vigor to alter the complexion of the almost all-white federal juries that would sit in judgment. What effect might have been obtained if in public places throughout Mississippi the Justice Department had posted "Warning!" notices clearly stating the criminal culpability of law officers who interfered with constitutional rights, and then had begun to prosecute any offenders against whom evidence could be obtained? When agents of the locally respected FBI came visiting the hometown to ask questions about old Tiny, when his fingerprints were made at the federal courthouse lockup, when the photographers from the nearby big city appeared with their flashbulbs and when the ugly facts of casual nighttime brutality were unfolded for all the old family friends and distant city cousins to see and read about—surely this would have served to caution other city policemen and sheriff's deputies to avoid such embarrassments for themselves and their families in the future. The public back-slapping that might come from the members of local Klavern 33 might seem small reward for the man wondering whether his children might believe some of that stuff the Harvard lawyer from Washington was saying about him in the big room at the federal courthouse. There might have been notable instances of non-response to this approach, of course, instances in which some officials chose to be local hoodlum heroes. But the most extensive trouble has never been with the tiny cluster of sheriffs who won national notoriety because of their public belligerence. Altogether, probably no more than a dozen of these figures emerged. The real trouble lay with less exhibitionist multitudes of sheriffs and others who, though they never were featured in double-page spreads in *Life* magazine, went on systematically repressing Negroes or at least leaving them second-class citizens in official dealings, frequently in direct violation of law—and who might not have done this if they had foreseen real trouble with the FBI and the United States government. Further, with juries selected in accordance with federal law and with vigorous prosecutions, probably more than a few convictions would have been obtained. Even a few might have had salubrious effects.

Collisions in Power

What was it, anyway, that the federal government was up against in these years? There was an unspoken tradition more than a century old in the South, a tradition at once subordinating law to custom and making law an administrative tool rather than a fundamental commitment. In this realm, the impact of the frontier remains stronger in the South than anywhere else in the country. The idea of swift, raw "justice" meted out by individuals or by a whole community outside the normal machinery of the court system is still present. For a century it was the rationale for lynching; the frontier concept of the posse is inherent in the night-rider phenomenon. And in isolated rural communities of even the modern South, as with earlier isolated settlements in the frontier West, there has been a sense of remoteness from the national halls of justice and an instinctive readiness to look first to one's own idea of what is proper in the local context—proper, or "right."

First there is a widespread, very personal application of law that removes normative standards and replaces them with a personal view of what may be best at the moment. We see it in the comment of a Mississippi legislator who, after passage of a criminal syndicalism bill intended for use against civil rights workers, defended it by saying: "I know it's not constitutional, but it can't hurt us." We see it again in what the mayor of one small Mississippi town had to say about its unorthodox method of electing mayors. He said yes, of course the election was not proper and legal, "but it doesn't matter because we have never had a legal election here and nobody is interested enough to set one up." Some of it is guileless, open rejection of a national law because it is not "practical." A white overseer in one of Georgia's old plantation counties, Baker, said in 1963: "It doesn't make any difference what Congress and the Supreme Court say the law is. It won't make a damn in Baker County, not during this generation." [21] In such a county, lawlessness often is all of one piece and consistent: Baker was noted not only for rejection of Congress and the courts on the big issues but also for raw harassment of rights workers by law officers themselves, for crimes never prosecuted, for speed traps on its highways, and for illegal gambling operations.

The rejection of national law often has been blithe and above-board, with a tone suggesting that, surely, any reasonable man would know we can't do that. In 1965 federal examiners were sent to Montgomery, Alabama, where Negroes had met unusual obstacles in efforts to register. By that time federal law clearly made it illegal to deny illiterates the right to vote in Alabama. But the chairman of the local board of registrars, Mrs. Barbara Dent, noted with some indignation that the federal examiners would register illiterates and added: "The ability to read and write is a necessary requirement to vote in Alabama." [22] It was as if Congress did not exist, or at least was subordinate to the Alabama legislature. Significantly, this stance could be taken at the same time the governor of Alabama, George Wallace, was noisily putting up the smokescreen for it. On the one hand, in September 1965 he was winning state court orders temporarily blocking state registrars from entering the names of Negroes who had signed with the federal examiners. On the other hand he was saying of the Supreme Court: "It is running the country by injunction, and instilling fear into the heart of every man by the threat of imprisonment." These words were an ironic bad joke, but they stirred many of the folks.

Spasmodically there has always been the reversal of the law's intent, even in criminal cases. Near St. Augustine in 1963, several Negroes were captured and thrown into a pile with threats that they were to be set ablaze by robed Klansmen. They were beaten but managed to escape. After their story was told, it was they who were arrested; none of the Klansmen were. There were no arrests in St. Augustine when shots were fired into the house occupied by Martin Luther King, or when one of his aides, Harry Boyte, was attacked on the street before numerous witnesses; but there were arrests of the Negro demonstrators. The same pattern emerged in many racial confrontations in the South in the early 1960's.

Law and legal method were used successfully so often to thwart higher legality that the process became respectable. Simple fact could be denied by contorted legalistic or procedural reasoning, and heads would nod in agreement. What else but the accepted respectability of this kind of perversion of law and simple truth could explain the testimony of the highest officials of the completely segregated University of Georgia in 1961, when with great dignity they stated under oath that the university had not discriminated against Negroes? District Judge Sidney C. Mize of Mississippi, to be sure, was saying nothing more preposterous than this when he commented during the James Meredith case that the University of Mississippi was "not a segregated institution." The Fifth Circuit Court of Appeals commented that word of this about-face would surely be a surprise to the people of Mississippi, and that the policy must have been set by "telepathic communication among the University's administrators. . . ." Others might laugh with the Fifth Circuit court, but to those who wanted to believe this kind of nonsense, and who were accustomed to denying plain truth on the basis of tortuous and fatuous legalistic fabrications, this kind of disgusting spectacle was acceptable. The pretense was not unique in the world, of course. While Negroes could not vote in his home state of South Carolina, Secretary of State James F. Byrnes had demanded "free and unfettered elections" for Poles, Rumanians, and Bulgarians.[23]

The extent to which violence was used by public officials is difficult to measure. It was talked noisily from the moment the Supreme Court outlawed school segregation, and there can be no doubt that when a governor predicted "blood will flow in the streets" and showed he was in agreement with those who would make it flow, his words were encouragement to the violent. This kind of encouragement had its logical culmination in such episodes as those that occurred during the Freedom Rides of 1961 and the integration of the University of Mississippi in 1962. When the Freedom Riders went through Anniston, Birmingham, and Montgomery, Alabama, local police abdicated. They arrived too late to prevent violence, despite ample warning of the Riders' schedule and certain knowledge of what local hoodlums might do. In the same way, Governor Ross Barnett's state troopers, despite the governor's pledges to the Justice Department to maintain order, absented themselves from the scene at Oxford; quite predictably, mob action broke out, resulting in two deaths. There was in these episodes an assumption that the federal government would retreat in the face of terror and violence. In these instances, the federal government did not retreat. Instead, the Justice Department moved carefully and forcefully. In doing so, in supplanting or reinforcing local officials in their responsibility to maintain order, the federal government was exercising a police authority usually reserved to the local communities.

The problem often was that the Justice Department simply would not act this decisively. One remembers from the Kennedy years the mind-pictures that created a national impression that the federal government was being forceful and decisive: the dramatic scenes of a big, straight-backed deputy attorney general, Nicholas Katzenbach, striding up to Governor George Wallace at Tuscaloosa for grim confrontation, citing his authority and rapidly clearing the governor out of the schoolhouse door; the scenes of troops and marshals in Oxford, Mississippi, there to make certain that the law was not evaded even though a whole state government's machinery was working to frustrate it. Even though these scenes were staged, they did leave a popular impression that the Justice Department and the administration were acting firmly. But these were the rare dramas. And in fact, for each of them, prior negotiations in a political context had carefully laid the plans. The law was not simply the law. It was a script. In between, there was the hard, grinding work of scores of Justice Department lawyers and FBI investigators putting together cases to advance public order by inches. And yet, even though on the part of the department's leadership there was a firm commitment to equality before the law, something was missing: realism about the South.

Consider the naïveté about some of the South's public officials, despite long federal experience since the 1954 school decision. In 1957 there had been the Little Rock crisis. Governor Orval Faubus, previously regarded as something of a liberal, chose to make the integration of Central High School in Little Rock occasion for a showdown with the federal government. In calling out the National Guard to preserve segregation there, he joined issue in a manner certain to make him a hero among the state's segregationists. He apparently had been impressed by their growing strength. His purpose was to shift himself dramatically in the political spectrum. In that context, then, and in view of the clear challenge to federal authority, it was a strange spectacle to see the defiant governor invited to confer with the President, and to see the resultant meeting described as a bargaining session. Next, President Eisenhower trusted the governor to do his duty, a reasonable kind of assumption ordinarily but the very kind that made the federal government often a dupe in its dealings with Southern officialdom during the height of the resistance. Mr. Faubus continued his defiance; President Eisenhower finally acted with resolve and federal authority prevailed.

Such unnecessary withholding of authority characterized the Kennedy administration more than once. In the University of Mississippi affair in 1962, Washington put its trust in a governor to do his simple duty. Attorney General Kennedy, after lengthy questioning in a series of telephone calls, pinned Governor Barnett to a commitment to preserve order with state forces on the Ole Miss campus when James Meredith arrived to enroll. Instead, the state troopers were withdrawn at a crucial moment and the rioting ensued.

In the same way, perhaps the civil rights strategists in Washington thought that, even though federal judges identified with the political forces of resistance in the South were appointed, they would follow the law as set forth by higher courts and, though somewhat unhappily, they would do what had to be done with reasonable dispatch. This was the same kind of misunderstanding of the South that was evidenced at Little Rock and Oxford and, in fact, on scores of occasions when Washington approached Southern officials with the assumption that they really knew the game was up and would now respond to the obvious requirements at hand. Even in 1967, thirteen years after the school desegregation decision, federal education officials were being dropped into traps like surprised beasts by Southern school officials, who often set the traps merely by force of habit. There was a complete difference in psychology. The federal school officials tended to assume, perhaps unconsciously, that all were now agreed that dual school systems really must be eliminated and that this was the immediate objective. Many of the Southern officials, however, assumed that all they really had to do was to somewhat extend token integration and token compliance with the regulations controlling federal school money, and that this would be showing the federals utmost cooperation.

The Justice Department's lack of familiarity with the South was understandable, and perhaps, also, its disposition toward procedures and styles that did not lend themselves especially well to the task at hand. This department was oriented toward Eastern law education and large Eastern law firms, and this raises questions. There is a difference between that great number of bright young law students who take up with intense interest the commerce clause or other special fields of law, upon which to build careers in corporate litigation, and those few who much more intensely grasp the equal-protection clause and the Bill of Rights as their chief interests. The former perhaps are more likely to be governed by fixed precedent and exhaustive administrative procedure; the latter, in this time of rapid re-evaluation of the human-rights parts of the Constitution, perhaps are more likely to be innovative and exploratory. The lawyers who were leading the Justice Department in the early 1960's were in the former category, but their chief domestic duty lay in the latter. For the most part, they were products of law schools largely oriented toward big corporate enterprise, and thus perhaps subtly oriented toward conservative style, manner, and expression. They were more cautious and more given to exhaustive piecemeal procedure than they needed to be. This characteristic, while perhaps a great virtue in corporate litigation, was one not likely to produce sweeping end-runs of innovation in law and policy. Perhaps, too, there was a patience and lack of the kind of expectation of immediate results that can produce fervid forward drive. And perhaps there was simply a lawyer's predilection for structure and preservation of order, for preventing "trouble." This alone would have made the chief instrument of justice of the U.S. government less sensitive to the needs of those in the civil rights movement, who were devoted to removal or drastic alteration of Southern structures and to the occasional use of "trouble" (insofar as possible, controlled "trouble") to bring this about. In 1965, after lengthy experience with intransigence, Burke Marshall wrote an article for the Los Angeles *Times* in which he stressed voluntarism and hailed small actions by the Justice Department that he said staved off trouble. His words reflect, seemingly, an assumption that it was desirable to prevent demonstrations in the Birmingham crisis, although it may have been only the demonstrations that finally moved that city to real change and, in fact, finally moved the country to the Civil Rights Act of 1964. Mr. Marshall heavily stressed Atlanta's voluntary efforts that paved the way for peaceful school integration, indicating that this process might spread through the South. Those familiar with Atlanta's initial school desegregation process, however, could not overlook the use of sheer force in the change—a kind of force often missing elsewhere in the South. White racist troublemakers in Atlanta were not removed by a dedication to some vague kind of voluntarism and a conversion to good will; they were responsive to the threat of prosecution and an awareness that desegregation was to take place no matter what they might do. The Klan had been infiltrated by police informers. One other extremist group was so ridden by police watchers and strict enforcement that it moved its headquarters to Birmingham in search of freedom. In short, the police in Atlanta knew what the Justice Department often seemed not to know: that certain enforcement, certain prosecution, and certain outcome are mighty discouragements for the lawless.

It is easy to look back and see errors of judgment in that era. After all, in those few years of struggle and introspection this country may have learned more about human rights under constitutional forms than the world had learned for centuries before. In 1967, men should be able to see clearly matters that were foggy in 1960 and 1961. So it is no condemnation of the Kennedy administration to say that, for example, the civil suit approach in the voting field was inevitably destined for failure from the start. That is clear now. Nor is it a condemnation to note the disproportionate influence of an inappropriate legal discipline, with its concomitant style and assumptions. Moreover, without the experience gained so harshly in the Kennedy years, the legislation that followed could not have been drawn as effectively and might not have been passed.

Failings in those years sprang principally from the fact that as the new national executive commitment emerged, the power of the old white South frequently was its match. Thus, even as the administration was deciding that the main thrust of all its civil rights policy was to be an extensive, determined campaign of civil suits to effectuate voting rights, it was being persuaded to appoint judges who would assure that those same suits were doomed to failure in exactly the court districts where the offense was worst. Here was an all-too-perfect example of how collisions in power rendered the federal government frequently ineffective even as it was slowly cutting away at the underpinnings of the opposing power. That opposing power—the Old South power, once rooted in Black Belt influence—was kicking hard as it was falling. Negro votes in the South would apply the final touch not to end, but to transform, that Southern political power in Washington.

NOTES

1. For an excellent summary, see Harold C. Fleming, "The Federal Executive and Civil Rights: 1961–1965," *Daedalus*, fall 1965, pp. 921–948. Crediting the Kennedys with the first clear executive policy in the field does not denigrate the importance of the role played by Harry S. Truman in boldly putting forward many admirable proposals which eventually were adopted and some of which, two decades later, still were ahead of what by that time had been accepted. Mr. Truman was President, however, before the onrush of Supreme Court decisions had placed before the executive branch an urgent challenge to exercise its powers broadly toward specific goals in the rights field.

2. In the spring of 1963, Mr. Marshall showed one of the authors a map of the South with varicolored pins indicating the locations and progress of these voter suits. He expressed strong optimism that these cases would result in the most significant rights gains of the near future. He said he expected great progress on this front by the presidential elections the next year, and in Mississippi, "some" progress. This was at the time when Dr. King had begun a general assault on segregation in Birmingham, where police violence and Negro rioting soon drew nationwide attention. Mr. Marshall, though reluctant to criticize Dr. King, conveyed the conviction that the general siege in Birmingham was of much less usefulness than the restricted pursuit of voter registration would have been. Second-guessing in retrospect is an easy indulgence, but we may see now that the Birmingham campaign succeeded in its intent to force federal legislation or a federal presence; surely the national attention it drew to the repression of Negroes in Birmingham, and the clear evidence that such Negro confrontations would continually be explosive, contributed substantially to Congress' willingness to pass the Civil Rights Act of 1964. By contrast, the Greenwood voter push, also intended to produce new national decisions on enforcement of voting rights, as we have seen, resulted in little—at least in part because the Justice Department de-fused it. A Justice Department attorney negotiated with Greenwood officials for the release of Negroes who had been jailed, and the dynamic tension which had been growing there subsided without producing any new national resolve on eliminating the obstacles confronted in Greenwood and elsewhere. Thus in the instances of Birmingham and Greenwood, Justice indicated a lack of sympathy with or a lack of understanding of the kind of use of massive, demanding confrontation which Dr. King used. It chose immediate order over an immediate tension that might bring long-term order of a more just kind.

3. Fleming, p. 938. The amount of work required for preparation of some of the resultant cases was extraordinary. Members of the Civil Rights Division were noted for the long hours they worked and for the urgency of their push in many of these cases. In Hinds County, Mississippi, department lawyers and their clerical assistants had to analyze 14,000 application forms and control cards to build evidence that there had been discrimination in the selection of test questions and in the grading of them. Burke Marshall pointed out that in cases filed under Section 1971 (a) of the U.S. Code, authorizing injunctive relief to secure the right to vote, it was necessary to count registration books; to determine the race of registered voters and rejected applicants; and to ascertain whether assistance had been given to white applicants or refused to Negro applicants. Sometimes, he noted, hundreds of witnesses had to be interviewed for the preparation of a single 1971 (a) case. Cases filed under 1971 (b) of the code, which prohibits acts of intimidation, threats, or coercion by

officials or private persons to interfere with the right to vote, also required lengthy preparations.

It is not difficult to understand why private agencies in the human rights and civil liberties fields could not effectively pursue these cases. The very nature of their preparation demanded large staffs and services costing hundreds of thousands of dollars. This factor, resting upon the nature of the law itself, made federally initiated suits the sole remedy available on a broad basis.

4. Fleming, p. 939.

5. *Report of the United States Commission on Civil Rights, 1963,* p. 13.

6. Fleming, p. 939.

7. *Report of the United States Commission on Civil Rights, 1963,* p. 21.

8. See Burke Marshall, *Federalism and Civil Rights* (New York and London: Columbia University Press, 1964), pp. 4–6, 44–50. On p. 50, Mr. Marshall refers to "the protest movement, whose members do not understand their rights."

9. "Law Enforcement in Mississippi" (Southern Regional Council, summer 1964).

10. The comments of a number of Southern federal judges on the Supreme Court's school desegregation decisions are summarized in Reed Sarratt, *The Ordeal of Desegregation* (New York and London: Harper & Row, 1966), pp. 201–203. One of those quoted is District Judge T. Whitfield Davidson, one of two judges who presided over the Dallas school desegregation case, who said from the bench: "The Supreme Court has placed your state, your country, and your schools . . . over a barrel . . . The white man has a right to maintain his racial integrity, and it can't be done so easily in integrated schools." Circuit Judge John R. Brown suggested some of the subtlety of unjudicial influences on some Southern federal judges' decisions when he said that ". . . lifetime tenure insulates judges from anxiety over worldly cares . . . but it does not protect them from the unconscious urge for the approbation of their fellow man, and fellow man most often means those of like interests and backgrounds, business and professional experiences and predilections and even prejudice."

11. See Alexander M. Bickel, "Impeach Judge Cox," *The New Republic,* September 4, 1965, p. 13.

12. In *Evers* v. *Jackson Municipal Separate School District,* 232 F. Supp. 241, 251 (S.D. Miss. 1964).

13. *Stell* v. *Savannah-Chatham County Board of Education,* 220 F. Supp. 667, 683 (S.D. Ga. 1963), rev'd, 333 F. 2d (5th Cir. 1964).

14. *Davis* v. *East Baton Rouge Parish School Board,* 214 F. Supp. 624, 625 (E.D. La. 1963).

15. Such personal and self-serving construals also, on occasion, have benefited Negroes. Registration workers in South Carolina told of one rural registrar who, old and tired and not anxious to have trouble of any kind, clandestinely allowed Negroes to take the registration forms home and return with them already completed. He cautioned them not to let anyone know. In Chatham County, Georgia, the county governing board passed a law barring from the courthouse the "courthouse worker" who had been stationed in the halls there by registration workers to guide Negroes to the registrar. After the Negro voter organization protested this new law, the county commissioners assented to let the "courthouse worker" keep at it. What about the law? the commissioners were asked. They replied that it would be left on the books but ignored. In one rural Georgia county, an older woman handled voter registration in her home. A young Negro registration worker, Beverly Lewis, made contact with the registrar to facilitate Negro registration. She was allowed to come into the registrar's home and administer the registration tests herself. The registrar seemed to like her young visitor. In fact, eventually the registrar tired of it all and on occasion

began to leave the whole office to her new helper. Thus, in the transitional South as in the Old South, personal relationships frequently softened and destroyed the rigidities of white supremacy.

16. "Albany, a Study in Rational Responsibility," by Howard Zinn (Southern Regional Council, 1962).

17. *Southern Justice*, edited by Leon Friedman (New York: Pantheon Books, 1965), p. 193. This volume provides an excellent summary of civil rights performances of Southern federal judges. See especially the chapter entitled "Judge William Harold Cox and the Right to Vote in Clarke County, Mississippi," by Gerald M. Stern, and "The Federal Courts of the South: Judge Bryan Simpson and His Reluctant Brethren," by Leon Friedman. We are indebted to the Friedman book for much of the information pertaining to judges in this chapter.

The influence of judges' past political identifications and social values has been established. One study of national scope, for instance, showed the relationship between judges' party affiliation and their decisions. Democratic judges were found to be above average in their courts in favoring the defense in criminal cases, the administrative agency in business regulation cases, the government in tax cases, and the labor union in labor-management cases. See Stuart S. Nagel, "Political Party Affiliation and Judges Decisions," *American Political Science Review*, December 1961, pp. 843-850. By the same token, it seems obvious that a federal judge's past identification with the Talmadge organization in Georgia or Eastland organization in Mississippi would likely indicate his leanings as a judge.

18. In dealing with local hoodlums for what they were when they appeared on the scene heavily armed and engaged in harassment, Judge Simpson seemed to be acting upon a legal principle once eloquently enunciated this way: "Judges are not necessarily to be ignorant in court of what everyone else, and they themselves out of court, are familiar with, nor was that unreal ignorance considered to be an attribute of the bench in early and strict times." *Lumly* v. *Gye*, 2 EL & BL, 216, 267, 118 Eng. Rep. 749, 768 (1953).

19. New York *Times*, October 7, 1963. "Registration in Alabama," Howard Zinn, *The New Republic*, October 26, 1963.

20. "Law Enforcement in Mississippi," special report of the Southern Regional Council, July 14, 1965, p. 24. The earlier quotations from the Notre Dame conference and the law professors' statement also may be found in this report, pp. 22-24.

21. The New York *Times*, July 10, 1963, in a dispatch by Claude Sitton.

22. *The Southern Courier*, October 9-10, 1965 (weekend edition).

23. While the irony of this may not have even occurred to Secretary Byrnes, in earlier days one of South Carolina's race demagogues, Ben Tillman, had made no effort to disguise the intent of methods used by his state to disfranchise Negroes. At the disfranchising convention of 1895 there was discussion of a new requirement that prospective voters be able to understand the state constitution, with the registrar as judge of their understanding. There was no doubt how this provision would be used. Tillman told the delegates: "Some have said there is fraud in this understanding clause. Some poisons in small doses are very salutary and valuable medicines . . . The [registration] officer is responsible to his conscience and his God; he is responsible to nobody else. There is no particle of fraud or illegality in it. It is just simply showing partiality, perhaps, (laughter) or discriminating. Ah, you grin." (From the journal of the convention, quoted by C. Vann Woodward, *Origins of the New South, 1877–1913* [Baton Rouge: Louisiana State University Press, the Littlefield Fund for Southern History of the University of Texas, 1951].)

9)
Victory?

The Voting Rights Act went into effect on August 6, 1965. On that day, across the Black Belt, across much of the South in Mississippi, Louisiana, Alabama, Georgia, South Carolina, Virginia, and some of the counties of North Carolina, literacy tests and other devices of administrative blockage dissolved.[1] In three of the states—Alabama, Mississippi, and Louisiana—federal examiners immediately opened offices. They were in fourteen counties, and lines of Negroes formed before them, the lines lasting all day long for several weeks, applying for the vote.

Here, come at last to a new day, were the people of the little churches, of the fear and "apathy," the people of courage. The office in Demopolis, Alabama, Marengo County, had opened on the morning of August 10. When the four Civil Service Commission employees serving as the examiners [2] had arrived at seven-thirty, at least 150 Negroes were already there waiting for them at the post office headquarters. When the doors opened an hour later, there were 250; by 10:00 A.M., 300; and when the doors closed at 4:30 P.M., there were at least 150 who had to be told to come back the next morning. The scene repeated itself day by day there for at least a month, and in most of the other examiner offices. It was notable that many who came to the examiners were older people,[3] and that many were people who had never tried to register before. A man ninety-two years old, gray-haired, with a cane, wearing from his farm home his Sunday-best clothes, sat attentively through the brief new process of becoming a voting citizen.

"Why didn't you ever try to register before?" the examiner, a Tennessean resident then in Georgia, asked him.

"I never believed in putting myself in the way of trouble comin'."

"Tell them," said the examiner, handing the old man his certificate which would allow him to vote in the next election, "that you've been waiting ninety-two years."

The new day had come, then. Negro Southerners at last were to be treated as other citizens—at least in this handful of places where there was a federal presence—in the most basic right of citizenship. The struggle had brought victory.

By the end of 1965, the federal examiners had been sent into twenty-three additional counties, including two in South Carolina. By August 1966, the anniversary of their appearance, they were in only five more counties—forty-two in all. They were still in no Georgia, North Carolina, or Virginia counties, and in only the two in South Carolina. This was to remain true into the year 1967. Then, in April, examiners were sent into three Georgia counties—Lee, Terrell, and Screven. They were also sent into Amite, Franklin, and Oktibbeha counties in Mississippi, and Bossier, Caddo, and De Soto parishes in Louisiana. As of September 1966, examiners had registered a total of 130,707 persons, more than 99 per cent of them Negroes, in those forty-two counties. The first onrush had soon ended, but business continued steady in most. (See Table I.)

Over all the South, Negro registration had increased from 2,174,200 in 1964 to 2,604,600 by August 1966.[4] This was a total increase of 430,000 in twenty months. The total increase during the thirty months of the first VEP (1962–64) was 668,800. Thus Negro registration was advancing at a pace not much, if any, faster than during the first VEP—even with the new voter law in force for 12 of the 20 months. And the increase that had been made was at least 25 per cent in the handful of counties where federal examiners had been sent.

The pattern becomes clearer in an examination of figures for each state. The over-all increase from 1964 to the summer of 1966 was from

Counties With Federal Examiner	1964 Negro Reg. Before Examiner	Number Registered By Examiners *	Negro VAP 1960 Census	Summer 1966 Total Negroes Registered **	Summer 1966 Total Whites Registered **
ALABAMA					
Autauga	50	1,285	3,651	2,308	6,932
Dallas	320	8,906	15,115	10,513	12,787
Elmore	400	1,670	4,808	2,813	15,710
Greene	275	2,094	5,001	3,927	2,001
Hale	236	3,535	5,999	4,096	4,515
Jefferson	23,992	23,007	116,160	62,992	175,087
Lowndes	0	2,688	5,122	2,758	2,823
Marengo	295	5,023	7,091	5,799	7,288
Montgomery	5,500	9,936	33,056	19,268	43,514
Perry	289	2,791	5,202	3,847	5,495
Wilcox	0	3,661	6,088	3,765	3,639
LOUISIANA (*parishes*)					
E. Carroll	119	2,525	4,183	2,735	2,577
E. Feliciana	1,821	2,041	4,102	2,195	5,378
Ouachita	1,744	5,429	16,377	7,596	31,044
Plaquemines	96	2,611	2,897	1,300	9,746
W. Feliciana	85	1,142	4,553	1,817	1,113
MISSISSIPPI					
Benton	55	517	1,419	956	2,419
Carroll	0	774	2,704	1,248	3,077
Claiborne	26	1,322	3,969	2,906	1,679
Clay	0	1,362	4,444	1,695	3,535
Coahoma	0	3,789	14,604	7,761	7,215
De Soto	0	1,141	6,246	2,129	5,592
Grenada ***	135	1,259	4,323	1,752	5,962
Hinds	5,616	8,070	36,138	15,663	63,952
Holmes	20	3,952	8,757	4,655	5,080
Humphreys	0	920	5,561	1,283	2,861
Jasper	10	530	3,675	976	4,643
Jefferson	0	2,049	3,540	2,049	1,913
Jefferson Davis	126	1,052	1,048	1,833	3,443
Jones	0	1,968	7,427	2,077 (est.)	N/A
Leflore	281	6,325	13,567	7,161 (est.)	N/A
Madison	218	6,193	10,366	5,991	6,334
Neshoba	0	514	2,565	953	6,783
Newton	0	540	3,018	1,127	6,198
Noxubee	0	1,797	1,789	N/A	N/A
Rankin	0	434	6,944	1,504	12,321
Simpson	0	1,194	3,186	N/A	N/A
Walthall	4	1,128	2,490	1,293	4,261
Warren	2,433	932	10,726	5,229	12,169
Winston	—	51	3,611	N/A	N/A
SOUTH CAROLINA					
Clarendon	523	3,384	7,735	5,339	5,436
Dorchester	1,750	1,166	5,370	3,941	8,624

43.3 per cent of the potential Negro voters in the South to 52.2 per cent. All but four states were over the 50 per cent mark. One of those which was not was Mississippi, where the greatest gain had to be made. Registration rose from 28,500 or 6.7 per cent to 139,099 or 32.9 per cent. This lived up to expectations of the great new day. But another state below 50 per cent was Georgia. Its increase had been from 270,000 to 289,545 or from 44.0 per cent to 47.2 per cent. A similar comparison showed for the other two states below 50 per cent—Louisiana and Virginia. In Louisiana, Negro registration increased from 164,700 to 242,130, or from 32 to 47.2 per cent. In Virginia, it increased from 200,000 to 205,000 or from 45.7 to only 46.9 per cent. All four were covered by the law and had been forced to abandon literacy tests and other barriers. One—but not the only—difference was that the examiners were in Mississippi and Louisiana, where gains had been great, and not in Georgia and Virginia, where gains had been slight. Obviously involved also was the fact that after the first 40 to 50 per cent of a state's Negroes are registered, it becomes increasingly difficult to motivate the remainder to overcome apathy and/or fear. Voter workers spoke of "skimming off the cream," and of getting down to hard cases.

Of the other states with federal examiners, results were spectacular the first year in Alabama, where the greatest gains were to be made and where the most examiners were sent in. In South Carolina, where the fewest examiners were sent, and where registration had already been at 39 per cent, the increase was to only 51.4 per cent, a climb from 144,000 to 190,600. In Alabama, the increase was from 23 to 51.2 per cent— from 111,000 to 246,396. The one other state besides Georgia and Virginia into which the examiners might have been sent but were not during the first year under the new law was North Carolina. It showed an increase from 46.8 to 51.0 per cent, a climb from 258,000 to 281,134.

The results in the Southern states not covered by the law were hardly more encouraging. Tennessee went from 69.4 to 71.7 per cent, or 218,000 to 225,000, and Texas from 57.7 to 61.6 per cent, or 375,000 to

←LEGEND

N/A—Not available
VAP—Voting age population
Reg.—Registration
* A very few, far less than 1 per cent of the total added by examiners, were white.
** These figures were compiled over a three-month period ending in August 1966, and do not reflect quite all of those registered by examiners.
*** Grenada County was designated for registrars following the Meredith march of June 1966.

400,000. In Arkansas—where the figures still reflected the last year of the poll-tax requirement of annual re-registration—Negro registration showed an increase from 1965's 105,000, or 54.5 per cent, to 115,000 or 59.7 per cent. Florida actually showed a decrease, apparently attributable to legitimate removal of voters' names from the register—from 300,000 in 1964 to 288,000 in mid-1966, or from 63.7 to 61.3 per cent.

In short, the great new day a-coming had not quite arrived. Indeed, except in the three states where repression had kept Negro registration scandalously low, it wasn't coming any faster than it had been. Nevertheless, over the South white politicians were jumping and switching about, and advocates of an equalitarian society were hopeful. They were all seeing what was potential as avidly as they saw present actualities.

Crucible in Selma

For a time, there had been the belief—so typical of the movement —that full Negro political participation would come overnight. That was in the early spring of 1965 when the voting rights law had been won at Selma. Everything had come together in Selma: voter registration and direct action, the courage of the little churches and the bestiality of the white resistance, the law's delay and the destructive consequences, the national conscience and its fixation on violence, the old militancy of the movement and the new radicalism, non-violence and seasoned, tough-minded Negro strategy, good intentions about the Constitution and the time-centered revolution (freedom now), the movement and the main-stream, democracy and its denial, the good guys and the bad guys. And then: murder and segregated justice. Somewhere in there still, occasionally, rarely now, shining out, was redemptive love.

Also: the North and the South. Wilson Baker, Selma's commissioner of public safety, a force generally for moderation in the little city, got mad at one point and arrested a group of Northern whites picketing the home of the mayor. The arrestees, priests and students and middle-class suburban types, were loaded onto a bus. Said the New York *Times*: "The occupants of the bus struck up an unmelodious version of 'We Shall Overcome.' Mr. Baker, his anger subsided, looked at his prisoners mournfully and said, 'This has ceased to be a Negro movement. . . . At least we had good music when the Negroes were demonstrating.'"

The big events of Selma had, even by movement standards, a small beginning. SNCC had started a voter drive in early 1963. It was one of the few in restrictive Alabama's hard core attempted by the civil rights organizations. The Reverend Bernard Lafayette and his new wife, Mrs. Colia Liddell Lafayette, began the work. They had both been in the movement, she in Mississippi, he in the Nashville sit-ins and the freedom rides. After their marriage, they came to VEP with a proposal to work in Selma together—saying they wanted to go to a new place where they could get off to themselves to begin married life. They were later joined by Frank Holloway and Worth Long. In his original proposal to VEP, Mr. Lafayette talked of the "fear-stricken" Negro population,[5] and the possibilities inherent in the fact that "if an effective program is initiated, overt violence from the white citizens can be anticipated." His sizing-up of assets also included listing of five militant Negro leaders in the town, including Mrs. Amelia Boynton, later to run for Congress, and a listing of "white liberals"—exactly two.

Vital statistics included 52 per cent of the town's population under the $3,000 income level in 1959, and Negro registration about 200 of a possible 15,115.[6] The registration office was open the first and third Monday of every month. The board of registrars, as Howard Zinn later pointed out, was never able to enroll more than thirty new voters a day. "At this rate even making the incredible assumption that the board accepted every Negro applicant, it would take the board ten years to enroll as many Negroes as whites," Zinn wrote.[7] In other words, it was a hard hard-core place. The SNCC workers found that a small registration effort was under way by the local leaders, but was being kept a secret, even from many Negroes. This was the town where the Alabama Citizens Council had been founded, with a speech at an early annual meeting warning: "The integration fight is going to be won or lost at the ballot box." [8]

Progress was the painfully slow, patient, nerve-racking kind on such projects. It took four months just to recruit youth workers. Voter classes started with one student, Mr. Major Washington, sixty-seven, who the next week brought another, and the next week, three more. Gradually the classes grew, with people coming in from surrounding towns. And gradually the impact was felt at the registrar's office. Then came the familiar pattern of violence (Mr. Lafayette beaten, a young worker hit from behind at the courthouse and then arrested for "action calculated to breach the peace") and the fearful withdrawal of the Negro community, and then a build-up to a bigger breakthrough.

This came in the fall of 1963, with big mass meetings featuring such celebrities as Dick Gregory, James Baldwin, and Dr. King himself, and "freedom day" demonstrations at the courthouse. Negroes stood all day in line to demonstrate their inability to get in to register, and here Sheriff Jim Clark began to be seen by the nation. By this time upwards of 1,000 Negroes had overcome their fear enough to go to the dreaded courthouse; more than 200 of them tried it even when it was flanked with the sheriff's men with their big clubs, big helmets, and threatening faces, and a local photographer taking their pictures. The sheriff's volunteer posse was in evidence, too—men calling themselves "squirrel-shooters" who were likely to turn up at any Alabama scene of racial tension to make it worse.

In the aftermath of these 1963 stirrings, Father Maurice Oulette, a white, thirty-seven-year-old Edmundite priest, head of the Catholic St. Elizabeth Mission for Negroes (operating schools and a hospital in Selma) declared: "The Negro community has turned to every possible group in this city and asked that they be allowed to speak concerning what they believe to be injustices against their race. Every group has turned its back on them . . . Will they allow a crime such as the one recently seen in Birmingham to come to Selma [a reference to the church bombing murders] and then belatedly utter pious prayers for the deceased to salve their own consciences?" A Citizens Council spokesman had already answered: "We are not going to give in. If we let them have one inch, they would want to go all the way."

Through 1964 efforts to register continued, largely unsuccessfully. The SNCC office was raided by the sheriff's department in January. Records and leaflets were seized, and nine workers arrested. Phones were torn off the walls and the office generally wrecked. Three Negro candidates ran for city council and Mrs. Boynton [9] for Congress, their vote totals less than 300. The Dallas County Bar Association advertised a resolution warning citizens they did not have to answer FBI questions in civil rights cases. Sheriff Clark in May sat in on a voter meeting, ignoring protests he was violating freedom of assembly. That same month, the Alabama Court of Appeals ruled out the $1,000-bonds being set in Selma for minor offenses, thus, in the words of the Selma *Times-Journal*, "strip[ping] local law enforcement of one of the most effective weapons employed here last year in restraining the activities of the Negro leaders in racial demonstrations."

In July the city obtained an injunction from state courts against *any activity* by civil rights organizations and numerous other groups. The Citizens Council advertised itself as an organization "whose efforts are not thwarted by courts which give sit-in demonstrators legal immunity, prevent school boards from expelling students who participate in mob activities and would place federal referees at the board of registrars. Law enforcement can be called only after these things occur, but your Citizens Council prevents them from happening. Why else did only 350 Negroes attend a so-called voter registration meeting that outside agitators worked 60 days to organize in Selma?" The strange injunction was in effect set aside by federal court proceedings against voter restrictions in Selma in late 1964, and on January 2, 1965, Dr. King and the SCLC opened their version of a voter drive in the little town with its old-fashioned cement bridge humping into the three square blocks of wide-streeted business section. SNCC had kept an outpost there, but it and activities of Negroes generally had been severely hampered by the injunction. Dr. King had meanwhile had his eye on the area for some time. There had been a decision after Birmingham (and after much discussion) that Alabama was the place for SCLC. The voter drive in Selma was to be the beginning, after plans for the 1964 "Alabama Freedom Summer" were dropped because of the build-up by SNCC for its Mississippi adventure.

The territory had been staked out. Selma, because of the previous activity there, and with knowledge of the potential in Sheriff Clark to become another Bull Connor (such lawmen were becoming less abundant in the South), was picked as a place to begin. On his arrival, Dr. King said: "We will seek to arouse the federal government by marching by the thousands to the places of registration . . . We are not asking, we are demanding the ballot." A month later, with 3,300 arrests recorded, he called for a new law establishing federal registrars and reforming Southern voter requirements.

Now the nation, still congratulating itself on having enacted the civil rights law, began to learn about Black Belt voter statistics, about the resistance and the fear. Now it read the questions on an Alabama voter test: "If no national candidate for Vice-President receives a majority of the electoral vote, how is a Vice-President chosen? In such cases how many votes must a person receive to become Vice-President?" [10]

Demonstrations continued through February. Negro teachers, 105 strong, lined up to register, and were shoved back with night sticks.

"We have never had anything like this before with teachers participating," exulted the Reverend Andrew Young, a King lieutenant; he went on to explain that they were risking their jobs. Young people, around 165 of them, some under 12, were taken by the sheriff and his posse on a forced march, between a fast walk and a run, for more than two miles into the countryside, on the way to jail for demonstrating. The sheriff's men poked at them with billy clubs, and burned them with the electric cattle prods to keep them going.[11] A few fell by the side, screaming. The familiar build-up was on. One could have almost predicted the outcome, stage by stage: concern expressed by the government, indignation and pressure mounting in the rest of the nation, worse and worse spectacles in Selma.

Demonstrations for voting began in nearby Marion, a sad-faced hamlet with the typical big courthouse square and a little ring of stores around it, and a scattering of ante-bellum mansions. In all, 1,315 Negroes were arrested there, almost half as many as in Selma, and on February 19 state troopers beat a night demonstration down with billy clubs, sending nine people to the hospital, injuring three newsmen. One demonstrator in the hospital was Jimmie Lee Jackson, who had been shot. He died a few days later. The first martyr.

On March 6, a little band of seventy white Alabama citizens, gathered from across the state, marched in support of the Negro's right to vote in Selma, the first such all-white demonstration by Southerners during all the movement. It was a brave act. And to say this is not to disparage those white Southerners who fought for racial sanity during the 1960's but could not bring themselves to demonstrate. This would probably include most of the whites who fought longest—those who were committed and often hurt in various ways for it—a decade, or two or three decades, before direct action started. They had of course other means of protest, closed to Negroes. It was a question for many of style and personality traits, rather than courage. In Atlanta, a Selma sympathy march attracted many whites, including some of the old white civil rights warriors—who looked self-conscious. One who didn't march told of standing on the curb, drawn to it, but somehow unable to take the step, thinking, Well I never did when it wasn't respectable. I don't have any right to, now.

In another episode of white sympathy, Mrs. Annie Mae Turner prepared a speech supporting Negro voter rights to deliver to the Alabama Education Association, as outgoing president of this white teacher's organization. She was pressured into canceling the speech, and wept over the suppression.

Then on March 9, came the attempt of some 525 Negroes to march from Selma to Montgomery in defiance of Governor George Wallace's order that they not do so, and the attack on them at the Edmund Pettus Bridge on the edge of downtown Selma. The nation saw their line on television standing there, orderly, asking the fifty state troopers [12] up ahead for a word, and heard Major John Cloud say, "There is no word to be had . . ." And: "You have two minutes to turn around and go back to your church." Then the awful moment of their just standing there, the troopers and Sheriff Clark's volunteer posse advancing on them with clubs, with horses, with whips, and with tear gas, and routing them the six blocks back to their church in helpless, defenseless terror, with attacks made again and again. This kind of thing had happened before—how many times in the voter effort alone across the South? But now the nation saw it, as it never had before, and responded, as it never had before. People dropped everything, many of them, that very Sunday night and flew to Selma, not planning ahead, just determined to do something about the outrage. There was a greatness to this sudden, spontaneous response of the nation—as much as it was to be later maligned.

The tough-minded of the Southern movement tended to see it as a necessary but nevertheless naïve intervention of unknowledgeable Northerners. The racists saw it as an invasion of Communists and worse, fantasying great sprees of mass drunkenness and public sex orgies. One whole paperback pamphlet with wide Southern sales was devoted to the latter. (The best reporters of the Southern scene, who were there through all of it, said the charges were not true. Some of the Southern basis for such fantasy was later exemplified in the highly publicized escapade of two white Selma dignitaries bilked by a Negro con man in their quest for Negro prostitutes in Washington, D.C.) The new left of the Southern movement was to ask scornfully afterward how a New Yorker who could afford to take time off from his work and afford to fly first class down to demonstrate could ever expect to have any solidarity with jobless Negroes of Selma living in shacks. "I'm getting sick of all these fly-by-night freedom fighters," said a young movement stalwart in the midst of one of the more artificial ceremonies of the March to Montgomery.

Why should there have been so much harsh criticism, so much questioning of motive? What is it in America that fears to accept or believe that people might act out of decent emotion, that idealism might move Americans? How many times, with tourist cars with the license-tag talismans of all the rest of the supposedly sympathetic nation flashing heedlessly by, had such scenes as the Pettus Bridge attack occurred in the South—on lesser scales usually, but no less brutal, no less against all America stood for? Almost the exact same scene of confrontation across a U.S. highway had occurred in the spring of 1963 when the ten "freedom walkers" of SNCC and CORE—in interracial protest of racist killings—reached the Alabama state line. Troopers stood before them, and a mob howled behind them, and they were ordered to turn back or be arrested. They stood there, and some fell to the pavement in nonviolent resistance, and they were arrested with considerable use of electric cattle prods. And the tourists rode right on by. How many times had Negroes looked to the rest of the nation, to the Justice Department, for real understanding of the terror, and not found it? Now at last the nation was responding, and those who came couldn't be faulted in the moment for not having come sooner, for not having done something already about the injustice behind the violence, the matter of voting. Nuns, businessmen and their wives, students, ministers, professors, a bearded patriarch of the Greek Orthodox church with his gold-headed cane, who impressed into silence even the jeering white teen-age toughs always attracted to places of racial tension—all of America was there.

And they found there what had eluded the fixation on violence before—the reality of the Southern racial anguish, and the feel of the idealism undergirding the coldly pragmatic, legalistic form the fight had by then taken—in which, on one level, they had become pawns. Three of those who came were set upon and beaten with iron pipe on March 9. The Reverend James Reeb, with the other pilgrims and their Negro hosts holding all-night vigils, died two nights later. He was the second martyr, a young man of that good part of a new generation which looks for meaning in life in the social problems of the age. He was a Unitarian minister, engaged in an American Friends Service Committee neighborhood project in Boston.

The violence, police and private, reached a new height of ugliness in Selma. It was peculiar. At the time of Dr. King's arrival, there was talk of a behind-the-scenes struggle between a more moderate element of whites in the town,[13] which had made important gains in the past spring's elections, and the forces represented by Sheriff Clark. There was awareness among the white leaders all the while that violence would make the campaign a success; otherwise it might, as in Albany, be defeated. For a time in January, this seemed about to happen. The campaign was losing steam. But the newspaper accounts indicated a strange inability of Clark and his men to keep away from the violence-prone confrontations. Sheriff Clark made a hostile gesture to Dr. King once, and a Negro woman flew at him and hit him in the face and he cracked her in the skull with his club, the echo sounding in the courthouse halls, and his picture was flashed to front pages across the country bending with his club over her prostrate body. The Reverend C. T. Vivian exchanged words with the sheriff over whether Negroes waiting to register could come in out of the rain, and called him "brutal" and "like Hitler," and dared the sheriff to hit him. The sheriff took the dare, hitting Mr. Vivian in the mouth with his fist. Aides had tried to talk him into going into his office, letting them handle it. He had spent two days in the hospital the previous weekend, exhausted from four weeks of the demonstrations. The children, some of whom had been on the forced march, had a demonstration and prayed for him to get well.

The obsessive quality of the violence of racist resistance in the South has been noted. As in other Negro advances, it directly forced the issue on voting rights. The unfair administration of voting procedures, alone, had been a terribly effective weapon. The violence, certainly in the latter stages, came from uncontrolled rage and hate rather than, as for a time, strategic calculation. Maybe there was a secret desire, too—as with certain kinds of criminals—to be made to stop. Whatever the hidden and Southern-muddled myriad of causes, violence it was, and violence it continued to be to the end.

Clashes of a different nature were also going on behind the increasingly frenetic scenes of Selma—between the young radicals and the other members of the movement. There had always been organizational rivalry [14] at the major demonstration crises, and it was operating in Selma, mainly over SNCC's old plaint that it had done the dirty preparatory work and SCLC was getting all the credit. But there were signs of more fundamental antagonism. At times it seemed that the young radicals were more interested in conflict with their movement brethren than in the exigencies of the campaign—a feel to this not unlike that of the behavior of the sheriff and his men.

For a time, the young radicals questioned the basic mode of the campaign (and of the movement)—the demonstrations. By this time SCLC had developed the mass marches and demonstrations, involving a cross-section of the Negro community, to an art, with predictable increasing of tension and disorder in clashes with white mobs and the law. (The technique was pioneered in Albany, proven in Birmingham, further refined in St. Augustine in 1964, proven again in Selma, and pushed against *de facto* segregation and Northern racism in Chicago in 1966.) The young radicals were out of a different tradition of demonstrations—the sit-ins and freedom rides, which involved single goals and a more direct encounter with the agents of the specific grievance. But in the years after 1962 they seemed to approach demonstrations in an exploratory sense—challenging various forms of racism just to see what manner of truth would emerge. They showed incredible courage (some said foolhardiness—like walking an interracial couple into a hot Fourth of July racist rally in Atlanta harangued by George Wallace and Ross Barnett) in this putting of their bodies where truth was, and showed also an increasing anger during confrontations, so that to call their resistance passive was stretching the word and concept. This anger (over too many unjust arrests, too many defenseless beatings) seemed to be as much behind their questioning of the Selma demonstrations as their more praiseworthy insistence that the local people decide for themselves whether to march, and understand why, and not be herded or pressured into it by mass psychology.[15] This sentiment on face value expressed the best of their radicalism—the respect for the people they worked and lived with in the voter effort. To whatever extent it was a use of such sentiment to gain their own ends in the organizational rivalry of the movement, it expressed the worst of what their experience had done to them.

Characteristically, when at the Selma bridge the confrontation with the truth of hard-core resistance to the vote did occur, a representative of the radicals, John Lewis of SNCC, was at the head of the line, alongside Hosea Williams of SCLC. Dr. King was out of town. And then after all the opposition to demonstrations, the young radicals were the ones who kept insisting in the following days that another try should be made at crossing the bridge. When they couldn't prevail, Jim Forman of SNCC and others set off to Montgomery and organized some of the most abrasive demonstrations of the movement, characterized by taunting and attempting to provoke violence from police and onlookers.

All of this, along with baiting of the liberals among the Selma pilgrims [16] and a SNCC-organized sit-in at the White House over Selma, added to the criticism of SNCC and a widening of the animosity among movement elements. This animosity was to break the movement apart, for the time anyhow, in 1966 on the Meredith March in Mississippi. It is worth noting that the argument then was not so much over what was said ("black power") but how it was said—over the belligerence and rabble-rousing of the young radicals.

The organizations were able to hold together in Selma, and on March 13, 1965, President Johnson announced he would send the voter rights bill to Congress. On March 26, the fifty-eight-mile march from the Edmund Pettus Bridge to Montgomery ended, with full protection of the United States Army enabling these marchers to do what the first group could not. Each day there were photographs of its drama and descriptions of dangers that didn't develop. By the end it took on the air of a great American production, a grand pageant, tents and the Army and all outdoors, something of the Fourth of July and Hollywood and the circus rolled into one, with the movement's idiom of song and suffering somehow assimilated. The night they arrived in Montgomery, there was a large outdoor meeting, with singing and "entertainment" brought from afar, and the inevitable starlet saying it was the greatest thrill of her life to be there, but moments of dignity, too, from such men as Leonard Bernstein, who acknowledged his introduction but did not presume to speak.

The next day the throng of 25,000—marchers, Montgomery Negroes who joined along the way, and thousands more pilgrims who had come for the last day—stood in front of the gleaming white capitol in downtown Montgomery, with its monuments to the Confederacy, the Confederate flag flying, and a line of Alabama state troopers standing protectively in front of it in pastel-colored helmets, a movie-set scene. Here again was the same mixture of a Hollywood production, including professional folk-singers, with the old spirit of the movement. A boy of about twelve, among a platoon of Negroes who had carried flags in the march, carefully furled his, and after holding it awhile, said to a reporter, "Could I please put it on your table there; I don't want it to touch the ground."

Among the most meaningful words of the day were Dr. King's: "Let us march on ballot boxes, until we send to our city councils, state legislatures, and the United States Congress men who will not fear to do justice, love mercy and walk humbly with their God. . . ." In a less spiritual vein, James Bevel of SCLC waved up at the capitol and said, "Those police up there on the steps know we belong inside. Thirty-four per cent of the seats in there belong to us. We don't want these steps.

We want the capitol." The crowd roared. Like the flash of the fierce sun on a marcher's canteen, the meaning of what the march was accomplishing was clear, and the wonder of it was that it hadn't really seemed to be before. Soon there would be the possibility of Negroes elected to the legislature up there. Dr. King spoke also that day of the old dream of Populism, again emphasizing the march's meaning by foreshadowing one of the larger possibilities it had thrown open. The movement had joined the mainstream. It sang "The Star Spangled Banner." The crowd, filling more than a block of wide pavement, all standing at attention, American flags waving, was in control there at the Cradle of the Confederacy. Only some of the state troopers and the few whites idling by the statue of Jefferson Davis were not standing at attention. They were the outsiders.

The killing that night of the campaign's third martyr, Mrs. Viola Gregg Liuzzo, shot on the highway where she had been ferrying Negroes back to Selma, restored reality—the reality, at least, of a still-enduring era. The voter rights law of 1965 was born in violence as murderous as any previous legislative breakthrough achieved by the movement.

The Law and Its Aftermath

The law itself, however, aimed most closely at the administrative aspects of voter discrimination. Its basic feature was to outlaw literacy tests and all other voter application tests, and to allow federal examiners [17] to accept voter applications where tests and applications had been used to discriminate. Such discrimination would be assumed in any state or county that used the tests as of November 1, 1964, and had less than 50 per cent of the voting-age population registered and voting. Alabama, Mississippi, Louisiana, Georgia, South Carolina, Virginia, and twenty-six counties in North Carolina, as we have noted, were thus covered by the law, and by a fluke, Alaska. Tennessee, Florida, Arkansas, and Texas of the eleven states of the old Confederacy thus escaped it by virtue of having had no tests, and their above 50 per cent performance on registration. As we have seen, their past records were not perfect. In ruling the law constitutional, the U.S. Supreme Court said, "It is irrelevant that the coverage formula excludes certain localities which do not employ voting tests and devices but for which there is evidence of voting discrimination by other means. Congress had learned that widespread and persistent discrimination in voting during recent years has typically entailed the misuse of tests and devices, and this was the evil for which the new remedies were specifically designed." [18]

As for the violence, the terror, and the fear, the law said that "no person, whether acting under color of law or otherwise, shall intimidate, threaten, or coerce, or attempt to intimidate, threaten, or coerce any person for urging or aiding any person to vote or attempt to vote, or intimidate, threaten, or coerce any person for exercising any powers or duties under [sections of the law]." Penalty was set at five years in prison or $5,000 fine or both. The law also allowed the attorney general to institute actions "for preventive relief, including an application for a temporary or permanent injunction, restraining order or other order . . ." against violating its various sections, including the one on intimidation.

So arrived the brave new day, the victory for which the voter effort had given so much. But to some who had given the most, the victory must have seemed as hollow as many other broken promises of the past. The situation in southwest Georgia a year after the voter law went into effect was in ironic contrast to booming totals in some of the other familiar Black Belt battlegrounds.

Lee and Terrell, how had these counties fared? After all the work, the terror, the courage in the little churches, Negro voter registration stood, at the end of the first VEP in November 1964, at an estimated 187 in Lee County and 340 in Terrell. No more. By July 1966, either because the 1964 estimate was high or a new estimate was low or because there had been unusual attrition or purges of voter lists intervening, the figure for Lee was 161 of the 1,795 Negroes eligible to vote there. In Terrell, eleven months after the arrival of the new day in voting for Negro Southerners, 429 of 4,057 eligible Negroes were registered. Federal examiners added 393 Negro voters in Lee County in a month and a half, and 1,122 in Terrell. During the first month and a half in the other Georgia county where they were sent—Screven—they added 961 Negro and 10 white voters.

Only Sumter among those early hard-fought campaign counties of southwest Georgia showed immediately anything like what might have been expected: 3,040 of 6,710 eligible Negroes registered in July 1966. There had been only 1,241 in November of 1964. SCLC had conducted a bitter and tempestuous registration and direct-action campaign there after the signing of the voting rights act; there were ostentatious efforts by white officials in Americus to show registration was accessible and federal examiners not needed. In a subsequent election, four Negro women were arrested when they refused to stand in a segregated voting line.

And in Albany, bruised and battered Albany, the county (Dougherty) total in early 1966 was 6,080 of 14,163 voting-age Negroes. In November 1964 the total had been 5,930. Here, for sociologists or historians, was a case study in the extreme damage done to the spirit and soul of a great people by the impact of stress during the first half of the 1960's. If the full implications of "apathy" were to be understood, here and the other cities of demonstration crises were the places to look.

In Baker County ("Bad Baker"), where Charles Sherrod finally penetrated, the total of Negroes registered in July 1966, was 722 of 1,285, an increase of 422 since November 1964. The July 1966 figures for other counties in this little pocket of the old South, most of them untouched by the movement, were: Calhoun, 509 of 2,393 eligible; Decatur,[19] 1,218 of 5,515; Early, 502 of 3,277; Grady, 809 of 3,364; Miller, 153 of 946; Mitchell, 1,242 of 4,971; Seminole, 418 of 1,255. None of the 1966 figures marked an increase of any significance attributable to the new law, unless it was Miller County. There, the increase from late 1964 to July 1966 was from eight Negro voters to 153 of the 949 potential. Other areas of rural middle and south Georgia were hardly better. Taliaferro, scene of a bruising 1965 SCLC direct-action campaign against the sending of all white pupils to high schools of surrounding counties instead of the local "desegregated" one,[20] had 984 of 1,073 eligible Negroes registered in the summer of 1966. But nearby Jones County had only 956 of 2,185; Monroe, 809 of 2,652; and Putnam 725 of 2,204.

What of some of the other battlegrounds of the first drive? In Mississippi's Sunflower County, site of the brave Ruleville registration work, a total of 2,325 of a potential 13,524 Negroes were registered in July 1966. Leflore, scene of so many battles, with federal examiners to help had more than 7,000 of a potential 13,567.

Negro registration performance in Georgia during the first year under the voter law suggested most of the strengths and weaknesses of the implementation of the law.

The federal government's own estimates showed, from August 6,

1965, to January 14, 1966, an increase of only 16,000 in Georgia.[21] By comparison, during the same period, federal examiners had registered 52,973 Negroes in eleven counties of Alabama, and local officials in all counties had registered 46,700 more, for a total increase of 99,763. Federal examiners in eighteen counties of Mississippi had registered 31,242 Negroes, and local officials in all counties had registered 45,600 more, for a total increase of 76,842. In Louisiana, the federal examiners in five parishes had added 13,499 Negroes to the voting rolls, and local officials in all counties had added 50,800 for a total increase of 64,299. And the examiners in two counties in South Carolina (sent in September 29, 1965) had added 4,364 Negroes, while local officials in all counties had added 21,400 more, for a total increase of 25,764. Of course, of the five states, Georgia had more Negroes registered to begin with—though the comparison with South Carolina in 1964 was close, 44 per cent of eligibles and 38 per cent. The contrast in gains was marked. By August of 1966, Georgia ranked above only three of the eleven Southern states in the percentage of eligible Negroes registered. (And Mississippi, from less than 10 per cent in 1965, had almost caught up with Georgia in one year.) Georgia's 47.2 per cent compared with 32.9 in Mississippi, 46.9 in Virginia, 47 in Louisiana, 51.4 in South Carolina, and 51.2 in Alabama. Alabama in a year had moved from next to last among the eleven states to sixth.

The same comparison might be made of Virginia—which might have had examiners but in the first year did not—with the states that did have them. The comparison suggests that the federal presence in a few counties encouraged Negro registration generally in a state. In all four of the states with examiners, local registrars alone had added more Negroes to the books than in Georgia, suggesting that there was both an encouragement to Negroes to try to register and a stimulus to local registrars to do their jobs in order to avoid having the federal examiners sent in. The impact of the examiners within a county, of course, was tremendous—involving the greater ease with which Negroes could register, and the better availability of officials to register them.

Pressures were building and southwest Georgia did finally in the spring of 1967 get federal examiners in the three counties. But why was Georgia able to avoid for a full year what it so obviously needed? Part of the answer lies in the good reputation the state achieved, under the administrations of Ernest Vandiver and Carl Sanders, among those who regard Southern race relations as good if only there are no intransigent showdowns of state and federal power manipulated by racist-opportunist politicians. There was perhaps a tendency to give Georgia a chance to reform its bad areas on its own. In places such as Atlanta the ballot had been available for many years. But a larger part of the answer would seem to lie in the obvious political implications, summed up in the immense power and influence of the state's congressmen, particularly Senator Richard B. Russell. Much the same sort of answer seemed inescapable in consideration of the charmed ability of Virginia to avoid examiners, and of such a place as Senator James Eastland's home county of Sunflower. As late as March 1966, there were still in Mississippi 30 counties, in Alabama 10, in Louisiana 7, in Georgia 29, and in South Carolina 2, where no federal examiners had been sent despite the fact that fewer than 25 per cent of their eligible Negro residents were registered. Of those counties, 24 in Mississippi, 2 in Louisiana, and 11 in Georgia had less than 10 per cent of eligible Negro residents registered.

Birmingham's experience emphasized what the presence of examiners meant. Registration in Jefferson County (which is mostly Birmingham) was 25,944 before the new law. From August 6, 1965, until February 12, 1966, local registrars added 17,917 Negroes to rolls. After SCLC-led demonstrations [22] demanded examiners and night-time registration, federal examiners were sent in on January 20, 1966. They quickly added 14,047 Negroes to the rolls, by February 21. This was almost as many in a month as the local officials had registered in seven months under the new law. These examiners, as many as twenty working at one time, were the first in the South to move out into a semblance of neighborhood registration and to conduct what amounted to night registration. An observer of the Birmingham registration who had seen many other moving moments in the struggle came away choked up by what he saw here—a mass response from the whole of the Negro community, many of the registrants previously untouched by the movement—older people, working men, average citizens. (Such a citizen was described in Atlanta during the initial days of the new law: Quite old, he had walked several miles to the courthouse to register. He had heard about how the law had been changed so that people like him who couldn't read or write could vote and he had, he said, always believed in doing his duty.)

Attorney General Nicholas Katzenbach had cited Birmingham as an example of local registrars' not making themselves available enough, saying that they weren't discriminating against individual Negroes, but weren't handling the mass of unregistered ones fast enough. He did not mention the SCLC demonstrations there as a reason for sending in examiners, and in private Justice Department spokesmen tended to say that the demonstrations had nothing to do with it. Yet Birmingham certainly hadn't been the only place in the South at the time where local registrars were dragging their feet.

Negro civil rights workers at a statewide conference on voter registration in Montgomery, Alabama, on October 2, 1965, sponsored by the Alabama Council on Human Relations, complained bitterly about many failures of federal enforcement of both voting rights and the civil rights law. Out of the Black Belt they brought the usual stories of physical and economic intimidation, unfriendly whites in control of the seats of local government, and administrative trickery. Federal government representatives from the U.S. Commission on Civil Rights and the Civil Service Commission were there, but the Justice Department, to whom most of the complaints would have been directed, though invited, was noticeable for its absence.

The complaints about voter registration could be heard all about the Black Belt, including the familiar reports of evictions of sharecroppers who tried to register. There was increased unrest among the sharecroppers and farm laborers of the Mississippi Delta. There on January 30, 1966, in dramatic evidence of the efficacy of demonstrations still, impoverished Negroes—men, women, and children, including many of the aged—seized a de-activated air base in Greenville. They were demonstrating chiefly the poverty in the eighteen-county region, worsened further in 1965 by a new agricultural act cutting back cotton crop-acreage allotments. By the middle of February, federal agencies launched a massive year-round food distribution program, started a new manpower training program at the Greenville base, and undertook a comprehensive labor survey of the Delta. There had been pleas for such action for months—indeed, years. With oceanlike persistence, various Mississippi counties were finding ways six months later to erode and crumble the year-round food distribution. One of the reasons was the old belief it inhibited the labor market.

Of the registration in Mississippi generally during 1965, Aaron Henry, the tough-minded veteran of the COFO battles and state president of the NAACP, said that things were, of course, much better than in the past. "But there is not as much registration as there might be if we had more examiners and the ones who are here were more accessible." As most other civil rights leaders were doing, he urged neighborhood and night registration, even door-to-door registration. He cited a bad county in Mississippi—Noxubee County, in the exact center of the eastern part of the state, bordering on Alabama, not far from dread Neshoba, where the three Freedom Summer workers were killed. "It's too tough for the Justice Department," Mr. Henry said. "It's too tough even for SNCC." SNCC workers had gone in there once in recent years, and come out after only two days. Registration of Negroes in Noxubee in March 1966, as ever since Reconstruction, stood at exactly zero. Examiners were finally sent there in April, and registered 1,800 Negroes in the first six weeks.

An interview by one of the authors with Richard Haley of CORE about the voter situation in Louisiana in the fall of 1965 was interrupted by a phone call from the town of Minden, Louisiana; a local Negro resident, very active in voter registration, had just been shot. When the Commission on Civil Rights held hearings in Thompson, Georgia, in February 1966, some witnesses interrupted accounts of their own troubles with landlords to point out that on the first floor of the Mc-Duffie County Courthouse, where the hearing was being held, a large sign designated a separate drinking fountain for Negroes, and that there were separate rest rooms for Negroes and whites. Such was the ragged face of democracy in the new South through 1966. There were reports of slowdowns from such diverse areas as rural Dorchester County, South Carolina, and New Orleans. In New Orleans and some other places there were reports of Negroes' being registered with no difficulty, but officials listed many as members of crank parties. This prevented them from voting in the next primary of Democrats or Republicans, and necessitated complicated party-changing applications.

There was still the old menace of violence. A Negro leader in Wilcox County, Ala., expressed apprehension that if Negro candidates should be elected there, they would be killed. He was driving at the time in a car with bloodstains all over the front seat. He had been first at the scene a short while previously when a white man had shot to death a Negro man over a traffic mishap in front of a Negro church. A newspaper reporter quoted an Alabama Black Belt white as saying of counties with Negro majorities, in the jocular way of such discourse, "They'll have to elect 'em a new sheriff every month."

For those who had observed the agonies of the South in its struggle toward something like equality for the Negro, and had seen the obvious implications of the first year's ragged enforcement of the voter law, who were convinced of democracy's efficacy and saw the vote as the key to success, the opportunity for full enfranchisement under the new law was a precious thing, not to be wasted. (The voting rights law's main provision—against voter tests—was limited to five years. After that, under the scrutiny of federal courts, the states might begin anew with equitable requirements. Even more perishable was the new mood of accommodation among politicians to the Negroes in their constituencies.)

Many Southern equalitarians would have agreed with a veteran of the civil rights movement who said that the federal government should have started at the topmost of the seven Southern states covered by the law, and taking a state at a time, sent examiners into every county, with neighborhood and night registration, with wide fanfare and efforts to reach every Negro eligible to vote. They would stay there until something like a normal percentage of each county's eligible Negroes was registered, and then they could move on to the next state, until all the South, in one equal, fast dose of it, should have achieved something like normal registration of all its Negro citizens. The job might have been completed well before the spring primaries of 1966, certainly by the general elections of the fall, according to this observer. But there was neither in the Justice Department a tradition for this kind of doing what the law seemed to say, nor in the politics or policies of the Johnson administration an inclination toward such sweeping action.

Enforcement

Attorney General Katzenbach, answering criticism of voter law implementation in a speech in Mobile, Alabama, in January 1966, promised increased voter registration efforts, more examiners where necessary, and swift, sure federal action against intimidation and terror. In another speech in Atlanta the next month, Mr. Katzenbach outlined a policy that seemed to say that Negro registration efforts had to be relied on for the necessary job, not exertions of the federal government. He did, however, promise more examiners wherever there were efforts to use voter tests, and wherever registrars made themselves inaccessible. This remained the policy into 1967, under Mr. Katzenbach and during the interim after his leaving the office to become assistant secretary of state. The attorney general cited Calhoun County, South Carolina, where there were no federal examiners and an increase from 14 to 44 per cent of eligible Negroes registered, and Anderson County, South Carolina, with presumably the same opportunity, but an increase of only .7 per cent (from 27.3 to 28.0). In Choctaw County, Alabama, the increase was 1,600 (to 63 per cent of eligible Negroes), compared with an increase of only 200 (to 18 per cent) in Chambers County—again with examiners in neither county. In counties with federal examiners, there were also notable variations. The percentage of Negroes registered climbed from 2 to 79 per cent of those eligible in West Feliciana Parish, Louisiana. But in East Feliciana, the increase was from 3 per cent to only 36 per cent. In some counties where the examiners were working, local officials also were accepting many Negroes, he went on. In Coahoma County, Mississippi, the federal examiners registered 3,100 Negroes. Local officials, who had enrolled only 1,000 Negroes prior to the new law, added 2,300 in the first eight months of its operation. Examiners added nearly all of the total in February 1966 of 2,696 Negroes in East Carroll Parish, Louisiana. But in adjacent Madison Parish, with no examiners, Negro registration increased from practically nothing to 2,666.

Katzenbach's point was that while examiners made a great difference, they were not the crucial factor. ". . . It is neither local compliance nor federal examiners which make the crucial difference . . . Counties which have seen extensive Negro registration, whether by local officials or by federal examiners, are counties in which registration campaigns have been conducted. In counties without such campaigns, even the presence of examiners has been of limited gain."

A study later in the year by the second VEP produced different findings. Results were best, it said, in counties which had both an organized voter registration drive in action *and* federal examiners. They were second best in counties with examiners alone, third in counties with a drive alone, and worst, of course, in counties with neither. A point that the attorney general may have made inadvertently was that not even federal examiners could wholly prevail against drastic intimidation and reprisal —the old terror. A movement veteran, lauding the presence of examiners, cited the difference between their efficiency and civility and what it is like to go to the courthouse and try to register in Neshoba County, Mississippi. The first thing you see there is Sheriff Lawrence Rainey, he said. But even with federal examiners, Neshoba had just under 1,000 of 2,565 eligible Negroes registered in July 1966.

In his speech, Mr. Katzenbach did acknowledge that "surely part of the reason for slight registration in a number of areas is evident. Negroes may be formally, legally free to register, but fear remains, fear well based on past experience and present threats. One answer is federal action—of the kind we already have taken in court and will, in all likelihood take in the future, not only regarding registration but also regarding the still more damaging intimidation that can occur at election time. As I observed to an Emancipation Day ceremony in Mobile last month, I have a message for those who may think of trying to frighten or coerce Negro citizens—or any citizens—from trying to register to vote. If they do, they will have the federal government to reckon with." Certainly, if the Justice Department lived up to this duty, his main point was apt: "The still more effective antidote to intimidation . . . flows directly from energetic registration efforts, and that is numbers. Two men or twenty can be threatened, fired, or harassed, but not a thousand. Not only is it impossible to intimidate large numbers, but large-scale exercise of the vote changes the attitudes that might otherwise breed intimidations." [23]

The old immediate goal of electing a better sheriff and getting a good chief of police was, indeed, closer or achievable for many Negro communities under the new law. But the basic problem of Southern justice was far from settled. One indication of this was the performance of the Justice Department itself in the use of the voter law's preventive and protective measures. This use was sparing during the first year of enforcement. There was a flurry of activity in the Alabama primary elections in May 1966. Federal examiners were on hand in seven counties to assure that Negro voters were not hampered in exercising their right, and to see that their votes were counted. A suit was filed by the Justice Department the outcome of which was to force acceptance of Negro votes that allowed Wilson Baker to defeat Jim Clark for sheriff of Dallas County. The federal representatives reported generally orderly and lawful polling across the state. They apparently did not look at such niceties of the situation as an obvious lack of preparation for the greatly increased number of voters in some all-Negro districts, like the Washington school precinct in Birmingham. There, some Negroes said they stood in line seven hours for the privilege of voting; it was the first time for many. Voting machines and personnel on hand were not increased from previous elections when the registration was considerably less. Otherwise, there had been in the first year two civil actions and one criminal under the new law. Two other civil actions were brought under the 1964 Civil Rights Act, successful injunctions against interfering with voting rights. Yet complaints of intimidation and reprisal seemed almost as frequent as before the new laws.

One of the reasons, surely, for this inaction was the knowledge that criminal cases would have to be tried before Southern juries, which would most likely be all-white, and which would be hard to convince (or reluctant to admit) of a causal relation between an attempt to register and an eviction, for example. It would be difficult enough before some branches of the all-white federal judiciary, where the preventive relief suits had to be brought.

The need for reform of the administration of Southern justice had been, in the aftermath of Selma, made in other ways frighteningly clear. Jonathan Daniels, a young Episcopal seminary student from New Hampshire, was shot to death in Hayneville, Alabama, on August 20, 1965. His companion, Father Richard Morrisroe, a Chicago Catholic priest, was severely wounded by the gunfire. They and others had just been released from the Lowndes County jail after arrests in a demonstration. Their main work had been voter registration, urging Negroes to avail themselves of the federal voter examiners in the county seat. A white resident of the town, Tom L. Coleman, was indicted for manslaughter in the case of Mr. Daniels and assault and battery upon Father Morrisroe. He was acquitted by an all-white jury of the manslaughter charge on grounds of self-defense. There was national criticism of Southern juries in the aftermath. "This is the price you have to pay for the jury system," said Attorney General Katzenbach, a statement much condemned. He did add, in at least some newspaper versions of the quote: "But I think it's too high a price." He later said there would be further federal investigation for civil rights violations. Malcolm Peabody, president of the Episcopal Society of Cultural and Racial Unity, which sponsored Mr. Daniels' work, talked of a license to kill, and said that if the federal government didn't act, "the racists in the South will have found the ultimate solution to the racial problem." A year later, John Morris, director of the Society, wrote in a newsletter: "There is ample reason that a federal indictment should be sought in [Mr. Daniels'] death, because of his involvement with voter registration efforts. Such is covered under the 1965 voter bill. I am afraid, though, that it will take constant pressure to obtain a satisfactory follow-through."

In the ten days before the shooting, federal voting examiners in

Lowndes County had been registering an average of 82 Negroes a day. In the thirty-two days after the shooting, the average dropped to 21 Negroes a day. The federal examiners began operating on a Saturdays-only basis. A Negro resident of Lowndes, active in voter registration, said this was partly because of the shooting, but partly due also to bad weather, and people's being busy.

Stokely Carmichael, who had been working in Lowndes County at the time of the shootings, subsequently organized an all-black political apparatus there, and developed his "black power" program. Some observers have suggested that the shootings were the catalyst for this development.

In the Liuzzo slaying, Collie Leroy Wilkins received one mistrial and then an acquittal on a murder charge by two all-white juries. He and two other Ku Klux Klansmen (one of whom subsequently died) were convicted by an all-white federal jury of conspiracy to violate civil rights statutes in the Liuzzo slaying, and were sentenced to ten years. They appealed. In yet another Alabama case, Willie Brewster, an Anniston Negro with no civil rights connections, was shot to death on July 15, 1965. He was driving home from work and was picked for death apparently at random. A white man was convicted by an all-white jury of second-degree murder and sentenced to ten years. Two others faced murder charges. The conviction came after considerable national publicity over the performance of Southern law enforcement in these and other cases of violence against Negroes. The nation recollected and rehashed the slayings, including the unsolved Birmingham church bombing in 1963 and going back to the 1955 lynching of Emmett Till in Leflore County, Mississippi, and back beyond that through well-known history of lynchings and unhampered violence to Negroes. Also cited was the 1964 slaying of Lemuel Penn, a Washington, D.C., educator who was returning home from reserve duty in Fort Benning, Georgia, and, like Mr. Brewster, just happened to be driving by at the wrong time and wrong place, near Colbert, Georgia. Three white men were indicted for murder, and two of them tried and acquitted in state courts. The three and three others were subsequently tried on federal charges of conspiracy to violate the civil rights of the victim. The two who had previously been acquitted of murder charges were found guilty of the conspiracy charges and sentenced to ten years in prison; the other four were acquitted.

The failings of not merely state and municipal courts, but of the federal courts in the South were called forcefully to public attention during 1965. A Southern Regional Council report showed that in the eleven Southern states in March 1965 there were no Negroes serving as federal judges or district attorneys, and that of 1,147 other jobs, from clerk to bailiff, only 14 (five of 158 assistant U.S. attorneys, and nine of 165 deputy U.S. marshals) were held by Negroes,[24] with a scattering of Negroes in 364 lesser jobs. Charles Morgan, Jr., director of the Southern Office of the American Civil Liberties Union, who had to give up a law practice in Birmingham after criticizing the community for the church bombing and otherwise showing sympathy for civil rights, contributed considerably to the criticism, particularly of state and federal jury selection. His organization filed suits in Alabama seeking jury representation of Negroes in proportion to population.[25] A potent series of articles in the Los Angeles *Times* by Jack Nelson further called attention to the problem. A Southern Regional Council pamphlet pointed up the perniciousness of the problem: ". . . In a manner of speaking, there is no such thing as 'definite acquittal' for the Negro . . . A given Negro is automatically a poorer risk than a white man at the bar of justice. That is a statistical certainty that hovers over every Negro and makes him never quite free. But, like Kafka's accused innocent, the Negro is not without a fretful, worrisome kind of hope. He is reminded constantly that he can buy insurance against the harshness of the system. One thing that most Negroes learn early is that a 'good nigger' fares better in times of trouble than a 'no 'count nigger.' By debasing himself systematically, a Negro can earn a reputation as a 'good nigger' and assure himself of favored treatment should he be called to account in a court of law." [26]

In his 1966 State of the Union address, President Johnson called for legislation "to establish unavoidable requirements for nondiscriminatory jury selection in federal and state courts—and to give the attorney general power to enforce these requirements; [and] legislation to strengthen authority of federal courts to try those who murder, attack or intimidate either civil rights workers or others exercising their constitutional rights—and to increase penalties to a level equal to the nature of the crime." Such legislation was introduced, and tied to an open-housing provision which set ill with even civil rights stalwarts in Congress. The performance of many of these men on a racial issue close to home was among the more unsavory aspects of the defeat of the bill in September 1966, one of the worst setbacks the movement had suffered. A similar bill was introduced in 1967. Until legislation guaranteeing equal justice in the South was passed, the voting law and the rest of the civil rights laws were in peril. And with each month of racist lawlessness in the South, there increased the likelihood of retaliatory violence from Negroes, self-defensive or, as in a riot, race against race.

The legislation had been given temporary impetus in the early summer of 1966 by the march through Mississippi of James Meredith, the individualistic young man who desegregated the University of Mississippi in 1962. On his second day out, despite Justice Department and other law-enforcement men on the scene, he was shot from ambush— his injuries fortunately not serious. (A white man from Memphis was arrested as the assailant.) The civil rights organizations continued his march, a happenstance revival of the large-scale demonstration. But it soon deteriorated in public opinion. Its visible inter-organizational rivalry, and the first public display of racist tendencies in the radical wing of the movement—the "black power" debate—diverted attention from Mr. Meredith's original goal, which was to encourage Negro Mississippians to register to vote. His fate underscored the points—that Negroes were not yet provided enough protection to do so, and that more federal examiners were needed in the South.

Mr. Katzenbach and others were correct, of course, when they asserted that ultimately, in the South's struggle for democracy, it was up to the Negroes. But such assertions could not be made blithely until justice was reformed and registration was in reality accessible to all.

Hope

Meanwhile, with the gains already made toward these goals, there were hopeful signs of progress against the old twin internal enemies, apathy and the fear. In Wilcox County, Alabama, a white Southerner and his wife were in a small town visiting Negro civil rights leaders, and were seen by the town police in a car with Negroes. As the couple were leaving town in their own car, a police car forced them over to the side of the road. One officer demanded the young man's driver's license, and the other, ostentatiously unbuckling his pistol holster, stood glaring. Just as the young man began to feel real terror, a car pulled up behind the police car, blocking it. Out stepped one of the Negro leaders the couple had visited, a big man. He came and stood, saying nothing, behind the two policemen. One of them, a small man, plainly nervous, finally said to the Negro, "It's just a routine license check." The Negro replied, "That's good. These are friends of mine. I'll wait." And he stayed until the police, hurrying through things, got back in their car and the young couple could drive away. This was in the spring of 1966; it was not the Alabama of even a year before. Such eventually could be the end of the fear everywhere.

The approach against apathy that promised the most real progress in the city and rural slums was that which the civil rights workers had pioneered—small-scale, highly personal community organization. In an Atlanta slum in 1966, Negroes got together on their own in a crumbling apartment to try to organize a protest over living conditions. In the scene was maybe one hint of the future of politics among Negro Southerners. By kerosene lamp (electricity had been cut off for non-payment of bills), before a feeble fire in an open grate, a man in overalls stood and said, without formality but no little dignity, "We'll have a meeting over what's wrong. Who wants to tell first?" They eventually organized a rent strike. Such was, perhaps, the promised shape of the new South.

There were all sorts of little enterprises in the air. One of the more hopeful was the effort of an integrated League of Women Voters in a small Alabama town (in the state of fear that remained in early 1966 the ladies asked that the town not be identified) to set up training sessions in voter procedures for newly registered Negroes and poor whites. They had first thought of having one class in a central location. Negro leaders pointed out how much more effective neighborhood classes would be. The ladies of the League made arrangements for a series of classes, complete with a sample voting machine owned by the county, in fire stations around the town and reached 2,500 new voters, 1,300 of whom were illiterate. Then they began work with a small VEP grant making television shows on citizenship for statewide showing.

In Atlanta, SCLC set up classes for Negroes from over the South who were running or planning to run for various local government offices. Instruction was in the duties and functions of such offices. Classes on election laws and procedure were held by the NAACP for Negro candidates and poll watchers in Alabama and Tennessee prior to the 1966 elections.

A volunteer group, white and Negro, in the Georgia Fourth Congressional District (mainly suburban Atlanta) set up a six-week registration drive in the fall of 1965. It pushed for neighborhood and night registration, and had its own workers deputized to register people. During the period, the group registered 4,250 new voters, white and Negro, and began plans for a new campaign. Mrs. Ross Green, its organizer, commented, "We feel that so-called voter apathy is an over-rated concept. Once people got used to the idea of neighborhood registration and realized that we were genuine deputies, they came in a steady stream to register—sometimes in very bad weather and often with babies and small children in tow . . . For families with one or no automobile, or where people work without time off, some sort of neighborhood registration is essential."

A new day—not the one dreamed of but somewhat better than before—had come. One of the earliest reports from southwest Georgia in 1962 had said: "We have to channel a frustration that has lasted a long time into an effective direction. We have to teach the lesson that the superintendents and boards of education aren't just for complaining about. They're to be visited, written to, questioned. You don't accept a raise in taxes that seems unjust with a shrug and bitter resentment. You write the appropriate authorities, check it out, build your case. Right now, it's a big step if people, instead of complaining to themselves of harassment, tell us. But some day, they won't even need us."

In Alabama, in 1966, they had added some new verses to an old bit of movement doggerel popular during direct-action campaigns. It used to go:

> If you look for me at Kiokee Church
> And you can't find me nowhere;
> Come on down to city hall,
> I'll be demonstrating there.

There were countless verses: "Come on down to the county jail, I'll be locked up there," etc. The new versions were:

> If you look for me on the paper mill truck
> And you can't find me nowhere;
> Come on down to Birmingham Courthouse,
> I'll be the registrar there.

> If you look for me in Miss Ann's kitchen
> And you can't find me nowhere;

> Come on down to Camden,
> I'll be the tax assessor there.
>
> If you look for me in city jail,
> And you can't find me nowhere;
> Come on down to Lowndes County,
> I'll be sheriff there.

A few days after the rout at the Pettus Bridge, Father Oulette told an audience what he had seen of it:

My memory recalls youngsters in the emergency entrance of Good Samaritan Hospital, youngsters frightened, gashed, battered, shocked. And adults in the same condition . . . I can see corridors lined with people waiting to be treated by doctors. I remember one man with at least five lacerations in the top of his head. I would say at least this long, and just laid open. And to get five licks in the head like that, somebody's got to stand over you for quite a while. And they've got to want to do it. I remember an old lady who came in to her daughter, a lady close to ninety years old, who came in to her daughter who was lying there with broken ribs and many bruises, and she said to her, "Girl, don't just lay there and hurt. Pray." I remember the young student nurse who turned to me with tears in her eyes and said, "Father what are we going to do? Who's going to take care of us? Who's going to protect us?" And all the despair of her people was written on her face. And I remember the little . . . girl that I picked up in my arms and she couldn't breathe and she couldn't see, and she had a cut on the side of her head. And I carried her and her face rested on my shoulder and with tears streaming out of her blind eyes, she said, "Father, I hurt." As I walked away I put my hand to the side of my face and it came away bloody. And later I went up to the mission, and I said Mass. And as I held in my hands the body and blood of Christ, for the first time in my priesthood I unashamedly wept. For just a little before, the blood that I now held in my hand had been on the side of my face. And He, Christ, had said to me through the mouth of a little girl, "Father, I hurt." Because she is Christ. And somebody else in the mystical body of Christ had done this . . . But for the first time since I came to Selma, I have seen a beaten people walking with their heads in the air, and this I had never seen before in Selma. A people who for the first time feel that there is hope . . . How was it done? It was done with love . . . I always all of my life responded to fear with anger. And these past years I have been frightened many times . . . And somehow I am still frightened, but I am no longer angry. And I was taught not to be angry by a group of Baptist ministers. Because I saw what they did for those who hated them. I saw them return love for hate . . . The Pettus Bridge was a Calvary. There was a crucifixion; there was a Peter; there was a centurion; there was a mob; there was the jeering; the blood and the hate. But on the cross there was a Christ who loved all of these, and this is our task—to love all of these, because they are Christ.[27]

The moments of epiphany were always that strong. The movement was the Negro people of the South, and its strength was their ability even as far along in acrimony and bitterness as Selma to breathe new life into old beliefs—in the priest's passionate metaphor, in the Bill of Rights, perhaps even in politics.

NOTES

1. A handbill distributed in Alabama in 1965 heralded the new day thus: "Don't delay longer! Register now to vote. No more test to register. You are eligible if you are 21 years of age or older, you have lived in the state one year, and never convicted of a felony . . . At the ballot box all people are equal. Beyond the ballot box lies the promised land with freedom and justice and opportunities for you."

2. The voter examiners were all Southerners, mostly from states other than where they worked, usually career Civil Service Commission men. Some spoke of a belief in what they were doing as an expression of democracy, regardless of their personal views on race. Others were less enthusiastic. There was some danger for them; bomb threats and unpleasant personal encounters were reported. But they were heavily protected by the Justice Department, as civil rights workers had seldom been. In their relations with local whites, some didn't discourage a prevalent mood of "they don't like it any better than we do; they're just doing their job." Some made subtle, sure-to-be-noticed gestures to prove their Southern credentials, like ordering buttermilk and collard greens at their meals. Some were obviously impressed, even awed with the quality of seriousness and dedication in the long lines of Negro applicants standing before them. At the end of the first week, one of them said, "I reckon it is history. Well, I'm glad to be a part of it."

About those who weren't glad to be a part of it, who still clung to white supremacy as an article of faith yet did their duty despite conviction, the moral problem posed by Eichmann seemed in turnabout perspective to apply, the problem of men who take orders that go against their conviction. Here was a new Southern paradox, apparent in many other areas of desegregation.

Negro applicants often approached the examiners warily, as they were wont to approach the county courthouse. Some remained nervous and distrustful; others mellowed and responded when there was politeness and an air of getting things done as quickly and easily as possible. "When you go to vote, vote for the best man," one of the examiners said to a middle-aged woman, smiling. "Who is that?" she asked suspiciously. "It's who you think is best. Not who somebody tells you." She smiled fervent agreement.

3. One report was that as high as 95 per cent of those registered in the first six months by the federal examiners were over forty.

4. The 1966 estimates had a precision that no previous estimates of Southern

Negro voting may have achieved; in many instances, the 1966 figures were based on checks by the FBI with local registrars. Even here, though, there was room for whatever distortion some registrars might have felt safe in giving to such reports, and also whatever errors they may have made unintentionally. The South-wide VEP total of 1964 was generally correct, but it balanced out some state totals that were too high and some that were too low.

5. "The Negro Voter in the South," p. 118, told of a 1956 survey of Negro attitudes in Dallas County. Negroes found in barbershops and poolrooms would not even talk about voting. Among the comments of those who would: "I don't want nothing to do with it." "If they don't want me to vote, I don't want to." "Leave them white folks alone."

6. There were some efforts in the project to branch out into surrounding counties of high Negro voting potential: Wilcox, 78 per cent Negro; Marengo, 62 per cent Negro; Lowndes, 81 per cent Negro; Perry, 66 per cent Negro.

7. "Registration in Alabama," in *The New Republic*, October 26, 1963.

8. The Citizens Council had a big office downtown, the SNCC reports said, and there were reports that much of its support came from local industry. Along with Macon, Barbour, Bullock, Wilcox, and Lowndes counties, Dallas County figured in another bit of segregationist history. Circuit Court Judge George Wallace, later governor, and county grand juries made efforts to prevent inspection of the voting records of these counties by the U.S. Commission of Civil Rights in its first big investigation in 1958.

9. A story in the Selma *Times-Journal* of March 23, 1964, recreates the atmosphere of that time in Selma:

> A television crew from the University of Georgia spent about three hours last night at the home of Negro Congressional candidate Amelia P. Boynton shooting a sound film, Sheriff James G. Clark reported. . . .
>
> Sheriff Clark said he was unable to find out the type of program which was filmed at the home of the Selma Negro woman, who is the first female member of her race ever to seek a seat in Congress from Alabama. . . .
>
> Sheriff Clark said he and State Trooper Capt. Robert Moore halted the three-vehicle, seven person convoy shortly after it left the Boynton woman's house and asked the members for their identity. . . .
>
> Sheriff Clark, who said members of his department kept the filming under surveillance from six to nine p.m. Sunday, reported that some six to eight other local Negro leaders were at the Boynton home during the period.

Which was worse—that such police activity should center on obviously legitimate activity at the home of a candidate for the United States Congress, or that the newspaper should describe such police methods with so obvious an attitude that they were neither extraordinary nor repressive? (The *Times-Journal* was in the 1965 demonstrations to make a favorable impression on the national press with generally competent coverage of the big story breaking under its nose, and for fairly enlightened editorials. Its previous performance had not been so praiseworthy.)

10. Some would argue that democracy over the nation might be served by requiring all voters to know such intricacies of our fundamental law. The effect of the 1965 Voting Rights Act has been to erode whatever foundation there might have been for such requirements, as well as for simple literacy requirements. But the real reason for this erosion was of course the South's shameful history of perversion of rational standards to disfranchise Negroes.

11. Louis Miller, twelve years old in 1965, a large-eyed boy with prominent front teeth, told one of the authors how it was in another Selma demonstration when the prods were used. "Yes, I marched . . . I got stuck with a cow prod. That's what they did to me. On the leg here . . . it hurts a little. It stung. We were getting on the bus, after we were arrested. They said hurry. And used the cow prod."

12. State troopers in Alabama, under Colonel Al Lingo, had become a particularly brutal instrument of police oppression of Negroes during the movement years. Their violence during various encounters of 1963 and 1964, including Birmingham, has been described and documented considerably. Colonel Lingo left the state patrol during the months after the Selma episode. He later emerged as a candidate for sheriff in Birmingham, showing up in a Negro church in quest of votes—and was defeated, with the help of a large Negro vote against him.

13. This moderate group, with Wilson Baker elected sheriff, emerged more in control in 1966. But none of several Negroes who ran for office in the 1966 elections won.

14. One reason that the Albany movement back in 1962 attracted so much press attention was that it was supposed to be the place for a showdown clash between SCLC, SNCC, and the NAACP. There was considerable behind-the-scenes antagonism, but, as elsewhere later, it was not allowed out in the open. In Selma, the rifts seemed rawer, more in the open, and maybe more fundamental. A 1963 report described NAACP and CORE rivalry in a north Florida town. The one was picketing stores for Negro employment, the other a theater for desegregated seating. The NAACP started helping CORE with its project, but CORE wouldn't allow NAACP's name on placards. But when there were arrests, CORE followers all wanted NAACP lawyers. Then NAACP, it was felt, didn't follow through on employment gains with enough voter registration. Meanwhile, there was criticism of one leader who was president of both the local NAACP branch and the local SCLC branch. He resigned both jobs and began moving a local organization into competition with all three of the national organization affiliates. "In general, there is no cooperation between the groups and people, but only rivalry, with everyone to blame for this state of affairs," the report concluded.

15. Al Ulmer in *New South* ("Ain't Gonna Let Nobody Turn Me Round," March 1965) described a youth meeting on the day when demonstrators thought they were going to be marched into the brutality of state troopers for a second time in Selma. A SNCC worker reminded the young people that he had asked them why they wanted to march a few weeks previously and they could give no reasons beyond the word "freedom," so he had refused to march with them. Now he wanted to know again if anyone could tell him. Finally a small girl, about fourteen, answered: "I have seven brothers and sisters and my father can't find work always, and all my life, I've had hand-me-down books and food not fit to eat and grow on. Freedom to me is maybe getting something when it is new sometime." After some less eloquent testimonials, the leader told them, "I asked you to decide as individuals why you're going, but when we face the posse—we face life or death. No individual break and run. If you're not together, you're dead. When the group moves, you move. Every boy in here has a responsibility to the girl nearest him."

16. Jim Forman was quoted in the New York *Times* of March 17, 1965, as saying, "Remember one thing. They aren't about to beat up white people. What do you think will happen to the Negroes when the white folks leave?" Of course white folks were beaten—one to death. An SCLC official was quoted in the same story as saying, "As much as I dislike middle-class whites, we need their help."

17. The law left up to the attorney general whether to send in examiners. He

was authorized to seek them at his discretion from courts if "(1) he has received complaints in writing from twenty or more residents of such political subdivision alleging that they have been denied the right to vote . . . and [if] he believes such complaints to be meritorious, or (2) [if] in his judgment (considering, among other factors, whether the ratio of nonwhite persons to white persons registered to vote within such subdivisions appears to him to be reasonably attributable to violations of the fifteenth amendment or whether substantial evidence exists that bona fide efforts are being made within such subdivision to comply with the fifteenth amendment), the appointment of examiners is otherwise necessary to enforce the guarantees of the fifteenth amendment . . ."

18. The suit that reached the Supreme Court had been filed by South Carolina. Alabama, Mississippi, Louisiana, Georgia, and Virginia joined the suit. In Alabama and Mississippi, actions had been taken to enjoin registrars of some counties from accepting on the voter rolls Negroes whose applications had been handled by federal examiners. Paul Anthony, executive director of the Southern Regional Council, pointed out in a 1965 memorandum the main import of the court actions: "The traditional Southern response to unpopular legislation is to declare it 'illegal' and 'unconstitutional' and to promise that it will be reversed by the courts. While these promises are never kept and those who make them know they cannot be, their importance is in the fact that citizens generally are encouraged to defy the law." The Supreme Court ruled on the act March 7, 1966, in time for Negroes registered under it to be assured of voting in the earliest primaries of the year, those in May in Alabama, for example. Justice Hugo Black dissented from the decision on one point—the legality of a provision calling for approval by the attorney general of any new laws on voter qualifications in the affected states. He said appeals of such a ruling would go to federal district court in Washington instead of to the Supreme Court, and also that the whole procedure "so distorts our constitutional structure of government as to render any distinction drawn in the Constitution between state and federal power almost meaningless." The majority of the court held the provision was justified by recent history, which showed how states could overcome federal anti-discrimination laws by passing a succession of new laws of their own.

19. Not to be confused with the town of Decatur, Georgia, a suburb of Atlanta. The county seat of Decatur County is Bainbridge, home of former Governor Marvin Griffin, an arch-segregationist.

20. This ruse was quickly broken up by the federal courts. The Taliaferro (pronounced Tolliver) demonstrations were marked by a sad episode when Negro lumber workers stopped a demonstration and turned it back on grounds it was disturbing peaceful relations of whites and Negroes. There were indications this had been set up by whites, reporters on the scene said. At one point, the whites appointed an unqualified Negro as chief of police with instructions to break up demonstrations. Such shenanigans give rise, in moods of darkest contemplation, to doubts whether parts of the South are capable of real self-government.

21. Again, indications of new registration in Georgia suggest either that estimates of total registration in 1964 were slightly high or that a considerable amount of attrition and disqualification had occurred.

22. These were participated in mostly by children who left schools and moved about on the streets with an impunity that would not have been dreamed of three years before. The new mood in another sphere, the art of condemning the federal government for such actions as the sending of the examiners, was demonstrated in a statement by Mayor Albert Boutwell, among similar ones by all Birmingham's self-righteously shocked officialdom. "I am sure," the mayor said, "the people of this

county share the feeling that citizens of whatever color should be permitted to qualify and vote if they possess the required qualifications. By the same token, I know that all of the people in the area—white and colored alike—resent this federal intrusion and exhibition of brazen power. We are called upon to endure actions that should never be directed by any government against its law-abiding citizens at the political demand of those admittedly engaged in discord and violence." Someday someone will compile a surrealist anthology out of such statements.

23. It was entirely appropriate for his audience, too—a gathering of registration leaders from over the South at a Southern Regional Council luncheon, shortly after launching of the second VEP.

24. "Racial Discrimination in Southern Federal Courts," published by the Southern Regional Council, April 1965.

25. Some method approaching the random sampling techniques used by public opinion polls was recommended in the suits. The outcome of one of the first, a three-judge federal court ruling that Lowndes County, Alabama, scene of the two slayings, had to redraw jury lists so as to include Negroes, fell short of this mark. The decree required use of a list of all names on the county tax assessor's list and qualified-voters list, including those registered by federal examiners. Negroes, by 1966, were half of both. In September 1966, under this ruling, a jury was selected for trial of a second Klansman, Eugene Thomas, in the Liuzzo slaying. Eight Negroes were on the twelve-man jury. The jury's verdict was for acquittal. Before the trial got under way, Attorney General Richmond Flowers had said white officials of the county "will allow only Negroes on the jury they can handle." He subsequently apologized to the court for the statement.

26. "Southern Justice: An Indictment," published by the Southern Regional Council, October 1965.

27. Father Oulette was transferred from Selma in June 1965. A New York *Times* story of June 26 pointed out that he was ordered to leave the Mobile-Birmingham diocese by Archbishop Thomas J. Toolen, rather than, as would ordinarily be the case, by his superior in the Edmundite Fathers. (This society specializes in work among Negro Catholics.) The story pointed out that he had been involved in the voter registration effort in Dallas County since 1962, and that prominent whites of Selma had put pressure both on him and Archbishop Toolen over a three-year period to try to stop this. The story said that he had asked the archbishop for permission to demonstrate, was refused, and did not take part in the Selma demonstrations of 1965 when nuns and priests from over the nation were doing so. He was told he could keep working on voter registration, however. When asked why Father Oulette was being ordered out, Archbishop Toolen was quoted as having told Edmundite officials that he did not have to give a reason; he just wanted him out. Father Oulette was quoted in the story as saying: "He said that I was a good priest, but that I was too wild on this racial question. But I never disobeyed one of his orders. I never demonstrated. I felt, though, like a man who had been allowed to walk out to the middle of a stream and then was forbidden to swim in either direction." In 1967 Father Brice Joyce, a forty-year-old white priest in Sheffield, Alabama, was ordered to leave the Birmingham-Mobile diocese by Archbishop Toolen. His friends charged that he was ordered out because of his role as a civil rights leader. Unorthodox behavior, such as the use of jazz-type music during Mass, was cited by the archbishop, according to the Los Angeles *Times*.

10)

The Future
of the Movement

W. J. Cash wrote that the mind of the South ". . . is continuous with the past . . . So far from being modernized, in many ways it has actually marched away, as to this day it continues to do, from the present to the past." [1] The past to which Cash referred was that of savagery, of tyranny.[2] Southerners (mainly black, but with a trailing of whites) who founded the most modern, and perhaps most radical, innovative development in American politics also looked back, but to something better; in fact, to the main forces fashioned to battle savagery and tyranny—namely, Western traditions of democracy and religion.

There were the inevitable pictures of Roosevelt in the shacks of the Negro poor, and in many a middle-class parlor. In recent years, it was often as not President Kennedy's picture. One such was cut from a newspaper and pasted on a crumbling plaster wall in a room whose floors literally sank down with each step. He wore a tuxedo. These pictures were part of the memory that includes Lincoln, and part of the feeling that the rest of the nation was different, and would help out if only it knew how bad things were. But more importantly, the memory of Lincoln was a part of faith in democracy, and this was bound up with their other belief, represented by the religious paintings and emblems on their walls and mantles.

Du Bois knew about this. He told of how abolition became a religion, and how they sang (as they were to do a hundred years later in the mass meetings) that "before I'll be a slave, I'll be buried in my grave, and go home to my Lord and be free." Then their religion lost freedom, like all else after Reconstruction. "But back of this," Du Bois concluded, "still broods silently the deep religious feeling of the real Negro heart, the stirring, unguided might of powerful human souls who have lost the guiding star of the past and seek in the great night a new religious ideal. Some day the Awakening will come, when the pent-up vigor of ten million souls shall sweep irresistibly toward the Goal, out of the Valley of the Shadow of Death, where all that makes life worth living—Liberty, Justice, and Right—is marked 'For White People Only.'" [3]

In 1960 the awakening seemed to have come. The Bible and the Constitution were the bedrock. But there was a duality. At its best the Negro movement in the South always contained in tight, tautly strained balance conflicting drives: the spiritual overtones of belief and the secular goal of immediately effecting, through subtle invocation of religious guilt and under protection of the Constitution, a revolution. Along with the beautiful spirit which forgave and asked salvation for a troubled America, there was also the knowledge that the mere presence of the most peaceful of demonstrations, or the mere attempt to register to vote in many Southern locales, would precipitate white violence and might produce federal action. Courage and love were willed in the face of the white enemy at the same time that fear and hatred shrieked loudest. Such duality within the movement, within individuals, must account for the amount of energy and power that was, for a time, released. For a time, there was a renaissance euphoria in the South. There was a feeling of hope in a land that had been hopeless. Thinking tended to be in absolutes, of a real integration in the South unique in the world, of total solutions to the never-solved regional social and economic problems, of truly democratic government—one man, one vote.

The movement lost its fine balancing of the spiritual and the practical. The nation, with its fixation on violence and its tendency to view a profound moral crisis as one more ball game, mainly missed the spiritual overtones. Few lamented the weighting to the secular.[4] Thomas Merton was to write in late 1963: "Washington is professionally capable only of seeing this as a political issue. Actually, it is a spiritual and religious one, and this element is by far the most important. But it is the element that no one is ready to see. . . . *What is demanded of us is not necessarily that we believe that the Negro has mysterious and magic answers in the realm of politics and social control, but that his spiritual insight into our common crisis is something we must take seriously.*" [5]

Non-violence, never fully perceived by white America, became for the Southern movement increasingly not a way of life but merely one more in an arsenal of subtle psychological weapons. The step to the use of real weapons was not a long one from this. For most of the years of the civil rights movement, some individual Negroes had been armed, and had fired back when they could. (A farmer in the Lee County, Georgia, voter effort was quoted in a 1963 report: "I believe in the Bible, the Lord, and my 30-30.") SNCC in 1963 concluded that field workers should not carry weapons themselves, but had no right to ask the same of others in danger of their lives, and shouldn't refuse to ride with or live with those who were armed. In one of the sporadic demonstrations of 1965 aimed at forcing the federal government to enforce the law it had been forced to pass, there emerged in Bogalusa, Louisiana, the first organized self-defense unit of Negroes, the Deacons for Defense and Justice. They would protect lives and defend homes where organized law enforcement would not; they would fight back, a burned home for a burned home. The organization and imitations of it spread across the Black Belt. But for all their talk, such groups did little real shooting; certainly they burned no homes. Perhaps the old conditioning against violence to whites was a factor.[6] Real retaliatory violence seemed more likely to come from another tradition, that of the underworld and youth gangs in the cities. These were a shadowy protective presence in many locales from the beginning. In Jacksonville, Florida, in 1960 and 1964 and 1966, rioting, spearheaded by youth gangs, broke loose, and in Atlanta, in 1966, lesser disturbances described as riots occurred. Those in Atlanta were encouraged by SNCC. This was as near as Southern cities had come to the wild rampages of ghetto rioting in the North. They were a warning.[7]

There is a difference between the two kinds of violence. A man, having reached a degree of self-realization and anger that he hadn't known before, takes down an old hunting rifle and says he will use it on any white man who attacks him. That is not the same as the roiling of rage in the riots of the ghettoes that points weapons at *any* white. This distinction was not always clear in the rhetoric of black power; if anything, the idiom of the ghetto predominated.

In the aftermath of what had seemed the great victories of the Negro movement, the winning of the Civil Rights Act of 1964 and the Voting Rights Act of 1965, despair and disillusionment set in among many Negro Southerners. Part of this was natural, the consequence of gradually discovering the magnitude of what the movement had set out to do in such a spirit of innocent optimism. As often in such striving, the moments of greatest success served only to show how great a distance there was yet to go. But part of the despair also reflected the conditions. In some of the worst areas of the South, one would have had to look hard in 1965 and 1966 to see much difference from the pre-1960 order of race relations. From public accommodations to the decade-old effort to desegregate schools, tokenism was the most that had been achieved anywhere. The principle of freedom of choice—which put law compliance at the initiative and risk of Negroes rather than society—at first characterized administration of most of the new legislation. Voter registration in the worst areas was still subject to harassment, intimidation, and less than full administrative cooperation. Reform of Southern law enforcement—that absolutely necessary accompaniment of enfranchisement—was unachieved.

Disappointment at the failure of the new law to reach into the lives of the most numerous class of Negro Southerners, the poor, spoke in the tendencies to blind retaliatory violence, and was reflected in what seemed to be a basic split of philosophy and strategy among the movement organizations. Both SNCC and CORE in 1966 had taken official stands in favor of armed self-defense for Negroes, abandoning even lip-service to the tradition of non-violence. Around the seemingly purposeful ambiguity in the rallying cry of "black power," they had set out a new and harsh rationale. Dispossessed Negroes, they said—North and South, ghetto and rural, the majority of Negroes—had not been helped by the movement's victories. America, the whole white nation, was racist. Negroes must develop their own inner resources and external power sources separately. If individual whites wanted to help, they should address themselves to racism in the white society and culture. The goal was no longer integration in the old sense of the Negro's wanting to move into the American mainstream. What seemed suggested was that the Negro develop power enough, if not to merge with the currents of the mainstream, then to stand securely aloof from it. The immediate black power to be developed was political, with the hope that it would lead to economic power. Negroes would elect all-black governments where they had majorities, and develop "power bases" where they did not. From such power they would then deal with conventional politics and politicians. The strategy had less to say for itself in the impoverished Black Belt counties of the South than in the increasingly Negro cities of the North, and in the arithmetic of the electoral college.

Radicalism and Black Racism

The seriousness of this departure of the young radicals was not to be measured so much in the degree to which it reflected grass-roots Negro thought in the South (it probably reflected little of thought, but more of the emotional tone), or in the amount of influence the new dogma might eventually exert on the masses of Negroes. The real importance seemed to be in what it showed of the corrosive effect of much that happened during the 1962–64 voter effort, and afterwards. Repetition of the familiar mistakes of those years continued in government policy and public opinion. In a new, grotesque way, the young radicals were putting their bodies where a certain truth was.

The voter effort was the formative experience for the young radicals. If one thing is clear from this study, it is that the decision to go into the small towns and rural areas with the vote, "sharing in the joy and suffering of the community life," had shaped them and the influence they had on the movement. Visceral involvement in poverty and terrorism at its Southern worst, the causes and effects of poverty, the blind, unmoving nature of white racism, failures of the federal government to protect voter rights—these, far more than the alarums and excursions of direct action, were their touchstones. Community organization, not demonstrations, became the mode of the movement for them. Obviously, there was no one-to-one relationship among the "young radicals" of black power and the "young radicals" who sought, through the movement, what they called "the beloved community" and, later, "freedom high" —that is, freedom of action bordering on anarchism. It was a loose movement; individuals entered and left and re-entered. But a core of those who began with the sit-ins or freedom rides were still in the ranks of the "young radicals" when the movement split over black power; most were in SNCC or CORE, but there were some in SCLC and the NAACP. The latter were, in the ways of these things, to become the moderates in the split.

Not only some of the veteran whites of SNCC and CORE left those organizations over black power, but some Negroes as well. These included John Lewis, who resigned soon after Stokely Carmichael was elected to replace him as SNCC chairman in the spring of 1966; he quit critical of black power. Julian Bond, SNCC's public information officer, also resigned soon after the election; his job had not been affected, and he maintained there was no connection. Charles Sherrod was no longer working through SNCC in the summer of 1966. Such stalwarts in the voter effort as Charles Cobb and Charles McLaurin stayed with SNCC, as did Jim Forman, replaced as executive secretary by Mrs. Ruby Doris Robinson, nee Smith. Mr. Lewis implied and others surmised that Mr. Forman was still powerful in the organization. Robert Moses, a mystical and powerful influence on SNCC thinking, had changed his name in 1965 to Parris and moved out of Mississippi to avoid "charisma." In 1966, he was refusing, literally, to speak to whites.

Mr. Carmichael, apparently relieved to be freed of administrative work, left the SNCC chairmanship in May of 1967 to return to SNCC work in the field, an old veteran at the age of 27. He was replaced by Rap Brown, a 23-year-old Negro who had been involved in SNCC work in the Black Belt of Alabama.

In CORE, James Farmer had resigned as national director prior to the black power outburst; Floyd B. McKissick, a movement veteran who replaced him, enunciated black power dogma with vehemence. Both SNCC and CORE had already been in serious financial difficulty; black power, not surprisingly, reportedly dried up most sources of white money.

From almost the start, the young radicals' best ideal was respect, indeed reverence for the humanity and dignity and potential of the despised poor. The worst result of this was whatever tendency they had to exploit these people in subtle, perhaps sometimes unconscious ways, and to exploit the various guilts and ignorances concerning them among more affluent Americans. "SNCC always does what the poor people say to do," said one local Negro leader, "so long as the poor people say what SNCC wants to do." But for a time SNCC's workers were almost the only ones in the movement in touch with the great unknown of the everyday life of these poorest people.

The young radicals were not, however, for the most part, themselves of this poor class. They were of the Negro middle class. In the South, this is not the neat economic classification that it is elsewhere. Because for so long nearly all Negroes were blocked from normal economic and educational opportunity, class was determined by standards (and perhaps aspiration). In a row of identical hovels, there would be general agreement among the equally poor dwellers on who among them was "middle class" and who was not. One gets a feeling of the golden age of middle-class life in America in the presence of the Negro middle class of the South, a hint of what "Life with Father" was really like, a sense of culture gap.[8] The young of this middle class, carrying the books and ideals and manners of the Southern Negro college, set the tone for the movement in the first year. But after that, after the sit-ins, the college students faded out. High-school students, drop-outs, even grammar-school youngsters, heartbreaking in belief and bravery, were the rank and file of much of the voter work.

One of the early workers in Selma told of the natural gravitation of young people to the movement as a novelty in a life of few diversions. The youngsters got their parents interested. There was a particular lure for jobless young people not in school, and many voter project reports told of the development of youth groups from school drop-outs, "the boys on the block." Charles Cobb of SNCC, describing the Greenville Student Movement as "probably the wildest crew of working freedom fighters in the state," told of efforts to "get them to recognize the importance and broadness of their movement, its national and international significance, as well as its local importance." John O'Neal, in a VEP report on a similar group in Hattiesburg, Mississippi, said: "From this group we have had the least formal or programmatic action, but needless to say they are potentially the greatest source of drive and energy. This is so for two reasons basically: because of their current lack of program and employment and secondly because of the strange kind of respect [people have for] these 'cool ones' . . . They have assisted us with canvassing in this area, they are invaluable sources of information, they help out around the office, and on occasion, they have provided us the much needed transportation." The opportunities for rehabilitation work with such youngsters on a large scale in the South need hardly be mentioned.

Richard Haley, formerly Southern director of CORE, said in early 1966 that it had been "quite difficult" during the past two or three years to attract Southern Negro college students to the movement. CORE was, he said, trying to correct this. It would attempt to introduce the idea of campus revolts, as in Berkeley, among other things. The main effort would be to correct the tendency to a "greater schism" between the movement and "the Negro leaders of the South of ten years hence." White college students from the South in civil rights work had been (another sad commentary) very few. Indeed, such young men as Sam Shirah and Bob Zellner, both formerly in SNCC, were something of movement curiosities because of their Southern backgrounds; both were out of Alabama. An organization for Southern white students interested in the movement and the new left, the Southern Student Organizing Committee (SSOC), was formed in 1964. Its membership was small but represented most Southern states. It seemed patterned after Students for a Democratic Society, and for a time seemed close to SNCC. It was considered a viable organization, but in its first years it was not a serious factor in civil rights work.

The changes in tone that came after 1960 and 1961 reflected, surely, the loss of the influence of the Negro college students among the rank and file. This was part of one of the sadder situations in Southern society, emasculation of Negro educators. Since education had been until the mid-1960's almost the only work available for educated Negroes, this meant the loss of much of the influence of an intellectual elite. This was reflected in the merciless contempt of the young radicals—many of whom had left behind both college and the middle class—for the Negro middle class, particularly the educators. Lillian Smith, whose death in September 1966 was as great a loss to the Southern movement as to American letters, in early 1966 lamented that in SNCC "there is no one of erudition, of philosophical depth, of historical sophistication." [9] This was a harsh truth, and applicable to much of the rest of the movement as well.

Nevertheless, perhaps paradoxically, one of the striking characteristics of the 1962–64 voter reports by the young radicals in SNCC and the other organizations had been their *intellectual* quality. Surely no other toilers in an American political adventure ever approached the commonplace of registering and voting with the thoughtful, abstracting, philosophical set of these youngsters of a people whom the racists had assured the world were innately inferior mentally. Of their life with the

Negro poor, their reports reflected or hinted truths and nuances of meaning that the best-educated intellectual would find difficult to express. Unfortunately, they never communicated at large much of the depth of their unique experience. The nation needed to know all they had learned. But the young radicals, a strain of anti-intellectualism building among them, ended up seeming to say that only the poor had virtue, and that a grass-roots Negro leader was great because of, not in spite of, inadequate education. No wonder that the nation and most of the movement, with their own stereotypes and prejudices about the poor, should only snort and continue to move on without understanding the poor—even in the poverty program.

A supposition about "power structure" entered into the alienation of the young radicals. There was early conviction that the power structures of the South's towns, cities, and states were the chief instrument of racist evil, rather than the violence-prone among the white people. The "power structure" was a figure of demonology, a symbol of many meanings, but most particularly it stood for the middle and upper class. With their drift toward class antagonism, the radicals had little trouble jumping to a view of the white liberals of the North in their very movement as pernicious elements of the power structure, too. After all, they were middle-class; they had power; like the Negro middle class, with their stake in the status quo, they had "sold out." And from here the concept of all American public policy as racist was not far off. The more sophisticated demonology of "the system," the naming of the enemy as corporate-military power in the nation, came later, and mainly from without the South. The two theories intertwined.

All of this was in the background of the movement's first major excursion into the harsh big leagues of professional politics, the fiasco at the Atlantic City Democratic National Convention. The roots and causes of despair and alienation were in evidence during all the 1962–64 voter drive. But until the summer of 1964, idealism and the sweet spirit of such campaigns as southwest Georgia and Ruleville still gave the predominant tone. The 1964 Freedom Summer brought, with the influx of Northern volunteers, a polyglot of radical idioms and who knows how much sophisticated cynicism. There was careful screening of the volunteers at an elaborate orientation at Oxford, Ohio, largely under church auspices, but after that, the gates were thrown open, and unscreened volunteers and ideologies appeared. All the nation's new-left versions of Marxism and the larger issues of international ideological struggle, including protest of the war in Vietnam, entered stronger than before into the Southern arena. Liberals who had always been able to dismiss the racist's espial of communism in the movement [10] began to take a second look.

But it soon became evident that not only did the Southern movement radicals mean it when they said communism was old hat and irrelevant, but also that the volunteers—most of them, despite it all, white, mainstream, middle-class college students—were themselves a source of annoyance and alienation to the movement regulars. There was friction in the coming together of ill-educated and striving young Negro Southerners with the confident and skilled young Northern collegians, not to mention clashes of Northern and Southern temperament and culture. Later, this all too human antagonism evolved into the proscription by SNCC and CORE of whites from work in Negro neighborhoods on grounds that whites in teaching roles discouraged black confidence and confirmed black stereotypes of white superiority.[11] Richard Haley gave some of the sounder rationale, telling of an old man in one community organization who said of a white college stripling, "He's like a daddy to me." But this rejection of whites who had been fellow sufferers was by far the most brutal and most racist of the black power manifestations. It seemed to incorporate that greatest evil of racism, the refusal to consider the individual. One young radical told of a white girl who broke with her family in Alabama to work with SNCC, and then was told a year later by SNCC to get out of the Negro community where she worked. Didn't he feel any compassion for her? "Sure," he said. "But"—with a shrug—"it's the wave of history." People interested in the communist question— whether accusing or defending the young radicals—seldom looked behind the question for these other real tendencies against the meaning of freedom.

The Break at Atlantic City

The challenge of the Mississippi delegation at the Democratic Convention at Atlantic City was the climax of the Freedom Summer of 1964, and the nearest to victory the voter effort had then come. It was also the turning point for the young radicals away from the hope of gaining their ends through the mainstream. Once again, as in Greenwood, a SNCC-dominated effort failed to gain what it sought. And SCLC went on six months later in Selma to win it in the form of legislation. The Freedom Democratic Party effort to hold county, state, and district nominating conventions was a demonstration with a difference. Its goal was to prove that FDP was the legitimate Democratic Party in Mississippi. "Thus the convention," said FDP literature, "must choose between a loyal delegation with no power and few votes and one of doubtful loyalty representing the state administration and a majority of voters." The regular party organization in Mississippi, as it had in 1962, voted to send uninstructed delegates and to hold off naming presidential electors until after the convention. It did, apparently because of FDP, promise to put the regular national Democratic ticket on the ballot, something that had been in doubt.

By July 30, the Washington *Post* was saying flatly that the regular Democrats would be seated. "This word from the White House sources fits the known effort of the President to conciliate the South on the racial issue and to keep the lines of communication open to Mississippi in order to obtain enforcement of the new civil rights law." To the young radicals and the movement generally, this meant conciliation with the forces that had murdered the three civil rights workers in Philadelphia, Mississippi, that summer. The New York *Times* supported editorially on August 16 a proposed compromise seating both delegations and splitting the votes between them, saying that otherwise President Johnson would "stand open to the charge that he chose silence in order to compete more effectively with his Republican opponent for Southern white racist votes." The choice, it said, was between "political tradition and political morality."

The legal counsel for FDP was Joseph Rauh. This fact indicates the degree then of SNCC's involvement in the mainstream of liberalism. Mr. Rauh was at the center of the militant wing of the AFL-CIO; the grown-respectable (i.e., the Americans for Democratic Action) wing of liberal intellectuals; and the right wing of the civil rights movement (i.e., the Leadership Conference on Civil Rights). In his brief and in appearances before committees, Mr. Rauh stressed the regular organization's disloyalty and Mississippi violence against the voter effort. "Are you going to throw out of here the people who want to work for Lyndon Johnson, who are willing to be beaten and shot and thrown in jail to work for Lyndon Johnson? Are we for the oppressor or the oppressed?" he asked the Credentials Committee. Politics cheapens. The profound experience of the voter effort was not communicated, except when Mrs. Hamer told the committee about the beatings at the Winona jail.[12] This highly emotional scene was interrupted on national television by a presidential press conference. Eugene Patterson, editor of the Atlanta *Constitution,* described the Mississippi regular party representatives before the committee: "They had stood aside and let beatings, burnings, bombings, and murder be committed while they denied guilt . . . Their closed society had insulated them from the accusing gaze of the race their political bullying had injured. Now the nation was staring at them. They couldn't have helped but look within . . . For the sturdy old men with pale heads and sunburnt faces are good men, not evil; they have simply been caught up in a system that will produce evil . . ."

Then came the compromise decision (to the young radicals, a compromise of a compromise) to seat all of the regular party delegation who would accept a loyalty oath and seat with full voting power two of the FDP delegates. There was also a pledge that participation of Negroes in party affairs would be required for seating of any delegation at future conventions. There was no Southern walkout. Mr. Rauh said it was a victory for FDP, more than had been hoped for. Senator Hubert Humphrey was given credit for working it out. There were repeated rumors that he worked under pressure of threatened loss of the vice-presidential nomination.

The FDP rejected the compromise out of hand. Aaron Henry, in an interview with the authors two years later, said he had no difficulty with that decision, but he did regret the rashness of its tone and the refusal of the FDP leaders, mainly SNCC, to let other civil rights leaders speak to the grass-roots delegation before it made the decision. He said he felt this denied all that such people as Roy Wilkins and Dr. King had done, and Mr. Rauh and Senator Humphrey, that it said that only FDP had been in the fight. The Leadership Conference on Civil Rights felt it had been used and then discarded. Out of all this, Mr. Henry said, came all the subsequent bad publicity and criticism. It would have been better if the country had understood why the compromise was turned down, he said—the feeling that it was not enough, that to accept it would betray all the idealism and suffering of the voter effort. There was also resentment that the compromise had named the two delegates to be seated, a violation of the credo of letting the people decide. Also, neither was of SNCC.

The FDP's rejection was based on its view of Atlantic City as an extension of the most beleaguered voter registration effort, and not as an exercise in the gives and takes of politics as usual. From the latter perspective, the compromise was—as many said—a remarkable victory for FDP. The FDP delegation had no tradition for seeing it that way. And surely it had some of the feelings described in the southwest Georgia VEP report on the need of the people to see their enemies punished, to taste blood. The other leaders were allowed to address the FDP delegates the day after their decision, to try to persuade them to reverse it. Bayard Rustin, organizer of the March on Washington in 1963 and longtime behind-the-scenes civil rights strategist, tried to explain to them the political facts of life—their need for allies. If you say, he told them, that a man who accepts compromise in politics is an Uncle Tom, the civil rights movement is doomed.[13]

The Atlantic City episode bears study. The young radicals always go back to it in explaining their breaking away from coalition and their deepened distrust and distaste for America. Little about it was pretty. By many accounts, the young FDP radicals' rush into rejecting the compromise came from an unwillingness to trust the delegates (and democracy) in a thorough airing of the issues. The insensitivity of the convention to the morality as opposed to the politics of the situation reflected the larger dilemma and narrowed choice of the nation at the time—beset by what the Republicans had done to the civil rights cause in *their* convention, where they nominated Barry Goldwater. Out of it all, the main message seemed not so much that racism in the future would not be tolerated, but that party disloyalty was to be punished.

A Strange Step Away

After Atlantic City, the young radicals, who had put their lives on the line for democracy, received lectures on the give and take of democracy, some of it from lecturers unwilling to put up even their livelihoods. If these youths came subsequently in their alienation to seem the apotheosis of much that democracy should not mean, if most tragically they seemed infected with the virus of the racism they had fought so valiantly, the reaction could only be sorrow and soul-searching for America. For they were among the best of a brave generation; they had lived what the movement believed. Here, in terrifying sum, was the extent of damage done America and a certain idealism. Not all of the damage, but much of it, was done by the white racism that was fought but not vanquished in the South. The terror, the fear, the anti-democratic forces of the South at their worst came to represent America to the young radicals.

There was resentment, not unlike the front-line soldier's, of those who hadn't been where they had been, who couldn't understand what they knew in their guts. It was easy to say they were victims of combat fatigue, as indeed they were, and correct to point out that they were abstracting the worst of the resistance as the meaning of America, and their experience with it as the meaning of life, rather than somehow integrating their knowledge into a broader understanding (though some, magnificently, did achieve this). But there was less talk of the equally fatal mental mechanism of pretending that the worst of the resistance didn't exist, of fitting it neatly into political conventions, of smoothing it out by calling it controversy with extremists on both sides.

What happened? America is a tough place; theory never really can handle all the hard surfaces of its daily routine. As late as the beginning of 1966, a white liberal of the South involved in its politics delivered himself of a long, private diatribe against SNCC, its wrongheadedness, its lack of political acumen. He had no good word for it, though it had been the chief instrumentality of his ever being in a position of effectiveness in politics. And if his hopes were to be fully realized, many more Negroes needed to be registered to vote, including those in one of the very worst of resistant counties. Somebody had to go in there and register them, he said. Who? He didn't have anyone. Someone gently suggested SNCC. He agreed. Sure, he said. Send 'em on in there. Just don't let them come around messing in the politics afterward.

In the struggle for the vote, the young radicals had working for them most of public opinion, the American creed, and, however reluctantly applied, the protection and sanction of the United States Constitution. But in their move to stubborn, uncompromising battle on immovable principle in an arena where the art is that of the possible, the creative form is compromise, and the archetype is the other-directed personality, about their only resource was what they had learned from Southern segregation about living through adversity. The fact that their new adversaries, including many liberals, reacted to them in a manner not unlike that of the white city fathers of Greenwood or Albany did not prove that they were right. But neither did the fact that they were defeated prove that they were wrong. All any of it meant was that they were in a new situation, with different rules, not all of which were any longer in their favor. All Negroes and most whites of the nation could agree on the clear-cut issues of democracy in which the movement first dealt. But when the radical wing made the jump from segregation as the only evil to segregation as only a symptom of a social system that was all evil, it had set itself against the majority who lived by that social system, including most liberals, and probably most Negroes.

Little that they said was really new. One of the very first SNCC proposals for a VEP grant in 1962 talked of "Negro control of the . . . rural counties in the Deep South in which there is a Negro majority . . ." No one could argue with the goal of developing a power base from which to deal effectively in politics. The movement had sought that from the beginning. What was new was the strident harshness, the racist overtones.

The metaphors seemed more appropriate for the 1962–64 years, and the dark ages before them, and even so seemed to retreat from the reality of the South in favor of theories about other realities. In the black power perspective, Negro Americans were a part of the exploited "native" populations of the world freeing themselves from white colonialism. Another key perspective was that of America as seen from the underworld of cities, particularly the ghetto jungle, where the only alternative to poverty was a life of hustling crime—dope pushing, prostitution, gambling—in daily battle with corrupt law enforcement. Out of this world the fanaticism of Malcolm X had come, a fanaticism that toward the end of his life had developed a streak of ambiguity in its hatred of all whites, though he perished without resolving the dilemma. That dilemma was that the only action appropriate to Malcolm's words was violence against the whites, who held all the superior troop strength and firing power. The young radicals tried to escape this dilemma by resort to the "native" perspective that whites and their workings are irrelevant, and by hedging their cries for white blood and the burning of white property (and the destruction of Western civilization) with the rationalization that they spoke figuratively, not literally. They had moved from reading such writers as Camus to reading the speeches and *Autobiography* of Malcolm, and *The Wretched of the Earth* by Frantz Fanon.

How much of black power was simply a new gimmick, this time in the vernacular of politics? The young radicals had been defeated in their first great political adventure at Atlantic City. They suffered subsequent political defeats in challenging the seating of the Mississippi congressional delegation; in FDP efforts in Mississippi, where only the few counties organized by the NAACP really delivered a vote in the 1966 elections; and in the refusal of the Georgia legislature to seat Julian Bond, then still in SNCC, after he endorsed a SNCC statement on Vietnam calling the United States action aggression and murder.[14] Having entered the mainstream of politics, the young radicals and their cry of black power would be judged by mainstream standards.

On the other hand, Mr. Rustin was among many who noted a "no win" despair in the strategy, a giving up of any hope for America. There was something of a feeling of, "If I have to die, I'll take some of the whites with me." The aspiration to instill self-respect and pride in a people whose cultural experience was deprived was praiseworthy. But the selection of nationalism, and the questionable nationalism of Africa at that, as the means was a strange step away from the direction in which the world was going. To find real significance, one had to go back to the truth the young radicals knew about Southern racism. The charge of a racist society had some empirical support in the South: in ten of its eleven states a majority of the white vote went to Goldwater in 1964. The euphemistically labeled "backlash" of Northern whites, including back-sliding liberals, fed their conviction. They were precisely correct in saying that it was the responsibility of whites, not of Negroes, to make the dangerous moral confrontations with white racism. We won't get our heads beat demonstrating for enforcement of laws that we got our heads broken to have passed, they were saying in 1965. After five years, they were still delivering the movement's old message that injustice, not the absence of white violence, was the issue. It was a grotesque reflection of the old spirit. They had started out believing the best that America said of itself; they had acted on this and came to believe the worst, out of experiencing it. The important warning was, of course, that more and more Negroes who already shared their disappointment and disillusionment might come to share their unfortunate ways of expressing it.

Black power embraced some of the worst features of American society, a mirror image of the movement's earlier evoking of the best. Some said the young radicals had appropriately found their place in the midstream of a violence-prone culture. Or maybe it was the Southern mainstream. A point-by-point comparison might be made of the fine qualities of the early SNCC and of the Confederate Army; a similar one could be made of black power and white supremacy politics. Sometimes it seemed to be black humor.

Black and White Together?

Bayard Rustin, soon after the fiasco at Atlantic City, had enunciated the alternative in his February 1965 call for coalition.[15] This call was for a continuation of the effective combination of the Negro movement, white liberals, and labor unions which had worked together in the March on Washington, in the successful drive to strengthen and then enact the civil rights bill of 1964, and in the campaign for Lyndon Johnson against the dread specter of Goldwater as president. He noted the need to "wrest leadership of the ghetto vote from the machines," but pointed out that because the Negro vote would always be a swing vote, "the issue is which coalition to join and how to make it responsive to your program." He described the young radicals at that stage of development, and addressed himself to them. Most perspicacious was his awareness then of the role of shock (particularly the shocking of white liberals) in their strategy.[16] A new approach nationally was urged by the coalitionists in late 1966 and publicized by Mr. Rustin. It was the $100-billion "Freedom Budget," drawn up by the A. Philip Randolph Institute and signed by a large number of liberals and labor and movement leaders, a blueprint for a ten-year attack on all the causes of poverty and results of discrimination.[17] Coming as it did in the midst of cut-backs in the modest-enough federal war on poverty and the general national demoralization caused in part by uneasiness about the Vietnam war, the proposal was sneered at by the new left, and looked at mostly wistfully by liberals. Its long-range significance, however, might have been greater.

Dr. King, in his speech at the end of the March to Montgomery, had urged coalition, and in 1966 and 1967, SCLC and the NAACP, with the Urban League, continued to support the coalition strategy. SCLC had the major summer volunteer program in 1965 (there was no major one in 1966), and at its orientation in Atlanta spent more time in praising the virtues of coalition than on survival lessons for the neophyte freedom fighters. The SCLC program was South-wide, involving five hundred volunteers, many of them Northern whites. Its main concern was voter registration. It developed far less violence (no serious violence) than other previous programs. Some of its workers, as in Choctaw, Alabama, stayed on a year or more beyond the summer. Its most enduring contribution was the building of community organizations that lasted. Though it was little noted in press reports, Dr. King had also invoked in the Montgomery speech the old, elusive Populist dream, political unification of the poor whites and poor Negroes on the basis of their shared interests and needs. This, too, was continued as strategy by SCLC and the NAACP—both of which were more active in the 1966 Southern elections than SNCC and CORE.

Thus on the crucial questions of political strategy, the movement was—for the time, at least—deeply split. It was different from previous wrangles over degrees of commitment and daring, over members and money, and over personalities. Indeed, it was possible to say that in the sense of its pre-1966 make-up, the movement was no more, or was two sets of organizations vying for support of the people. Further division of the movement centered on the question of opposition to the Vietnam war. In 1967, Dr. King spoke out strongly in opposition to the war, enunciating a moral and partly pacifist position. This was generally considered a strategic mistake, and was considered by some a step toward the position of SNCC and CORE on the war. The latter castigated it as a white man's war against colored people. As during direct-action days, much of the nation seemed incapable of seeing the war in the moral terms presented by Dr. King. The NAACP and Urban League reacted to his stand by saying that strategically, peace and civil rights should be kept separate.

The goal of real integration without anyone's calling it that (which would be the way of a neo-Populism) had probably occurred more often in politics during the movement years than in any other sphere. The white politicians in towns beset by the movement or Negro opponents for office came to know their Negro antagonists in the searching, telling way that such battles necessitate. To hear one describe the Negro individual he fought was to realize that for him never again would it be possible to say, "They're all alike," and when all Southerners (black and white) find it impossible, racism is dead. Grudging respect was not the least of the human-relations gains of such battlings.

Representative A. W. Willis of Memphis, elected in 1964 as the first Negro in the Tennessee Legislature since Reconstruction, summed up another side of the matter when he told those attending a VEP meeting of Negro Southern legislators in Atlanta in late 1966 that they would soon learn that not all those white politicians who acted friendly could be trusted. They should not be fooled by gestures of acceptance, or speeches of praise. Take all that, he said, "but go right on voting right." The main thing, he said, is not to be liked but to be respected by them. And he described ways he had earned such respect, as by careful research on his fellow legislators, so that when one opposed his minimum-wage law while praising the principle, he could point out that this gentleman was attorney for a large laundry that paid below the minimum wage. He told of getting gubernatorial support for his bills and a pick of committee assignments by letting it be known he would otherwise introduce legislation designed to cause a showdown vote on race. Another at the meeting, Senator Leroy Johnson of Atlanta, elected in 1962 as the first latter-day Negro state legislator in the South, gave the main meaning of this new status. He told of his first attendance at a committee meeting where his vote was needed to break a tie: "When they saw me walk in the door, they didn't see a black man. They saw a vote."

But not all the political recognition was hopeful. A white policeman, listening to a Mississippi Negro leader haranguing a fervent political audience, whispered to a reporter in admiration: "Why, he's just another damn Bilbo. He tells 'em what they want to hear. But when it comes down to dealing, he knows what he can get."

The development of a bi-racial government in Tuskegee (Macon County), Alabama, was something of a showcase for the good-faith approach, and harked back to the old, balanced spirit of the early movement. By dint of court cases against gerrymandering and on voter registration, Macon was the first county in the Black Belt to achieve Negro majority registration, this in 1964. Leaders of the Tuskegee Civic Association—who had fought the court cases and registered the voters—with their Macon County Democratic Club pushed through a bi-racial slate in the first city and county elections under the drastic new conditions. This was against an all-black opposition slate. The strategy was a deliberate one—to show other such counties they did not have to fear their Negro majorities. But in the calculations also was awareness that an all-white administration overthrown by an all-black one was capable of leaving the government bankrupt and blaming it on the Negroes, saying that's what comes of letting them vote. (Black power advocates did not address themselves to this problem.) In the next elections, in 1966, a similar bi-racial slate was successful—though Negro voters departed in important ways from the moderate leadership. In the primary, they rejected the Macon County Democratic Club's endorsement of Carl Elliott for governor and gave a majority to Richmond Flowers. In several local races they were split enough to defeat or put into a run-off club-endorsed candidates. These cases seemed more a rejection of the leadership's choice than a racial manifestation; in other local races, the club's choices were accepted. A far more serious breach of Tuskegee's experiment in a harmonious Southern bi-racial social order were the riots that occurred in January and December 1966. Young Negroes, mostly students, were in the midst of a voter drive in December 1965, and one of their number, Samuel Younge, Jr., was slain by a white man in a filling station altercation—setting off the January riot. The second riot occurred when the white man was acquitted of second-degree murder charges in connection with the slaying.

Dean C. G. Gomillion of Tuskegee Institute (his name is in history as a plaintiff in the gerrymander suit that led the Supreme Court into the "thicket" of reapportionment) was a major architect of the bi-racial strategy. He analyzed the move for all-black government in Macon County in 1966 as deriving from four sources. One, it was being urged elsewhere; it could spread like direct action. Two, a small group wanted to retaliate, to show whites how it felt to be left out. Three, another group felt that if power could be had, it should be grabbed. (Dr. Gomillion demurred. Parents don't always exercise the power they have over their children, he said. Sometimes it is better for their growth to withhold it. The Negro's plaint against whites through the years had been that they made unbridled use of power; might was not right then.) Four, a small group felt that since Negroes in this Negro college town were better qualified academically, they deserved office. Yet in rural counties, Dr. Gomillion said, Negroes were saying that even if they were not as well qualified as whites, they should have the opportunity to participate in government. He agreed with the latter—for whites as well as Negroes. The first two years of integrated government in Tuskegee, Dr. Gomillion said, had been educational for both races. Whites learned they could be defeated in political maneuverings by Negroes, and Negroes learned that some city and county problems that hurt Negroes are not easily solved.[18]

Coalition and Community Organization

Black take-overs of local governments had been one of the racist specters haunting the white South since Reconstruction. The number of counties where this was possible in 1900 was 284 out of the more than a thousand in the South. In 1920, the number had been reduced to 221, in 1940 to 180, and in 1966 to 85. Table II indicates how far along toward realizing their voting potential they were a year after passage of the voting rights act.

The further job of political organization—of welding such voting strength behind either an all-black or coalition strategy—was indicated in performance of some of these counties in the 1966 Alabama elections. This was an election notable for elimination of Negro office-seekers. Of 51 such candidates in all, only 24 survived to the primary run-off. In Wilcox County, where some 3,691 Negroes were registered—slightly more than the 3,639 white registration—five white candidates with Negro opposition were able to win. Interracial friendships, political obligations, fear of touching off white anger, and irregularities in the vote-count were cited by Negroes as the reasons. "It was too early for us to have a colored sheriff," a fifty-four-year-old Negro told the New York *Times.* Only four of all the Alabama Negro candidates survived the run-off. For whatever it says of the efficacy of the coalition strategy, three of them were in Macon County, including the first Negro sheriff in the Black Belt since Reconstruction. This was Lucius Amerson, a thirty-two-year-old man, who was not fully supported by the Gomillion leadership, but was not a black-power man either. Also elected was a Negro tax collector, another first, L. A. Locklair.

The work of Stokely Carmichael in setting up the Lowndes County Freedom Organization in Alabama (called the Black Panther Party, after its symbol) was the source apparently of his emergence as the new leader of SNCC and chief apostle of black power. This first showcase for black power was a failure in the 1966 elections. It illustrated the difficulty of the all-black strategy in even an area where it might seem most justified. (There virtually were no moderate whites with whom to coalesce; power in the hands of whites had been an instrument of oppression.) Observers cited as reasons for the defeat the economic hold of whites on some Negro voters, instances of intimidation, and instances of genuine conviction in selection of whites by some Negro voters. Certainly, too, at work was the resistance of the Southern Negro culture to the harsher tones of black power, its inherent appeal to racism which has for so long been anathema to that culture. In the aftermath, SNCC spoke of directing such organizational efforts in the future in the city slums, where, though majorities were lacking, the breeding ground of anger might be greater.

Increasingly elsewhere, the problems within Negro communities and Negro mass psychology were in the forefront. Apathy persisted. A report from Albany back in 1963 had pointed out that those who had been asked to register and decided against it "are harder to persuade than those not unearthed before, to whom the idea is a new one." On the other hand, Hosea Williams had maintained that same year that Savannah was proving that Negroes "at the bottom of the barrel" were just as ready to register and "vote intelligently" as those who had regis-tered at the first opportunity. Such contradictions were being tested by the second VEP, which, in the words of its director, Vernon Jordan, was "aimed at the slums, the poverty pocket, rural and plantation communities." The masses in these places, he went on, noting failure of civil rights legislation to help them, "seem to have a feeling of resigna-tion, estrangement, and defeatism because they see politics as irrelevant and meaningless to them." Mr. Jordan prescribed voter education and organization, and urged that the greatest responsibility for working with the poor lay with the Negro middle class of the South.

Patient, individual-oriented community organization work was the obvious need—the kind of effort against apathy the young radicals had made against fear. The experts in this recommended what amounted to traditional methods of ward-heeling politics, the organization of people around issues that mean something to them: sidewalks, playgrounds, paved streets, street lights, police protection, jobs. (In Ruleville, the first step was forming a committee of the already-registered voters to go down and talk to the mayor about paving the streets. The already-registered at that time numbered six.)

The prognosis of community organization work of this kind seemed good but slow. After more than a year of work in an Atlanta slum, Al Ulmer wrote in a Southern Regional Council report: "The community is aroused and interested but the organization thus far has been a paper one; two or three active people have carried the burden of the work. More people must participate in the decision making. Yet, for all the lack of organization, all the personality clashes, all the mistakes, and all

TABLE II
COUNTIES WITH LARGER NEGRO VOTING AGE POPULATION

County	Negro VAP 1960 Census	White VAP 1960 Census	Mid-1966 Negro Registration	Mid-1966 White Registration
ALABAMA				
Bullock	4,450	2,387	3,197	3,323
Dallas	15,115	14,400	10,513	12,787
Greene	5,001	1,649	3,927	2,001
Hale	5,999	3,594	4,096	4,515
Lowndes	5,122	1,900	2,758	2,823
Macon	11,886	2,818	7,130	4,997
Marengo	7,791	6,104	5,799	7,288
Perry	5,202	3,441	3,847	5,495
Sumter	6,814	3,061	3,392	3,775
Wilcox	6,085	2,624	3,765	3,639
ARKANSAS				
Chicot	5,555	4,817		
Crittenden	12,871	10,569		
Lee	5,957	4,545		
Phillips	12,208	10,431		
St. Francis	8,403	7,963		
FLORIDA				
Gadsden	12,261	11,711	4,237	6,338
Jefferson	2,600	2,383	1,540	2,470
GEORGIA				
Baker	1,285	1,139	722	1,517
Burke	6,600	4,358	1,595	3,835
Calhoun	2,393	1,654	509	1,895
Crawford	1,611	1,596	354	1,468
Hancock	3,576	1,727	1,706	1,661
Lee	1,795	1,427	177	1,373
McIntosh	1,823	1,643	1,935	1,612
Macon	4,077	3,171	1,644	3,514
Marion	1,609	1,353	236	1,563
Peach	4,562	3,650	1,011	2,930
Quitman	707	581	160	670
Randolph	3,663	2,878	867	2,598
Talbot	2,507	1,437	661	1,406
Taliaferro	1,073	917	1,165	1,052
Terrell	4,057	3,038	449	3,305
Twiggs	2,255	1,969	317	1,749
Warren	2,224	1,911	1,380	1,938
Washington	5,451	5,373	1,672	5,367
Webster	975	775	231	826
LOUISIANA				
De Soto	6,753	6,543	2,317	5,866
E. Carroll	4,183	2,990	2,735	2,577
Madison	5,181	3,334	2,734 *	2,971 *
Tensas	3,533	2,287	719	2,237
W. Feliciana	4,553	2,814	1,817	1,113

* Race is not indicated for 280 persons registered in Madison Parish.

County	Negro VAP 1960 Census	White VAP 1960 Census	Mid-1966 Negro Registration	Mid-1966 White Registration
MISSISSIPPI				
Bolivar	15,939	10,031	5,732	6,209
Claiborne	3,969	1,688	2,906	1,679
Coahoma	14,604	8,708	7,761	7,215

County	Negro VAP 1960 Census	White VAP 1960 Census	Mid-1966 Negro Registration	Mid-1966 White Registration
De Soto	6,246	5,338	2,129	5,592
Holmes	8,757	4,773	4,655	5,080
Humphreys	5,561	3,344	1,283	2,861
Issaquena	1,081	640	446	768
Jefferson	3,540	1,666	2,049	1,913
Kemper	3,221	3,113	369	3,342
Leflore	13,567	10,274	7,161 (est.)	N/A
Madison	10,366	5,622	5,991	6,334
Marshall	7,168	4,342	2,562	4,741
Noxubee	5,172	2,997	N/A	N/A
Quitman	5,673	4,176	1,382	3,391
Sharkey	3,152	1,882	433	1,768
Sunflower	13,524	8,785	2,325	8,287
Tallahatchie	6,483	5,099	1,174	4,913
Tunica	5,822	2,011	505	1,558
Washington	20,619	19,837	5,094	12,683
Wilkinson	4,120	2,340	1,127	2,777
Yazoo	8,719	7,598	1,050	7,580

NOTE: Race is not indicated for many recent registrants in 51 of Mississippi counties. Where these figures occurred, they have been divided between the races in the totals above. Three-fourths are counted as Negro registration, since it is thought that most of these recent registrants are Negroes. N/A indicates statistics not available when these figures were assembled.

NORTH CAROLINA

County	Negro VAP 1960 Census	White VAP 1960 Census	Mid-1966 Negro Registration	Mid-1966 White Registration
Bertie	6,261	6,156	3,879	5,925
Hertford	6,102	5,606	3,025	4,605
Northampton	7,304	6,178	4,016	6,062
Robeson	21,424	20,851	9,401	12,904
Warren	5,490	4,439	2,562	5,207

NOTE: Non-white figures include Indians, but these are not a major portion of the statewide total.

SOUTH CAROLINA

County	Negro VAP 1960 Census	White VAP 1960 Census	Mid-1966 Negro Registration	Mid-1966 White Registration
Allendale	3,205	2,531	1,626	3,018
Calhoun	3,318	2,623	1,621	2,663
Clarendon	7,735	5,223	5,339	5,436
Fairfield	5,536	4,975	2,227	4,894
Jasper	3,333	2,689	2,079	2,879
Lee	5,446	4,394	2,564	4,616
McCormick	2,248	1,915	972	2,153
Orangeburg	17,355	16,381	8,397	16,039
Williamsburg	10,535	7,560	5,810	9,285

TENNESSEE

County	Negro VAP 1960 Census	White VAP 1960 Census	Mid-1966 Negro Registration	Mid-1966 White Registration
Fayette	7,215	4,437	4,113	5,563
Haywood	6,295	5,497	4,579	2,605

TEXAS

None

VIRGINIA

County	Negro VAP 1960 Census	White VAP 1960 Census		
Brunswick	4,734	4,637		
Charles City	2,126	582		
Dinwiddie	8,587	5,212	NOT	
Nansemond	9,806	6,965	AVAILABLE	
Southampton	7,435	7,239		
Surry	1,842	1,479		
Sussex	3,706	2,662		

the lack of people involved, the people of Vine City have started to get together to help themselves." [19] Charles Sherrod, directing (still in southwest Georgia) in 1966 and 1967 one of the larger registration and community-organization efforts in the South, said of this later work that its focus was even more on individuals than in the past. The content of political developments, wins and losses, he said, was not considered important—only the fact that people were involving themselves in political action. In the end, it seemed to be a matter of work with individuals, and this, inevitably, seemed to promise more than ward-heeling politics had ever achieved. It was a work barely begun, and in its entirety beyond the resources of the movement.[20] And—as the experience of the young radicals so abundantly proved—it was not without physical and psychological danger.

There were similar indications of the will of the Negro people to take hold and work their way out of the various traps of Southern culture. Many such efforts were directed at the economic trap. Many cooperatives—from little quilting ventures to sewing cooperatives to multi-county farm marketing-and-buying combines—were being formed. The civil rights organizations were encouraging such work. A Southern Rural Action Project was begun in August 1966, under auspices of the UAW-supported Citizens Crusade Against Poverty, to encourage economic self-help ventures. Randolph Blackwell, formerly with VEP and then SCLC, was its director. He said that by early 1967, it had assisted in development of twenty-eight projects, including a small (twenty-seven people) employee-owned sewing factory. As with other reachings out to what the people themselves wanted to do, there were many more opportunities for such projects, he said, if there were people and funds to assist them.

The Issues

The issues around which to build political awareness among Negroes in the South were all too obvious. They were in fact a catalogue of the failures of leadership for more than a century. After World War II, the region shed two of its greatest handicaps: It became predominantly urban and industrial, and its agriculture shifted from the one crop of cotton to a diversity that included more cattle and poultry. In the process, sophisticated boosterism bragged continuously about Southern bootstrap lifting-power and of growth. The truth of the matter was that most of the growth was a reflection of national growth; much of the industry attracted by non-union labor, tax favoritism, and other subsidies, was of the kind any area would be better off without; and the growth did not keep up with the rest of the nation and was not as great as it should have been. The South was ever adept at looking away from such facts, but the economists who offered them had the selfsame and self-evident remedy for them—improvement of the lot of the people.[21]

Per-capita income in the Southern states in 1940 ranged around 57 per cent of the national level. By 1964 it ranged around 75 per cent. Florida, the best, with $2,251, ranked twenty-ninth. Mississippi, with $1,438, ranked fiftieth. The national average was $2,566. In 1960, with $3,000 the poverty cut-off for family income, Mississippi's median was below the poverty level, and that of the rest of the Southern states just barely above it. The poverty program of the federal government, which might have alleviated such basic need, was serving the South least well of all regions. The South during the first year of the program contained 44 per cent of the nation's poverty; it received only 20 per cent of the total poverty-program expenditures. "Millions of dollars available for services and jobs in the southern states are not being claimed, while most of the better-off states of the North are getting all that is due them and asking for more," the New York *Times* reported on January 2, 1966, pointing out that the communities and states had to initiate requests for the poverty funds. A similar disinclination of leadership to request available grants for research into the ills of the area was noticeable through 1965, but was being somewhat alleviated after that.

In education, the South, as late as 1964 and with little improvement afterward, had no state spending on elementary and secondary schools as much per pupil as the national average of $455. This was part of the old, dismal statistical story. Another index pointed up its poignancy. In school years completed, the Southern states clustered near the national median. The range in 1960 was from 10.9 in Florida to 8.7 in South Carolina, compared with the national median of 10.6. The people of both races believed in education, indeed had a mystical faith in it, the whites refusing in almost every instance to abandon public education rather than segregation. They sent their children to school; on the whole the schools happened to be the sorriest in the nation. And the economists said, that—as in the other underdeveloped countries—education was an absolute necessity for attracting the kind of industry that would enhance the economy. This meant education for more than the assembly-line skills, which automated factories will not need. In the long view, it meant true and full education, the development of a people capable of building and responding to the highest achievements of the age. It meant, in the true sense, culture, and this meant more than the likely as not garish culture centers that the better-off Southern cities were building as feverishly and unknowledgeably as their forebears built cotton mills in quest of a magic remedy for the economic ills of an earlier time.

If there was awareness of the central facts and difficult problems of the real economic solution among the business and political leaders of the South, it was not, for all their good intentions, very evident. (The very first step would have to be a real elimination of racism.) There was more awareness, but hardly more political skill, in the deliberations and political action of the movement. All the classical analyses of the South and all the arithmetic of the new politics pointed to a basis for consolidation of the poor white and poor Negro votes, in coalition with the still relatively few white liberals. The young radicals, while talking of organizing both, were slow in doing more than talk about it—even in the Negro end of it. For all the hullabaloo about black power in 1966, SNCC's work that year was confined to Lowndes County, a sporadic effort in Atlanta which seemed bent more on stirring up trouble than registering voters, and a competent Arkansas operation (which in its dissent from the all-black concept was regarded by 1967 as out of SNCC). SNCC had accomplished very little in the way of program since 1964. CORE was doing little more. The mainstay of voter registration and what little organization there was continued to be the local groups, with SCLC and the NAACP providing some leadership. By the end of 1966, there were indications that SCLC would further withdraw to the North. Aside from a few sporadic, local ventures and the ministrations of the Ku Klux Klan, no one was doing anything toward organizing the poor whites.

There was a need for a real native radical voice in the politics of the South. And all along, the movement had engendered a real radicalism, something beyond books and the imposition of global theory on its small corner of the globe. Such a move as the Southern effort for jury reform, seeking peers of the poor, would revolutionize American jurisprudence. Attention to the abuses of consumer credit and to consumer education stirring in the poorest parts of the South struck at the heart of an American way of life that had developed since World War II. Nowhere more than in the Negro movement (and the ghetto riots) was the need for rethinking of the role of American policemen made more evident. One of the striking proposals from a delegate at the 1966 White House Conference on civil rights was for "de-militarizing" them, de-emphasizing their guns and uniforms, and re-introducing the concept of policemen as public servants.

Belief by the Negro people of the South in the founding principles of American democracy and the moral imperatives of Western philosophy was the well-spring of this real radicalism; such belief in an age of unbelief was itself a radical act. The old beliefs, with life breathed into them, were as in their origins a radical, indeed revolutionary force. Not to be overlooked, either, was the ability of these people to think.

Negroes and those whites with them who began to overthrow the administrative forms of Southern racism in the 1960's were breaking with their culture. For the Southerner, the goals of the movement were not the automatic and thoughtless allegiance that many other Americans pay to national ideals. Applied to the Negro, these ideas were contradictory to the South's ideals and way of life. They meant a tearing away from the powerful hold of childhood conditioning, with all the doubt and pain and terrible conflict this implies. People who do this in one area of life are less likely to accept at surface value beliefs about the other areas. They are cast off into a sea of uncertainty where it is necessary to look anew at every old truth and examine with care each proffered new one. It becomes necessary to think things through, and such thinking, in any age, is of the essence of radicalism, and in our own age, a rarity.

"The poverty and suffering which we see around us are man-made and man can abolish them," said a 1963 report from a nameless young volunteer in Clarksdale, Mississippi, who had put his mind to examining the existence he had always known. "But the remedies which touch only the surface will not do for this purpose. We will have to change the entire structure of our society. We do not aim at doing acts of kindness but creating a kingdom of kindness. Kindness comes and goes even in a kingdom of wickedness but only as a pinch of salt does in bread."

Bayard Rustin was celebrated for his championing of the cause of coalition. But basic to his advocacy was the belief that coalition had to achieve "radical programs for full employment, abolition of slums, the reconstruction of our educational system, new definitions of work and leisure." He made clear that he was "talking about a refashioning of our political economy." The movement's role would be "to agitate the right questions . . . The questions having been asked, motion must begin in the larger society, for there is a limit to what Negroes can do alone."

Confronting Compromise

In its great legislative victories, the movement and its allies had proved adept at lobbying for passage of bills, but less so at assuring that the laws and the crucial administrative procedures for enforcing them worked out as expected. The most glaring example was the wan tokenism in the South that at first came out of all the grand promises of the 1964 civil rights law. The voting rights law in its first year of existence had not achieved what the nation had demanded after Selma. And these failures were at the heart of the disillusionment and alienation among Negroes in the South.

Failure of Congress even to pass the 1966 civil rights bill was among many other disquieting things, another indication of the movement's political failure. Coalition in its highest responsibilities had not worked. There was a feel in the air of a repetition of the nation's turn-of-the-century failure of will in doing its duty toward Negro citizens. Not unsurprisingly, a chief reason cited for the bill's failure was the violence of Negroes. This seemed to say that as Southern whites had been punished with civil rights legislation for their violence, Negroes would be punished for theirs by withholding of it. To force attention and conscience to the alleviation of the conditions behind both kinds of violence remained the greatest challenge of the new Negro political strength. Could it be harnessed?

Leslie Dunbar summed up some of the larger dangers in 1963: "Success breeds hard problems, and it seems to me that the Negro movement is courting two very serious ones. There is disquieting evidence that a great many Negroes, naturally imbued with the excitement and the power of having led America's first sustained experiment in government by the street, are oblivious to the fact that their guiding rule and their indispensable ally has been the Constitution. Secondly, the availability of the political process has been so long withheld from them that they may not learn soon to value it." [22]

It was probably no accident that Atlantic City's demonstration of the movement's inability then to cope with high-powered politics centered on a question of compromise. American democracy's historical struggle with this key mechanism for the adjustment of conflicting interests has been highlighted by the racial problem. The nation broke apart when the issue of slavery was finally defined as one of those moral issues about which there can be no compromise. Compromise had been in the very names of the stratagems that sought to avoid this moral showdown, and was, to the further discredit of the term, what the betrayal of the Negro and the South—"The Compromise of 1877"—was called.

The movement would not be dealing in such issues of no-compromise morality in many of its political stances. Yet it might be inclined to continue acting as though it were. On the other hand, the nation had an overwillingness to evade morality in its politics, to compromise that which is uncompromisable. The movement forced the issue on the compromise of constitutional rights of Negroes. Could it continue to define such issues for the nation? That, as Merton said, would be the kind of distinctive political achievement to look for from it. In its negativistic way, the black power aberration may have been in this tradition.

That the movement had come to its deepest breach over political strategy was also no accident. Negro Southerners had been able to transcend all their diversities and disagreements in the great surge for freedom. But the condition of freedom that they had sought meant of course the ability to break apart in all their splinters of conflicting interests; that is what democracy is all about. Freedom and democracy would mean for Negroes and their organizations the luxury of being able to blunder; the necessity for never being wrong was of the cruelest burdens placed on them by racism. Freedom means, to defined limits, even the freedom to do evil.

It is not pleasant to be judged on the basis of the color of your skin. Whites subjected to this in the increased racial animosity of unresolved problems of segregation and poverty learned emotional truths Negroes have known since childhood. Negroes, those who were dangerously close to taking on the burden of race hatred's many irrationalities, might pause in it for a moment and gain something of new understanding of the historical forces that had blighted their lives. The purest of the nonviolent demonstrations had always been castigated by most white Southerners as Negro violence. If whites attacked such demonstrations, they said the Negroes were to blame for so provoking them. When Negroes moved to violence in the riots of the cities, it was on one level as if they felt a compulsion to do as the Southern whites had said all along they would. On another level, the riots were again stimuli to the fixation on violence. How much knowledge of this boiled in the mind that mindlessly raged in the riots?

The Movement's Future: The People

"The word love is suspect," said Stokely Carmichael. "Black expectations of what it might produce have been betrayed too often. But those were expectations of a response from the white community, which failed us. The love we seek to encourage is within the black community . . ." [23]

"The cry for black power," said Dr. Martin Luther King, Jr., in a newspaper interview, "can incite bitter anti-white feelings among Negroes and it can intensify white prejudices and resistance. Every ethnic group has sought power—sought it legitimately and gained it. This is what we are seeking. But we shouldn't . . . incite people or estrange friends."

"We all recognize the fact that if any radical social, political, and economic changes are to take place in our society, the people, the masses, must bring them about. In the struggle we must seek more than mere civil rights; we must work for the community of love, peace, and true brotherhood. Our minds, souls, and hearts cannot rest until freedom and justice exist for all the people," said John Lewis. Or rather he wanted to say it; incredibly, this was among passages deleted by movement moderates as too radical from a speech he prepared for delivery at the Washington March of 1963.[24]

"These Negroes," said Merton in 1963, "are not simply judging the white man and rejecting him. On the contrary, they are seeking by Christian love and sacrifice to redeem him, to enlighten him, so as not only to save his soul from perdition, but also to awaken his mind and his conscience and stir him to initiate the reform and renewal which may still be capable of saving our society. But this renewal must be the work of both the white and the Negro together." [25]

Of all the new rights, the one that came with the least personal trauma to white Southerners (regardless of all their resistance to it) was the vote. It was the one with which they had the longest (since 1944) familiarity. "I think it's only right that they should have the vote," a Louisiana sheriff told a Negro official of the federal government. "And I'll support 'em to get it. But just let 'em come marchin' down the street yonder hollerin' an' singin', and I'll lock ever last one of 'em up!" Myrdal was most impressed by the allegiance—paradoxical and illogical, given political and social reality at the time—of the white South to the American creed. More than one observer has suggested that the white South, with perhaps its own secret picture of Lincoln up alongside Robert E. Lee on the mind's living-room wall, seemed to want to be made to do what is right about race. Some saw the white counterpart of the Negro Southerner's religiousness as a similar hope.[26]

The opportunity for a more rational Southern society was at least discernible in the potential of new politics of the South. Whites showed little inclination to take the necessary initiatives. The impetus seemed with the Negro movement, which had accomplished so much. Could it continue what it had started, cope with the complexity of social and economic problems with the same sureness with which it had fought the stubborn inflexibility of institutionalized segregation?

The movement was, first, the organizations—the national and regional ones, NAACP, SCLC, SNCC, CORE, Urban League. In the press, in the in-group writings of civil rights enthusiasts, in popular culture, the movement was generally treated as no more than these organizations with their leaders and images. Upon them were fitted all manner of sophisticated stereotypes and conventional analyses; the American norms of organizational in-fighting and personal self-seeking were enough in evidence to feed the mechanical journalistic practice of seeking such, and describing it. Also the tendencies of intellectuals to atomize and dissect human creation into wearisome and tedious meaninglessness was allowed full scope, so that in some circles to read and discuss the movement was like reading and discussing Marxism or modern art, an exercise in memorized minutiae and endless hair-splitting.

One of the interesting fallacies in such writing, almost from the beginning, was the tendency to nationalize what was essentially a Southern phenomenon. Mainly this amounted to lumping together what were, in important ways, the different problems of Northern and Southern Negroes of the first half of the 1960's, and assuming that the campaigns against the Southern problems of institutionalized segregation had direct bearing on the Northern problems of *de facto* segregation and ghetto poverty. There were of course echoes and offshoots of the Southern movement in the North, but what happened in the South was a concerted and broad-scale social upheaval whose counterpart did not develop contemporaneously in the North. Moreover, the techniques and spirit of the Southern movement had specific aims which were not relevant to the Northern problems. In effect, its achievement was to move the South, in terms of law and institutions, to the point of equality that theoretically was supposed to have existed all along outside the South. After the Southern victories were won, the fallacy persisted in gloomy assessments, including those of the black-power theorists, that the Southern movement had failed because it had not solved the problems of the North. The Southern movement succeeded in the limited goals that it first sought—the overturning of legal segregation.

Part of the confusion has been one of terms—particularly imprecision in the use of the term "movement," for it was far more than the big five organizations. There were the local organizations—in existence, many of them, for many years before the larger scope of the movement gave them a feeling of unity and a degree of communication one with the other. These were ready units for the regional revolution that spread so rapidly. The larger organizations were catalysts (though often it took no more than reading in the paper or hearing on television what was happening twenty miles or two thousand miles away), the style-setters, and in varying degrees they serviced the local groups—with workers, literature, training, and the like. But much that happened was spontaneous, with no direct link between the local group and the larger organizations.

Then there were the people. Some the organizations touched; some touched off the formation of local organizations. Beyond all the minutiae and super-complication of analysis and commentary, it seems certain from simple observation that had the people not been ready, had the people not had, no matter how dimly in the subconscious, the logic of the Southern civil rights revolution within them, there would have been no movement. Some, as in the descriptions of southwest Georgia and Mississippi, had to be skillfully guided to expression of what was within them. But finally it came down to what was within them, and all that grew and built in the organizations was of them. It might be a little brown-skinned middle-aged woman like the one encountered in a federal examiner's office in the Black Belt of Alabama, working day after day helping the people in the lines, reassuring them, answering questions, working with the examiners where they needed local information or understanding of local phenomena. She was of the movement, she said, yet knew not even the names of the state leaders of the SCLC with which her local organization was affiliated. Her essential characteristic —and this is discernible immediately in individual Negro Southerners one meets in any group, any city, any town, across the South—was freedom. Jaunty, cocky, able to look the stranger in the face, to laugh, and to speak indignation at injustice immediately, she stands out as one strong product and at the same time creator of the movement. The federal examiner finishes an old man's application, and asks him "Do you like Alabama?" "Yes," he answers gravely. "I was born here. It's a good place." The woman, head high, eyes scornful, grunts. "I don't think it's a good place." The old man shakes his head. "We have some nice white peoples here." She snorts. Between these two were the countless others who, without drawing attention to themselves, had come to know what was wrong, and something of what they wanted to do about it. These were the real movement in terms of spirit and in terms of real work done—this nowhere more true or important than in voter registration.

By 1967, if one had to look to the larger organizations only, it would have been proper to pronounce, as many were doing, the movement in the South nearly dead, or dormant. SNCC and CORE, for the time anyhow, had degenerated into talking societies. SCLC gave every indication of further abandoning the South for adventures like that of 1966 in Chicago, a direct assault on poverty in its ugliest breeding grounds. The NAACP and Urban League—as before 1960— remained, with their network of largely middle-class local affiliates and their largely middle-class political methods.

But all that from within the people and the local organizations had built the impetus of the early 1960's was still alive. As late as the end of 1965, one could go to a movement-organization office in a Black Belt area and learn immediately the names and addresses of the "active" people, the leaders in a given community. But by 1966, there was likely no office, no contact man. The "active" people, maybe six families at the end of a dirt road in a little town, were still there, still active. But it was more difficult to find them, to communicate with them.

The second VEP, involving mostly the continuing work (all along the most productive) of the local groups, remained one of the few region-wide movement activities of 1966 and 1967. Some indication of the energy yet stirring in the movement was the number of requests for funds received during 1966 by VEP, more than 400. It was possible to make grants to only 106 of these. Not all of the reason was lack of funds, but the following figures indicate the disparity between what was being requested and what the second VEP was able to grant: During 1966, an estimated total of more than a million dollars was requested, and a total of $183,875 was granted. Given the normal American tendency to ask for more than you expect to get, and given the scrupulousness of the second VEP's financial policies, still there was here evident a need not being fully met. And given the vacuum in other organizational movement activity in the South, given the feebleness of federal voting rights enforcement, and given the crucial importance of increasing Negro registration, seriously lagging in ten of the eleven states, the situation seemed to call for more resources, either for VEP or some other broad-scale registration, voter education, and community organization program.

Probably the strongest and certainly the most dramatic example of the movement's vitality at the source of its strength, the people, was the Child Development Group of Mississippi. This was a Head-Start program, part of the "war on poverty," that survived a fund cut-off at the end of its first summer (1965), until it was recognized that the need and spirit of the people would continue the Head-Start schools without federal money. Then in 1966 it survived what seemed clearly a political effort to cut the funds off on such far from proven grounds as inefficiency and all-black policies. The stemming of this effort, involving behind the scenes a showdown fight between certain of the liberal forces of coalition and Sargent Shriver, director of the Office of Economic Opportunity, was one of the few hopeful developments of national significance during the depressing second year of the Johnson administration, despite continued bickering over the settlement.

But the real importance of CDGM was that, whether federal funds continued or not, it seemed strong enough and sure enough of its purpose to survive. This was what struck most observers—that the 121 schools operated in 28 counties, serving 12,000 children and taught by local Negro adults, many of whom themselves suffered from deprival of decent education, were places where very real education was taking place. The teachers were more than dedicated workers. They were aware of their technical lacks, and eager to learn, themselves, all that they could about the vital techniques for training children. They were aware of children as few adults ever are and as all good teachers must be, attuned to the greatness of potential in them, and individuality of each. Parents of the children were deeply involved in planning and operating the program. And all had achieved a vision of what these children might be and must be, and of what education means.

This was how the poverty program might have worked over the country. Mainly by default (white Mississippians had been conditioned to resist federal programs), the program came alive in the hands of the Negro people, became far more in its individual units and individuals than the headquarters and bureaucracy supporting it, and showed itself, strong enough to endure on its own. Like the poverty program itself, the CDGM had roots in the "freedom schools" of the 1964 Mississippi Summer. But there was a crucial difference. The freedom schools had imported teachers; the CDGM units drew directly on the resources and strengths of the local Negro people. These were the resources and strengths that would sustain the hope for a continued reformation of politics and government in the South, which would be the future of the movement, if there were any. Indeed, the people and organizational network of CDGM were a potential political organization themselves. CDGM possessed what the FDP lacked—permanent, viable grass-roots organization. How much of awareness of this was the real reason for the powerful political effort in 1966 to wreck CDGM?

The movement was the people. They were a people not fully known, the black mass of the Black Belt and all the South's "niggertowns." They were spoken of uneasily in the old classical studies as needing preparation for the duties of citizenship, but they had seldom been seriously studied.[27] Many stories and commentaries upon the people attest to the strengths that indicate why the real movement will go on. "They take a long time," wrote Robert Moses with gentle fondness of the people in Mississippi during the years of struggle, "before trying to register, studying for the test. . . . If they fail it, they take this to mean they should study it harder . . . not seeing it as a technique for denying their rights."

In an Atlanta slum not touched by the so-called Atlanta riots of 1966, there was immediate revulsion and condemnation of the role ascribed to SNCC in contributing to the trouble. There was talk of running SNCC out of the community. Then there came evidence that forces from outside the community were trying to encourage this. And the people, gathered in their community organization meeting, came to this conclusion —that SNCC people or anybody else had a right to be there whether you agreed with them or not. They would be no part of running anybody out. They had come to precisely the same conclusion a few months before when SNCC had tried to talk them into getting rid of a white community worker and his family living in the area.

And, finally, there was a poem signed C. W. in the Choctaw (Alabama) *Freedom News* in late 1965: "We are not going to vote for a black man because you are a Negro./We are not going to vote for you because you are white./Whether you be black or white/We will vote for you to give us a chance."

What one Negro candidate told his audience in what was formerly one of the worst areas of white resistance of the Alabama Black Belt presumably, in the ways of the politician, was at least partly inspired by his knowledge of their standards and beliefs. "Why are Negroes seeking office?" he asked. "Why has the white man held office all these years? This is our great opportunity to correct the mess the white man has created. But we're not going to abuse him. Though he's been cruel to us, we'll be kind to him. The best way to destroy an enemy is to make him into a friend."

A young Negro woman of a small Georgia town, mother of three— like most Negro Southerners, never involved actively in the movement —said that well, yes, if she could see a white hated her, she hated back. "In church, the way Dr. King means, I can love them. But in my heart, I hate them when they hate me."

"I may be naïve," said Dr. Gomillion of Tuskegee, "in thinking human beings intelligent enough—a large enough number of them—to do what is good for the greatest number. Over the years I've been more interested in cooperation than in the possible consequences of conflict. I recognize that some good comes from conflict. But I do not believe that only through conflict can good come. My conception is of Negroes and whites electing to public office persons best qualified for the positions and then instead of fighting them after they are elected, helping them to carry out good programs for the best interests of the total community."

The movement in the form of organizations and programs had all along been a tiny and sometimes thin abstraction of such voices as these. The real movement had been the people, and these voices probably still spoke for the majority of them. That as much of their great faith was still alive after the years of struggle and after the vicissitudes of "victory" seemed the best hope that it would force fulfillment, and that America might partake of its strength. But such faith could not be indefinitely disappointed by the routines of American democracy.

N O T E S

1. Cash, p. x.
2. Cash, pp. 137–138:

> The final great result of Reconstruction we have to consider in this chapter (a result which stands as a sort of summation of the things we have been seeing) is that it established what I have called the savage ideal as it had not been established in any Western people since the decay of medieval feudalism, and almost as truly as it is established in Fascist Italy, in Nazi Germany, in Soviet Russia— and so paralyzed Southern culture at the root.
>
> Here, under pressure of what was felt to be a matter of life and death, was that old line between what was Southern and what was not, etched, as it were, in fire and carried through every department of life. Here were the ideas and loyalties of the apotheosized past fused into the tightest coherence and endowed with all the binding emotional and intellectual power of any tribal complex of the Belgian Congo. Here was what might frame the Democratic Party, as potent an instrument of regimentation as any totemic society that ever existed. In a word, here, explicitly defined in every great essential, defined in feeling down to the last detail, was what one must think and say and do.

3. W. E. B. Du Bois, *The Souls of Black Folk* (Greenwich, Connecticut: Premier Americana, Fawcett Publications, 1961; originally published 1903), p. 151.
4. Lillian Smith, James Baldwin, Thomas Merton, a few others wrote of it. Vincent Harding, in a more recent look at the subject ("Where Have All the Lovers Gone?" in *New South*, winter 1966), asked: "Is it possible that dependence on federal power, a conservative, manipulative power, has actually sapped the *elan vital* of nonviolence? Could it be that the movement that began with a promise to match 'physical force with soul force' may well have found too easy a way out in matching instead the physical force of the federal government against the terror of Al Lingo's state troopers? . . . Is it possible that the movement that sang 'God is on our side,' was really more happy with the national guard around it, and thus may have chosen the lesser part? In the process many a strategic battle has surely been won, but no one seriously speaks any longer of 'redeeming the soul of the South' or of America. Has the task been given up as hopeless or have the victories been confused with redemption?"
5. Thomas Merton, "The Black Revolution," in *Ramparts*, Christmas, 1963. Italics added.
6. Several times on the last day of the Meredith march, as it wound through Jackson, Negroes broke ranks and made hostile responses to heckling whites. But no blows were struck. One white man was surrounded in his front yard by at least fifty Negroes angrily shouting at him. His son of about ten ran in terror into the house; the man

stood his ground, face red, fists balled up. No one hit him. In racially reversed circumstances, he would have been lucky to escape with his life.

7. The Atlanta disturbances grew out of the usual background of urban decay, of long-time police bullying, of neglect of housing needs, and were sparked by the shooting of a Negro car-theft suspect by a white policeman in one area, and the random slaying of a sixteen-year-old Negro boy by a white man in another. SNCC's role was to encourage anger and outrage and anti-white sentiment, and to organize "protest demonstrations" in the immediate aftermath. In 1959, James Baldwin (*Nobody Knows My Name*, p. 98) warned of the national race riot that would start in Atlanta and "spread to every metropolitan center in the nation which has a significant Negro population." The non-violent demonstrations started the next year; the race riots that came in 1963 and immediately afterward were not in the South.

8. Out of the voter effort in Albany came the script of a play, "Help for Mr. Whitney," by Brownie Wright, apparently a Negro high-school youngster. The play, performed at a voter registration meeting in Albany, is about Mr. Eli Whitney's being cheated out of the proceeds of his famous invention, and being urged by a young man of the voter movement to register to vote to prevent such exploitation. He resists. The character development gives insights into what is perhaps a Negro middle-class archetype. Mrs. Whitney says at one point: "Sometimes Eli don't have a sense of humanity." Mr. Whitney paces about, saying things like, "Ain't nobody gonna force me to anything." The voter worker and his family talk to him of God. He says: "Oh, God is going to do what He wants to do." One of his children says that Father just may not understand that his vote will be counted. Another: "I think Father should have a little more sense of humor." Mrs. Whitney says hopefully: "Yes, he'll change."

9. Letter to the Editor, Atlanta *Constitution*, January 14, 1966. Miss Smith also said: ". . . I can see why the young Negroes have accepted the advice of men like Staughton Lynd and others who came South and infiltrated the movement (it was at first such a starry-eyed and pure-hearted movement but alas there was no Gandhi to lead and discipline them. . . .). They've been listening for three years now to a mixed-up mess of nineteenth-century anarchism and 1930's communism (several of their most popular young northern helpers are children of the old Commies well known in the '30s)." Miss Smith was later to resign from the board of CORE in protest of black power policies. Some of the young radicals did finish college, dividing their time between campus and social revolution. Among these were Stokely Carmichael and Charles Sherrod, both of whom did graduate work.

10. The ironies of this were wearing. A report told of how Clinton, Louisiana, set out to destroy a CORE unit with a restraining order against all forms of demonstration and free assembly, and then sought to prove in court that CORE was a part of the international communist conspiracy. Here is the wording of a law proposed in the United States in 1963: "An ordinance setting forth the purposes for which streets and sidewalks are maintained by the town of Itta Bena and making it unlawful for any person or persons with certain exceptions to parade or march or to sit, kneel, or recline, or to engage in public speaking, group shouting, or group singing, or to assemble in organized groups carrying signs, on the sidewalks or streets of the town of Itta Bena, Mississippi, or to interfere with the normal use of sidewalks and streets without written permission of the marshal of said town and making it unlawful to place debris on streets and sidewalks and providing that this ordinance be effective on the date of its passage." Punishment for the "crimes" described was $100 fine and/or 30 days in jail.

August Meir ("New Currents in the Civil Rights Movement," *New Politics*, summer 1963) suggested that "socialists and particularly the more militant revolutionary Marxists" early considered the student movement a "golden opportunity." They talked the same language of revolution, but with different meanings. "Undoubtedly the white radicals added to the revolutionary, anti-Negro-bourgeois, anti-white-liberal psychology of the Movement. Their presence was welcomed by many, though fully understood by only a few . . . Attending the SNCC meeting in 1962 was like going to a Popular Front affair in the 1930's." As early as 1963, he pointed out that the movement regulars distrusted white liberals and were beginning to cool toward white radicals. He went on to say that the revolutionary Marxists of the movement "regard it as regrettable that Negroes would be satisfied with the ballot, a home, and a car. But they have really missed the point of the Negro protest movement. After all, the vote, a job, and decent standard of living, the right to come and go like other American citizens are what Negroes are really striving for." Myrdal (p. 510), before the movement came along, wrote: "But there is, I have become convinced, a still deeper reason why Negroes are so immune against Communism. Negroes are discriminated against in practically all spheres of life, but in their fight for equal opportunity they have on their side the law of the land and the religion of the nation. And they know it, down to the poorest stratum. They know that this is their strategic hold. No social Utopia can compete with the promises of the American Constitution and with the American creed which it embodies."

11. The white field workers were not discharged, but a number resigned, leaving only a few in SNCC. When reporters at a press conference questioned whether any whites were left, one such was trotted out like nothing so much as a token "whitey." The Arkansas SNCC rejected the Negroes-only policy, saying conditions were different there.

12. "Mrs. Hamer's story is too fantastic to be typical of other Negroes in the Freedom Party . . ." said a story out of the Washington Bureau of the Miami *Herald*, August 24, 1964. The trouble was that her story was typical of the fantastic world of the worst resistance, which never was, really, communicated.

13. In "Waiting for '68" in the *New Leader*, September 14, 1964, Stokely Carmichael of SNCC was quoted as saying, "Some people are confused by the FDP decision. Some people when they go into the hall, trade in their principle for politics. Some people, eager for office [the reference apparently was to Humphrey], compromise. They must come out holding their heads down. We will never place politics above principles. We can hold our heads high."

14. Mr. Bond had been elected from a district consisting of a slum and part of the Atlanta University complex. He had campaigned for such things as minimum wages for domestic workers, birth-control centers for the poor, and repeal of right-to-work laws. One of the ringleaders of the move to deny him his seat was notable for previous efforts to have Governor Wallace address the Georgia General Assembly. In past years, Georgia's legislative branch had been not loath to pass resolutions against the federal government in racial matters. Fourteen members who voted for interposition in 1956 were still in the legislature in 1966, and seated without question. On the other hand, SNCC's charge that the action against Mr. Bond was motivated purely by race seemed to ignore the other nine Negroes seated that term, including Ben Brown of Atlanta, a former direct-action stalwart. At one point in the episode, Mr. Bond might have saved his seat by performing a ritual of recantation. To his credit, he refused. Some saw in his refusal to play the game, to make a deal, a harbinger of the freedom that Negro-supported politics might develop. Subsequently, in court action against the ouster, Mr. Bond and SNCC treated voluntary attorneys from the American Civil Liberties Union in a shoddy way, dismissing them in mid-

case in favor of leftist New York attorneys. While the case was pending, Mr. Bond won a special called election for his seat, was refused seating again, and then won re-election for a "second term." In December 1966 the U.S. Supreme Court in a precedent-setting decision ordered him seated, and this was done in January 1967. Following is some of the language of the SNCC resolution which, though he had no hand in writing it, he readily endorsed:

> . . . Samuel Younge [a civil rights worker in Tuskegee] was murdered because United States law is not being enforced. Vietnamese are murdered because the United States is pursuing an aggressive policy in violation of international laws. The United States is no respecter of persons or laws which run counter to its needs and desires.
>
> We recall the indifference, suspicion and outright hostility with which our reports of violence have been met in the past by government officials.
>
> We know that for the most part, elections in this country, in the North as well as the South, are not free. We have seen that the 1965 Voting Rights Act and the 1964 Civil Rights Act have not yet been implemented with full federal power and sincerity.
>
> We question, then, the ability and even the desire of the United States government to guarantee free elections abroad. We maintain that our country's cry of "preserve freedom in the world" is a hypocritical mask behind which it squashes liberation movements which are not bound, and refuse to be bound, by the expediencies of United States cold war policies.
>
> We are in sympathy with, and support, the men in this country who are unwilling to respond to a military draft which would compel them to contribute their lives to United States aggression in Vietnam in the name of the "freedom" we find so false in this country . . .

15. "From Protest to Politics: The Future of the Civil Rights Movement" in *Commentary*, February 1965.

16. "Sharing with many moderates a recognition of the magnitude of the obstacles to freedom, spokesmen for this tendency survey the American scene and find no forces moving toward radical solutions. From this they conclude that the only viable strategy is shock; above all, the hypocrisy of white liberals must be exposed. . . . While they admit [Malcolm X] has no program, they think he can frighten white people into doing the right thing. To believe this, of course, you must be convinced, even if unconsciously, that at the core of the white man's heart lies a buried affection for Negroes—a proposition one may be permitted to doubt."

17. The full title of the proposal was "A 'Freedom Budget' For All Americans. Budgeting Our Resources, 1966–1975, To Achieve 'Freedom From Want.'" Copies of the 84-page pamphlet were available from the A. Philip Randolph Institute, 217 West 125 Street, New York, New York, 10027.

18. There is always the danger in the recording of speech that the subleties and depth of personality that speech conveys will evaporate. This kind of distortion has been common to coverage of the movement. The Negro of the situation often emerges unreal, a kind of saint, a stereotype in its way as damaging as the unkinder ones. Dr. Gomillion should emerge as the man of immense subtlety that he is, not as saint or, for that matter, as Negro. He smiled at one point in the interview and said, "It's difficult to tell why I feel as I do. Perhaps it is things that I remember reading long ago. Like 'She Stoops to Conquer.' And 'A living person can do more good than a dead person . . .'" At another point he remarked, "The golden rule is pure

selfishness. As I say to my students, I'm not sure of the difference between egoism and altruism. . . ."

19. "A City Slum: Poor People and Problems," Southern Regional Council, March 1966.

20. The movement's efforts at community organization beyond those centered on the vote in the hard-resistance areas had been sporadic and thinly spread. Notable were citizenship and literacy classes of SCLC at various places, including Greenwood during the 1963 drive, and the continuing citizenship training program of SCLC in Dorchester, Georgia, and of the Highlander Center in Tennessee, both for students from over the South. The Citizens Crusade Against Poverty, a United Auto Workers offshoot, was developing a program in 1966 whereby Northern groups would sponsor indigenous organizations across the South. But the emphasis here seemed on economics, as indeed had much of the community activity during 1965 and 1966. There were various "cooperative" schemes in manufacture and agriculture which sought self-respect as avidly as sales, and which seemed sadly handicapped by the lack of the main requisites for success—capital, managerial skill. (See "Cooperatives, Credit Unions, and Poor People" by Al Ulmer, published by the Southern Regional Council, 1966.) In Mississippi, among the numerous offshoots of SNCC, a Poor People's Corporation emerged to organize co-ops. CORE, before the black-power eruption, was also developing co-ops in various places. A number of free-lance enthusiasts were urging co-ops and credit unions as panaceas, with little practical knowledge about them. When such ventures failed, a useful idea was discredited in the minds of participants. Domestic worker unions cropped up here and there, an old dream.

21. See "Four Decades of Thought on the South's Economic Problems" by Clarence H. Danhof in *Essays in Southern Economic Development*, edited by Melvin L. Greenhut and W. Tate Whitman (Chapel Hill: University of North Carolina Press, 1964): "Throughout it has remained true that the economy of the South has evolved as the capabilities of its citizens to respond to their environment has been enhanced. That experience suggests that persistent adherence to the fundamental task of upgrading human capabilities is the region's best guarantee of continued growth." (p. 68.)

22. "The Changing Mind of the South: The Exposed Nerve," in *The Journal of Southern Politics*, February 1964.

23. "What We Want" in *The New York Review of Books*, September 22, 1966.

24. Howard Zinn, *SNCC: The New Abolitionists* (Boston: Beacon Press, 1964), p. 217.

25. Merton, "The Black Revolution."

26. Walker Percy, a novelist and kinsman of the late Mississippi author William Alexander Percy (*Lanterns on the Levee*), wrote in "The Failure and the Hope" (*Katallagete*, publication of the Committee of Southern Churchmen, December 1965): ". . . At least in [this] Southerner's opinion, the ultimate basis for racial reconciliation must be theological rather than legal and sociological and . . . in the South, perhaps more than in any other region, the civil and secular consciousness is still sufficiently informed by a theological tradition to provide a sanction for racial reconciliation."

27. Du Bois, in *Souls of Black Folk* (p. 105), wrote:

We seldom study the condition of the Negro today honestly and carefully. It is so much easier to assume that we know it all. Or perhaps, having already reached conclusions in our own minds, we are loath to have them disturbed by facts. And yet how little we really know of these millions—of their daily lives and longings, of their homely joys and sorrows, of their real shortcomings and the meaning of their crimes! All this we can only learn by intimate contact with the masses, and not by wholesale arguments covering millions separate in time and space, and differing widely in training and culture. Today, then, my reader, let us turn our faces to the Black Belt of Georgia and seek simply to know the condition of the black farm laborers of one county there.

11)

The Future of
Southern Democracy

Political leadership among white Southerners, as among most Americans, is largely middle-class. It usually rises out of the civic and business organizations of a community, where a leader finds political encouragement in the fact that he is known to a sizable stratum of his middle-class peers, or out of the legal profession. Where is political leadership to come from for ten million Negro Southerners, many of whom live in areas where white supremacy prevented the development of an extensive middle class? Of the first ten Negroes to be elected to the Georgia legislature in the post–Jim Crow era, four were lawyers, four executives of social work and civil rights agencies, and one a minister. There was doubt about the middle-class status of only one, who lacked college credentials but who listed himself as an unemployed undertaker. The first Negro officeholders elsewhere in the South, too, were usually well-established members of the middle class. But what of the large areas where hardly any Negro middle class had really emerged? In the whole state of Mississippi, as late as 1966, there were only four practicing Negro lawyers in a Negro population of almost a million.

The Negro Southerner's world is different and the kind of leadership he needs in order to become a full political participant is different. No mere replica of the white model will do more than scratch the surface in the years immediately ahead. The commonly accepted laws of voting suggest relatively little future participation by Southern Negroes. If low income, low education, lack of a large middle class, and lack of a sense of identity with the larger community are necessarily deterrents to voting, as they seem to have been with whites, and perhaps with Negroes in the past,[1] Southern Negroes will come to the polls very slowly indeed. But the dynamics of the rights movement, which thrust forward a new kind and style of leadership, and which aroused many Negro communities, make these past correlations questionable indications of the future. So did, by the mid-1960's, the voter registration figures for a number of areas of the South.[2]

In the politics of the immediate future, substitutes must be found in many places for traditional middle-class leadership. *Students who worked on voter registration and other civil rights causes in the Deep South in the 1960's often were, in effect, substitutes for a non-existent or paralyzed middle class. In truth, this was their most important role.* Their function as the shock troops of the rights movement has been widely recognized, as when they broke the block of Mississippi; but their functional role as an imported middle-class leadership filling a void has not been so recognized. It was certainly not seen in these terms by the visiting legion itself, so many of whom were preoccupied with rejection of the superficial appearances of middle-class society. It was sensed, intuitively at least, by the thin middle-class elements of some Negro communities. These sometimes protested the style and emphasis of the outsiders, and in Mississippi in 1964 and 1965 the local NAACP chapters also protested that the young imports of SNCC in particular were seeking to undermine them.

The paralysis or non-existence of middle-class leadership was what had given rise to the kind of direct-action leadership that came into many Negro communities from outside. Full-time civil rights activists worked systematically to arouse a beaten, wary, defeatist community, then to channel this arousal toward certain ends, and then to control the force as it propelled itself. They understood as well as anyone the difficulties which had limited local middle-class leadership: the legacy of fear among the leaders as well as the people at large, the internal barriers that kept men from moving, and the real threats that existed for a local

Negro leader who offended the white community and then had to go on depending upon it.

How relevant will politics seem to be to Negro Southerners? Does it answer the pressing questions for Negroes, those immediately related to disadvantage because of race as well as those bread-and-butter issues that transcend matters of race? Many Negroes simply do not share most whites' view of voting. They are not inclined to vote simply because this is what one does; social conformity, in many places, has been less of a factor.[3] Robert Coles, who has spent much time getting to know Negroes on lower economic levels, has spoken from the viewpoint of a psychiatrist and a sensitive white observer who knows the limitations of what a white man can see: "We see that Congress has passed a law and Negroes can vote. Or *we* see that if Negroes would only organize and push, they can do this or that. If they don't do so, we call them apathetic, divided, or afraid. But I think we really don't want to look at *our* laws and our notions of what can be done by organizing through *their* eyes, and their experience with laws and police and even with organizing for their own self-protection. To vote is a social act, and requires some sense of belonging to the community and believing that it makes some difference to belong, that there is something useful (or 'right,' if you're an intellectual) about participating in the political life of one's town or state. . . . I think, for all the empathy we sometimes feel we have for Negroes, we simply forget the historical facts of their condition and quite naturally fail to see their view of mayors, cops, judges, the whole bunch of people who are the human expressions of the 'political process.' *We* are often doubtful about what our flimsy vote means. Well, 'folk culture' is known for its calculating, sly humor and awareness, and I think many Negroes really know the score—at least as it has been—and in some respects feel as we do; namely, what difference does it make? I'm not sure I'd care to vote if I knew the facts of our society as only a poor man can. *We* know about our corrupt leaders, or 'system,' but we go on anyway, joining and voting and participating, because it works for us, makes sense to the thrust of our lives, and generally seems to be a not-so-bad 'essential' to make everything 'run smoothly.' What if there were a few signs that it might not be, or didn't seem to be?" [4]

Negroes have not heard, for decades, exhortations on the virtues of voting.[5] Southern Negroes soon may adopt such a general civic view, as many already have, but the difference between Negroes and whites in the South on this point of social conformity may remain for some time. Voting must seem relevant, then, not just a civic formality. How relevant will politics seem to the new voters and potential new voters—the teen-ager torn between "the movement" and "the Block" in Greenville, Mississippi; the old woman in Terrell County, Georgia, who said she had always been a slave and always would be; the young family man with a new skill, looking for a better neighborhood and a better job?

In this time when chaos sometimes has been the price paid for lagging politics, when rising expectations outrun sluggish realizations, a real question remains about whether politics, in effect, will be fast enough. There are pessimists about this. "Because of the structure of American politics as well as the nature of the Negro community," James Q. Wilson wrote in 1965, "Negro politics will accomplish only limited objectives. This does not mean that Negroes will be content with those accomplishments or resigned to that political style. If Negroes do not make radical gains, radical sentiments may grow. How these sentiments will find expression is perhaps the most perplexing and troubling question of all." [6]

Lower-income, poorly educated Negroes in areas of heavy Negro population have hardly ever had anyone to vote for. "I don't see no difference between these crackers," a Negro political cynic whose services were for sale said in that recent past that is fading. "They're all crackers and when they get elected, they are still going to be crackers." [7] Every white man who has ever given some measure of trust or enthusiasm to a particular mayor, governor, or other political candidate should understand a little of how it might have been never to have felt able to risk that kind of commitment.

In areas of repression, Negroes often have a strong desire (though often repressed) just to confront. That desire, built into a man by his cultural condition, sometimes can move him to the polls when, by the usual probabilities of voter behavior, he is not likely to be there. "If we could get ten thousand people into the streets of Birmingham but only two thousand to go register in Birmingham, does that suggest that there is less interest in voter registration than in marching?" a leader in the movement asked. "It doesn't. You can explain it just by the desire of frustrated people to confront. The desire for confrontation can be channeled into voter registration and voting, and in many places it already has been." [8] In Negro communities, the yearning to confront may become more powerful than any of the usual factors that influence voter behavior.

Generalizations about voter behavior, too, usually have been based upon individual motivations and independent individual influences. In the case of Negro Southerners, immediate group influences often are more important. It is much easier to move people in a group than as individuals when they have been intimidated. The fear of the court-house, that ominous fortress of the sheriff and the jail and self-appointed courthouse-square guardians of white privilege, may be more easily overcome by a group than by an individual. The group also may over-come those economic, educational, and cultural factors that might normally influence an individual not to vote.

Voting by Illiterates

One of the foremost of these obstacles is illiteracy. White illiterates have voted throughout the South in the past. General white manhood suffrage was extensive before there was a comprehensive educational system. Great concern about voting by illiterates did not come until after the Civil War, when the illiterates who turned up at the ballot box were Negroes. When the white politicians of the South first proposed stringent literacy requirements, they did not usually bother to conceal their purpose, which was simply to disfranchise Negroes.

At Mississippi's disfranchising convention of 1890, a delegate cal-culated that literacy qualifications would bar 60 per cent of the Negroes and 10 per cent of the whites. In the 1890's, when it had become ap-parent that Negroes' educational level was rising and many more were becoming eligible to vote even with literacy tests, Mississippi white leaders began to talk about other devices to stop them. At the Virginia disfranchisement convention of 1901–1902, the "threat of rising Negro literacy" was noted, and one delegate commented on the hazards of rest-ing white supremacy only on literacy requirements: "One half of all the Negro electorate in the state can read and write. . . ." In Alabama, a convention delegate reasoned in 1901 that the "grandfather clause," intended to enable white illiterates to vote while Negro illiterates were being barred, might encourage whites to remain illiterate and encourage Negroes to read and write. "Followed to its logical conclusion," he warned ominously, "this deplorable law might easily result in the end in raising up a majority of Negro voters in Alabama." It was not the barring of illiterates which these delegates wanted most; it was the barring of Negroes, illiterate and literate, and the perpetuation of all-white rule. The places in the South where Negroes have had the greatest difficulty in voting also have been the places where literate Negroes encountered major obstacles.[9]

Most Southern states in the past made specific provisions for the voting of illiterates. In Louisiana, candidates were (and still are) numbered on the ballot so that an illiterate might choose by this simple identification. In Tennessee, an illiterate could request a printed slip with the name of his candidate, this to be pasted on the ballot (though he himself, and not an election official, must do the pasting). In Arkansas, illiterates always could vote, and a new elections law approved in 1965 continued this tradition, omitting any literacy requirement and providing for lifetime registration of illiterates as well as literates. South Carolina excused anyone from the literacy test if he could show payment of taxes on property assessed at $300 or more, and other states provided a variety of escapes from the tests. State laws in a number of cases stipulated the procedure by which those conducting elections were to mark the ballots of illiterates as requested, with witnesses.

Throughout the South, strong strains of opinion traditionally have risen against the barring of illiterates as such from the ballot box. Especially in such areas as the mountain regions, the Piedmont, the "hill country" and those flatlands that were mainly white-populated, there always was fear that the plantation counties wanted literacy requirements not just to bar many Negroes but also to bar many poorer whites whose interests were different from those of the Black Belt's privileged classes. When Negroes were being systematically disfranchised to accommodate the Black Belt, the other areas or Southern states exacted protections against practices that would stop their own poorer whites from voting.

In recent years the South has become more concerned about voter literacy simply because sizable Negro registrations were imminent. Louisiana, therefore, by constitutional amendment, stopped registering illiterates in 1960, though it did not generally remove those who had been registered previously. In 1956 it had had 30,661 white and 19,346 Negro illiterates on the voting lists; by May 1965 the numbers were 20,235 white and 12,921 Negro. Louisiana's literacy requirements, like those of Alabama, Mississippi, Georgia, and South Carolina, were set aside by the Voting Rights Act of 1965. The racial division of illiterate registrants then was reversed. After the first wave of registration under the new act, the count of illiterates on the rolls had become 27,628 Negroes and 19,962 whites. Most white illiterates who had wanted to register evidently already had been on the rolls at the time of the 1960 cut-off, which subsequently had served principally to bar Negro illiterates. U.S. District Judge Frank Johnson of Montgomery took note of this kind of effect when he ruled in the Tuskegee case that the local registrars must certify all Negroes whose literacy was equivalent to that of the least-qualified white registrants.

In Leflore County, Mississippi, in the heart of the Delta plantation country, young registration workers prodded, cajoled, and persuaded an increasingly willing local Negro population in 1963 to attempt to register. Their reports were studded with notations beside the figures for those who went to the courthouse to register: On April 14, 23 went, "15 can't read or write." In the same county, and across the rural South, scattered small classes were being held for Negro adults to promote basic literacy. The civil rights movement was trying to fill, in an extremely limited way, a gap of monstrous size left by the failure of the South to educate its people. Here, again, was the trail of its disaster with political leadership, for certainly the South of the first half of the twentieth century was not so poor that it could not afford universal education of a basic kind.[10] Yet, to choose only one abysmal example, in Lee County, Georgia, as late as 1960, half the Negroes had a third-grade education or less.

Were Negroes to be penalized now on voting only because they had been penalized before on education? Robert Moses, the young Negro intellectual who had started the student movement in Mississippi, wrote in the winter of 1963 to Burke Marshall that a sheriff had complained because registration workers were taking illiterates to the registration office. Moses noted that the purpose was more than to build a record on registration efforts. It was good, he said, because it helped teach Negro illiterates to face the white man and ask their just due, and to tell the registrar that they knew of white illiterates who voted. That was good for the Negroes involved, vote or no vote. It also was arguable under the "equal protection" clause, Moses said, that these Negroes should not have to take literacy tests, because they had been denied equal education when they were children.

Many illiterates, one can believe, are more capable of arriving at logical and reasonable decisions than are literate men whose thought processes are heavily encumbered by mental snarls and kinks left from a lifetime of racial nonsense. Examples from the tortured and tragically absurd logic and expression of men who fought white supremacy's battles in Congress come quickly to mind.[11]

Modern democratic political theory has been heavily influenced by eighteenth-century ideas. Literacy is the handmaiden of philosophical rationalism. Before Freud and the Bilbos made it less possible for us to extoll the rational processes as the all-encompassing light of the present and the future, an occasional optimistic democratic theorist had envisioned a world in which each citizen would be continuously interested in government and politics, well informed on all their workings, deliberate in his decisions about them, and motivated by detached dedication to the public interest. It did not turn out that way. Students of voting know that relatively few voters change their minds during presidential campaigns, no matter how lively the issues and how prolonged the stimulus; that campaigns mainly "reinforce the faithful," charging their interest and arousing a few more to get to the polls than otherwise might, to vote the way they were inclined to all along; and that if one changes from one election to the next, it is more likely to be due to a substantial change in one's social position or income rather than "the dialogue." Bernard Berelson has noted that political decisions "are relatively invulnerable to direct argumentation and vulnerable to indirect social influences," and wishful expectation may weigh heavier than cool prediction of consequences. "Indeed, it can be said that for many citizens the decision as to how to vote is not really an individual matter at all but a kind of collective decision in which a whole group of people, from the family to the social stratum, work their way to final position without much conscious or deliberative thought." Berelson comments that in justification of democracy we tend to place too much emphasis upon the virtuous wisdom of individual voters, and too little on the working of the democratic process as a whole.[12] Would an infusion of even substantial numbers of uneducated voters be damaging or helpful to the working of the democratic process as a whole? That, rather than whether one uneducated voter can choose as intelligently as one educated voter, is the question. If the democratic system is founded upon the idea of fair and orderly reconciliation of all interests, and we assume that all legitimate interests must be represented, there can be no justification for preventing an illiterate man from voting. If his judgment is not needed, or wanted, he nevertheless has interests. He is entitled to have them weighed in the same proportion in which they exist in society and the only way to make that genuinely possible is to give each man one vote. It is not reasonable to suppose that at the polls he would not represent his own interests and that without his participation someone else would. If we assumed this about illiterates, we could assume it about pawnbrokers, or automobile salesmen, or millionaires, and for one good reason or another bar them all. And if we may assume that a sixth-grade education is necessary for acceptably intelligent voting, we also may assume that a ninth-grade education or a college education is necessary for it. Universal suffrage ought to recognize that votes are the best means found yet for reconciling all interests.

Manipulated Negro Votes

Throughout the South in recent years there have been pockets where Negroes voted freely or, at the least, extensively. In many cases, the Negro communities have seemed to derive little benefit. No doubt the general climate of the region has been a severely limiting factor: Though he may desire the votes, a mayor may be reluctant to obviously do much for Negro constituents directly when the posture of "the South" is belligerent insofar as Negroes and the federal government are concerned. White tempers that may be gone tomorrow flare today. In North Carolina, an entire city council was swept out in retribution after it had integrated a public swimming pool. Fear of this kind of swift reprisal, fear of the quicksilver nature of racist tempers, has paralyzed many a politician in the South. But often when Negro votes have brought few benefits, the reasons have been more complex.

In Liberty County, Georgia, a sheriff two decades ago began to marshal Negro votes against his opponents. Registration was easy for Negroes. In the mid-sixties 63.4 per cent of the Negro adults in Liberty, a flat-land county on the Georgia coast, were on the voting lists. They had been, intermittently, a majority of the county's registered voters. Yet their benefits from this were limited. The principal result, apparently, was benign police practices on the part of the long-time sheriff and the son who succeeded him. Police brutality and mob violence were not characteristic of Liberty. But a racial report on the county in 1961 noted that, although Negroes had consistently appeared on lists from which juries were drawn, only two were believed to have served on juries in many years. No Negroes were among the jury commissioners. Courtroom and jail facilities were segregated. Three of the sheriff's eight-member staff were Negroes, but part-time and without the authority to arrest whites. They were considered political appointees. The county in general was thoroughly segregated after many years of voting. Liberty's county hiring practices were not better than those of nearby counties where Negroes did not vote. In Liberty, as in a number of Black Belt counties studied in 1961, the U.S. Commission on Civil Rights reported, the situation for Negroes was "one of general deprivation with only relatively minor variations." [13]

The same situation prevailed in a county adjoining Liberty, McIntosh, which also had a sheriff's dynasty. The sheriffs of McIntosh stayed in office partly because of strong Negro support, which they cultivated. McIntosh had a tradition of Negro voting on into the twentieth century; as late as 1917 it still had a Negro representative in the Georgia legislature, the last Negro there until 1962. Negroes, a majority of the population, constituted half the electorate long before the Voting Rights Act of 1965. As they were finishing high school in the county seat of Darien, Negro students of legal age (Georgia law permits voting at eighteen, and registration of seventeen-year-olds who will be of age by the next election) were taken in groups to register. Their principal, a Negro, was a member of the county board of registrars.

The Negroes' support of Sheriff Tom Poppell was a bitter pill for reform elements in McIntosh.[14] This county was widely noted for its bizarre law enforcement practices, operation of tourist traps and toleration of criminal elements. The anti-Poppell forces, repeatedly defeated, maintained that the sheriff bought Negro support in part by a rural Georgia version of a city ward-heeling system: he named numerous Negro special deputies who, his opponents complained, were sometimes given *carte blanche* authority in law enforcement in their areas in exchange for their political support. Welfare rosters in McIntosh were unusually big in relation to population, with Negroes the most numerous beneficiaries. The sheriff's faction maintained a close identification with these benefits. But all of this was within a system of rigid segregation. Negroes held no full-time public offices before 1966, when one was elected to the County Commission, and what they received for their votes principally was toleration of small-time rackets such as illegal bars and the numbers game, relatively benign police treatment in general, and relatively easy dispensation of welfare funds, which largely are paid for by the state and federal governments.

In Florida, a 1964 study by a University of Florida team in several small cities pointed up approaches used in a number of Southern communities. "Hell," a county judge was quoted as saying, "the federals are interested only when you try to keep the colored from voting, and we're voting them to the hilt." In one of the towns, where Negroes were 14 per cent of the total registered vote, the city judge and sheriff, aided by a police chief working under the sheriff, organized Negro voting. Their principal method was to hold barbecues on the judge's ranch before an election. Negroes were taken there in trucks and treated to spreads of free barbecue, fish, beer, and liquor. On election day a crew of hired Negro helpers toured the Negro neighborhoods working up a good turnout. Each had a list of registered Negro voters, with the responsibility of getting them to the polls. Individual voters apparently were not paid for their votes. Designated workers were given some funds for their canvassing.

In another of the Florida towns, the white manipulators had ties with Negro credit groceries that helped them get votes. A white lawyer who was the chief organizer of Negro votes in his town placed local Negro voters in four categories: an old, established group with recognized leadership that simply went along, usually, with the white organizers, seemingly seeing no better choices; transient workers in pulpwood and citrus industries whose relatively few votes could be obtained with the help of their employers and foremen; petty criminals involved in numbers, moonshine, and other rackets; and "working class" Negroes approached through petty racketeers and through the lawyer's firm, which handled many Negro cases.[15]

It may be argued that permissive law enforcement on the numbers or moonshine racket is a positive benefit for a Negro community when normal means of capital accrual are lacking. Money from a racket sometimes has sent a child to college when no others or few others could go. But the only other positive gain for Negroes after a decade of voting in the Florida cities studied was elimination of offensive police practices. Sheriffs were personally friendly rather than hostile; officers did not regularly enter homes without warrants; and police brutalities and abuse were minimal or non-existent. None of these gains, of course, cost the white community anything. Few of the streets in Negro residential areas were paved. Municipal services in general were minimal. There was no integration of schools, restaurants, recreational facilities, or hotels. Negro leadership was not created by voter registration and voter participation; most of the Negro registration was organized by the white politicians who expected to be the beneficiaries. This white manipulation has existed in many places. Often it has been the only reason Negroes were registered. One white faction would lower voting barriers so that it might enlist Negroes on its side, and then its leaders became the chief political leaders of Negroes.

This is application of traditional political-manipulation methods to a community not well prepared to resist or alter those methods and not prepared to require the "higher" forms of reward, which might be received by middle-class whites, such as low property-tax assessments. Poorer whites often have been manipulated with methods similar to those used in the Negro communities. Many an elected sheriff has been maintained in office only because he has allowed a large segment of the white community to traffic in bootleg whisky, or simply to indulge in a sizable amount of "good-ole-boy" carousing that might bring immediate arrest in a city. The established white middle class usually looks upon these activities with disdain, and seldom takes the sheriff into its country club or its Lions Club; but neither does it stop him as long as it is not victimized by his permissiveness with "the boys" (or the jeans-clad ladies-of-the-night). In smaller cities where the manipulated Negro vote is sizable, middle-class Negroes tend to look upon the spectacle with the same disdain as middle-class whites.

There is no evidence that easy manipulation of lower-income Negro voters is more extensive than similar manipulation of lower-income whites in the South. Still, in places where the big manipulative vote is white, as it often has been in the mountainous or cotton-mill parts of the non-urban South, the non-manipulated part of the white community remains. It may garner the regular benefits of local government and the more desirable type of special privileges. Because this part of the white community remains, those whites in the easily manipulated sector can get out of it and can join the other whites in such middle-class benefits. Negroes often have had no such alternatives. The manipulation of their votes tends not only to perpetuate officeholders who are of little real service to them; it also tends to perpetuate their own community disorganization. In becoming subservient politically, they make it more likely that they will remain subservient in other ways. This practice becomes a powerful influence for weakness and disorganization in

Negro communities. It becomes the predominant element in the Negro community's relationship with the whole community and, perhaps most tragic of all, it chokes out the kind of unorthodoxy that Negro communities sometimes have used to move against their own situation.

Increased Negro registration in the South will not put an end to manipulation of Negro voting. In Mississippi, as registration grew in 1965, some Delta planters began to talk about the situation in a new light. The new Negro voters would give their counties more votes in future governor's races, and therefore more influence at the state level. Some planters expressed confidence that plantation employers and foremen could "deliver" these votes. In Alabama, legislators from the Black Belt talked confidently of controlling the new Negro votes in their areas. One of the most arresting Southern political commentaries of 1965 was, surely, the result of a Birmingham *News* interview with legislators from the Belt. The *News* reported: "In the past years, they may have pressured the Negro on their lands not to seek voting status, legislators point out, but they are now advising their employees and tenants to go ahead and register. . . . Negro voting was controlled after Reconstruction and before disfranchisement in 1901, legislators say, and it can be controlled in years to come. . . . A white landlord presumably would have just as much right to appeal to his Negro worker to vote one way as others would have to ask him to vote another way. In such cases, bread and butter probably would have the stronger appeal. According to the way some Black Belters look at it, a large Negro vote could turn out to be a political asset rather than a liability." [16]

The Birmingham *News* story assumes some conditions, one of which is that landowners can strike back at Negro employees who vote freely. This would be a violation of the Voting Rights Act of 1965, and subject to redress by the Department of Justice. But the Justice Department began enforcement of the new act with the same insensitivity to the political dynamics of the South that it has repeatedly displayed. The first voter intimidation suit under the new act was not filed by the Justice Department until four months after the law took effect. Three days later a federal judge temporarily restrained a group of Louisiana landowners from evicting some Negro tenants who had registered to vote. A typical affidavit in this suit was that of a man who said he had lived on one plantation in West Feliciana Parish for sixty-seven years, had been warned of an eviction when he registered, and subsequently had received a letter from the owners telling him to leave, without stated cause. Similar statements were received from a number of Black Belt areas soon after the voting act went into effect. As it often had in the past, the Justice Department in the first intimidation case took the more passive of the approaches open to it. It sought only an order to end interferences with the vote in the locality involved; it did not use the opportunity to obtain an injunction of broader application; and it did not initiate criminal prosecutions, a course which might have discouraged other violations. Continuing action by the Justice Department seems the only means of effectively combating economic intimidation of this kind. In view of the department's past performance, this is a sobering thought.

If Negro voters cannot ultimately be manipulated by economic pressures, what of their seduction by corrupt appeals? There is no reason to think a Negro voter more likely will be "bought" under a free electoral system than under the one that has prevailed. Every evidence is to the contrary. The preacher who can be paid for his support is certainly not gone in the South; but where he still exists he is suspect and, frequently, worth relatively little.

"That the Negro vote is singularly ignorant, venal, and corrupt is a widely held generalization in American politics," Henry Moon of the NAACP wrote in 1948.[17] He was expressing not his findings, of course, but a popular white conception, at a time when many stereotypes remained to be shattered by the forthcoming rights movement. Such generalizations are not so widely held today, just two decades later. We have to remember, too, that they have been held before. In the 1840's one large body of Americans was subject to precisely the same generalizations lately made in the South about Negro voters: that they were inherently inferior, immoral, happy in their poverty, frequently drunk at election time, and inclined thoughtlessly to vote Democratic (when not selling their votes). These were the Irish.[18]

Negro Majorities

Negro majorities already are exerting themselves in some places, and not in the old pattern under white manipulation. Macon County, Alabama, was the first Southern county where Negroes became a voting majority as a result of recent litigation.[19] Among the whites of Tuskegee, a dusty cotton town typical of that part of east-central

Alabama, some relief followed the 1964 elections. White racial extremists had been largely eliminated from office, but Negroes had not sought exclusive control. Bi-racial groups went to work on local problems. In the face of Negro voting power, whites quickly agreed to changes that the Negroes had never been able to win before. The new Tuskegee City Council moved immediately to pave and light streets in Negro neighborhoods. Businesses began to open "white" jobs to Negroes.

Not all was rosy as this went along. "Some whites are glad to see this administration doing what it's doing," C. M. Keever, a white storekeeper who had been elected mayor of Tuskegee, said a year after taking office, "but that's a minority, of course. I have a good number of whites who don't speak to me." [20] It had not been long since Tuskegee whites had drawn the city limits in a way that put virtually all Negroes outside the city, an action later overturned by the U.S. Supreme Court.

A similar spirit was evident in some other counties. But it seemed notably missing in others, at least on the part of the whites. East and West Feliciana parishes in Louisiana provided an example of early white intransigence in the face of prospective Negro election-day majorities, while Jefferson County in Mississippi was an example of a place where rather startled whites began to make some adjustments to the new situation.

In West Feliciana, Negro registration reached a majority soon after passage of the voting act. In East Feliciana, Negroes became almost half the electorate. Both rural parishes, bordering the southernmost counties of Mississippi's Black Belt, had had little Negro voting before and were areas of strong white supremacist sentiment. The suddenness of Negro political power was not accompanied by sudden change of the Felicianas' leading politicians, at least outwardly. "They're just like children," State District Judge John R. Rarick said as the lines at the examiner's office were producing the Negro voting majority. "They get something to show up the white people and they play it awhile and then they get tired of it." He said he planned to ignore the Negro vote. District Attorney Richard Kilbourne indicated he would make no new pitch to attract Negro votes. The judge and the district attorney, whose jurisdictions were composed of both the Feliciana parishes, faced elections in 1966. They were showing no indications of a move to new Negro-white alignments in politics. The comment of Louisiana's House speaker, Vail M. Delony, seemed to epitomize the thinking of many intransigent white officeholders: "I won't stoop to entice the niggers. They either vote for me or they don't." [21] None of this offered much encouragement to representatives of the Congress of Racial Equality working in the area, who were saying they hoped not for all-Negro rule but for a coalition of Negroes and white moderates.

As white politicians in the Feliciana parishes were expressing their disdain for this kind of equitable change in the face of the new registration, and thus making Negro-white cooperation more difficult, some in a similarly situated Mississippi county only fifty miles away were facing an earlier expression of the new Negro power. Jefferson County, one of the old plantation areas that more recently has turned to timber and cattle, had 1,500 registered voters as of November 1964. All were white. Negroes, who were 75 per cent of the population, had not voted in this century. But under a more liberal Mississippi registration law passed in the face of federal legislation, almost 800 Negroes were registered in 1965. Then a federal examiner arrived, and shortly Negro voters were an overwhelming majority. They immediately pressed their advantage with a boycott, demanding hiring downtown, desegregation of public facilities, the use of courtesy titles for Negroes at stores and public offices, appointment of Negro officials, police and other, and removal of separate rest rooms in service stations and other places. Some of these, of course, were not political goals, but they suggested what may be required in the future because of political power. Private hiring policies are not decided in local elections; but local elections decide on officeholders who can have a big say about private hiring when a community-wide practice of discrimination prevails. Negroes in Jefferson had tough leadership, strengthened by the help of Charles Evers, state field director of the NAACP. With their new voting majority, Jefferson Negroes made it clear that in the next elections, they would not re-elect white officials who failed to help them attain the goals of the boycott. In June 1966, six months after it had begun, the boycott was ended with total victory for the Negroes.[22]

In a revealing combination of interviews, Roy Reed of the New York *Times* quoted the seventy-year-old mayor of Fayette, county seat of Jefferson, as saying soon after Negroes had gained the majority: "I've tried to be good to our niggers every way that I know how . . . I don't think that I should have an enemy in the colored race." The mayor, R. J. Allen, was asked about Ferd Allen, president of the local branch of the NAACP. He brightened and said warmly: "He's a very good nigger. In fact, he used to work for my father-in-law." Then he remembered the new state of things and the changed relationships the new electorate dictated, and he added thoughtfully: "But he's turned out to be president of this thing, and they are all behind him, I guess." When the NAACP leader in turn was asked about Mayor Allen, the *Times* reported he replied: "Mr. R. J. Allen? He seems to be a very nice fellow. He never has denied me anything . . . 'Course, he's a Southerner. You know?" [23] In the Black Belt, such personal relationships rooted in the past will not necessarily now be meaningless simply because that past is disappearing. The R. J. Allens and the Ferd Allens of the rural South will sometimes be sitting together and working out community affairs, aided in part by a shared past and a personal regard established under very different conditions.

Although white employers may continue to influence Negro employees, the kind of prolonged white domination suggested by Alabama's Black Belt legislators seems extremely dubious in the light of situations such as the one in Jefferson County, Mississippi. When the legislative delegations arrive in Montgomery in future years, they are more likely to be the most integrated and the most racially liberal delegations that ever sat in the old Confederate capitol building.

Alliances and Third Parties

In the days of Populism, objectives were equalitarian and Negroes found allies principally among the poor whites, mainly outside the cities. In more recent years, the objectives have been libertarian, and Southern Negroes have found allies principally among middle-class whites in the cities. When the issues have been segregation, harassment, or intimidation, or direct repression and denial of other kinds, many middle-class whites in Atlanta, Memphis, Durham, and other Southern cities have found Negro goals tolerable even when these were not their own primary political goals. Alliances of Negroes and middle-class whites thus have been workable, frequently against poorer whites whose primary political motivation was opposition to any gains for Negroes. But the thrust of the rights revolution, nationally, turned in the mid-1960's. A libertarian revolution became, in 1964 and 1965, an equalitarian revolution.[24] To what extent the white professional man and the well-to-do white matron can be allied with Negroes under that aegis remains to be seen.

In the more comfortable all-white wards of Atlanta, many a white man has voted exactly the same ticket as his Negro yardman without being in real agreement with him on the most important issues.[25] Perhaps the white man voted for election of the mayor because he is an honest and efficient businessman, despite his racial liberalism; perhaps the Negro man voted for the mayor because he has been sensitive to the needs of Negroes, or because for the Negro man this year there was no other choice. Such joinings of voters are the rule rather than the exception in this country, the South included. Frequently the ruling coalition of the past was the rural rustic (who had no electric power) and the power company president (who did not find it feasible to extend the lines); the farmer (who had to pay interest when he borrowed every year on his next crop) and the banker (who wanted higher interest rates); the textile worker (who was paid less than the worker of any other industry) and the Klansman of the 1930's (who wanted to keep the "socialistic Northern unions" out). The foregoing is, in fact, an accurate enough description of the Talmadge camp in Georgia over a span of three decades. We should not look, too much, for complete consistency in political alliances.[26]

In a city such as Atlanta, it is difficult to imagine that most Negroes would choose in the foreseeable future to abandon a long-tested alliance with middle-class whites in order to experiment with an untested equalitarian alliance with the poor whites they had always voted against. In fact, this combination seems less likely to develop effectively in most Southern cities than an occasional alliance of middle-class and poorer whites against specific Negro goals. Coalitions of Negroes and poorer whites were being seriously proposed in the South and elsewhere in the mid-1960's. Among the Southern states, only Texas, with its working political organization of Negroes, Latins, liberals, and labor, had such a force formally organized. Equalitarian demands may temporarily heighten the chances for such formal alliances; but equalitarian results, such as increased ascent of Negroes into this country's standard-setting, value-setting, subtly all-powerful middle class, will lessen the lasting chances.

A formal coalition of Negroes and poorer whites is presently unlikely, but election-day alliances of Negroes with poorer whites are not. Another real possibility is the all-Negro political party.

As for the Negro third party, Mississippi was the first to experience such a turn. The Freedom Democratic Party took shape during a proliferation of rights organizations in Mississippi in 1964. Insofar as they had any political thrust, and some seemed to have none, the "freedom schools" which emerged at the same time and under the same auspices were radical. On August 6–8, 1964, delegates from the schools attended a Mississippi Freedom School Convention in Meridian and drew up a 1964 platform. Perhaps it suggests the nature that a program-oriented radical party might have in Mississippi. The platform called upon the federal government to lend funds "to set up industries and whole towns which shall be publicly owned by the communities. . . . textile and paper mills, stores, schools, job relocation programs for those put out of work by automation, job retraining centers, recreational facilities, banks, hospitals." It demanded "preferential treatment for the Negro in the granting of federal aid in education . . . until integration is accomplished," a guaranteed annual income of $3,000 for every citizen, freedom for teachers "to join any political organization to fight for civil rights without fear of being fired," rent control laws requiring that rents be "according to the condition of the house," housing codes that would require that every house contain central heating, "a laundry room and pantry space," "a basement and attic," and numerous other parts.

The Freedom Democratic Party, although its leaders did not think so, had a certain initial success: It did, at the Democratic National Convention of 1964, present a dramatization of the faithlessness of the regular Mississippi Democratic Party insofar as the national party was concerned. It even won seats on the convention floor. Subsequently, in part because the FDP seemed to be offering the only challenge from the left to the established state Democratic forces and it seemed too radical to many, new coagulations of loyalist Mississippi Democrats came into being to challenge the segregationist leadership of the state party. Thus the FDP had some impact in pushing Mississippi Democrats toward being national Democrats. The whole idea of a truly separatist FDP was discouraged by organized labor and white moderates in Mississippi, and nationally by organized liberals such as the leadership of the Americans for Democratic Action. It received its principal encouragement from the radical wing of the civil rights movement. This was very thin support, indeed, in Mississippi. By 1966, its role as an alternative to the established state Democratic leadership having been pre-empted by others less radical, it hardly seemed to exist except on paper.

Third parties, or more accurately, new Negro-dominated parties, may be temporarily the ruling forces in some small Negro-majority areas where Negroes have not been permitted to participate extensively in regular political party channels. Such a local party, the Lowndes County Freedom Movement (called the Black Panther Party because of its symbol) appeared in 1965 in one of the most repressive Black Belt counties of the South. It was principally the creature of the Student Nonviolent Coordinating Committee. It was born after the county's Democratic Party powers continued to exclude Negroes from all party processes. Negroes had gained a voting majority in Lowndes by 1966. To avert the possibility that Negro candidates might win in the Democratic primary, the county Democratic Party leaders renominated the incumbents at a "convention" at which Negroes were excluded. The white leadership also raised entrance fees substantially. The Black Panther Party was a means of entering Negro candidates for the general election, since they could not make their way into the Democratic Party. Initial efforts had little success, however. Black Panther leaders failed in attempts to persuade local Negroes to boycott the regular Democratic primary. Then in the November general election all the Black Panther candidates were defeated by segregationist whites. Many Negroes did not vote; and some voted for the white candidates.

The prospect appears to be that such local third parties may be successful on occasion in the future, but that they would function more as local factions rather than as bedrock for expansive political parties. In most states the rules of elections are determined at the state level. How many signatures will a state require of a third party to get its candidates on the general election ballot? The ruling party at the state level could make it 5,000, or 100,000. These would be formidable obstacles. A greater possibility would be the fleeting use of third-faction candidates simply to damage or to persuade the major-faction candidates. If a state has two major candidates running for attorney general, one a "moderate" who hopes to win with Negro votes but who refuses to show any reasons why he should get them, a Negro third party may deprive him of the office he seeks. But in the final elections (whether these be primaries or general elections), these episodes are likely to be only occasional and aberrational. Our political system is not built upon the desirability of "spoiling" or losing elections.

On the other hand, there will be sacrificial Negro candidacies having a kind of third-party function. Sometimes there has been good political justification for such candidacies. The very possibility of them strengthens the Negro bargaining position. And in areas where Negro registration is very low, the candidacy of a Negro, however hopeless, can serve as a stimulus for increased Negro participation. During the first years of the Voter Education Project, registration workers repeatedly noted the helpfulness of such candidacies. They were not intended primarily to alter the outcome of the election, or to create a separatist force, but to stimulate participation of Negroes. By conventional political standards, the 1964 Congressional candidacy of C. B. King, a Negro lawyer in Albany, Georgia, was foolish. But a registration worker reported in July: "Prior to the May 2 registration closing date, registration was significantly increased in the Georgia second district as a result of Attorney King's announcement that he would run for U.S. Congress. The last week of registration in Albany 235 people were registered [substantially higher than the other weeks]. Most of us feel the increase was caused by C. B. King's announcement." Slater King, who ran for mayor of Albany in 1963, when Negro registration was 4,600 of a 16,646 total, said of his reasons: "I am really interested in freeing the minds of Negroes because many of them feel that no black man should aspire for high offices." He said he also thought his candidacy would help young Negroes feel they are a part of the democratic process. "We've had almost no training politically," he said. "This helps the Negro to think politically. . . . It also makes white politicians, when you can deliver a sizable bloc of votes, a little more cognizant of giving more recognition to the Negro community. . . . The way the city is run you wouldn't think we had any Negroes living here." [27] In North Carolina, Mrs. Sara E. Small, a thirty-eight-year-old Negro housewife, after running unsuccessfully for Congress in a 1965 special election, said that her candidacy was a "starting point for Negroes." She said she was pleased about getting a good Negro vote "because Negroes don't bother too much with politics." She and her managers were aiming not at Congress but at increased Negro interest in politics.[28] Similar effects were obtained from a number of Negro candidacies in Mississippi.

What are the chances for equalitarian alliances that would exist within an established party, or that would move from one party to another? In 1965 Bayard Rustin called for new coalitions of labor, Negroes, and liberals as "potentially the most important development" for the movement? The three primary needs of Negroes, he said, are jobs, better schools, and better housing. All would require government action and thus political influence. Negroes alone would not have that influence, but would have with strong allies. He cited leaders of the religious faiths and labor as the potential allies for these particular goals. "I think the AFL-CIO is as anxious for this alliance as we are, because the fundamental objectives of the labor movement at this moment precisely coincide with the economic needs of the Negro," he said.[29] As he spoke the AFL-CIO was assisting with a new project for registering Negroes in the South under auspices of Dr. King's Southern Christian Leadership Conference. This kind of coalition may very well develop effectively in the South on the state level. It has existed in some elections, but the violence of racist thought among many white union members often made such alliances ineffective.

James Q. Wilson has noted the potential loss in attempting to form such alliances where other, workable alliances already exist for Negroes: "The Negro is already a partner in a set of tacit, though unorganized, coalitions. . . . to break existing alliances, tenuous though they are, in favor of a new alliance which may be impossible of realization may be a costly experiment. This is particularly true in the South; it is to a lesser extent true in the North." [30] It would seem folly at this point for Negroes in Atlanta, for example, to abandon their alliance with white business and financial interests for an attempted alliance with labor. The existing alliance is workable and fruitful; the alternative would be, at best, uncertain of success and effectiveness.

How Much More Liberal?

How much more liberal are Southern Negroes than Southern whites? They are undoubtedly a great deal more liberal insofar as "liberal" in the modern context suggests support for welfare-state positions.[31] In the presidential campaigns of 1952 and 1956, however, Adlai Stevenson certainly had a more liberal posture than Dwight Eisenhower, but the large Atlanta Negro electorate went for Eisenhower in both elections. So did Negroes in many other Southern cities, especially in 1956. By a thin edge, Richard Nixon was the choice of Atlanta Negroes in 1960, when, again, John F. Kennedy's program and party were more "liberal." Nor did low income swing Southern Negroes to the Democratic camp, where they might have been expected to come to rest. Among Negro voters with annual incomes under $1,000, according to a study of urban Negro voting in five South Carolina cities, Eisenhower received almost twice as many votes as Stevenson in 1952 and 1956.[32] Sometimes such Republican voting by Southern Negroes has been explained as merely a continuation of traditional Republicanism that was mainly a rebellion against their states' white supremacist Democrats. But real Republican strength still exists among Southern Negroes in many places, despite the Goldwater wing's purges of Negroes from Republican officialdom in 1964. Not much of it, of course, is "conservative" Republican strength. But sometimes it leads to Negro support of relatively conservative Republicans, and sometimes it results in white conservative Republicans' support of Negro Republicans. In Atlanta, where the Republican leadership was badly divided on the Goldwater campaign, the party afterward continued a steady push into the Negro community for support. Republican candidates locally fared unusually well with Negro voters. The local party's singular success at a time when Negroes had dropped away from the party nationally brought national Negro Republican leaders flying to Atlanta in late 1965 to study some of the reasons. Here was an example of a working alliance growing between a large segment of the Negro community and white Republicans ranging from liberal to arch-conservative. Such alliances are possible where politicians are adroit and Negroes can see meaningful gains. In such circumstances, ratings on a welfare-liberalism scale become less important than party rewards for the Negro faithful, and whether a local candidate goes down the street to shake hands in the shops and manages to get a new street light installed at a Negro neighborhood's school crossing. "My white friends ask me what I say to Negroes when they ask me why they can't eat at the Commerce Club," a white Republican politician in Atlanta said. "I've never been asked a question like that. They want to know when we're going to get a street marked, or a light put in, or some better garbage pickup." [33]

These are the signs warning against suppositions that the new vote is a kind of predictable bloc. Politics continues to be politics, Ike father-images, handshakes, and all. But there will be more liberalization of politics with the increased Negro vote. Negroes in a general way will have more "liberal" views than whites, at least for some time. The voter on the street can be influenced by what is done about the street light, but he also will be interested in more government action in such fields as housing, employment opportunity, and health.

Two Liberal Candidacies

In the elections of 1966, the appearance of two candidates for governor, Richmond Flowers in Alabama and Ellis Arnall in Georgia, had significant implications. Each seemed to be a product of the new era of fuller Negro political participation. In Flowers' case, there also were flickerings of Populism, which had been kept alive in Alabama by Governor James E. Folsom in the 1950's.[34] In Arnall's case, there was a clear coloration of economic liberalism and friendliness toward organized labor. More important, each man announced for governor knowing that he had no chance of election without solid Negro support. Probably neither would have entered except for confidence that he would have that support.

Flowers' campaigning was the more remarkable. As attorney general of Alabama, he had staked off a position of militancy against Governor George Wallace and the governor's white supremacist radicalism. Flowers succeeded in moving the Alabama Democratic Executive Committee to strike from its official seal the words "White Supremacy, For the Right"; he intervened to press prosecutions in racial murders; he took an unqualified and open position in favor of advancing Negro rights. In the Democratic primary, his campaign strategy was based on giving highest priority to solidifying support among Negroes, with the idea that a Negro bloc, even with little white help, would be sufficient to make the attorney general one of the two leaders in a large and divergent field of candidates. Thus he would be in a runoff, presumably against Governor Wallace's wife, Lurleen, whom the governor had entered because he could not succeed himself. Then, the reasoning went, with solid Negro support again, Flowers could win with as little as 38 per cent of the white vote. The whole strategy rested upon winning the governorship despite an overwhelming white vote against Flowers.

This was a new kind of arithmetic in Alabama politics [35] and it produced the kind of campaign the Deep South had not seen before. Flowers, a tall, red-headed man who spoke with a rural flavor, traveled the back sides of towns all over the state, speaking in Negro churches and making handshaking tours of Negro areas no state-level politician had ever visited. He promised full Negro participation in state government, and he spoke about helping with the economic needs of Alabama's poorest people. He was defeated overwhelmingly. He did carry a substantial part of Alabama's Black Belt because of the Negro votes, but the segregationist appeal and powerful political forces of Governor Wallace surprised almost everyone by winning a majority in the first primary, thus obviating a runoff.

In Georgia a few weeks later, the candidacy of Ellis Arnall suddenly came alive when the man who had seemed the strong favorite for governor, former Governor Ernest Vandiver, dropped from contention because of his health. Arnall had been governor from 1943 through 1946. His administration had been decidedly liberal by Southern standards, and he looked to Georgia's Negro registration of some 280,000 to help put him in again. Most of the state's Negro political leadership joined his forces, as did the AFL-CIO leadership. Arnall was seeking political vindication after two decades out of politics, during which he frequently had been a chief whipping boy for white supremacist politicians. He confided to friends that he hoped "to make it popular again to be liberal in Georgia." His campaign was decidedly different from Flowers'. Arnall assumed he had virtually all Negroes' approval. He worked privately to solidify their support, but he did no campaigning in Negro communities. Nor did he publicly call himself a liberal. Despite all this caution about his political identification, his race, too, was a disaster. In the first Democratic primary he won 29.4 per cent of the votes in a field of six candidates. In the runoff two weeks later, he was overwhelmed by an ultra-segregationist and quixotic rightist, Lester Maddox, a man who had been unsuccessful in three previous political races, and who was running this time with a promise to emulate Governor Wallace. Maddox two years earlier had defied the Civil Rights Act of 1964, refusing to desegregate a restaurant he owned. Having armed friends with ax handles, he had waved a pistol and chased away Negroes who sought to enter his establishment. Obviously the nomination of such a man, against anyone, reflected the force of an enormous white supremacist sentiment remaining in Georgia. Arnall's total vote was about 45 per cent, a proportion attained only by almost total support from Negro voters. In the general election, write-ins for Arnall prevented either Maddox or his conservative, segregationist Republican opponent, Howard H. Callaway, from receiving the required majority. The Georgia Legislature, acting under a state constitutional provision dating from 1820, then elected Maddox governor.

The Alabama outcome undoubtedly discouraged future campaigning of the kind done by Flowers, and the Georgia outcome was a heavy blow against racial moderation. But neither outcome said any final word about how valid were the bases of the candidacies involved. In 1966, white racism—"the white backlash"—was running strong in many parts of the country, having been stirred by Negro rioting in some of the larger cities, Negro advances under the civil rights acts, and new Negro thrusts in the field of housing. In the Deep South, white resentment against the Washington administration seemed to be at fever pitch, benefiting reactionary and racist forces. All of this was a powerful aberration of the kind felt in the 1964 presidential race in the South, and in the wake of the 1954 schools decision. Its future extent was uncertain.

Political Money and Political Distribution

We cannot measure the impact of Negro votes without considering two factors that often influence and divert the force of votes: campaign financing and special-interest lobbying. Will these two factors halt, cushion, or turn Negro political power?

Conventional politics is a business of perpetual adjustment, of reconciling interests and distributing advantage and services. But equal advantage cannot come without equal, or equitable, power. The white politicians' idea of what would satisfy demands for equal schools was not really equal schools; it was merely what would look like equal schools to the white politicians (and maybe the courts). Across the South one may see, repeatedly, that the most imposing school building in a county is a new Negro school; and in many places one may hear local white people say pointedly, Look, the only school in the county with air-conditioning is the new Negro school. Not just political cynicism but genuine good faith by local whites often produced these results. Yet the slightest examination would show that the schools could not conceivably be called equal. Negroes had little to do with the "equalizing," and so the project was reduced to what the white man might think was equal, what looked equal to him, or equal enough. Fair political distribution cannot be attained without fair political power.

In the past, a rural legislature might inaugurate a new kind of "farm-to-market" road system specifically intended to benefit the residents and voters of rural areas. This was a distribution of goods and services in response to voting power. Never in Southern legislatures has there been a similar plan to benefit residents of city areas by good streets. Now there may be: legislators who concentrated as late as 1960 on establishing an authority to issue bonds and spend $100 million on farm-to-market roads may concentrate in 1970 on creating an authority to spend $100 million on residential street construction in cities. Unskilled people now are sometimes trained by Southern states to meet the needs of a specific industry that is moving in; that is a program intended to please industrialists. What if the system were geared more to please and benefit the presently unskilled? What if, after assessment of their particular qualities, they were offered the kind of training that seemed most likely to suit them? That is only a change of emphasis, but it is a big change. Training would become a service primarily to individuals rather than primarily for industry. Nor will such new distribution by politics always be offensive to campaign financiers, for these forces are not generally concerned with big directions as much as with smaller applications. If a road is to be built, the cement industry's concern is not over where the road will go but over whether it will be made of concrete or asphalt. And this suggests the central fact about political money and lobbying on the state level: money for state and local political campaigns, unlike much of the money given for national political campaigns, is seldom related to a state's general direction.

Business frequently gives heavily for a presidential campaign with the idea that its candidate will be "better for business." Unions do the same with the idea that their candidate will be "better for the working man." But seldom is such reasoning applied to a gubernatorial candidate or a candidate for the legislature. The kind of business that gives heavily to a gubernatorial candidate, most often, is not one contemplating the general welfare of "business" but one contemplating state contracts, or one desiring advantage at the hands of a specific state regulatory agency, or one desiring a change in banking laws. Union money in such races is usually directed toward a candidate who will move on a few very specific issues by which labor bureaucracy may measure its victories or losses: the repeal of a "right-to-work" law, or an increase in unemployment compensation. These have little more than peripheral bearing upon the general welfare of working men, and so labor political money usually has no more to do with the general welfare of working men than business political money has to do with the general welfare of businessmen.

Money for state and local campaign financing almost always has been divorced from any direct relationship with racial or even general social and ideological considerations. A utility wants higher rates from the state utilities commission. A trucking firm wants permission to lengthen trucks. Insurance companies want a higher rate structure. A railroad wants limited taxation of its rights-of-way. A bank wants a law permitting it to establish branches in other cities without local capitalization.

A concrete maker wants fewer asphalt roads and more concrete roads. A telephone company wants someone else to bear the costs when it must relocate lines because of urban renewal. An oil company wants to block an increase in gasoline taxes. A soft-drink concern wants the sales tax to start at 15 cents, not 10. These are, for the most part, the "great issues" of state legislatures and city councils. None has any direct relationship to race and problems created by the American racial situation. There is no indication that black politicians will smoke fewer cigars, take fewer questionable legal retainers, reject fewer retainers, or wrestle with more or less conscience than have white politicians on all these special-interest questions. So it seems unlikely that an infusion of Negro participation of itself will alter the answers to many such questions. There is no reason to believe the special interests involved will have any great interest in whether the representation is white or Negro, or any great interest in what questions it raises on other matters or what answers it gives.

On the other hand, a governor answerable to an electorate of a new complexion will have some new freedom. He may be bound by one set of his campaign contributors to avoid a sales tax on new industrial machinery and by another to increase unemployment compensation payments. But in the future that surely lies close beyond the Wallaces, Barnetts and Maddoxes he is not likely to be bound, ideologically, to "keep the Negroes from taking over" or to "get the state government out of private business." Because of the kinds of money that influence politics on the state level, he may be a captive on numerous smaller specifics but probably free on broad directions. The road contractors or their equivalent will still be around to give him money.

The Role of Business

In recent years, there has been only one instance in which business as such has consciously redirected Southern governments in broad fashion. The role of business throughout the racial revolution has been one to baffle ideologues. More often than not it has been business which, in the throes of local turmoil or in fear of it, has led the way within the white community for orderly change.[36] This has been begrudging response more frequently than committed initiative. When merchants and industry leaders, concerned about some local action of the picketing-boycotting-marching kind, are moved to sit down with Negro leaders, it may be that they do so only because a mayor with an eye fixed on Negro votes has urged them to. Usually in the South, however, the business-men have not been slower to change than the mayors. Especially as the drama has proceeded with a kind of controlled chaos in the Birming-hams, Albanys, and St. Augustines, a clear message has gone out. Brunswick, Georgia, peacefully desegregated its downtown in 1962 and 1963; its eye had been on a city of similar size not far away, Albany, which had suffered economically from racial demonstrations. Demon-strations often have turned on the spotlight; and in the spotlight and with the stimulus, Negroes have gone to register, white community leaders have reckoned with the fact that "whether we like it or not it's here," and cities have risen to make it over the first hurdle without disaster. Sluggish, fearful, self-conscious, business almost always could have moved much faster; but within the white community it frequently has been the principal reason for any move at all in time to avert chaos. Pinched first, it usually has understood before other segments of the white community that the change must be made, now, this afternoon, or the price will be high. In Georgia, a human-relations council leader, looking back from 1965, concluded that such problems as police harass-ment and brutality were reduced more often because of the spotlight that demonstrations produced than because of added voting strength. Business had reacted to that spotlight. Georgia had five bi-racial com-mittees by 1965, all but one originally the result of a need to negotiate with demonstrators.[37]

Political writers in Southern states in 1965 had a common refrain in their appraisals of the impact of Negro voting: politicians had changed because of a general belief in their states that hard-nosed resistance to desegregation is bad for business. In South Carolina in 1963, business-men talked about the urgency of avoiding a "Mississippi image." The Mississippi resistance at Oxford the previous year had sent a tremor through South Carolina on the eve of its own university's integration. Businessmen interested in industrial development feared the impact of such events upon South Carolina; and in general, some pride grew that South Carolina had not been the scene of swinging billy clubs, tear gas, snapping police dogs, and roving bands of take-charge white hoodlums. This negative kind of pride became a text for orderly change, but the main reason for the change at times seemed to be simply a business-men's consensus that resistance would be costly. That altered political dialogue. The same was happening in North Carolina. A political writer there told of one ramification for politicians because of businessmen's attitudes: "Those who yell 'nigger' defiantly most likely will find themselves calling for money desperately." [38] So in considering the role of political money and lobbying in Southern politics of the future, it is worth noting that only in this one way has business broadly and systematically helped redirect state governments in the South in the recent past, and redirection in a way was simply a neutralizing of passions. Business' devotion to order has been a subtle and amorphous factor, always, in the Southern political situation. Not the status quo, really, but order has been business' political credo. The Bourbons who regained control of the South after Reconstruction had order and peace to offer; with everything under control again, there would be fewer uncertainties and disrupting changes. In the long years of political white supremacy, the demagogues at least did not disturb the local business climate, and so business leadership as such was not a force for removal of demagoguery. But more recently, order has required change rather than preservation of the status quo. Peaceful orderliness in the South no longer was possible, as it had been for decades, without change; and so change was given business priority.

The Two-Party System

The two-party system may be Negroes' greatest ally in their thrust into Southern politics. The leaders of the old Bourbon class knew of this when they solidified one-party control at the same time they were disfranchising Negroes. Let the whites be divided, a delegate to the Virginia disfranchisement convention of 1901–1902 said, and "you will have the white men of your state bidding for the Negro vote against each other." [39] This was a common theme of white politicians everywhere in the South at that time.

The principal escape for Negroes under the one-party South was the non-partisan primary, adopted by many cities. It enabled Negroes to vote meaningfully in the years when Democratic primaries made their votes useless in state elections. In Atlanta, a non-partisan primary was installed under Mayor William B. Hartsfield. Most Negroes in Atlanta were Republicans, and this election system enabled the Democratic mayor to profit from their votes (and from the votes of white Republicans, business executives, principally, who supported the mayor). The non-partisan primaries were the most important vehicles for political gains by Southern Negroes in the 1920's and 1930's. A number of aspects of city government, in particular, gave Negroes advantages. Among these were the frequency of municipal elections in many cities and concern with referenda on tax and bond matters, in which no white supremacy issue could negate Negro votes. In 1921 Negroes successfully used their political muscle for the first time in Atlanta. A bond issue which Negroes voted against was killed twice. Negroes were not satisfied with its provisions for Negro schools. The purpose of the issue was redrawn to their satisfaction and the bonds were approved in a new referendum.

Bidding for Negro votes (as well as for white votes) is likely even between factions within a one-party system when the franchise is free. But in a matured two-party system each party has an entire slate of candidates; a program of sorts; and usually a more continuing commitment to certain ends than is the case in personality-centered factionalism. Thus Negro political leadership may demand not just favors of one candidate but benefits of the party and then its entire ticket. It can seek "ticket balancing" with Negroes. And if a Democratic ticket for statewide offices should include a Negro Democrat running for a secondary state office, thus tending to pull most Negro votes to that ticket, the Republican Party is likely to respond in kind in order at least to neutralize the pull of the Negro Democrat. In a true two-party system, this very situation is a likelihood rather than a possibility. For if both parties take this course, neither can generally suffer the wrath of anti-Negro white voters. It may be that negative racial considerations on statewide Negro candidacies will not be neutralized until this happens. Barring some fluke of circumstance, the South's first elected Negro state attorney general or lieutenant governor since Reconstruction will be the creature of the two-party system.

We have seen a form of this ticket-balancing already in the big cities of the South. In Atlanta, a Negro real estate operator, Q. V. Williamson, won election to the Board of Aldermen in a 1965 city-wide election, in part because he was on an informal, unpublicized, and non-party "mayor's slate" loosely supported by the incumbent mayor; and in part because he was a Republican. Both factors are suggestive of the future. By being on a "ticket," he was satisfying a general demand by Atlanta Negroes that the city-at-large election system be made to accommodate them. To win their support, a "ticket," no matter how informal, had to begin including Negro candidates. As for party identification, it had no direct significance in a non-party city primary. But by virtue of being even an unlabeled Republican, Williamson received heavy support from white members of his party. His campaign was financed in large part by the usual big contributors of the party, who included right-wing conservatives. Moreover, he was the beneficiary of aid from numerous white Republican volunteers. In a sense, then, he was on this "ticket," too. And although he would not have won the city-at-large election without his heavy Negro support, he did take a substantial portion of the white votes, especially in the area of the city where Republicans have their greatest strength. In a legislative election the same year in Atlanta, the Republicans "balanced" a three-man ticket in county-at-large elections of legislators with a Negro clergyman. He ran against a white Democrat and, although he lost (the white Democrat received half the Negro votes) he pulled—an especially noteworthy fact—a sizable number of Negro votes to the Republican ticket in the year that Barry Goldwater headed that ticket. These conventional appeals to voters by having representative tickets will have for some time the dual effect of extending Negro officeholding beyond what it might be without party tickets, and of limiting Negro officeholding to a "representative" level.

Party lines give Negro voting a more general kind of impact. In Virginia, in 1965, the Byrd organization's candidate for governor, Mills Godwin, won by a margin approximating the Negro vote for him. Taken from him and given to his Republican opponent, Linwood Holton, these votes would have certainly changed the outcome. A year earlier anyone might have supposed that a moderate Virginia Republican such as Mr. Holton could count on this vote. Lieutenant Governor Godwin had been one of the mainstays of Senator Byrd's "massive resistance" against desegregation in the 1950's. The Byrd organization in general had always been either outwardly negative or at best cool to Negro and labor votes. Mr. Holton, by contrast, had sought Negro support for the Republicans. But in 1965 the changing Byrd machine, which already had deserted its patriarch by endorsing Lyndon Johnson for president despite Senator Byrd's noncommittal stance, suddenly competed for Negro and labor votes. The Negro political leadership, then, at last had a choice. Most decided to go with the old machine because of this consideration: it probably would win, and if they could elect a "converted" Byrd man, he would be in a much better position than a lonely Republican to control the state apparatus, and thus in a better position to satisfy Negroes' political needs.

Godwin was promising expanded state services and state jobs for Negroes. He had undergone, one liberal Democratic supporter declared, "a transformation as dramatic as Saul on the road to Damascus." [40] But probably the Negro political calculators were persuaded more by the Byrd organization's power to deliver than by wondrous transformations. Godwin apparently won 50,000 of about 70,000 Negro votes cast; the old Democratic organization had bent sharply in order to survive the increasing onslaught of Republicanism. Here was a Negro political decision, or collection of decisions, that turned upon the existence of party organization and substantial expectations from it. Such is the kind of consideration a two-party system introduces. Neither party is likely to fail to court Negro Virginians, along with white Virginians, hereafter.

Struggle over the Framework

How will counties be grouped to make up a state senatorial district or a state judicial district? The answer often will determine whether Negroes can decide who is to be the senator or the judge. How will county commissioners or county supervisors be elected—on a county-at-large basis, or by districts within the counties? The answer may tell whether two Negroes will sit on a given five-member board, or none. How, in fact, will a county be governed—by a board making policy, or by a professional county manager? That is a question that heavy Negro political participation may bring to the fore in some counties. Will a county be governed by a five-member board, or by a one-member "board"? By three commissioners or five? In Atlanta, some Negro leaders in 1965 called for an increase of the county board from three to five members, primarily as a means of seeking at least one seat for a Negro. Will a city elect its aldermen by ward or by a city-at-large vote? With the latter system a city with 40 per cent Negro population may have an all-white board of aldermen, but it would not with a ward system of electing, because of segregated housing. Will the chief law enforcement officer be appointed by an elected board, as are most police chiefs, or elected in his own right, as are most sheriffs? That question may arise sharply after Negro communities gain representation on city and county governing boards.

The answers to these and similar questions will partly determine the degree of Negro influence through Negro votes. Some of the answers will come by local decisions, some will come from the courts, and some will be made at the state level because the state may require consistency from one county to another in such matters as how county commissioners are chosen or how law enforcement officers are selected.

These matters may give the South a constant shifting and rearrangement of power on local and state levels in the next few years. They may create such a drumbeat of immediate issues that soon no one may ignore the meaning of Negro votes, for Negro votes and white votes will be at the center of these issues over how votes are to be applied. Although the old "nigger-nigger" campaigns of overt racism seem to be about over, there will be some whispered "Negro-Negro" campaigns and whispered "watch Whitey" campaigns because of these manipulations of the local governmental system.

Hardly any of this kind of struggle had begun by the outset of 1967. In Mississippi, there had been some attention to the means of electing county supervisors [commissioners] and some strained congressional-district gerrymandering because of the growing Negro vote; but in most of the South these issues were still latent. For anyone familiar with the white South's artful and almost instinctive manipulation of legal structure, public policy, and public morality for a century, to keep Negroes from getting a political foothold, there could be little hope that these struggles would not take place.

Direct action, which so often has been Negroes' only means of breaking out of systems set against them, may yet be required in places throughout the South, and the federal courts may continue to be busy with new constitutional issues, many of them now related to manipulations of local political structures for the specific purpose of reducing Negro influence.

"Negro Candidates" and "White Candidates"

When all is said about the changing issues of the Southern Negro's coming into politics, the full truth of it is still not told. He will be coming into the value-determining places as well as the council places; into the white man's presence, at eye level, as well as into the polling places. He will change something because of his own unique experience and unique familiarities, and of course, his own unique values and unique warps. But he will change more than just what his own votes will require, for his presence alone ultimately calls for a choice. To some extent, he faces that choice, too. Encrusted by our past, we have been looking through racial prisms and, contemplatively, measuring and projecting this degree and that degree of white-black; this and that likely throwback to a racist past; this set of political circumstances (founded in racial considerations) and that set (founded in racial considerations). We cannot do otherwise, and it is not spurious contemplation, for the world does not abruptly change and the racial prisms are not gone. For a long time some white men will be elected to office for no reason but their race, and some black men for no other reason. Tickets will be "balanced" for no reason but race, and many votes will be cast or not cast for no reason but race. There will be "Negro candidates" and "white candidates," "Negro majorities" and "white majorities." We cannot escape it. The past will be past, but the present will still reflect it. It leaves its mark not only upon a region and a nation, but also upon our eyes and our thought processes. The strange snarls of mind and emotion through which we view people will be no less strange because we now perpetually see black-and-white instead of black here and white there, or because we have replaced artificial barriers of segregation law with artificial ties of the mind, still seeing races always, and men only sometimes. "Integration" of politics, like "integration" of everything else, only makes the unraveling of the snarls begin to be possible, and barely starts the process. The new sharing of power only removes an old negative. We can move on at this point with only a different degree of ensnarlment than that which possessed and obsessed other Americans in the past, moving some good men to double-think on the Senate floor and other good men of more humble circumstance to commit symbolic murder of their neighbors by denying them mere acceptance of their humanity. What happens after this?

Perhaps what will come first in this new political and social world of the South is a kind of integration in the public sector, the kind discussed here in terms of officeholding, candidacies, and public debates. Then perhaps there will be such an incessant survival of the old snarl that we will truly sicken of it. For the white Southerner, there this other fellow will be, not behind but before him, every day, at eye level, with no possibility at all that he will go away. The only escape will be to get rid of the snarl.

The Negro's political arrival also will bring a better look at all the things which Negroes in the South know best: exclusion, prejudice, slums, rural poverty, and in general the extent of society's unfinished business in a time when a great many people are self-satisfied, comfortable, and conformist. At such a point, surely any kind of new force will have value just in being less comfortable and less digestible, less immediately reducible to organized conformity. Here, again, the new presence of the Negro brings confrontation of what we are and where we are.

Will the rights movement now provide the genius for truly innovative political change, to overcome the remaining resistance and hasten the new day? At this point, one may not be certain; it may be too early. The Negro politicians in the machines of Chicago and New York came of age and accepted a pattern before the existence of those latter-day creative forces in the civil rights movement which moved mountains, and the new Negro legislators of Georgia, Tennessee, and Texas have only begun to serve. By 1967 there were strong new evidences, in the slum response to Martin Luther King, Jr., in Chicago, for example, that Negro electorates in the North no longer were tolerant of the conventional participation of their politicians in the conventional political acts, with the conventional rewards. Increasingly there was realization of the limitations of these accepted political ways.

What will happen now with those (and their successors) whose genius produced the powerful Christian non-violent resistance born at Montgomery; the audacious use of unwelcome presences that began with the first student sit-ins in 1960; the rough-edged creative confrontation of Birmingham in 1963; the cohesive in-gathering of the nation for a rededication to its ideals, through a Washington March; and the personal awakenings of forgotten men and women in the Black Belt? The movement in 1967 faced the necessity of finding new genius in political action; it would have to be a genius and an impetus immersed in, though not necessarily encased by, traditional political factors. The old and the new had been mixed, in the movement, all along. While thousands marched and thousands went to jail, others also moved on as before with older styles, making headway and even breakthroughs, often abetted by what was going on far away in Birmingham or Albany. Never, in the movement, have the older means and outlooks been really divorced from the newer ones. So it will be in politics.

NOTES

1. In an extensive team study of 1,000 counties, Professors Donald R. Matthews and James W. Prothro of the University of North Carolina have examined many

aspects of Negro registration and voting in the South. They have offered their find-ings with caution, stressing that correlations do not necessarily mean causes. They concluded that there is relatively strong correlation between Negro voter registration in Southern communities and the percentage of middle-class Negroes who reside there, the median number of school years completed, and the median income. "Small increases in the size of the Negro middle class are associated with large increases in Negro voter registration, and these higher rates cannot be attributed simply to the registration of white-collar workers themselves," they have written. Each percentage point of increase in the Negro middle class was accompanied by a 3 or 4 per cent increase in voter registration (up to 42 per cent registration of eligible Negroes). See *Change in the Contemporary South* (Durham: Duke Uni-versity Press, 1963), Allan P. Sindler, editor; chapter by Matthews and Prothro, "Negro Voter Registration in the South."

2. One of the announced goals of civil rights organizations in the South after passage of the Voting Rights Act of 1965 was to bring registration to at least 70 per cent of the age-eligible Negroes. That figure seemed unrealistic to some. It was, for instance, almost exactly the percentage of age-eligible Georgia whites on the registration rolls in 1964; they, of course, had not faced the deterrents of Negroes. But on the other hand the Negro registration already was 69.4 per cent of the adults in Tennessee, 63.7 per cent in Florida, and 57.7 per cent in Texas. These three were not, of course, states where the plantation system had prevailed. That does make a difference. When the Civil Rights Commission in 1961 analyzed four heavily Negro counties where there was high or relatively high Negro registration, it found that in three of them cotton was not the main crop, farm ownership was more prevalent among Negroes than elsewhere, and agriculture was not the dominant source of income. Sharecropping and tenant-farming were comparatively limited. Negroes obviously had greater independence. The four counties examined, all of which had Negro population majorities, were: Liberty County, Georgia, 87.6 per cent of voting-age Negroes registered; St. James Parish, Louisiana, 58.4 per cent registered; Hancock County, Georgia, 42.4 per cent registered; and Charles City, Virginia, 36.6 per cent registered. See *1961 U.S. Commission on Civil Rights Re-port*, Book 1, "Voting," p. 145.

3. See "Negro Voting in Atlanta 1953–1961" by Jack Walker, *Phylon*, winter 1963, p. 380.

4. Robert Coles, interview with the authors.

5. Confronted by ballots that include numerous races, Negro Southerners sometimes have voted in fewer contests than did whites in the same elections. This, too, is related to a difference in attitude about the validity or importance of voting as such. For a discussion of this point, see H. D. Price, *The Negro in Southern Politics* (New York: New York University Press, 1957), p. 77.

6. James Q. Wilson, "The Negro in Politics," *Daedalus*, fall 1965, p. 970.

7. Quoted by Harry J. Walker, "Changes in Race Accommodations in a Southern Community" (unpublished Ph.D. dissertation, University of Chicago, 1945), pp. 197–198.

8. Randolph T. Blackwell, then of the Southern Christian Leadership Conference, interview with the authors. Albany was such a place. The marches there in 1962 and 1963 were accompanied by and followed by substantial increases in voter regis-tration. The arousal of a community through mass meetings and confrontation marches can be the beginning of registration breakthroughs.

9. The Virginia and Alabama delegates are quoted in Lewinson, p. 84 and p. 261n. The frequent candor of the Charleston *News and Courier* over the years

has been a refreshing departure from the hypocrisy in some other quarters. There is, of course, sincere and unbigoted concern by many people about voting by illiterates. But for some newspapers, the argument for voter literacy has been a transparent cover for long-standing opposition to Negro voting. The *News and Courier*, forgoing such sophistry, commented on June 24, 1936, that "the 'negro question' in South Carolina and in most of the Southern states is a question of numbers." It added: "About three-fourths, which is to say 300,000, of the Negro adults in this state are defined by the census as literate. Hence, with an undiscriminating enforcement of the state's suffrage qualifications about that number of them could register for a general election." That, obviously, would not do; other means must be used besides literacy tests. The *News and Courier* explained on August 26, 1937, that it opposed equal treatment for Negroes as voters because it favored aristocratic government. ". . . The *News and Courier* is not a democrat," it said. "It fears and hates democratic government." In November of 1965, as Negroes were being registered on a large scale in South Carolina, the *News and Courier* was still saying in one editorial after another that it opposed the entire principle of "one-man-one-vote." It favored a republic and not a democracy, it said enigmatically. Democracy it defined as mob rule.

White illiterates often have received whatever help they needed to register. In Issaquena County in Mississippi's Delta, for instance, a registrar accepted absurd answers to questions on "constitutional interpretation" when they came from whites. He also accepted answers from successive whites that were identical, indicating collusion. The registrar reserved for Negroes a very complex section of the Mississippi Constitution dealing with corporate taxing power. In Plaquemines Parish, Louisiana, according to testimony in a 1962 Justice Department suit against voter discrimination, the local political boss, Leander Perez, Sr., told the registrar to administer the literacy test by offering applicants a selection of one card from twenty-five. She also was given twenty-five answer cards. She testified that she did not think it was unusual when white applicants turned in their test cards with answers almost identical to those on her answer cards. A government handwriting expert testified, on another aspect of voter registration in Plaquemines, that registration officials had sometimes filled out the forms for whites. Negroes were rejected for minor errors.

10. During the first wave of voter registration in Mississippi under the Voting Rights Act of 1965, an outspoken moderate, J. Oliver Emmerich, editor of the McComb *Enterprise-Journal*, proposed a state-sponsored voter education program. In a front-page editorial, he noted that Negro Mississippians would and should be participating on a broad scale in public affairs and said it would be for the welfare of all if the state would begin a massive program of citizenship classes for adults. See the Atlanta *Journal-Constitution*, December 18, 1965.

11. Father Theodore M. Hesburgh, a member of the Civil Rights Commission, said in 1965: "I am aware that some are concerned that in acting upon our strong conviction that literacy tests must be removed as a discriminatory impediment to voting, we may somehow impair the foundations of good government based upon an informed electorate. While I can appreciate this concern, I do not think that this legislation [to remove literacy tests] will produce such a result. In an era when citizens can and do inform themselves by means of television and radio, literacy no longer seems an important qualification for voting. . . . During the Mississippi hearing, we heard scores of witnesses who had little formal education and who did not meet all of the traditional standards of literacy. Nonetheless, these were people who by their interest and awareness were eminently qualified to participate in re-

sponsible democratic government. Their concerns for good citizenship and good government have been sharpened by years of deprivation and denial. When they are permitted to register and vote, democracy will be stronger for their contributions." *Voting in Mississippi, A Report of the U.S. Commission on Civil Rights*, 1965, p. 63.

12. See Berelson et al., *Voting, A Study of Opinion Formation in a Presidential Campaign* (Chicago: University of Chicago Press, 1954), and "Voting Behaviour," by Berelson (*Encyclopaedia Britannica*, 1961).

13. The commission found a different situation in one Black Belt county. In Charles City County, Virginia, where Negroes were 83.3 per cent of the population, the commission estimated that 36.6 per cent of the adult Negroes were registered. Two Negroes had served as county commissioners, and the Negroes also had been registrar, election judges and clerks. Four sat on the twelve-member county Democratic committee.

14. A similar situation was noted in another south Georgia county, with indications of blatant illegality. Registration workers reported that Negro farm workers sometimes were hauled into the county seat on election day to vote for the town's incumbent political powers and against reform elements.

15. "The Manipulated Negro Vote: Some Pre-Conditions and Consequences," Alfred B. Clubok, John M. De Grove, and Charles D. Farris, *Journal of Politics*, February 1964, pp. 112–129.

16. The Birmingham *News*, September 15, 1965.

17. Moon, p. 39.

18. Noted by James W. Silver, in his speech accepting the Sidney Hillman Award at the annual luncheon of the Sidney Hillman Foundation in New York, April 28, 1965.

19. Negroes of Macon County attained their voting majority before the Civil Rights Act of 1965, after conclusion of a sweeping voter discrimination suit.

20. James K. Batten, Chicago Daily News Service, in the Atlanta *Journal*, September 18, 1965.

21. All three politicians were quoted by Jules Witcover, "Who's Afraid of Those New Negro Voters," *The New Republic*, October 20, 1965, p. 10.

22. See the New York *Times*, December 23, 1965, and June 10, 1966, and the Jackson *Clarion-Ledger*, June 9, 1966.

23. The New York *Times*, December 23, 1965.

24. For discussion of this point, see James Q. Wilson, "The Negro in Politics," *Daedalus*, fall 1965, pp. 949–973.

25. Atlanta has had several kinds of "bloc votes." A typical example of its political past may be taken from the mayoralty race of 1961. Ivan Allen, Jr., a businessman whose racial outlook was moderate and moving to liberal, received 99 per cent of the Negro votes in some precincts in a runoff against Lester Maddox, a hard-line segregationist. There were white "blocs" also. In white precincts of Atlanta's middle-to-upper-income Northside, Mr. Allen received majorities as high as 89 per cent. In white precincts of less-prosperous Southside, Mr. Maddox' vote ran as high as 74 per cent.

26. For that matter, we should not look for them in individuals. "Rich suburbanites will favor free medical care for the indigent if the issue is stated in terms of building a new county hospital and voted on locally but not if the issue is called 'socialized medicine' and is voted on in Washington." Wilson, *Daedalus*, p. 960. See also Wilson and Edward C. Banfield, "Public Regardingness as a Value Premise in Voting," *American Political Science Review*, December 1964, pp. 876–887.

27. Associated Press report in the *Arkansas Gazette*, December 20, 1965.

28. Associated Press report in the New York *Times*, December 20, 1965.

29. Bayard Rustin, interview with the authors.

30. Wilson, *Daedalus*, p. 950. Professor Wilson has cited Detroit as a rare example of organized coalition of labor and Negroes. The United Auto Workers and the United Steel Workers, through their integrated locals, have supported balanced tickets of Negro and white politicians. The alliance has led to no extensive social welfare program, but it has strengthened both Negro and labor representation and influence.

31. See Matthews and Prothro, "Southern Images of Political Parties: An Analysis of White and Negro Attitudes," *Journal of Politics*, February 1964, pp. 82–89.

32. The sample for this study included 530 urban Negroes of voting age in five South Carolina cities. They were interviewed by Negro teachers in 1958. See John H. Gauntlett and John B. McConaughy, "Some Observations on the Income Factor on Urban Negro Voting in South Carolina," *The Journal of Negro Education*, winter 1962, pp. 78–82.

33. Jack Sells, interview with the authors.

34. "The accident of color can make no difference in the interests of farmers, croppers, and laborers . . ." Tom Watson of Georgia, Populist leader, had said. "You are kept apart so that you can be separately fleeced of your earnings."

35. The new arithmetic may have another, immeasurable effect. J. Oliver Emmerich, McComb, Mississippi, editor, has noted: "For 100 years many responsible people have shunned politics in Mississippi because race has been the dominant issue. Emotion reduced the most intelligent man to the level of the most unintelligent, so there was no premium on being an intelligent man in politics." He said talk of irresponsible government had arisen among Mississippi whites because of registration of Negroes with little education. "We have *had* irresponsible government in Mississippi," he said. "We are not going *from* highly responsible government." Negroes voted in Tennessee, and it seemed to have no worse government than Mississippi, he said. (Interview with the authors.)

36. Downtown businessmen of McComb, Mississippi, after they finally had rallied against the Ku Klux Klan and the extremist Americans for the Preservation of the White Race, issued a "Statement of Responsibility." One of the signers later said: "The trouble is we represent the bosses, the middle and upper level. The people who run the Klan are trying to manipulate the workers against us. And there are more workers than bosses." (Quoted by Paul Good, "A Bowl of Gumbo for Curtis Bryant," *The Reporter*, December 31, 1964, p. 22.)

37. Survey of human relations councils.

38. Survey of political writers.

39. Quoted by Lewinson, p. 89.

40. "The New Byrd Men," *The New Republic*, November 13, 1965, p. 9.

APPENDIX I

The Winona Incident

An Interview with Annelle Ponder and Fannie Lou Hamer, June 1963

At Winona, Mississippi, in June 1963, seven civil rights workers were arrested and several were beaten. The incident, similar to many others that occurred during voter registration activity, attracted little attention at the time. But later the voice of one of those severely beaten, Mrs. Fannie Lou Hamer, uneducated but eloquent wife of a Mississippi Negro sharecropper, was heard across the country. Before network television cameras she told her story when Negroes who had been excluded from the Democratic Party in Mississippi sought representation at the Democratic National Convention of 1964.

The story encompasses many of the recurrent themes of the rights movement in the South: police-state suppression; beatings; sadism; involvement of state police; clinical detachment of FBI men in their dealings with the victims, but good-faith cooperation with local police who obviously were suppressing constitutional rights; the deep religious faith of many of the Negroes in the most desperate circumstances, and, finally, their growing despair. This was the despair that preceded the "black power" cries of 1966, which first came from those parts of the South where the bitterest seed had been planted.

The following telephone interview, between the victims at Winona and staff members of the Voter Education Project of the Southern Regional Council in Atlanta, took place on June 13, 1963. Those interviewed were Mrs. Hamer and Miss Annelle Ponder. Others arrested were Misses Rosemary Freeman, Euvester Simpson, and June Johnson; James West; and, later, Lawrence Guyot, who subsequently was chairman of the Freedom Democratic Party in Mississippi. All at the time were local participants in voter registration except Miss Ponder, a Southern Christian Leadership Conference worker.

1ST INTERVIEWER—Can you tell me, if you feel up to it at the moment . . . what happened to you from the time you went into the bus station?

MISS PONDER—Let me see—well, this is what happened. We got there in Winona at eleven-fifteen Sunday morning, and then three or four of us got off the bus and went in the café to be served, and we sat down at the lunch counter and when we sat down—there were two waitresses back of the counter—and one of them just balled up her dishcloth she had in her hand and threw it against the wall behind her and said, "I can't take no more," you know? And so right after she said that, the chief of police and highway patrolman came from the rear area of the café . . . and came around and tapped us on the shoulder with the billy clubs, and said, "Y'all get out—get out." . . . So, when he got to me—we all stood up as he tapped us . . . when he got to me I stood up, and I said, "You know it is against the law to put us out of here, don't you?" He said, "Ain't no damn law, you just get on out of here!" . . . So, we went on the outside and stood and talked about this . . . for about five to eight minutes, and two other people, Euvester Simpson and Rosemary Freeman, joined us out there . . .

1ST INTERVIEWER—Had they been on the bus?

MISS PONDER—. . . As I understand it, they had been in the restaurant —Euvester had tried to go to the rest room and a police officer or the chief of police . . . one of them, had told her to go to a segregated one and pointed out which one for her to go to, and so she came out and was telling us about that . . . and we stood around talking for a few minutes, and then I started—I went back to the door and looked in . . . to get a better look at the patrolman, at the officers, and . . . they saw us looking in, and then we came back out and stood and talked some more, you know, we were just discussing it, what happened. And I said, well, we ought to get something to make a report on them. So then I happened to think that the patrol car was right out front there, so I said, well, we can get the license tag number off the patrol officer's car, and went around the back to get this, and as I was writing it down, the patrolman and the chief of police came out of the restaurant, and the chief of police said, "Y'all are under arrest—you are under arrest—get in that car, there!" And they had us to get in the patrolman's car. And, as we were getting in the car, Mrs. Hamer got off the bus and asked us if we wanted them to go on down to Greenwood. So I said yes. Then the police chief hollered out to another officer, and said, "Get that one there; get that one there—bring her on down in the other car . . ." So, he got Mrs. Hamer and brought her on down in the other car. . . . [They] took us all down to the jail, and when we got down there he didn't say what he charged us with. He said, "Y'all raising hell all over the place," you know. And then they took us inside and had us standing up and then started asking us some questions, and then they separated us . . . put some of us in cells, and never did say what they were locking us up for. And, . . . all of us were put in a cell except June—June Johnson, she was the last one out, so they started talking to her and asking her questions. And, I understood one of them to say something like, "What do you think we are supposed to do about that?" . . .

1ST INTERVIEWER—Who said that?

MISS PONDER—One of the officers. He said, "What do you think we are supposed to do about that?" And I could hear her say, "You all are supposed to protect us and take care of us." . . . And after that, I heard her screaming . . . and we could hear sounds of blows . . . being passed. And I guess they beat her a few minutes and then they came and got me out, and sent her where I was, and I passed her on the way out . . . and she was bleeding from the face, and she was crying . . . There was blood on the floor . . . over there where she had been, and they told me to stand over there where she had been . . . And then I went over and stood . . . around about a half a minute . . . and then they started in asking me questions and started hitting on me. One man said, "Y'all just stirring up . . . shit and making it stink"—the more we stirred, the more it stank, you know. "Y'all were doing a demonstration." We weren't planning a demonstration at all, we were just going in there to eat, and so we tried to explain this . . . And, they kept worrying me to say, "Yes, sir," you know. "I want to hear you say, 'Yes, sir,' nigger," and before they had separated us into the cells, one officer in a blue uniform . . . he wanted to know if I had enough respect for him to . . . say, yes, sir, . . . and I told him I didn't know him that well . . . and he looked at me, . . . with a kind of amazed look, and then after that they kept trying to get me to say, yes sir, and I wouldn't and they kept hitting me from one to the other, around, and it went, off and on, for about ten minutes . . . talking and beating. I'd say there were at least three . . . the highway patrolman, the blue-uniformed officer, and I guess the local policeman, and then there was a man there that did not have on a uniform . . . He was a short man, but we saw him—he was there yesterday . . . when we got out. I could identify him easily. And there was one fellow . . . A guy from down in Greenwood had some good pictures we can use to identify him later on. Anyway, at least three of them kind of gave us the runover with blackjacks, and a belt, fists, and open palms. And at one point the highway patrolman hit me in the stomach. So, that went on, I guess, off and on, for about ten minutes, talking . . . They really wanted to make me say yes, sir . . . and that is the one thing I wouldn't say.

1ST INTERVIEWER—Then what did they do?

MISS PONDER—After they got through beating me, they took a white fellow out of a cell and put him in a cell with some more white men, and put me in the cell he was in because the other cells were full . . . There were two to each cell, and I was in that one.

1ST INTERVIEWER—Who was in the cell with you?

MISS PONDER—I was in a cell by myself.

1ST INTERVIEWER—O.K. And then? By this time it was Sunday afternoon?

MISS PONDER—Yes. And Sunday afternoon, well, they woke us up at that time to eat; at least they brought us supper, and I ate. And the man kept saying, "You black African-looking son-of-a-bitch." That's what they kept saying and calling me, you know. Even after I'd passed the room, the man in the blue uniform would look in and yell that out . . . He *kept* insisting that I call him mister. So I asked him at one point, I asked him why it was so important, and then . . . he would get angry again and just start hitting me again . . .

1ST INTERVIEWER—How long were you in the jail after dinner?

MISS PONDER—We were in there until yesterday [Wednesday] afternoon. I guess we got out about four-thirty.

1ST INTERVIEWER—Were you or any of the other prisoners beaten after Sunday?

MISS PONDER—After Sunday? No, not that I know of. Now whether Guyot and the young man were beaten after Sunday, I don't know, but none of the ladies were.

1ST INTERVIEWER—How about Mrs. Hamer?

MISS PONDER—She was not. You can talk with her about the trial. We thought that Wiley [Branton][1] would have been there. Did he know about it?

1ST INTERVIEWER—Yes, he knew about it; he was on the phone most of the last two or three days with kids from Greenwood trying to get the thing straightened out. And then he finally got in touch with Andy Young, and he was in touch with Andy most of yesterday. In fact, he was in touch with him most of the night before, too.

MISS PONDER—The thing is, they had this trial Tuesday, and we didn't know anything about it until late Monday night, very late Monday night. And we were under the impression that everybody else knew that the trial was going to be. So we thought that Wiley would have been there, or someone from the Justice Department, and we went in prepared to have somebody there. But they didn't have anything like a trial—they just asked us questions, and nobody recorded anything, and we—I just said just enough to—what was necessary to say, you know, since I didn't feel it would be very important to try to say more . . . in the way it was.

2ND INTERVIEWER—What happened, Annelle, was that Wiley, I think, learned about this for the first time Monday afternoon around four o'clock, and he was in contact with the people in the Greenwood office immediately to arrange for bail bonds, and he did not find out until ten o'clock Monday night that bail bonds had not been arranged. And, it was, as I recall, he tried to make connections to get out there, and there wasn't any way that he could get there—I believe that was the way it was, and then, of course, there were other things breaking here.

MISS PONDER—But, really, that trial was nothing but a farce. And we just said as little as was necessary.

2ND INTERVIEWER—Well, of course, that trial was only a preliminary affair. I'm not saying that you shouldn't have been defended, but that trial can be completely re-enacted then in the circuit court—you can get a completely new trial. Did Andy put up appeal bonds, or did he pay your fines?

MISS PONDER—Appeal bonds. We are supposed to appear in court in October sometime. October 15, I think—I don't remember the date.

2ND INTERVIEWER—Wiley was in contact with the Justice Department attempting to get them to come in and do something.

MISS PONDER—Yes. Well, that's it; we thought that somebody would be there.

2ND INTERVIEWER—They kept telling him that they were investigating. And that was about all, apparently. Did you talk to any FBI people in the jail at any time?

MISS PONDER—I talked to some yesterday, yes.

2ND INTERVIEWER—Yesterday. That's Wednesday. And that was the first time you had talked to them at all?

MISS PONDER—The first time. And there were some in there Tuesday. And they happened to be there at the time Willie Peacock called me to ask if they were investigating or interrogating me . . . And so then I asked them if they were the FBI. They were just taking pictures of Guyot and maybe one or two others, I'm not sure, and they were getting ready to close up when the jailer called me. I had to answer the phone, and they were getting ready to close up, and I asked them were they with the FBI, and they said, yes, and they asked me who was calling . . .

2ND INTERVIEWER—They had not even identified themselves as FBI men?

MISS PONDER—They had not talked with me at all. They were in there talking to other people . . .

2ND INTERVIEWER—Were you close enough to be able to hear what they were talking about?

MISS PONDER—Not very. I could hear them talking to Guyot, and I could hear them taking pictures. But they had closed the little door to the cell so I couldn't hear too well what was going on. But they said, after I asked them, they said they were FBI men, and I told Peacock they hadn't had a chance to talk with me . . . Before they left, they said, "The chief [emphasizing *chief*] says that we can talk with you tomorrow," you know, and they didn't bother to take time to talk or take any pictures, and it was pretty early in the day, then, before five, I'd say. And, anyway, it seems to me they were cooperating with the chief, in a way.

2ND INTERVIEWER—How many of them were there? Two?

MISS PONDER—There were about four or five in there that day.

2ND INTERVIEWER—Is that right? And that was Tuesday?

MISS PONDER—Yes. And then yesterday, you know, the same number came back and they finally got around to talking to us. To me.

2ND INTERVIEWER—And what did they do? Did they take a written statement from you?

MISS PONDER—I gave them a statement and they wrote it down.

2ND INTERVIEWER—And then you signed it?

MISS PONDER—I didn't sign it . . .

2ND INTERVIEWER—They didn't ask you to sign it?

MISS PONDER—No.

2ND INTERVIEWER—Is that right?

MISS PONDER—That's right. They said they were going to turn it in and . . .

2ND INTERVIEWER—They didn't ask you to sign the statement, Annelle?

MISS PONDER—They didn't ask me to sign it, no.

2ND INTERVIEWER—And they identified themselves to you as FBI men?

MISS PONDER—Yes.

2ND INTERVIEWER—They showed you identification?

MISS PONDER—Yes.

2ND INTERVIEWER—And you looked at it and saw that it was an FBI identification card?

MISS PONDER—Yes. And I would be able to recognize them if I were to see them again.

2ND INTERVIEWER—Were you there when they were questioning any of the other people yesterday? Do you know whether or not anybody signed a statement for them?

MISS PONDER—No, I don't. One other thing is, on Tuesday, after our trial, they told Willie Peacock—somebody told him—that they had gotten secondhand—that only one person had said that he was not guilty at his trial they had . . . and that took a lot of running around to pin that down because Willie thought then that he would have to go out and get these fines, you know. But they didn't ask us until that night . . . some of them asked Mrs. Hamer, some of them that night, whether they had pled guilty or not—They were going on the word of some people up there . . . So it's . . .

2ND INTERVIEWER—Now, did you all plead guilty at the trial, or not?

MISS PONDER—No, none of us did, that I know of. Everybody said not guilty.

2ND INTERVIEWER—They had you charged with what?

MISS PONDER—Disorderly conduct and resisting arrest.

2ND INTERVIEWER—I sure thank you, Annelle. Mrs. Hamer, I wonder if you would describe what happened from the time you were arrested on?

MRS. HAMER—It was the mos' *horrifyin'* experience I have ever had in my life. You see, I was on the bus . . . Annelle and the others was off—part of the others—was off the bus. And when I saw the policemens carrying them to the car, and I knowed it wasn't going to be too long before we supposed to be on our way to Greenwood, I just stepped off and asked her what did she want us to do, and she motioned for me to go on, that they would have to go down to the station. So, by this time, a man told me to wait, and I stopped, and he come round to the side of the car—it was two men in there—and he told me to come round there and get in, and when I went to get in—

2ND INTERVIEWER—This was one of the officers?

MRS. HAMER—That's right. And when I went to get in, he kicked me.

2ND INTERVIEWER—He kicked you?

MRS. HAMER—Yes, so I got in the car, and he drove me on round, just me—it was him and another person, so we went on round to the place where they had carried Miss Ponder and the others, and after we had gotten there it wasn't too long before I heard screamin' and I was in a cell then . . .

2ND INTERVIEWER—By yourself?

MRS. HAMER—No, it was me and one other girl with me. Her name is —she is a Simpson—Euvester Simpson—that's right.

2ND INTERVIEWER—She had been on the bus?

MRS. HAMER—That's right. She was one of them, too. We were put in the room together. After I heard the hollerin' and going on, I saw this girl pass the window where I could see her, and I didn't—I really didn't know what was going to happen. So, after a while, they had Miss Ponder. And you know—that screamin' and all of that will always follow me—I never will forget it. They whipped her, and after a while she passed by where we were in the cell, and her mouth was bleedin', and her hair was standin' up on her head, you know, it was *horrifyin'*. Then after they decided to stop, well, this man asked me where was I from.

2ND INTERVIEWER—One of the officers asked you that?

MRS. HAMER—That was the state highway patrolman. He asked me where was I from, and I told him I was from Ruleville. And he say, "I'm gonna check and see." And I figures, you know, well, I figured there wasn't going to be nothing to happen to me because, you know, I told him, I say, "Well, after all, I was born, I think it was, in this county. Montgomery County," and he say, "And you stay in Ruleville now?" and I say, "Yes, sir," so he say, "Well, I'm gonna check—I'm gonna see where you from." So, I know by me being one of the persons that works with this voter registration, when he checked—well, that was really going to put me on the spot for sure. So, when he walked back in, he says, "Yes, you live in Ruleville," and says, "You the big . . ." and I have never heard that many names called a human in my life, and he told . . .

2ND INTERVIEWER—He used curse words, you mean?

MRS. HAMER—Oh, all *kinds* of curse words. So, one of the officers called me "Fatso," and then he told 'em, "Let's take her in here." So, they carried me in a room, and it was two Negro boys in this room. So, the state highway patrol[man] gave them a long blackjack, and it was wide, and he told one of the boys, he said, "Take this." And he said, "This is what you want me to use?" He said, "That's right." And said, "If you don't use it on her, you know what I'll use on you." So, then the boy told me, say, "Get over there." And I say, "Where?" And he said, "On that cot." I said, "You mean you would do this to your own race?" And this state patrolman told him, "You heard what I said." So, then I had to get over there on the bed flat on my stomach, and that man *beat* me—that man *beat* me until he give out. And by me screamin', it made one of the other ones—plainclothes fellow, he didn't have on nothing like a uniform—he got so hot and worked up off it, he just run there you know and started hittin' me on the back of my head. Well, my hand—I was trying to guard some of the licks, you see—and my hands, they beat my hands till they turned *blue*, and after he had finished, my clothes . . . quite naturally, beating me like that, my clothes come up, and I tried to pull them down, you know. It was just *pitiful*. And then he—one of the other white fellows—just taken my clothes and just snatched them up, and this Negro, when he had just beat me until I know he was just give out, well, then, this state patrolman told the other Negro to take it. So he taken over from there. And they just beat till—and anywhere you could see me, you can see I'm not lying, because I can just set down—I been sleeping on my face, and I'm just as hard as a bone. It was just hard. When they stopped, when they turned me aloose, I was as hard as a bone.

2ND INTERVIEWER—Then you went back to the cell?

MRS. HAMER—Yes. They carried me back to the cell.

2ND INTERVIEWER—Were you able to walk when you got off the bed?

MRS. HAMER—I was *drunk!* Look like somethin' nother happened to me —look like I must have passed out, or somethin'. But I did, 'cause he said, "Hell, you can walk." Oh, it was all kinds of language used.

2ND INTERVIEWER—How many white men were in the room at the time this happened, Mrs. Hamer?

MRS. HAMER—It was the jailer, the state highway patrol[man], another man with a blue—he was a police[man], but he was off duty that day —and then there was that man had on the dark trousers and white shirt, and then it was this sheriff that carried me over there, and the two Negroes, and me.

2ND INTERVIEWER—Now, was that the only time that they beat you?

MRS. HAMER—That was the only time, but it was enough to last me, 'cause it still is lastin'.

2ND INTERVIEWER—I'm sure it was. Did they take you back to the same cell?

MRS. HAMER—They taken me back to the same cell.

2ND INTERVIEWER—Now, do you know whether or not they took anybody else in and beat them?

MRS. HAMER—Over in the night, I heard screamin'—I heard the scream-in'—I said, "O, Lord." I say, "Somebody else gettin' it, too." So, it was later that we heard that Lawrence Guyot was there. You know, all the way we could do, is just every once in a while, you know, maybe see somebody passing; we just didn't know nothin'. We was there and we begged for cold water, and the only thing that was *kind* of nice there—the jailer's wife and the jailer's daughter—we could tell when the jailer and the other men was out—they would bring us cold water; they would bring us ice . . .

2ND INTERVIEWER—Is that right.

MRS. HAMER—And I told them, "Y'all is nice. You must be Christian people." The jailer's wife told me she tried to live a Christian life. And I told her I would like for her to read two scriptures in the Bible, and I tol' her to read the 26th Chapter of Proverbs and the 26th Verse. She taken it down on a paper. And then I told her to read the 7th Chapter of Acts and the 26th Verse. [The two verses read: "Whose hatred is covered by deceit, his wickedness shall be showed before the whole congregation." And: ". . . Hath made of one blood all nations of men for to dwell on all the face of the earth, and hath determined the times before appointed, and the bounds of their habitation."] And she taken that down. She never did come back after then. I think—I don't know what happened, but I told the jailer when they carried us to the trial—Annelle was able to walk, but I wasn't able to walk. You see, a long time ago I had polio, and I don't know, it had me where I couldn't hardly make it, so this man who carried me down was the same man that pulled my dress up, but you see, he didn't know it. He didn't know I had sense enough to *know* him. You see, he was bareheaded that Sunday, and then the next day, when the day—that Tuesday—they had to carry us to that trial, well, he had on a cap. I asked him, I said, "Do you people ever think or wonder how you will feel when the time come you will have to meet God?" He said, "Who you talking 'bout?" I said, "People who treated us like we was treated in jail." He said, "Well, hell, don't say me, because I was off duty." But it was the same *man!* So, I talked so nice, I actually chiseled him out of his name, you know. He was unaware of what I was trying to do, and I acted so *dumb*, you know, I would get to get their names, and they wouldn't be aware of what was happening.

2ND INTERVIEWER—Now, when was the first time that the FBI talked to you?

MRS. HAMER—The first time he tried to talk to me was yesterday. That was a little before we got out of jail. But you know, I had been through so much I just told him, you know, after all that shooting . . . last year, after those FBI's, look like, did not get nothin' straightened out from Ruleville, I don't know—it looks like I just don't *trust* 'em, you know? So, they wanted to know what I was going to say. I say, "I can tell you one thing, *I want to get out of here now*." I say, " 'Cause this just a death cell." And, he say, "Well, we would like to talk to you," and I said, "Well, I just can't do it." You see, I didn't know whether if I said what had happened to me then he could tell the jailer, and I just couldn't do it—I just *couldn't!* But we sho' wanted—if we could have just seen anybody, I said, well, I reckon now God is the only refuge we have because there wasn't nobody there from the Justice Department, nobody there to say *nuthin'*—just the Negro out by theirself. I just wonder how long will we have to keep on sheddin' blood and be *beat*—you know, that is just *pitiful*—women like that and everybody can have guards *but* the Negro, you know? Now, we were just women there loose in that jailhouse being *beat* like *criminals* and hadn't *done* nothin'!

2ND INTERVIEWER—Now, you did not see any of the things that happened to Guyot?

MRS. HAMER—No, I didn't see nothin' but Guyot's back yesterday. I talked with him, you know they had him out in the little hall and I begged them to let my door stay open, you know, not the cell part, but the other big door. I was in the cell, but I could walk as far as the door, and I asked them to leave that door, please, so we could get a breeze of fresh air—everyone was hot—so that is how we got to see Guyot.

2ND INTERVIEWER—Did he look like he was in pretty bad shape?

MRS. HAMER—Yes, he did. Guyot looked like he was in a bad shape and it was on my nerve, too, because that was the first time I had seen him, you know, and not smiling. Once I glanced at him, and I don't know where they were carrying him to, but he crossed and I was just looking through a crack at him, you know, one of the bars, and he had his hands behind him. But that is a death place down there. I don't see how in the *world*—I don't see how under the *sun*—that people could do human beings like they do them—it was just a *death* trap.

2ND INTERVIEWER—We tried to call you in Ruleville, Mrs. Hamer, and they said you were on your way to Washington. Are you going up there to talk to the Justice Department, or what?

MRS. HAMER—I just don't know exactly. I am supposed to go to New York, too. But you know, something is going to have to be done! It really is! You know now . . . What we get is give to us—me, you know; you know this. All right, my tax money go just like anybody else's, but still we don't have *no protection*. At the same time, mister, if it was *your* wife, and you thought one *small* lick had been hit, it would have been one thousand and fifty soldiers there to protect that woman. But *me* . . . and I don't know how long we can keep on going like this, and then after I got out of jail yesterday, half dead, to find out that Medgar Evers had been shot down in his own yard—well, things—somethin' got to break!

2ND INTERVIEWER—Yes, yes, I certainly agree with you, Mrs. Hamer.

MRS. HAMER—And just keep on saying *wait*—and we been waitin' all of our lives, and *still* gettin' killed, *still* gettin' hung, *still* gettin' beat to death—now, we tired waitin'!

2ND INTERVIEWER—[very low] Yes, ma'am.

MRS. HAMER—Now, you know, ain't that right? We is tired!

2ND INTERVIEWER—Absolutely! Absolutely! I'm tired with you.

MRS. HAMER—That's right.

2ND INTERVIEWER—And I'm with you any steps you take. I think all of you know that.

MRS. HAMER—O.K. [Friendly laughter exchanged.]

2ND INTERVIEWER—I sure enjoyed talkin' to you, and I want to certainly —it doesn't do *you* any good, I know—but I certainly want to express my personal regrets that this happened.

MRS. HAMER—O.K. Well, any time somebody say that, well, that gives me, keep me with more courage.

2ND INTERVIEWER—Well, you are certainly doing a wonderful job, Mrs. Hamer, and I think everybody knows it.

MRS. HAMER—Well, thank you.

2ND INTERVIEWER—We wish there were something that we could do to make the job that you and your friends are doing a little bit easier.

MRS. HAMER—I wish it was . . .

2ND INTERVIEWER—You know, many of us with pale faces are up against much the same thing that you are . . .

MRS. HAMER—I know that . . .

2ND INTERVIEWER—The only difference is, we can retreat and y'all can't.

MRS. HAMER—That's right . . .

2ND INTERVIEWER—Well, it has been awfully nice talking to you, and I want to wish you the very best of everything. Thank you so much.

NOTES

1. This was another example of the voter effort's dependence on VEP Director Branton for legal assistance, reflecting the movement's lack of legal counsel in hard-core areas.

APPENDIX II

Voter Registration in the South—1962, 1964, 1966

State	White VAP	Negro VAP	Whites Regis. 1962	% WVAP Regis.	Negroes Regis. 1962	% NVAP Regis.	Whites Regis. 1964
ALABAMA	1,353,058	481,320	883,732	62.4	68,317	13.4	925,000
ARKANSAS	850,643	192,626	506,799	57.1	68,970	34.0	553,665
FLORIDA	2,617,438	470,261	1,819,342	67.0	182,456	36.8	1,958,499
GEORGIA	1,797,062	612,910	1,152,707	60.8	175,573	26.7	1,183,181
LOUISIANA	1,289,216	514,589	934,862	69.3	151,663	27.8	1,027,981
MISSISSIPPI	748,266	422,256	390,000	49.6	23,920	5.3	525,000
N. CAROLINA	2,005,955	550,929	1,861,330	88.0	210,450	35.8	1,856,497
S. CAROLINA	895,147	371,104	480,793	50.7	90,901	22.9	703,000
TENNESSEE	1,779,018	313,873	930,198	49.8	150,869	49.8	1,297,026
TEXAS	4,884,765	649,512	658,198	41.2	111,014	26.7	1,720,183
VIRGINIA	1,876,167	436,720	940,115	47.5	110,113	24.0	940,811
TOTALS	20,096,735	5,016,100	10,566,111	52.5	1,344,519	26.8	12,690,843

% WVAP Regis. 1964	Negroes Regis. 1964	% NVAP Regis.	Whites Regis. 1966	% WVAP Regis.	Negroes Regis. 1966	% NVAP Regis.	% NVAP of VAP	% Negroes of Total Regis.
68.4	110,000	22.8	1,192,072	88.1	246,396	51.2	26.2	17.1
65.1	80,000	41.5	598,000	70.3	115,000	59.7	18.5	16.1
74.8	299,960	63.8	2,093,274	80.0	286,446	60.9	15.2	12.0
65.8	270,000	44.1	1,378,005	76.7	289,545	47.2	25.4	17.4
79.7	163,041	31.7	1,071,573	83.1	242,130	47.1	28.5	18.4
70.2	28,500	6.7	470,920	62.7	139,099	32.9	36.1	22.8
92.5	258,000	46.8	1,653,796	82.4	281,134	51.0	21.5	14.5
78.5	144,000	38.8	718,061	80.2	190,609	51.4	29.3	20.9
72.9	218,000	69.4	1,375,000	77.3	225,000	71.7	14.9	14.1
35.2	375,000	57.7	2,600,000	53.3	400,000	61.6	11.7	13.3
50.1	127,000	29.1	1,159,000	61.8	205,000	46.9	18.9	15.0
63.1	2,074,461	40.8	14,309,704	70.2	2,620,359	52.2	19.9	15.4

LEGEND—
    VAP—Voting age population
  NVAP—Negro voting age population
WVAP—White voting age population

ACKNOWLEDGEMENTS

We are grateful for the assistance of Mrs. Janet Shortt, formerly with the Voter Education Project and secretary, typist, and valuable consultant during preparation of the manuscript; Mrs. Barbara Patterson, formerly of the Southern Regional Council research staff; and Mrs. Glenda Bartley, Miss Susan Friedman, Mrs. Doris Reed, Mrs. Bernice Morrison, presently of the Southern Regional Council research staff; Wiley Branton, director of the Voter Education Project, 1962–1964, and his staff, including Randolph Blackwell and John Due; Vernon Jordan, director of the Voter Education Project, 1966 to the present, and his staff, including Marvin Wall, director of research; Leslie W. Dunbar, director of the Southern Regional Council, 1961 to 1965, who contributed valuable editing and insights; Paul Anthony, director of the Southern Regional Council, 1965 to the present; and all those whose field reports provided the fundament of this book.

INDEX